Destination Papua New Guinea & Solomon Islands

'One of the last frontiers' is an expression that couldn't be closer to the truth where Papua New Guinea and the Solomon Islands are concerned. Whether nature or culture excites you (or both), these are some of the most diverse and untouched lands on earth. The white-sand beaches and islands are as attractive as you'll find anywhere, and the underwater scene is better: sunken relics of WWII, colourful coral reefs and majestic marine life make the region arguably the world's best diving destination. Papua New Guinea is blessed with relatively undisturbed rainforest and trekking is becoming more popular. The famous Kokoda Track increasingly draws people for a thoroughly challenging pilgrimage.

As anthropologists will testify, these two small countries offer more culture than you could experience in a dozen lifetimes. More than 900 distinct languages reflect the diversity. The Asaro mud men, the Polynesian-influenced Trobriand Islands Yam Harvest festival, the menacing masks of the Sepik, the underwater volcano at Marovo Lagoon and a head-hunter king's coral fort are all available to the visitor.

With so much to see, it's hard to believe Papua New Guinea and the Solomons are among the least-touristed countries on earth. Parts of Papua New Guinea can be dangerous, but the country is not as bad as commonly perceived. If you use common sense you're more likely to be smothered in smiles than encounter difficulties.

So set fear aside – the last frontiers await.

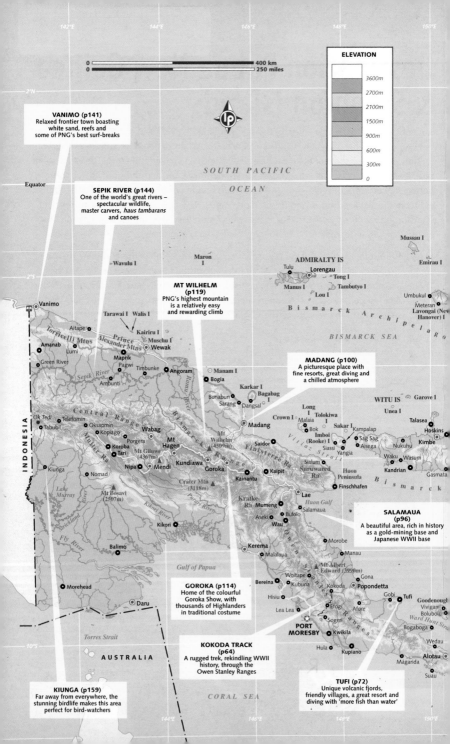

ELEVATION

3600m
2700m
2100m
1500m
900m
600m
300m
0

VANIMO (p141)
Relaxed frontier town boasting white sand, reefs and some of PNG's best surf-breaks

SEPIK RIVER (p144)
One of the world's great rivers – spectacular wildlife, master carvers, *haus tambarans* and canoes

MT WILHELM (p119)
PNG's highest mountain is a relatively easy and rewarding climb

MADANG (p100)
A picturesque place with fine resorts, great diving and a chilled atmosphere

SALAMAUA (p96)
A beautiful area, rich in history as a gold-mining base and Japanese WWII base

GOROKA (p114)
Home of the colourful Goroka Show, with thousands of Highlanders in traditional costume

KOKODA TRACK (p64)
A rugged trek, rekindling WWII history, through the Owen Stanley Ranges

TUFI (p72)
Unique volcanic fjords, friendly villages, a great resort and diving with 'more fish than water'

KIUNGA (p159)
Far away from everywhere, the stunning birdlife makes this area perfect for bird-watchers

Papua New Guinea
& Solomon Islands

Andrew Burke, Rowan McKinnon, Arnold Barkhordarian
Sean Dorney, Tim Flannery

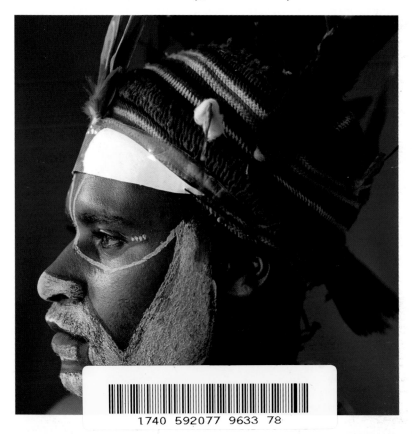

Contents

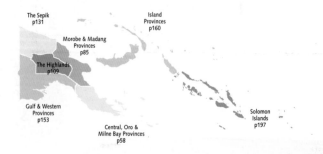

The Sepik
p131

Island Provinces
p160

Morobe & Madang Provinces
p85

The Highlands
p109

Gulf & Western Provinces
p153

Solomon Islands
p197

Central, Oro & Milne Bay Provinces
p58

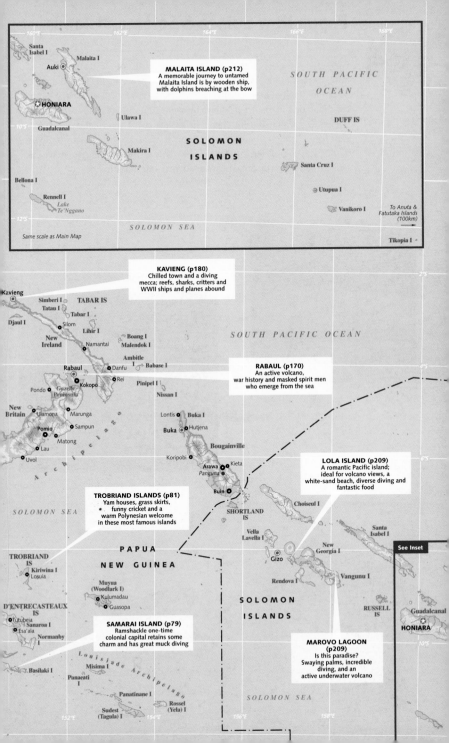

MALAITA ISLAND (p212)
A memorable journey to untamed Malaita Island is by wooden ship, with dolphins breaching at the bow

KAVIENG (p180)
Chilled town and a diving mecca; reefs, sharks, critters and WWII ships and planes abound

RABAUL (p170)
An active volcano, war history and masked spirit men who emerge from the sea

LOLA ISLAND (p209)
A romantic Pacific island; ideal for volcano views, a white-sand beach, diverse diving and fantastic food

TROBRIAND ISLANDS (p81)
Yam houses, grass skirts, funny cricket and a warm Polynesian welcome in these most famous islands

SAMARAI ISLAND (p79)
Ramshackle one-time colonial capital retains some charm and has great muck diving

MAROVO LAGOON (p209)
Is this paradise? Swaying palms, incredible diving, and an active underwater volcano

SOUTH PACIFIC OCEAN

SOLOMON ISLANDS

DUFF IS

Santa Cruz I

Utupua I

Vanikoro I

To Anuta & Fatutaka Islands (100km)

Same scale as Main Map

Tikopia I

Santa Isabel I

Malaita I

Auki

HONIARA

Guadalcanal

Ulawa I

Makira I

Bellona I

Rennell I

Lake Te'Nggano

SOLOMON SEA

Kavieng

Simberi I

Tatau I

TABAR IS

Tabar I

Djaul I

Silom

New Ireland

Lihir I

Namantai

Boang I

Malendok I

Ambitle

Danfu

Babase I

Rabaul

Kokopo

Rei

Pinipel I

Pondo

Gazelle Peninsula

Nissan I

New Britain

Ulamona

Marunga

Pomio

Sampun

Matong

Lau

Uvol

Lontis

Buka I

Buka

Hutjena

Bougainville

Koripobi

Arawa

Kieta

Panguna

Buin

SHORTLAND IS

Choiseul I

Santa Isabel I

TROBRIAND IS

Kiriwina I

Losuia

PAPUA

NEW GUINEA

Muyua (Woodlark I)

Kulumadau

Guasopa

D'ENTRECASTEAUX IS

Tutubeia

Sanaroa I

Esa'ala

Normanby I

Basilaki I

Louisiade Archipelago

Misima I

Panaeati I

Panatinane I

Sudest (Tagula) I

Rossel (Yela) I

SOLOMON ISLANDS

Vella Lavella I

Gizo

New Georgia I

Rendova I

Vangunu I

RUSSELL IS

Guadalcanal

HONIARA

See Inset

SOLOMON SEA

SOUTH PACIFIC OCEAN

If the rugged outdoors is your caper, then you'll love Papua New Guinea and Solomon Islands. For divers, **Tufi** (p72), **Samarai Island** (p79), **Madang** (p100) and the Solomon's magnificent **Marovo Lagoon** (p209) will get the blood pumping. Surfers will be stoked by breaks at **Vanimo** (p141) and **Kavieng** (p180). To experience the local culture, check out the Sepik region's *haus tambarans* (p150), stay in a **village** (p104) or play a game of **Trobriand Islands Cricket** (p82). Or laze about on romantic beaches such as **Lola Island** (p209).

PETER HENDRIE

Rowing in the Middle Sepik (p148)

Parrot from Solomon Islands (p212)

SIMON FOALE

Tuvurvur Volcano, New Britain Province (p162)

PETER HENDF

ROBERT HALSTEAD

One of the beautiful beaches along Milne Bay, Milne Bay Province (p73)

A Huli wigman at a *singsing* (p130)

ROWAN McKINNON

Red ginger plant from a local garden (p23)

MARY L PEACHIN

ANDREW BURKE

A trekker, carriers and local children climb the Kokoda Track towards Isurava Memorial (p68)

SIMON FOALE

Cardinalfish is one of the tropical fish seen when snorkelling (p101)

Male and female tree kangaroos, Rainfore Habitat in Lae (p91)

PAUL BEIN

JERRY GALEA

Sepik carving is a mix of traditional motifs and popular styles (p134)

Getting Started

Travelling in PNG and the Solomon Islands does not follow a conveyor-belt tourist routine. Even though travelling there isn't exactly a walk in the park, the striking natural beauty and myriad of cultures offer some riveting experiences. Reading some of the limited range of books and websites beforehand will dispel misconceptions and help you understand what you'll see when you arrive.

WHEN TO GO

PNG has one of the most variable climates on earth, which can make travel planning difficult. The wet season is roughly from December to March and the dry is from May to October. April and November are anyone's guess. There are, however, plenty of exceptions to this pattern (Lae and Alotau are wet when everywhere else is dry); see the regional chapters for details. The months from June to September are cooler, drier and better to visit PNG.

It's worth scheduling your trip around a festival or event (p226), such as one of the unforgettable cultural shows that are held between July and October. If you plan on trekking (p220), diving (p218) or looking for that elusive bird, it's best to research when are the best times to go.

There are no real high and low seasons in PNG and the Solomons. At Christmas, Easter and other major holidays (p226), hotels and transport can fill up, and you'll need to book your accommodation (p215) ahead if you're in a town during one of the cultural shows.

See Climate (p222) for more information.

HOW MUCH?

Mid-range hotel room
K100–400/S$200-400

1hr online K30/S$15

Bilum (string bag)
K50/S$110

Meal in a cheap restaurant K10/S$25

'Compo' for running over a dog K250-14,000/ S$500-8000, depending on the dead hound's alleged hunting skills and your negotiating skills

COSTS & MONEY

You'd think PNG, being a developing country next to dirt-cheap Indonesia, would be an inexpensive place to travel. It's not. The reason is that the cost of doing *anything* in PNG is unreasonably high. Loan interest rates are high and repayment periods short, virtually everything is imported, there's little competition and some businesses take a 'high risk, high reward' attitude.

For the traveller, this means sleeping (p215), eating (p40) and getting around (p240) are all relatively expensive, with flying being almost prohibitive. Backpackers are doing well if they can get by on less than K157 (US$50) per day, staying in guesthouses and eating mostly in cheap restaurants and *kai* bars (cheap takeaway food bars), with a couple of flights thrown in. For a few days in a resort, with good food, activities and

---

DON'T LEAVE HOME WITHOUT...

- Valid travel insurance, noting the emergency phone and policy numbers (p226).
- Antimalarial prophylactics (p251), a mosquito net and a screw-in hook to hang it from.
- A snorkel and mask (p218).
- A small umbrella and/or a plastic poncho for weather protection.
- A bottle of sweet-chilli sauce (or some other condiment) to spice up the village diet (p40).
- A small torch (flashlight) for late-night toilet expeditions (vital in a village).
- A sense of humour and a deep well of patience – your best plans *will* go awry at some point.

TOP TEN BOOKS & FILMS

Many books and films on the region have a distinctly anthropological slant because the truth about PNG and Solomon Islands cultures is often stranger than fiction. The films are hard to find; try www.roninfilms.com.au, or see p28.

- *Throwim Way Leg* (1998), written by Tim Flannery
- *Village on the Edge* (2002), written by Michael French Smith
- *The Sky Travellers: Journeys in New Guinea 1938–1939* (1998), written by Bill Gammage
- *Happy Isles of Oceania* (1992), written by Paul Theroux
- *In a Savage Land* (1999), directed by Bill Bennett
- *First Contact* (1983), directed by Bob Connolly & Robin Anderson
- *The Shark Callers of Kontu* (1987), directed by Dennis O'Rourke
- *Bridewealth for a Goddess* (2000), directed by Chris Owen
- *Since the Company Came* (2000), directed by Russell Hawkins
- *Robinson Crusoe* (1996), directed by Daniel Defoe

DIVES & TREKS

There are hundreds of exciting dive sites and dozens of challenging treks. Here are a few that should please those who travel there.

- Samarai Island Wharf (p79)
- Marovo Lagoon (p209)
- Manta Ray Cleaning Station (p80)
- B17 'Black Jack' (p72)
- Around Jais Aben Area and Madang's northern coast (p105)
- Kokoda Track (p64)
- Mt Wilhelm to Madang (p120)
- Mt Wilhelm (p119)
- Crater Mountain Wildlife Management Area (p117)
- Black Cat Track (p98)

DIY CULTURAL EXPERIENCES

The Melanesian experience can be as culturally rich as you allow it to be. Go ahead and try:

- Learning new dance steps at a Highland *singsing*
- Watching the Asaro mud men
- Playing *garamut* (a hollowed-log) and *kundu* (hour-glassed shaped, lizard-skin) drums, nose flutes and jew's-harps
- Chewing betel nut
- Drinking the juice of a green coconut
- Setting a fish trap in the Sepik River
- Eating freshly slaughtered pig at a village celebration
- Learning to prepare sago and a *mumu* (underground oven)
- Sleeping in a *haus tambaran* (spirit house)
- Commissioning or buying a piece from a Sepik master carver

flights, you'll spend as much as K942 (US$300) per day. There's plenty of in-between options and couples or pairs pay less per person.

Your expenses depend on how far off the beaten track you get. Wandering off to a lesser-known village is not only a fantastic way to see the country and witness the culture, it's also inexpensive: food and lodging will cost you about K50 per night, often less (p217). Apart from the occasional local handicraft, there's virtually nothing else to spend your money on in a village, so it can't help but be cheap.

The steady devaluation of both the kina in PNG and the Solomon Islands dollar make travelling slightly cheaper. But as tourism facilities tend to use imported goods, the savings start when you get out of town.

Unlike PNG, the Solomon Islands can be relatively inexpensive. Resorts are more costly, but transport, hotels and food are cheaper.

TRAVEL LITERATURE

Michael Moran's recently published *Beyond the Coral Sea* sees the author retrace the steps of some of the colourful characters and empire-builders who were so influential in forming the country you see today.

Solomon Time: An Unlikely Quest in the South Pacific, by Will Randall, is an unassuming and well-written tale of a naive Englishman who somehow finds himself on a remote island in the Solomons, breeding chickens.

Four Corners: Into the Heart of New Guinea, by Kira Salak, presents the 1927 journey of British explorer Ivan Champion by foot and canoe, and his meetings with missionaries, cannibals and incredible landscapes.

Legendary swashbuckler Errol Flynn's autobiography, *My Wicked, Wicked Ways,* covers the actor's six formative years in New Guinea. It's engaging and relevant, particularly as it was so influential in developing the world's idea of PNG.

Into the Crocodile Nest keeps you turning the pages as author and masochist-traveller Benedict Allen becomes the first white man initiated into an obscure crocodile cult on the Sepik river.

INTERNET RESOURCES

There isn't a vast array of websites about PNG and the Solomons, but new ones are appearing and existing sites are improving. Some worth looking at before you leave include:

Australian National University PNG Page (coombs.anu.edu.au/SpecialProj/PNG/topics/Ww2 .htm) A wide range of links to PNG-related sites.

Lonely Planet (www.lonelyplanet.com) The Thorn Tree bulletin board and Postcards have invaluable up-to-date information and tips.

PNG Business Directory (www.pngbd.com) PNG's busiest site can be awkward to navigate at first. It's full of handy information with plenty of photos that give you an idea of where you're going.

PNG Tourism Promotion Authority (www.pngtourism.org.pg) PNG's official tourism website. Has good links to tour operators.

Post Courier (www.postcourier.com.pg) Website of the *Post Courier* newspaper, with the day's news and a 'What's On' link.

Solomon Islands Visitors Bureau (www.visitsolomons.com.sb) Travel information and visas.

LONELY PLANET INDEX

Beer in a bar ('SP brownie') K4/S$6.50-9

Green coconut (for drinking) K1/S$2

Litre of bottled water K2/S$3-8

Litre of petrol K2.70

Souvenir T-shirt K40/S$90

Itineraries
CLASSIC ROUTE

MAINLAND ODYSSEY
Two weeks / Port Moresby to Madang

This grand tour of mainland Papua New Guinea gives you a taste of the coast, the Highlands and the Sepik. It's busy, and with so many flights it can be pricey, but if you want more time and/or want to save money cut out the Alotau leg and fly straight to Lae.

After a day in **Port Moresby** (p44), fly east to **Alotau** (p74) on the waters of Milne Bay. Take a boat out to the colonial-era capital of **Samarai Island** (p79) and snorkel or dive around the world-famous piers before returning via **Kwato Island** (p79). Fly to **Lae** (p89) and spend a couple of days checking out the **Rainforest Habitat** (p91) and **Salamaua** (p96). Take a PMV (public motor vehicle) up the Highlands Hwy to **Goroka** (p114) and celebrate your arrival by watching the **Asaro mud men** (p117) do their thing.

From Goroka go to **Mt Hagen** (p121), enjoying the spectacular scenery of the Wahgi Valley and stopping en route for a game of Highlands darts. Stay at the excellent **Haus Poroman Lodge** (p123) and spend a day hiking through the bucolic surrounding forests. If there's no clan warfare going on (p127), continue on the highway to **Tari** (p129) via **Mendi** (p126), but if arrows are flying you'll have to fly too...you wouldn't want to end up as supper! Whichever way you come, Tari and, more to the point, the beautiful **Tari Basin** (p126) are worth it. Don't miss the **Huli Wigmen** (p130).

From Tari, fly out of the Highlands to coastal **Wewak** (p135) and the Sepik area. Take a boat up the mighty **Sepik River** (p144) seeing villages and the *haus tambarans* (spirit houses). Fly from Wewak to a luxury resort in picturesque **Madang** (p100) and dive on reefs or wrecks, and relax.

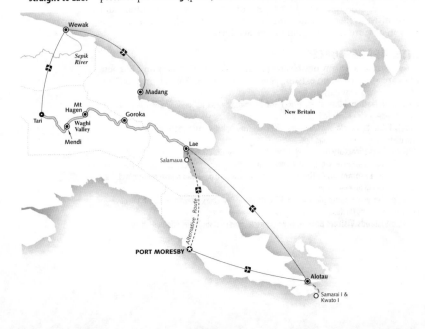

ROAD LESS TRAVELLED

BOUGAINVILLE & BEYOND   Three to four weeks / Lae to Honiara

This nautical extravaganza has something of a Joseph Conrad feel to it; taking slow boats to remote places, crossing borders without showing passports, living and moving as locals do. In **Lae** (p89), find a boat to **Kimbe** (p177); you might have to wait, but you'll get used to waiting on this trip. From Kimbe head down to the **Walindi Plantation Resort** (p178) for some diving or snorkelling with (if you're lucky) killer whales, and return for the twice-weekly boat to **Rabaul** (p170).

In Rabaul, head out to **Matupit Island** (p175) to check out **Tuvurvur** (p170), the volcano that ate the city, before getting under the water at the WWII-era **Submarine Base** (p175). Sleep in the excellent-value **Hamamas Hotel** (p173), a great place to chill out until the boat leaves for **Buka Island** (p194).

At booming Buka take in **Sohano Island** (p194) and buy supplies for the next leg of the journey; that leg takes you across the Buka Passage to Bougainville Island and beyond. Head down the east coast to **Arawa** (p196), and via Aropa on to **Buin** (p196) for the quasilegal border crossing known as the **Gun Run** (p244), because it was once used by Bougainville Revolutionary Army rebels to smuggle guns from the Solomon Islands. Spend your waiting time on Buin trekking to **Admiral Yamamoto's aircraft wreck** (p196).

After the three-hour canoe ride to the mangroves of the Shortland Islands, fly from Ballalae Island to **Gizo** (p205), where the diving and WWII history is amazing (and you can pass through immigration). Island hop from here all the way to **Honiara** (p199), via **Munda** (p208) and the wildlife wonderland that is **Marovo Lagoon** (p209).

Being on a boat or under a palm tree for at least three weeks, covering more than 1200km, should give you plenty of time to read. For relevance, we recommend *Beyond the Coral Sea* by Michael Moran. The seas are much cheaper than the skies, so this is possible for budget travellers.

TAILORED TRIPS

BATTLEFIELD NEW GUINEA   Three weeks / Port Moresby to Rabaul

PNG is littered with rusting relics of WWII both above and below the water. Start in **Port Moresby** (p44) and get a feel for the challenges faced by the troops by walking the **Kokoda Track** (p64).

From Kokoda, continue on to **Popondetta** (p70) and spend a day visiting the overgrown remains of the Japanese bases at **Buna and Gona** (p71).

Take the boat to **Lae** (p89) and visit the moving **Lae War Cemetery** (p91) before tracking back down the coast to **Salamaua** (p97). Check out the Japanese guns and tunnels on the Salamaua peninsula and trek up part of the **Black Cat Track** (p98) to the battlefield at Mt Tambu.

Returning to Lae, ride in a PMV to **Madang** (p100), crossing the Finisterre Ranges through which Allied troops pursued the retreating Japanese after the fall of Lae. In Madang visit the **Coastwatchers' Memorial** (p101) and head out to **Alexishafen** (p106), where bomb craters and rusting Japanese bombers can be seen around the wartime airstrip.

Fly to **Rabaul** (p170), which was at the heart of Japanese operations in the Pacific. Visit the **East New Britain Historical & Cultural Centre** (p166) in Kokopo, snorkel around **Submarine Base** (p175) and check out the **Japanese Barge Tunnels** (p169).

DIVER'S DELIGHT

If you've got the money hiring a live-aboard yacht (p218) is easily the best way to approach this diving paradise. Milne Bay is where 'muck diving' (diving in silty water) was invented and from **Alotau** (p74) you can dive the **Samarai Island** (p79) wharf, the *Muscoota* in **Wagawaga** (p78), plus some unforgettable open-water dives, such as the **Manta Ray Cleaning Station** (p80).

Around the coast **Tufi** (p72) has a fine dive resort, interesting reef and WWII wreck dives. **Madang** (p100) also has many WWII wrecks, with those in **Hansa Bay** (p106) offering a rare mix of history and natural beauty.

Over in New Britain, Kimbe Bay and the seas near **Walindi Plantation Resort** (p178) have some of the PNG's best reef diving, while **Rabaul** (p170) has lots to interest wreck divers. Advanced divers will be thrilled to dive with schools of barracuda at Big Fish Reef close to **Kavieng** (p180). Nearby Three Islands Harbour boasts the *Sanko Maru* and a preserved Japanese minisubmarine.

There's also Solomon Islands, where **Lola Island** (p209), the **Marovo Lagoon** (p209) and **Gizo** (p205) are a few of the world-class dive sites that are unsullied because they see so few divers.

For detailed descriptions of most of these dives, read Lonely Planet's *Diving & Snorkeling Papua New Guinea*.

The Authors

ANDREW BURKE
Coordinating Author, History, Food & Drink, Port Moresby, Central, Oro and Milne Bay Provinces, Morobe, Gulf & Western Provinces, Directory, Transport

Ever since he was given a carved Sepik mask in the late '80s Andrew has been interested in Papua New Guinea. On this trip, he combined another interest: testing the perception of countries that have bad reputations with the real thing. His verdict is that coverage of PNG in the Australian media is damaging in its ignorance. Andrew has worked for newspapers in Australia, the UK and Hong Kong, and when he's not on the road for Lonely Planet he is based in Phnom Penh, Cambodia.

The Coordinating Author's Favourite Trip

To get away from big-city tensions, I'd like to take a series of PMV boats down the Huon Gulf coast (p95). Busama would be my first stop, where, if I'm there at the right time, I'd see giant leatherback turtles coming ashore at night (p96). Just inland is Gwado, and from there, I'd walk a few hours south to Salamaua (p96) to take in its jungle-full of history. I'd keep heading southeast to Lababia (p96) and enjoy the wonderful diversity of the Kamiali Wildlife Management Area (p96). Another few hours down the coast is Pema, from where I'd trek to Bau and hang out with the entertaining ladies of the Tulip Women's Guest House. These places are truly remote and incredibly rewarding.

ROWAN MCKINNON
The Culture, Highlands, Sepik, Madang, North Solomons

Rowan caught the islander bug early. As a kid, for a time he lived in Nauru, a tiny Micronesian island long before Australia shamefully interned asylum seekers there. He's been to PNG and the Solomons regularly since his first visit in 1988, as part of the arty rock band Not Drowning Waving. Rowan coauthored the previous edition of this guidebook and has contributed to various Lonely Planet titles on the South Pacific and the Caribbean. Rowan is a passionate Melaneasian art collector, wannabe fiction writer and (coming full circle), these days he plays guitars in the garage. He lives in Melbourne.

ARNOLD BARKHORDARIAN
Island Provinces, Solomon Islands

Arnold has authored several books on the region and is a keen scuba diver, bushwalker and environmentalist. His passion for taro chips, reef breaks and exotic creatures made PNG and the Solomons a natural choice.

CONTRIBUTING AUTHORS

Jon Cook & Fiona Young wrote the boxed text 'Volunteering in PNG' (p234). Jon is a doctor, who has worked in various hospitals in Victoria, plus he's worked for a short stint in a Zimbabwean hospital and has done voluntary work in Southern India. Fiona is a community development worker, having a degree in Asian & Pacific studies as well as a Masters in Public Advocacy & Action. Before going to PNG in 2003, she worked and volunteered for various community organisations in Melbourne.

Tim Flannery wrote the Environment chapter. He's a naturalist, explorer and author of a number of award-winning books, including *The Future Eaters* and *Throwim Way Leg* (an account of his adventures as a biologist in New Guinea) and the landmark ecological history of North America, *The Eternal Frontier*. Tim lives in Adelaide, where he is Director of the South Australian Museum and a professor at the University of Adelaide.

Sean Dorney wrote Snapshot. He spent 20 years in Papua New Guinea, 17 as the Australian Broadcasting Corporation's PNG correspondent. He was deported in 1984 after the ABC broadcast a programme on PNG's troubled border with Indonesia. Despite the temporary expulsion, PNG later awarded Sean an MBE for contributions to 'broadcasting and sport'. Back in 1976 he captained the national Rugby League team, the Kumuls. Author of two books on PNG, Sean is currently Radio Australia's and the ABC's Pacific correspondent based in Brisbane.

Michael Sorokin wrote the Health chapter. He was born in South Africa, graduated from the University of Witwatersrand in Johannesburg, and holds a Fellowship of the Royal College of Physicians of Edinburgh. Having travelled widely in the West Melanesian region, he was a district medical officer in the Solomons, lecturer at the Fiji School of Medicine, consultant physician in Lautoka, Fiji, and was awarded the Fijian President's medal for medical services in that country. Currently he is a tutor at the University of Adelaide's Medical Education unit and consults in a travel medicine clinic.

Snapshot Sean Dorney

In Papua New Guinea, you should not judge the country by its capital. Port Moresby has a rotten international reputation and despite complaints from PNG politicians that this is the media's fault, unsavoury situations continue. PNG can be a bewildering place where the generosity of the villages is masked by the disaffected unemployed in the country's urban squatter settlements. Even in the ugliest of these settlements people grow flowers. Papua New Guineans love the soil and seem able to grow almost anything, as displayed by the patchwork of gardens on the barren hills around Port Moresby. Despite people drifting to urban locales, they retain strong links with the villages. There is a fierce determination to defend traditional 'land rights' that frustrates economists who regard tradable property as economic progress. In PNG, however, few people go hungry and those who still live in their villages can feed themselves. The *wantok* system (p24), where clanspeople look after each other, is both a blessing and a curse here.

At the national level, PNG's economy relies upon huge resource projects. First it was the Bougainville copper mine, majority owned by Australia's CRA (Conzinc Riotinto of Australia); the PNG government owned 19%. But that closed after plunging Bougainville into a secessionist war. The Ok Tedi copper mine followed but it was built in the geologically unstable Star Mountains where constructing a waste dam was so risky the waste was dumped into the Fly River. Other big projects – the Porgera and Lihir gold mines and the Kutubu oilfields – have provided sorely needed export revenue. China could be the next big mining investor. PNG is also desperately hoping a gas pipeline to Queensland will be its economic saviour. These huge projects employ relatively few locals so for most families cash comes from agriculture – coffee, cocoa, copra, oil palm and vanilla.

PNG's biggest problem is neither crime nor corruption (although both are serious) but a dysfunctional political system that cannot accommodate Papua New Guineans' 867 languages. Unfortunately, the Australian-inherited Westminster system was not designed to run the construction of the Tower of Babel. No prime minister in the 30 years of independence (since 1975) has served a full, five-year term. Survival, not policy is the focus. PNG politics is bewildering because most of the 109 MPs are basically free agents who believe they have been elected to lead rather than represent their people, resulting in 109 cross-purposes.

Most Papua New Guineans are hoping Australia's Enhanced Cooperation Program treaty (whereby more than 200 Australian police and other officials will work within the PNG police force, public service, border control and transport security) will work because their faith in their major state institutions has been rocked. But some resent the intrusion and query whether Australia, the old colonial power, will make a useful contribution in view of past expensive yet unworkable Australian initiatives with police advisers. This new, hands-on approach is a bold experiment under Australia's new cooperative intervention policy, which led to the (so far) successful Regional Assistance Mission to Solomon Islands. But the Solomons was a British colony. And when it got into deep trouble it wasn't Britain it turned to for help.

FAST FACTS – PNG

Population: 5.7 million

GDP: US$3.6 billion

GDP growth: 2.3%

Inflation: 7.5%

Languages spoken: 867

Languages spoken per adult: 3

Land border with Indonesia: 820km

Parliamentary political parties: 18

Indigenous counting systems: More than 50 (one is based on joints on of the body and the nose)

Number of airports: 559

FAST FACTS – SOLOMON ISLANDS

Population: 524,000

GDP: US$394 million

Economic contraction 2000–02 (post-ethnic tension): 23.6%

Weapons destroyed after July 2003 intervention: 3730

Languages spoken: 90

CIA phrase for government: Parliamentary democracy tending towards anarchy

People per telephone: 79

American and Japanese warships sunk in Iron Bottom Sound: 67

History

THE FIRST ARRIVALS

Archaeological evidence suggests humans first reached New Guinea, and then Australia and the Solomon Islands, by island hopping across the Indonesian archipelago from Asia more than 50,000 years ago. The migrations were made easier by a fall in the sea level caused by an ice age, and by a land bridge that linked PNG with northern Australia. Subsequent migrations over many years account for the different language groups: Austronesian and non-Austronesian.

Evidence of early coastal settlements includes 40,000-year-old stone axes found in Morobe Province. It is believed humans reached the Highlands about 30,000 years ago. At Kuk (or Kup) Swamp in the Wahgi Valley in Western Highlands Province, archaeologists have found evidence of human habitation going back 20,000 years and there is evidence of gardening beginning 9000 years ago, which makes Papua New Guineans among the world's first farmers.

New Ireland, Buka and the Solomon Islands were probably inhabited around 30,000 years ago and Manus Island 10,000 years ago.

EUROPEAN CONTACT

The first European impact on PNG was indirect but important. The sweet potato was taken from South America to Southeast Asia by the Portuguese and Spaniards in the 16th century and it is believed Malay traders then brought it to Papua Province (West Papua), from where it was traded into the Highlands. Its high yield and tolerance for poor and cold soils led to its cultivation at higher altitudes, thus expanding the population.

Europeans started arriving in 1512, when Portuguese sailor Antonio d'Abreu sighted the coast. However, it wasn't until 1526 that another Portuguese, Jorge de Meneses, became the first European to set foot on the main island. Unconcerned by the fact they'd never seen most of it, in 1660 the Dutch East Indies Company claimed sovereignty over New Guinea.

The British East India Company explored parts of western New Guinea in 1793 and even made a tentative claim on the island but, in 1824, Britain and the Netherlands agreed the latter's claim to the western half should stand. A series of British 'claims' followed; every time a British ship sailed by, someone would hop ashore, run the flag up the nearest tree and claim the whole place on behalf of Queen Victoria, which would be repudiated by the Queen's government only for the next captain to sail by and go through the whole stunt again.

German interest in the northeast coast spurred the British, in 1884, to finally announce they were getting serious about New Guinea. In response, the Germans quickly raised the flag on the north coast. A compromise was reached – a highly arbitrary line was drawn east–west in the 'uninhabited' Highlands between German and British New Guinea.

New Guinea was now divided into three sections: a Dutch half protecting the eastern edge of the Dutch East Indies, a British quarter to keep

DID YOU KNOW?

Sixteenth-century Portuguese explorers named New Guinea, Ilhas dos Papuas (Island of the Fuzzy-Hairs) from the Malay word *papuwah*. Later, Spanish navigator Ynigo Ortis de Retez likened it to West Africa's Guinea and named it New Guinea. The names were combined at independence in 1975.

50,000 BC	1526
An ice age allows the first humans to island hop their way to New Guinea	Portuguese explorer Jorge de Meneses is the first European to land on New Guinea

the Germans (and everybody else) away from Australia and a German quarter because it looked like it could be a damned good investment.

But the Germans would have to wait. For 15 years the mosquitoes were the only things to profit from the German New Guinea Company's presence on the north coast. The company moved its administrative base from one centre to another until 1899, when it threw in the towel and shifted away from the threat of mosquito bites to the happier climes of the Bismarck Archipelago and quickly started to make those fat profits it had always wanted. Many German-initiated plantations are still operating today.

In 1888 Sir William MacGregor became British New Guinea's administrator and established a native police force to spread the benefits of British government. He instituted the policy of 'government by patrol', which continued through the Australian period. In 1906 British New Guinea became the Territory of Papua and its administration was taken over by newly independent Australia.

Despite being in demise elsewhere, slaving was thriving in New Guinea and especially the Solomons during the late 19th and early 20th centuries. Known as 'blackbirding', men were carted off to provide plantation labour in northern Australia and Fiji. More than 29,000 people were taken from the Solomons alone.

DID YOU KNOW?

In 1927 a 17-year-old Errol Flynn arrived in PNG. He worked as a cadet patrol officer, gold prospector, slaver, plantation manager, copra trader, charter boat captain, pearl diver and a diamond smuggler for six years. Later, he promoted New Guinea, once calling it one of the great loves of his life.

1914–41

When WWI broke out in 1914 the British government asked Australia to occupy German New Guinea. An Australian force was dispatched and, after a few brief skirmishes, the Germans surrendered. In 1920 the League of Nations officially handed German New Guinea over to Australia as a mandated territory.

Australia was quick to eradicate the German commercial and plantation presence, baulking only at the German missions. Australia enacted legislation aimed at restricting the commercial exploitation of Eastern New Guinea to British nationals, and (more precisely) Australians. Copra, rubber, coffee and cocoa were the main earners, but indigenous production was largely ignored and the majority of the population continued to exist on subsistence agriculture.

The discovery of large deposits of gold at Edie Creek and the Bulolo Valley in the 1920s brought men and wealth to the north coast; and after 400 years of coastal contact, some of those white men finally made it into the interior (see 'The Land that Time Forgot', p20).

Under the Australian administration, government-by-patrol was the key to both exploration and control. Patrol officers, or *kiaps*, were usually the first Europeans to venture into previously 'uncontacted' areas but were also responsible for making the government's presence felt on a regular basis. This situation continued until independence. But in the Solomons the first prominent rejection of European values occurred in the 1927 Kwaio Rebellion (p199).

For a look at relics from WWII, check out the well-researched www .pacificwrecks.com. It has plenty of information on downed planes, sunken ships, including details on their whereabouts, and MIAs.

WWII

Having raced south through Asia and the Pacific, the Japanese occupied Rabaul in January 1942 and most of the Solomon Islands shortly after. But their success was short-lived. Australian troops fought back an advance

1876	1930
Italian adventurer Luigi d'Albertis charts the Fly River in a tiny steamer, using fireworks to scare off menacing-looking locals	The Leahy brothers 'discover' the Highlands and about one million people – living completely unaware of the outside world

---

THE LAND THAT TIME FORGOT

When Mick Leahy ventured inland in 1930 he was looking for gold. Instead, on that and nine subsequent expeditions during the next five years, Leahy, his brother Dan and Jim Taylor 'discovered' about a million people living in the secluded valleys of the New Guinea Highlands.

New Guinea's white colonialists had previously thought the area uninhabited, but it was the most densely populated part of the country. In the age of aeroplanes, radio and international telecommunications, the discovery was stunning. It didn't take long for the 'land that time forgot' to be dragged into the 20th century. The Leahy brothers introduced coffee, and before long missionaries and aircraft were also arriving. The Highlanders, who had only known a barter economy, were quick to adapt to cash.

Mick Leahy's meticulous recording of events – in his diary, several hours of 16mm film and more than 5000 photographs – can be seen in the acclaimed 1983 documentary *First Contact*.

Through the accounts of Japanese, Australian and American war veterans and Papua New Guinean villagers, *Angels of War* (1982) portrays the plight of villagers who lived through some of the most brutal fighting of the Pacific campaign.

along the rugged Kokoda Track (p69), which the Japanese were using in an attempt to reach and take Port Moresby, the only remaining Australian stronghold on the island. In a flanking move, the Japanese landed at Milne Bay (p73) but were repulsed after a bloody 10-day battle with Australian troops. At the same time, US forces landed on Guadalcanal (p199) in the Solomons, initially suffering heavy casualties but, after months of fighting, eventually taking the island.

The Japanese came within 50km of Port Moresby, but an unsustainably extended supply line and heroic resistance by Australian soldiers with local help turned the course of the whole Pacific war. By September 1942 the previously undefeated Japanese were in a slow and bloody retreat. During the next 16 months Australian and American forces battled their way toward the Japanese strongholds along the north coast, eventually taking Salamaua, Buna, Gona and Lae (see p87) at a cost of thousands of lives.

The Japanese, however, refused to surrender. It took until 1945 to regain all the mainland from the Japanese but New Ireland, New Britain and Bougainville were not relieved until the Japanese surrender.

Most Melanesians were militarily neutral in the conflict, although they were used extensively on both sides as labourers, guides, carriers and informers. But some were heavily involved. It is estimated that almost a third of Tolais, from northern New Britain, were killed.

A Bastard of a Place (2003) by Peter Brune accurately details fighting on the Kokoda Track and the bitter struggle to recapture the Japanese coastal positions, and criticises some of the senior Australian and American officers.

THE END OF COLONIALISM

While masses of abandoned war equipment was soon put to use in developing both the Solomon Islands and New Guinea, the war's main impact proved to be social and political. The colonial rulers, who had been seen as the only possible form of government, lost that status.

An influx of expatriates to PNG, mainly Australians, fuelled rapid economic growth. The expatriate population grew from about 6000 to more than 50,000 in 1971. Today it's about 20,000.

Colonialism wasn't popular in the 1950s and '60s and Australia was urged to prepare Papua and New Guinea for independence. A visiting UN mission in 1962 stressed that if the people weren't pushing for independence, then it was Australia's responsibility to do so. Australia's policy of

---

1942	1975
The invading Japanese face US and Australian troops in PNG and the Solomons	PNG gains independence from Australia, with Michael Somare as the first prime minister

reinforcing literacy and education was wedded to a concerted effort to create an educated social group that could run government.

In 1964, a House of Assembly with 64 members was formed. Internal self-government came into effect in 1973, followed by full independence on 16 September 1975.

In the Solomons the Marching Rule nationalist movement was crushed by the British in the early 1950s, but self-rule was slowly introduced, culminating in independence in 1978.

AFTER INDEPENDENCE

Even today, PNG is one of the least nationalist countries on earth – ask anyone where their allegiances lie and they'll name their clan or tribe and laugh if you suggest they are 'Papua New Guinean'. Yet despite this, the years immediately following independence were relatively trouble-free.

Law and order (p223) was not a serious issue until the 1990s and the mineral-rich country began to develop large-scale mining operations. These fast became the greatest contributors to the economy, but also social, environmental and political burdens that, in the 1980s and '90s, took a heavy toll. First the giant Ok Tedi gold and copper mine (p158) poisoned much of the Ok Tedi and Fly Rivers, and then conflict over profits from the Panguna copper mine in Bouganville descended into war (see p193).

The Bougainville conflict drained resources and divided PNG along tribal lines for years, and strained relations with the Solomon Islands. In 1996 the government hired mercenaries to try to crush the separatists. What became known as the Sandline Affair was a disaster, but military intervention led by Australia and New Zealand brought peace. The Solomons, meanwhile, had its own war in the late 1990s. Groups from Guadalcanal and Malaita squared off along ethnic lines, but Australian- and New Zealand–led intervention brought peace (see p199). The 1980s and '90s saw PNG face a series of challenges: a volcanic eruption in 1994 buried much of Rabaul (see p174); ongoing border problems involving the Organisasi Papua Merdeka (Free West Papua Movement) strained relations with Indonesia and saw thousands moved to refugee camps in PNG; and a growing level of corruption and government misspending sucked money away from where it was needed most – education and health. All this served as a backdrop to the revolving door of prime ministers and no-confidence motions that continues to characterise PNG politics.

THE 21ST CENTURY

In 2001 a peace deal providing the framework for an autonomous government was signed in Bougainville (see p192). So far, the peace is holding. Sir Michael Somare, PNG's 'father of independence', returned in 2002 for a third stint as prime minister and promptly introduced much-needed electoral reforms that will hopefully create a more stable political climate, and in turn help the economy. By mid-2004, however, Somare's government was avoiding the familiar no-confidence motion by prematurely adjourning parliament. For more on PNG's current political state, see p17.

DID YOU KNOW?

Barely recovered from WWII's devastation, in 1951 the district headquarters of Central Province, Higaturu, was flattened when Mt Lamington erupted, killing more than 3000 people. The new capital, Popondetta, was built further from the volcano.

The Sandline Affair by veteran Pacific correspondent Sean Dorney is a thorough account of the Bougainville war and the disastrous mercenary affair that ultimately precipitated its end. Details of the corruption involved are impressive, though the early years of the war are not so well explained.

1978	1994
Solomon Islands becomes independent	Mt Tuvurvur erupts, burying Rabaul in volcanic ash until most of the town collapses

The Culture

REGIONAL IDENTITY

The people of Papua New Guinea and the Solomon Islands are almost all Melanesians but the background of the population varies greatly. Those that aren't Melanesians share many Melanesian habits. Increasingly, there's European and Chinese blood in the mix, more so in the towns.

Some people have typical urban lifestyles with mobile phones and comfortable homes. Others inhabit remote areas and may never have seen a town or a white person. In traditional PNG societies, despite their sophisticated agricultural and maritime skills, tools and artefacts were made of wood, bone, pottery or stone. There was no metal working, nor domestic animal power nor wheel. Extensive trading networks existed and rare shells were used as currency. People traded widely in pottery, stone tools, obsidian (dark, glassy volcanic rock), dyes, salt, sago and smoked fish. Some people still live this way and, while the hard currency and cash crops have replaced kina shells, traditional valuables still hold value and certain ceremonial objects are revered.

In just a few generations since European contact, the people of Papua New Guinea and the Solomon Islands have found themselves in independent island states in the age of information and the Internet. Along the way they've been browbeaten by Bible-thumpers and exploited by colonial power. Most claim to be Catholic but European religion is often blended with traditional beliefs. The primary obligation that Melanesian people have is to their *wantoks* (see p24), which is taken very seriously and gift-giving is highly formalised. You might think nothing of giving somebody a small gift but in Melanesian culture that person is then indebted to you.

There's cynicism about politics, especially among those in remote areas (where roads and services are in decline) who regard politicians as corrupt. But PNG has a young demographic – the median age is 19.7 years – and the energy, hope and Melanesian optimism are shown in their music, friendliness and ready laughter. One of the many things that confounds outsiders is the warmth of people who were forever at war; ritually killing and eating each other. These people's many facets no doubt contribute to anthropologists' attraction for this region.

Young, urbanised Papua New Guineans and Solomon Islanders wear Eminem T-shirts but prefer their own home-grown sounds to the Western pop charts. Many travel overseas and stay with relatives in Cairns and Brisbane. They almost all chew *buai* (betel nut), go to church, worship dead ancestors and fear *masalais* (malevolent spirits).

LIFESTYLE

Melanesians are laid-back, at least on the coast where it's too hot to get overly fussed. Highlanders are a bit more feisty and passionate. Everyone seems to walk slowly, but they've got this climate worked out – cling to the shade, sleep through the midday heat and save physical exertion for village rugby late in the day.

Most rural people are subsistence farmers or growers and traders of cash crops, such as bananas, betel nut and coffee. In the towns and cities, unskilled work pays about K120 to K150 per fortnight; skilled middle income earners earn K400 to K500 per fortnight.

Most people live very simply by Western standards. In the bush people have very few possessions and often no cash income. In the cities a

DID YOU KNOW

Shark-calling in Malaita in the Solomons involves boys handfeeding sharks and riding on their backs. For more details, see p186.

DID YOU KNOW?

After the great American military machine left at the end of WWII, cargo cults began to sprout. People built runways for imaginary planes to land on and deliver *kago* (material goods). Locals ritually mimicked military officers sitting at desks shuffling paper. See p187.

number of educated people lead sophisticated middle-class lives, other people live in squalor in city-fringe settlements. PNG lifestyles range from the rarefied cold-weather climes of the Highlands to life on the coast in stilt houses above the shifting tide.

Both PNG and the Solomons are changing quickly and locals want development. Particularly in PNG, people have married outside their traditional clans and homelands, and Tok Ples ('talk place' clan language) is increasingly being replaced in the villages with Tok Pisin (the Pidgin language). Isolated communities are suddenly being confronted with huge mining and logging operations. These bring new roads and facilities – remote areas are opened to Western influences, good and bad.

In the cities are also people who drift in from the villages looking for work – there aren't any unemployment benefits in PNG and these people often commit petty crimes to eat. Those who are engineering graduates can't get always work and they too fall into gangs of *raskols* just to survive. Poker machines and home-brew alcohol are problems, and AIDS is a looming disaster.

Arsegras is Tok Pisin for that bit of grass or tanket leaves that covers your arse. Your *maugras* is your beard.

Traditional Lifestyle

In the village, *bigmen* or chiefs traditionally presided over the affairs of the clan. Most villages were small, comprising several generations of just one extended family. They were typically isolated and this is why so many distinct languages evolved (there are 90 in the Solomon Islands). One of PNG's features is its extraordinary number of mutually unintelligible languages – 867 at last count – but many will die out. Ownership in the Western sense didn't exist in traditional societies, rather ownership was a concept tied up in family and clan rights, controlled by the male elder.

For those who continue to live the traditional life, there are three main areas of everyday importance – prestige, pigs and gardening. A village chief shows wealth by owning and displaying certain traditional valuables, or by hosting lavish feasts where dozens of pigs are slaughtered. *Bigmen* don't inherit their titles, they earn them by accolades in war, wisdom in councils, magic-practice skills and the secret arts that are *tambu* for women. Particularly in the Highlands, people have to be made aware how wealthy *bigmen* are, so ceremonial life in this region focuses on ostentatious displays and in giving things away. There are various ways in which this is formalised; it's part of a wide circle of exchange and interclan relationships. Wealth is never really given away in the Western sense. Your gifts cement a relationship with the receiver, who then has obligations to you. Obligation and payback are deadly serious in Highlands culture; Melanesia has no privileged classes, but individuals still inherit land through their parents (often their mother). Village life in PNG and the Solomons is usually egalitarian, and ownership continues to be a concept tied up in family and clan rights.

Sorcery and black magic have had a strong resurgence in recent years.

Pigs are extremely valuable, they're regarded as family members and lactating women sometimes suckle piglets. People can be seen out taking their pig for a walk on a leash, patiently waiting as the pig grazes and digs by the roadside. Large pigs can be worth K1000. Dogs, on the other hand, are mangy, fly-blown creatures left to scavenge for food.

People in both countries still maintain animist beliefs. Despite the inroads of Christianity, ancestor worship is still important. The netherworld is also inhabited by spirits, both protective and malevolent, and there are creation myths that involve animal totems. More so in certain areas; islanders from Malaita in the Solomons worship sharks while some Sepik River people revere crocodiles. Christianity has a tight grip on most people, but it

DID YOU KNOW?

Trobriand Islanders worship yams and build elaborate yam houses many storeys high. Everywhere there is great art and ritual involved in gardening.

hasn't supplanted traditional beliefs. They coexist – Jesus is alive in people's hearts and minds without conflicting with their traditional ideas.

Bride price is the formalised gift-giving of money and certain traditional valuables to the father of a would-be bride. It often comprises shell money, but can also include cash, pigs and SP Lager. Part of becoming a man and commanding respect in traditional societies is to work hard and raise a bride price so you can marry. Bride price is common, but these days many men compile their bride price *after* they're married.

POPULATION
PNG

PNG people are closely related to people from other parts of the Pacific. There are Papuans, the first arrivals; Melanesians, who represent 95% of people and are related to people from the Solomon Islands, Vanuatu, Fiji and New Caledonia; Polynesians, related to New Zealand Maoris, Tongans, Samoans and Hawaiian islanders; and Micronesians, related to people in the Marshall Islands, Kiribati and Nauru.

Only 15% of people live in urban areas, while most of the rest are subsistence farmers. Nearly two million people live in the Highlands, the most densely populated part of the country. Most cities have many people who weren't born there. Many Highlanders migrate to Port Moresby and elsewhere, but few coastal people move into the Highlands. Melanesian people still identify more strongly with their clan links and their origins than with the people they come to live with, so enclaves exist in the settlement areas of the big cities, and there is a traditional distrust between Highlanders and coastal people. During the Bougainville war, dark-skinned *bukas* (Bougainvilleans) used to be harassed and vilified around PNG, but this doesn't seem to happen now.

Only Port Moresby, Lae and Mt Hagen have a real big-city crush. The other provincial capitals are not so crowded (except on provincial show

THE WANTOK SYSTEM

Fundamental to Melanesian culture is the idea of *wantoks* (meaning 'one talk' in Tok Pisin) and your *wantoks* are those who speak your language. Every Melanesian is born with duties to their *wantoks* but they also have privileges. Within the clan and village, each person can expect to be housed and fed, and to share in the community's assets. Regardless of whether clanspeople are in Wewak or Warsaw, all *wantoks* can expect to be accommodated and fed, until they can make a more permanent home.

This is a social security system, and the plague of both democratic politics and enterprise. Some say that the *wantok* system is the best and worst thing about PNG and the Solomon Islands. For villagers, it is an egalitarian way for the community to share its spoils. In rapidly changing circumstances, the village and the clan provide basic economic support as well as a sense of belonging.

When these ideas are transposed to politics and social affairs, it becomes nepotism and, at worst, corruption. In the public service, the police, the army and especially in politics, this is a scourge. Candidates don't get to run without the support of their fellow *bigmen*, who expect that when 'their' candidate is elected, their generosity will be repaid. The *wantok* system is also the greatest disincentive to enterprise.

The *wantok* system is a microcosm of the battle being waged between the modern and the traditional in PNG. It is so deeply entrenched that some educated youngsters choose to move away from their families to avoid the calls for handouts. And without it life would be much harder for many others. Just saying 'no' to a *wantok*, especially from your extended family, is rarely an option.

day). Land pressures have caused people to leave the villages and seek work, and great urban squatter settlements have appeared around many major cities. In 2002 Madang authorities burnt down a huge Sepiks' settlement on the outskirts of town after giving the residents some resettlement compensation.

Solomon Islands

The Solomons people are 94% Melanesian and otherwise made up of Polynesians, some relocated Micronesian communities and a few expatriates.

Malaita has more than twice the population of rural Guadalcanal and only Honiara has many people. Here too land pressures have forced locals to move, most notably Malaitan islanders to Gaudalcanal, and this in part brought on the ethnic tensions that began boiling over in 1999. Since then 20,000 people have been coerced into returning to Malaita, exacerbating its overpopulation problems.

Expatriates

In both PNG and the Solomons there are relatively large numbers of expats, but this is in decline. There are 19,200 noncitizens in PNG, down from a 1971 peak of 50,000, and about a quarter of these are West Papuan refugees living in border camps.

Most expats are Australians, Brits and Germans, but there's a large Chinese community that has been in PNG a long time and it has intermixed with the local population more than any other group. Around Vanimo there are significant numbers of Indonesians and Malaysians.

Expats fall into three groups – those who are in PNG and the Solomons for a long time or even a lifetime, expat workers who come in on lucrative two-year contracts with international companies and younger people who come in for a period as volunteers, aid workers and NGOs.

There are no more *mastas* in oversized shorts and knee-length white socks building empires with cheap local labour. Today's expatriate community is a varied group; some are involved in the fledgling tourism sector as hotel proprietors or scuba-diving instructors. There are religious zealots, people fleeing broken marriages or dodgy business activities, obsessed scientific nerds studying insect larvae, and adventurers.

When independence came in 1975, many Australian and Chinese residents were eligible for PNG citizenship, on the condition that they renounced their original citizenship. Many did and some now hold positions of considerable political and economic importance.

SPORT

Organised sport is in its infancy in PNG and the Solomon Islands. Papua New Guineans are proud of their nationals doing well in sport overseas – Mal Michael is a successful Australian Rules footballer, and Marcus Bai was a very successful rugby league player in Australia, and now plays in England. Stanley Nandex from Erave district in Southern Highlands Province is the world super-middleweight kickboxing champion.

Melanesian people love sport, and ball games of all kinds fit into their communal outdoorsy culture. There are raggedy volleyball nets in many villages and impromptu rugby games are played in village *singsing* grounds. Local netball and rugby competitions are played on weekends in parks and fields everywhere. Soccer and softball are now popular.

Televised sport is of paramount importance and everybody aligns themselves fiercely (and arbitrarily) to the Blues or Maroons for the Australian Rugby League's state-of-origin match between Queensland

'There are religious zealots ... obsessed scientific nerds studying insect larvae, and adventurers.'

and New South Wales. The fervour for this big event sees a rash of T-shirt sales and vast amounts of money wagered on the outcome.

If you get to the Trobriand Islands (p81), make sure you take in a game of Trobriands cricket. Cricket was introduced in 1903 by Methodist missionaries to reduce ritual warfare, and in the century since, has been adapted to include many local rules as well as magic, war paint, feasting and ritual.

'Cricket has been adapted to include ... magic, war paint, feasting and ritual.'

MEDIA

The media is vigorous and fair-minded in PNG. People write to the newspapers expressing free opinions and many people buy newspapers. This edginess has escalated a couple of times when newspaper offices in Moresby and Buka were raided and vandalised.

The two main newspapers are majority-owned by Murdoch and a Malaysian company. A third local daily is published in Tok Pisin by a Christian organisation. The content is not overtly churchy, but still conservative in manners of religion and anything strongly sexual. There's thorough national coverage in the daily newspapers, as well as reasonable overseas news.

There are several FM radio stations in each town that play local music and two national radio broadcasters. Local content is strong.

The one Solomons daily is published and owned by local John Lamani. This region has had more breathing room for journalists since the Regional Assistance Mission to the Solomon Islands (RAMSI) was established.

For more information on television media, see p28.

RELIGION

Both the PNG and Solomon Islands constitutions declare that they are Christian countries. The churches have played an important role in developing the countries' health and education services, as well as infrastructure. But they have also sought to repress traditional knowledge and cultural practices.

About 28% of people are Catholic, 23% Evangelical Lutheran, 13% belong to the Uniting Church, and there are significant numbers of followers of the Evangelical Alliance, Seventh-Day Adventist, Pentecostal and Anglican churches. In the Solomons 35% are members of the Anglican-affiliated Church of Melanesia and 20% are Catholic. Regardless of where people align their Christian beliefs, they retain many of their beliefs in traditional religion and customary practices.

In most areas of PNG and the Solomons traditional life continues but Christian churches are extremely influential. American hellfire fundamentalists come to save the lost souls. They have seminars and give public speeches in the marketplaces of Port Moresby and Honiara. Local soapbox preachers, common in many towns, give the word of God in Tok Pisin, which can be quite interesting.

WOMEN IN PAPUA NEW GUINEA & THE SOLOMON ISLANDS

Sexual politics is complicated in traditional Melanesian society. In some places in the Highlands husband and wife don't live together at all and sexual relations are not to be taken lightly. Some Melanesian men have two or more wives. In many belief systems, women are considered dangerous (in terms of black magic) especially during menstruation. Women often live in a house alone with the young children, or with sisters and their nieces and nephews. In many places land rights pass through the mother and older women can wield great power in the villages.

Women carry *kago* (cargo) in *bilums* (string bags) home from the market while the man walks unburdened. Women do most of the food gardening, although men grow magnificent decorative gardens. Traditionally, men practise arts that are exclusively their domain and, although these can sometimes be shown to women travellers, they are still *tambu* for local women.

Domestic violence is a major problem. A World Health Organisation report into PNG in 1998 claimed that 56% of women have been victims of domestic violence, and this means that PNG has the second-highest level of violence against women in the world after Uganda. PNG is a patriarchal country and the payment of bride price often leads to the belief that the husband has a right to beat his wife. Public awareness campaigns in recent years have really brought the issue to the surface, but unless police are prepared to enforce tougher laws the problem won't go away. Although alcohol is banned in parts of PNG, home-brew alcohol – sometimes 90% proof – and resulting violence is a major problem.

Physical dislocation and poverty drive some women into prostitution and this is particularly noticeable in Port Moresby, Lae and Mt Hagen. An explosion of HIV/AIDS is said to be imminent and this places these women at special risk. The exposure of the HIV/AIDS risk is very real to many women because their husbands are often promiscuous. Once infected, HIV/AIDS sufferers are ostracised from their communities, and infected children are abandoned

ARTS

Papua New Guinea's arts are regarded as the most striking and varied in the Pacific, and Solomon Islanders, being great carvers, are part of the same cultural tradition. The lack of contact between different villages and groups of people has led to a potent array of indigenous art.

Contemporary art is also vividly expressed – the death of Mathias Kauage, PNG's world-famous painter, in May 2003 was a huge national loss (see p30).

In traditional societies, dance, song, music, sculpture and body adornment were related to ceremonies. Art was either utilitarian (such as bowls or canoes) or religious. Since European contact, art has become objectified. There have always been master carvers and mask-makers but their role in traditional cultures was to enable the ceremonies and rituals to be performed correctly, and to serve the clan and chief.

The production of artefacts is often ritualistic. On some of the islands secret men's societies build *dukduks* (spiritual costumes) or carve *malangan* masks (totemic figures honouring the dead). Women are forbidden to look upon a *dukduk* or *malangan* until it is brought to life in a ceremony by a fierce anonymous character. But a *dukduk* is regarded as a spirit entity.

'The lack of contact between different villages and groups of people has led to a potent array of indigenous art.'

Cinema & TV

Despite the fact that there's no local film production, there's a rich tradition of documentary films made in PNG – and in the Solomons to a lesser degree. Some of the finest films are listed in the boxed text below. Errol Flynn spent time in PNG and more recently Madang's north coast was the setting for Pierce Brosnan's portrayal of *Robinson Crusoe*.

Australian Mark Worth was born in PNG and spent most of his professional life there as a pioneering 'guerrilla' journalist and film maker. While shooting his 1995 film *Raskols,* Worth got embroiled in a Highlands tribal war. He had just finished making *Land of the Morning Star,* about the struggles in West Papua, when he died in Jayapura in 2004.

TOP DOCOS

Bob Connolly and the late Robin Anderson made a trilogy of excellent documentaries about PNG. *First Contact* is an extraordinary film, using footage shot by the Leahy brothers when they went into the Highlands in 1933 in search of gold. Instead they found 100,000 people living in the Wahgi Valley who had no idea that the outside world existed. It's truly brilliant cinema and made from old scratchy black-and-white images showing amazing scenes of Highlanders in traditional gear. They look completely bewildered when the Leahy brothers land a plane, play music on a wind-up gramophone and when they see themselves in little mirrors. *Joe Leahy's Neighbours* shows a traditional society slowly coming to terms with the modernised world. Joe is the son of Mick Leahy (with one of his Highlands concubines) and his profitable coffee plantation in the Highlands sets him apart from the neighbouring Ganiga clanspeople, whose subsistence lifestyles remain almost unchanged. *Black Harvest* completes the trilogy, showing Joe Leahy's coffee plantation expanding in partnership with the Ganiga clan. Just before the first harvest (after a five-year maturation), international coffee prices plummet and clan warfare breaks out.

Since the Company Came, made in 2000 by Russell Hawkins, is about logging Rendova Island in the Solomons, land disputes and clan troubles.

Dennis O'Rourke's *The Shark Callers of Kontu* is justifiably famous. O'Rourke's film explores the ancient New Ireland art of shark-calling. He also looks at the bewildering dichotomies for Kontu villagers between their traditional ways and the impact of a rapidly arriving 21st century.

Also set in a New Ireland village is Chris Owen's splendid documentary *Malangan Labadama,* which depicts the preparations, rituals and festivities surrounding the death of the village *mimi* (elder and chief) Buk Buk in the island's Mandak region. It provides a wonderful insight into Malangan culture. Owen, an expat Australian, also created *Bridewealth for a Goddess* in 2000, which tells the story of Amb Kor, a goddess who comes to Highlander chief Ru Kundil in a dream and his attempts to woo her through elaborate rituals.

Ronin Films (www.roninfilms.com.au) in Australia distributes many of these titles.

EmTV is PNG's national broadcaster in PNG, but the Solomons doesn't have one. Satellite dishes in both countries pick up CNN, BBC World and Australian programmes, as well as other subscription TV. EmTV is very watchable – for a little while. It has its own news and sport programmes, cheesy local ads in Tok Pisin, local music-video shows and some lightweight 'lifestyle' programmes which mostly advertise outdoor furniture from Brian Bell stores. Otherwise it carries Australian programming. Watching EmTV is a good way to pick up some Pidgin language skills. The conservative influence of the church ensures that TV carries no overtly sexual content (but violent Rambo-style vigilante movies are very common and popular).

Music

Melanesians are incredibly musical people and some local artists have had international success. They are great singers – listen to the church singing early on a Sunday morning – and natural guitar and ukulele players.

TRADITONAL MUSIC

In recent years there's been some revival of traditional music, but the impact of missionary workers has meant many traditional musical forms have been lost. The *kundu* drum is the most widely used traditional instrument, shaped like a tall, narrow egg-timer and covered with lizard skin. Many cultures use *garamuts* (hollowed-out logs from wrist-size up to tree-trunk size). *Garamut* drummers play astonishing rhythms in hierarchical ensembles where the senior drummers play the trickiest patterns. The rhythms are specific to the region and are very complex.

Shells and bamboo panpipes are blown, while rattles are made from gourds and bundled banana leaves. Highland flutes (simple throwaway bamboo tubes) are played in pairs and do an eerie call-and-response routine. Sepik flutes are highly decorated and hollowed from solid timber. Jew's harps are also indigenous to PNG. Other instruments include bull roarers and ceramic whistles from the Highlands.

CONTEMPORARY MUSIC

It's exciting that countries as small as PNG and the Solomons can support such strong local music scenes. Local radio is very supportive of local music (which is readily for sale as cassettes and CDs). Stringband music is played by four or five guitarists and a ukulele player and based loosely around a 12-bar blues structure. The guitars are tuned in unorthodox ways and are often played with an arpeggiated, hammer-on action. The stringband sound has a real swing to it in a lazy South Pacific kind of way, but it varies widely from the bright and happy Tolai (East New Britain Province) sound to the more dirge-like and sombre Manus stringband music. Virtually every village has its own stringband and most PNG pop music comes out of this tradition. Reggae is also a strong influence in modern pop music.

In the '70s and '80s Sanguma was a pioneering band that fused jazz-rock with indigenous sounds – and had some international success. Another artist, George Telek has been touring and working in Europe and Australia. Ben Hakalitz and Baruka Tau (Yothu Yindi's former band member) performed with Yothu Yindi in stadiums in Brazil and to close the 2000 Sydney Olympics.

Theatre & Dance

There are community-based drama groups as well as those associated with the universities and colleges. National funding for theatre has dried up, and some great initiatives have had to stop. Theatre groups commonly work on local-legend themes and stories, bringing to life traditional stories.

RECOMMENDED LISTENING

■ George Telek's *Serious Tam*, recorded at Peter Gabriel's Real World Studios, is an evocative record that features Telek's extraordinary voice. His 1999 album *Telek* won an Australian ARIA Award and he recorded *Amete* in Melbourne 2003. Telek is a Tolai from Rabaul.

■ Quakes have had more than 20 No 1 hits in PNG, and had hits in Fiji, the Solomons, Vanuatu and New Caledonia. Theirs is a very traditional stringband sound supplemented by a drum machine, and emphasises melody and vocal harmonies. *Best Hits Volume 2* is a good compilation.

■ Hausboi from Manus are the most interesting new act, and their *Diriman* CD is great. Crosby, Stills & Nash harmonies meet stringband rhythms via some boy-band soul and a little hip-hop (with traditional flutes and *garamuts*). Highly recommended.

■ O-Shen grew up in Lae and America, son of an American father and Central Province mother, and he's the current superstar. His music derives from American hip-hop and, although he sings in Tok Pisin, there's not a strong Melanesian feel in it. Still *Kanaka Pasifika* was the hottest record of 2004.

■ *Tabaran* was a collaboration between Australia's Not Drowning Waving and Rabaul-based musicians at Pacific Gold Studios (pre–volcanic eruption days), including George Telek. A great mix of cultures and music, this 1988 recording is a classic and pre-dates the worldwide explosion of 'world music'. Stringbands and funeral chants meet arty atmospherics, electric guitars and wall-of-sound percussion.

The Raun Raun Theatre in Goroka occasionally has performances by the resident ensemble. The Kaikuali Theatre Group in Alotau is another long-established group of performers, and Drum Drum Theatre Group is based in Port Moresby (www.drumdrum.com.au).

Architecture

Modern architecture is a relatively new concept in PNG and the Solomons. *Haus tambarans* were the traditional expression of formal architecture and there are incredible *haus tambarans* in the Sepik and in the Highlands. Yam houses in the Trobriands are another interesting traditional form (see p150). An emerging style blends traditional forms and materials into modern structures on a large scale. The towering façade of the PNG parliament house takes its shape and big decorated prow from Sepik *haus tambarans*. Another individual piece of architecture is the Raun Raun Theatre in Goroka. On a smaller scale, some of the upmarket lodges around the country exhibit this building style quite successfully, such as Ambua Lodge in the Southern Highlands (p129) and Karawari Lodge in the East Sepik Province (p152).

Painting & Printmaking

PNG painting is typically 'flat', with no sense of perspective or receding backgrounds. Themes often combine elements of traditional and modern culture or the illustration of local legends, such as the shark or turtle spirit. Printmaking evolved from the Melanesian tradition of tapa cloth production and textile design is often reminiscent of tapa designs. Silkscreening is common and Papua New Guineans do fantastic T-shirt art (although this seems to be less common than a decade ago). The Faculty of Creative Arts (also known as the National Art School) was established at the University of PNG in Port Moresby in 1972. With a strong emphasis on printmaking and painting, some of its graduates have earned international reputations. Mathias Kauage, Jakuba, Cecil King, John Siune and Akis have works hanging in overseas galleries; Kauage, in particular, became world famous (see the Mathias Kauage aside below).

Pottery

The village of Aibom, near the Chambri Lakes, is virtually the only place on the Sepik that specialises in pottery. Aibom pots are noted for their relief faces which are coloured with lime and made by the coil method (as opposed to using a pottery wheel).

MATHIAS KAUAGE

I met Mathias Kauage in 1997 – he was asleep on the concrete path outside a Port Moresby hotel, his head resting on his folded forearms. His paintings were laid out near the door with a pebble on each corner, all for sale. They were very striking and filled with vivid images of helicopters and planes with huge faces in the windows.

A self-taught artist from Simbu, Kauage started painting in the '70s and was so successful that many artists copied his style, and eventually there was a 'school' of Kauage-style naive–primitivists.

In 1994, when Kauage was invited to exhibit his work at the Glasgow Museum of Modern Art and a London gallery, he was granted an audience with Queen Elizabeth II. He presented her with the portrait *Misis Kwin*, in which she's depicted with a tribal headdress and a bone through her nose – it hangs in Buckingham Palace. He was awarded an Order of the British Empire in 1998, and died in 2003 aged 66. His paintings are now more valuable than ever.

Rowan McKinnon

Other interesting pots can be found near Madang, in the Central Province, made by the Porebada people, and at Wanigela in Oro Province. The Amphlett Islanders in Milne Bay also make delicate pottery. Pottery is not glazed in Melanesia and often poorly fired – it can be extremely fragile.

Carving

Carving is the main art of Melanesians and is what they are renowned for. It can take many forms from tiny pieces to giant *garamut* drums.

BOWLS & STOOLS

The Trobriand Islanders are prolific carvers of everything from stylised figures to decorated lime gourds and beautifully made bowls. The bowls are generally carved from ebony or rosewood and laboriously polished with a pig's tusk. The rims are patterned, often featuring a fish or turtle.

The Tami Islanders near Lae are renowned for their carved bowls. Further offshore the Siassi Islanders carve deep, elliptical bowls which are patterned with incised designs coloured with lime.

Trobriands stools are wonderful, carved from a single piece of timber and incorporating intricate detail.

SHIELDS, BOARDS & PROWS

Some of the most interesting Pacific art manifests in shields, canoe prows and Sepik storyboards. Trobriands splash boards and canoe prows are magnificent and have a unique design. Traditionally, shields were often thought to be inhabited by dead ancestors who brought power and protection to a warrior in war. These days, shields are produced for decoration and are often too unwieldy to stave off an incoming spear or arrow.

MALANGAN & GOGDALA CARVINGS

In New Ireland, master carvers create *malangan* figures for mortuary rites. *Malangan* refers to more than just the carvings – it's a complex system of spiritual beliefs and rituals. There are a few master carvers on Tabar Island and Libba village near Konos. These are spectacular pieces but often large and terribly fragile.

In the Balimo area Gogodala pieces are also unique, carved like a totem pole. They can represent humans and spirits, crocodiles and snakes.

CULT HOOKS & SCULL RACKS

Classic Sepik pieces, cult hooks make good souvenirs. The small ones are called Yipwons, while larger ones are Kamanggabi, and they're carved as hunting charms. Food hooks hang *bilums* of food from the roof to keep them away from rats, but they also have a spiritual significance.

Traditionally, the sculls of both enemies and relatives were kept, over-modelled with clay and decorated. Ancestors were worshipped and enemy skulls were war trophies – both had spiritual power. Skull racks were traditionally made to display the skulls, but they're quite beautiful objects in their own right.

NGUZUNGUZUS

The Solomons most famous carved motif is the ubiquitous *nguzunguzu* (pronounced 'noozoo-noozoo'). These can be very beautiful objects and originally made to be placed on the prows of canoes especially in times of war – nguzunguzus ward off water spirits and strengthen the raiding party. Native to the Solomons' Western Province, nguzunguzus have been adopted as a national symbol and embossed on the one-dollar coin.

'Traditionally, shields were often thought to be inhabited by dead ancestors who brought power and protection to a warrior in war.'

Masks & Headdresses

Masks in PNG are generally used for decoration rather than something to be worn. They are prevalent along the Sepik River, but also in other parts of the country. The Chambri masks from the villages on the Chambri Lakes are the most contemporary of the Sepik masks – recognisable by their elongated design and glossy black finish with incised brown-and-white patterns.

At Korogo, in the Sepik region, masks are made of wood, then decorated with clay in which shells, hair and pigs' teeth are embedded. Other distinctive Sepik mask styles are found at Kaminabit and Tambanum, and masks from the Murik Lakes have an almost African look. At Maprik the yam masks are woven from materials such as cane or rattan, but they are also carved at Kiwai Island, near Daru on the southern Papuan coast.

Some masks and headdresses are made of woven wicker-style material – middle Sepik people produce the most famous ones. Bainings fire dancers wear a mask made of bark sewn to a wooden frame, often with huge eyes and a duck-like beak.

Aspiring Huli wigmen can spend four years at hair school learning the fine arts of wigwork. See p130.

Jewellery

A classic form of jewellery that figures in traditional ceremonies from Kavieng all the way down the islands to Makira in the Solomons is the *kapkap* – open-worked turtleshell over a white shell disk worn on the forehead. Teeth and tusks are highly valued and worked into various forms of jewellery. Highlanders especially invest great value in large kina and baler shells worn on the chest.

Textiles & Weaving

The weaving loom was unknown in the Pacific before European contact, but there has been a long tradition of Melanesian tapa cloth produced by women. Tapa cloth is coarse paper made from soaked and beaten tree-bark and decorated with various designs. Some tapa is very sacred and highly valuable.

Other Crafts

The Chambri Lakes carvers produce decorative spears that are very similar to their masks. In the Highlands, the ceremonial Hagen axes are half-tool, half-icon; there you'll also see lethal cassowary-claw-tipped Huli picks, while in the Sepik region you will find equally nasty bone daggers.

DID YOU KNOW?

Penis gourds are still *de rigueur* for many men in PNG's remote parts. See p230.

Bilums are colourful string bags which are made in many parts of PNG. They are enormously strong and expandable. They are time-consuming to make since the entire length of string is fed through every loop. *Bilums* are now also made of synthetic cords which can be garish and sometimes beautiful. There's a variety of styles – Highlanders make big 'woollen' ones made of cuscus fur. Highlanders also make Highland hats, essential headwear for Highlands men.

Buka baskets, originally from Buka Island in Bougainville, are the finest baskets in the Pacific. Wicker-work figures of various types are made around Murik Lakes, the Yuat River and the Trobriand Islands.

Further recommended reading and films on PNG and islander culture include the following:

■ *Village on the Edge* (2002), Michael French Smith, is a thoughtful book about a village on a volcanic island and changing lifestyles as it confronts modernity.

- *Contemporary Art in Papua New Guinea* (1997), Susan Cochrane, is an excellent book showing how powerful Melanesian creative energy has produced great painters like Kauage and Siune.
- In *Beyond the Coral Sea* (2003) Michael Moran retraces the steps of some famous early visitors to PNG and offers some thoughts on the modern country. A fine book.
- See the film *First Contact* before you die.
- Bill Bennett's *In a Savage Land* (1999) was shot in the Trobriands about couple of anthropologists in the 1930s and their take on the 'Islands of Love'. David Bridie's soundtrack won a bunch of awards.

34

Environment Tim Flannery

The island of New Guinea, of which Papua New Guinea (PNG) is the eastern part, is only one-ninth as big as Australia, yet it has just as many mammal species, and more kinds of birds and frogs. PNG is Australia's biological mirror-world. Both places share a common history going back tens of millions of years, but Australia is flat and has dried out, while PNG is wet and has become mountainous. As a result, Australian kangaroos bound across the plains, while in PNG they climb in the rainforest canopy.

Tim Flannery is a naturalist, explorer and writer. He is the author of a number of award-winning books, including *Throwim Way Leg* (1999) and the landmark ecological history of North America, *The Eternal Frontier*. Tim is Director of the South Australian Museum and a professor at the University of Adelaide.

A MEGADIVERSE REGION

PNG is one of Earth's megadiverse regions, and it owes much of its diversity to its topography. The mountainous terrain has spawned diversity in two ways: isolated mountain ranges are often home to a unique fauna and flora found nowhere else, while within any one mountain range you will find different species as you go higher. In the lowlands are jungles whose trees are not that different from those of Southeast Asia. Yet the animals are often startlingly different – cassowaries instead of tapirs, and marsupial cuscus instead of monkeys.

The greatest diversity of animal life occurs at around 1500m above sea level. The ancestors of many of the marsupials found in these forests were derived from Australia some five million years ago. As Australia dried out they vanished from that continent, but they continued to thrive and evolve in New Guinea, producing a highly distinctive fauna. Birds of paradise and bowerbirds also abound there, and the forest has many trees typical of the forests of ancient Gondwana. As you go higher the forests get mossier and the air colder. By the time you have reached 3000m above sea level the forests are stunted and wreathed in epiphytes. It's a formation known as elfin woodland, and in it one finds many bright honeyeaters, native rodents, and some unique relics of prehistory, such as the giant long-beaked echidna. Above the elfin woodland the trees drop out, and a wonderland of alpine grassland and herbfield dominates, where wallabies can often be seen, and tiny, confiding birds like the alpine robin. It is a place where snow can fall and where early morning ice coats the puddles.

Lowlands

Making sense of New Guinea's spectacular diversity is not easy, for the environment is so varied and its animals and plants so abundant that identifying creatures can be difficult. Let's start with a sample of what you might find in the lowlands.

Flying into Port Moresby you'll encounter grassland – a far cry from the eternally wet forests that beckon from the distant ranges. Such habitats exist in a band of highly seasonal rainfall that exists across southern New Guinea, and the fauna you'll see there is much like that of northern

KEEP AN EYE OUT

Papua New Guinea is still very much a biological frontier so it's worth recording carefully any unusual animal you see. A photograph, local name, and description of where it was found will help a specialist identify it. In little-visited regions, there's a chance that it will be an undescribed species. There are still lots of species – especially frogs, reptiles and insects – waiting to be discovered.

Australia. Magpie geese, brolgas and jabirus occupy the floodplains, as do sandy-coloured agile wallabies, Rusa deer (which were introduced a century ago) and saltwater crocodiles.

Where the dry season is shorter, however, the savannah gives way to lowland jungles and there you are in another world. The largest native land animal you'll encounter there is not a mammal or a reptile, but a bird – New Guinea's southern cassowary. Weighing as much as a human, they are secretive creatures, but they can be awesome. The males care for the nests and chicks, and if you disturb either, you're likely to hear a sound like a steam-train bearing down on you; it's the call of an angry cassowary and the creature can burst from the forest with surprising power and speed. Its kicks are what must be guarded against, for on each foot it bears a 15cm-long claw – as wicked and sharp as any stiletto.

It's the nature of rainforests that their inhabitants form intimate relationships, and the cassowary stands at the centre of an intricate web. It eats the fruit of rainforest trees, and it can fit objects as large as a grapefruit down its throat. Its stomach strips the pulp from the fruit but passes the seeds unharmed, and from them new forest trees can grow. Unless a sinister-looking parrot is nearby. The vulturine parrot is a cockatoo-sized bird with the colours of an Edwardian gentleman's morning suit – a sombre black on the outside, but with rich vermilion linings. Its head is naked and bears a long, hooked beak– hence its common name. Until recently no-one knew quite why its head was so odd – then one was seen neck-deep in cassowary faeces. The bird specialises, it seems, in picking apart reeking cassowary droppings in search of the seeds, and for such an occupation a bald head (which prevents the faeces from sticking) and a long pincer-like beak are essential requirements.

Cassowaries are reputed by some villagers to be able fishermen. They wade into a forest pond and then, using their loose feathers as a net, walk backwards into the shallows, trapping tiny fish and crustaceans. When they reach the shallows, with a flick of their rear-ends, they fling the creatures onto the shore. Among their catch are some of the most beautiful of all freshwater fish, the rainbowfish. Some of these sardine-sized creatures are bright red, others are striped with the colours of the rainbow, while still others are bicoloured, with the front half being entirely different in colour from the rear half.

If you really wish to understand the lowland jungle, smother yourself in mosquito repellent and take up a comfortable post at dusk. The sun sets rapidly in the tropics, and the insect chorus, which has been drumming away all day, alters with the light. An eerier buzzing sound (reminiscent of the sound supposedly made by alien spaceships in B-grade sci-fi movies) announces the awakening of the 'six-o'clocks' – cicadas that sing briefly twice each day, at dawn and dusk. Then, as the harsh sounds of the day die away, the subtle sounds of the night chime in – frogs that sound like bells, crickets that chirrup incessantly, and the low note of the frogmouth, a large owl-like bird with gouty feet and a huge, gaping bill.

By now bats are on the wing, and New Guinea has a huge diversity of them, from the moth-sized, insect-eating Mosia which may flit around you while the light is still strong, to the great flying foxes with wingspans of more than a metre and a weight of 2kg, the largest flying mammals ever to have evolved. Because some species roost in huge colonies near towns, most Papua New Guineans know such creatures well, and indeed have been kept awake at night by their raucous quarrelling during the fruiting season. Many of the smaller, insectivorous bats spend the day in caves. It's best not to disturb them there, both for their own sake and because

Brian Coates' two volume *Birds of Papua New Guinea* (1985 and 1990) is more suited to the coffee-table than the field. It is filled with magnificent photographs and is encyclopædic.

Ernst Mayr and Jared Diamond are the world's greatest living ornithologists. Their *Birds of Northern Melanesia: Speciation, Ecology and Zoogeography* (2001) is a unique work, brimming with evolutionary insight as well as detail for the serious amateur ornithologist. It covers the Bismarck Archipelago and Solomon Islands.

caves can be unhealthy places (they abound with lung-clogging fungus among other unsavoury microorganisms). It's worth looking around the entrance of bat caves, however, for you will often find geckos, tree-frogs and snakes there. All are waiting for the bats to pass by at dusk, when they will try to grab one or two.

New Guinea's snake fauna includes some extremely venomous species, such as the taipan and king brown snake, which are limited to the savannahs. Generally speaking the higher up the mountains you go, the fewer venomous snakes there are. The largest of New Guinea's snakes are pythons, and some are simply enormous. While nonvenomous it's wise to give them a wide berth, as they are immensely powerful and have been known to swallow children.

Tim Flannery's books *Mammals of New Guinea* (revised 1995) and *Mammals of the South-West Pacific and Moluccan Islands* (1995) provide a species-by-species account of all mammals found in Melanesia.

Mountain Forests

The forests of New Guinea's mountains including its high-mountain elfin woodland, on first acquaintance, are more sedate places. There is often a distinct chill in the air at dawn, and out of the mist you might hear the pure tones of the New Guinea whipbird, or the harsher calls of any one of a dozen birds of paradise. Just why New Guinea is home to such an astonishing variety of spectacular birds has long puzzled biologists. Part of the answer lies in the lack of mammalian predators on the island. The largest – a marsupial known as the New Guinea quoll – is only kitten-sized. Thus there are no foxes, leopards or similar creatures to prey on the birds, which as a consequence have developed such astonishing colours and spectacular mating rituals as to beggar belief. Some species clear a miniature stage upon which they dance with all the precision of a prima ballerina, while others build metre-tall towers decorated with colourful fruit and flowers to attract a mate. They are living jewels, but to see them you will need to enlist the skills of an experienced New Guinean bushman; these days, such people are often older men who speak no English, for the younger generation spends less and less time in the forest.

If you can get well away from the villages, perhaps by accompanying experienced bushmen on a two- or three-day walk to distant hunting grounds, you might get to see a tree kangaroo. These creatures are relatives of Australia's rock wallabies which, five million years ago, took to the treetops. There are eight species in New Guinea, but in the central ranges you are likely to see just two. Goodfellow's tree kangaroo is a chestnut-coloured creature the size of a Labrador. It has blue eyes, two golden stripes running down its back and a tail ringed with gold. An eater of fruit, it is most commonly found in forests between 1500m and 2500m elevation. Higher up you may encounter the bear-like Doria's tree kangaroo. It is shaggy, brown and immensely powerful, and lives in family groups.

DID YOU KNOW?

Rainbowfish are among the most attractive of all freshwater fish and they are particularly diverse in New Guinea. GR Allen's and NJ Cross' *Rainbowfishes of Australia and New Guinea* (1982) is the definitive guide.

Walking through the mountain forests at night you enter another environment. The trunks of great fallen trees, which by day are invisible under a mass of leaf-litter, are lit up by luminous fungi. You can often follow the shattered trunks through the forest for tens of metres. And everywhere are the glowing green parasols of luminous mushrooms. In the trees you might spy some of New Guinea's marsupials. Among the more common are the cat-sized, coppery ringtail possum. Its name comes from its fur, which appears to be tipped with burnished copper. It's a peaceful leaf-eater, which lives in tree-hollows or even in burrows underground. If you're fortunate you'll see a triok, a black-and-white striped animal the size of a kitten. It has a long, skeletal finger, which it uses to 'fish' for wood-boring grubs, a raucous screech, and it stinks like a skunk.

Alpine Regions

Where the elfin woodland gives way to the alpine regions yet another world unfolds. There the tiger parrot, its breast striped the colour of moss and dry grass, calls from stunted umbrella plants. Rhododendron bushes and tufted orchids are covered with flowers, and any woody plants are festooned with ant plants. These relatives of the coffee-bush resemble misshapen bottles more than plants, and are honeycombed with passages that serve as home to colonies of ants. In a perfect example of the intimate ecological relationships that abound in the forest, the ant protects the plant, while the plant provides shelter for its tiny defenders.

You'll see well-worn tracks winding through the alpine tussocks. Some are made by diminutive wallabies, others by giant rats. New Guinea is home to a spectacular diversity of rats, which comprise fully one-third of the mammal fauna. These distant relatives of the laboratory rat are spectacularly varied: some look like miniature otters and cavort in mountain streams, others resemble small, tree-climbing possums, while still others look, and smell like, rats from elsewhere. Among the most spectacular are the giant woolly rats, which arguably are the largest rodents in the world. Several species inhabit the alpine zone, where they eat vegetable matter and live in burrows below the tussocks. They can grow to almost 1m long from nose to tail-tip, and have teeth that could snip a thumb off without trying, yet they are gentle creatures that never attempt to bite unless harassed.

In two of the highest mountain regions in PNG – the Star Mountains in the far west and Mt Albert Edward near Port Moresby – one of the country's most enigmatic birds can be seen. Known as McGregor's bird of paradise, it is a velvet-black bird the size of a large crow which makes a distinctive rattling sound as it flies. Under each wing is a large orange spot, and behind each eye a fleshy, flapping orange wattle of skin. It's a strangely trusting bird, making it easy to get a good look at if you are lucky enough to stumble across one. Although long classified as a bird of paradise, genetic studies have recently indicated that it is a highly specialised honeyeater!

Other Regions

New Guinea's more isolated mountain ranges and islands are biological places of their own. The Torricelli Mountains in New Guinea's Sepik region started out as an island archipelago, but now form part of the mainland. The mountains are home to a unique array of creatures, such as Tenkile, a black tree kangaroo that is one of the rarest creatures on earth. Perhaps just a few hundred survive in the forests south of Lumi, where a conservation programme is based which is trying to protect this last remnant. Even rarer is Weimanke, a relative of Goodfellow's tree kangaroo which has a white face and golden ears; it is among the most beautiful of all mammals and only a handful survive to the east of Lumi. If you're fortunate enough to hike into the mountain forests that are home to these creatures, you'll find a misty wonderland of abrupt gullies and ridges, the summits of which are adorned with grand palms bearing bright red fruit. Here the black sicklebill dwells, its explosive call of *blak, blak* drawing attention to this long-tailed creature, whose dark plumage glistens with the colours of the rainbow.

The islands of southeastern New Guinea hold their own wonders. Muyua Island (Woodlark), the most remote of the Trobriands group, is home to a primitive cuscus, each individual of which is – rather like a tabby cat – differently marked. Goodenough, just south of Kiriwina

Little by way of definitive works are currently available on Melanesia's herpetofauna. Mark O'Shea's *A Guide to the Snakes of Papua New Guinea* (1997) and Mike McCoy's *Reptiles of the Solomon Islands* (1980, now available on CD) are both highly useful.

WILDLIFE SPOTTING

Good places to see wildlife:

■ **Ambua Lodge** (p129) In comfort; in the Tari Gap, Southern Highlands.

■ **Crater Mountain Wildlife Management Area** (p117) For the more adventurous; in the Southern Highlands area.

■ **Karawari Lodge** (p152) In pristine lowland rainforest in the foothills of East Sepik Province.

Island, is a huge spire of rock whose mountain forests give refuge to a unique mountain wallaby whose outer fur is black while the underfur is white. It's a long-isolated relic of Australia's Pliocene period of five million years ago, but to see it you will need to climb hard for two days to reach its habitat.

The Bismarck Archipelago is home to spectacular fruit bats, including the largest of them all – the great flying fox, whose wingspan can approach 1.5m. The more petite Bismarck flying fox is the size of a pigeon and has a boldly patterned black-and-white face as if it's wearing a mask, and unusually among mammals, the males' breasts produce milk.

Solomon Islands

The Solomon Islands represent a whole other environment, for they are an ancient island archipelago that has never been connected to a continent. The cuscus found there only reached the islands a few thousand years ago with people. The true endemics are giant rats, monkey-faced bats, and unusual birds such as the Guadalcanal honeyeater. The giant rats are rare now, but you might be fortunate enough to spot one of the half-dozen species in dense, virginal forest. One of the largest species makes nests like those constructed by eagles, in the tallest rainforest trees. One other aspect of the Solomons fauna is a radiation of frogs that is unique. Some look like dead leaves, others like lumps of moss, while one genus, which is often found in caves, is gigantic, reaching over 20cm long.

Tim Flannery's *Throwim Way Leg* (1999) is a tremendously enjoyable account of his adventures as a biologist in remote New Guinea. It's rich, rollicking and imbued with an appealing sense of wonder; don't land without having read it.

NATIONAL PARKS & WILDLIFE MANAGEMENT AREAS

Land is protected in various ways in PNG. There are few national parks; the most accessible is Varirata National Park (p56), although you may also find yourself in national park areas at Mt Wilhelm (p119) and Lake Kutubu (p127). There are also various regional parks, wildlife sanctuaries and, arguably of most interest to visitors, wildlife management areas, such as that at Crater Mountain Wildlife Management Area (p117). Rennell Island (p211) in the Solomon Islands is World Heritage-listed.

Creating 'national parks' as such has proved ineffective in Melanesia, largely because the main form of land tenure is clan-based ownership. As a result Melanesian conservationists have now turned to the development of wildlife management areas as the main tool for conserving the environment. In these areas, local landowners have agreed to set land aside for wildlife on the basis that tourism or some other form of income generation will make this worthwhile.

ENVIRONMENTAL ISSUES

Threats to the environment of PNG and the Solomon Islands are, to the outsider, rather surprising in nature. The media frequently run stories on how mining and logging are the main threats. These differ in their impact, so they need to be treated separately. Mining often has a very adverse local impact, notorious examples being the destruction of the Carstensz Meadow and pollution of the Aikwa River by mining company PT Freeport Indonesia (in neighbouring West Papua) and pollution of the Ok Tedi River by Ok Tedi Mining. Overall, such activities are so limited in scope that they do not threaten the extinction of entire species. Changes in local culture following the advent of mining, however, can have larger impacts. Bulmer's fruit bat almost became extinct in the 1970s when traditional taboos broke down and shotguns became more available in the Ok Tedi area (it is reported that shotguns were given as payment for the company's exploration geologists).

Logging has a more widespread impact, but is mostly limited to lowland areas. Because New Guinea's lowlands are extensive, and log quality is generally poor when compared to forests elsewhere, logging has not as yet directly threatened species with extinction. In the Solomon Islands, logging is much more of a threat, both because more of the land area is slated to be logged and because some species depend on very large areas of virgin forest.

So what are the main threats to Melanesia's biodiversity? An inexorable growth in human population, especially in the highlands, has already caused the extinction of many populations of larger animals and without doubt represents the most immediate threat. This has occurred in concert with a breakdown in traditional taboos that previously protected many species. Tree kangaroos, harpy eagles and other larger animals have declined precipitously in recent decades and many are slated for extinction unless something is done. In the Solomons this has been exacerbated by the introduction of cats, black rats and other exotics that have caused extinctions. The recent establishment of macaques in West Papua may threaten a similar wave of extinction in New Guinea.

The greatest long-term threat to Melanesia is global warming. Most of the region's biodiversity lives in the mountains, so when the earth warms these species will be pushed off the mountain summits, a process that could destroy 20% or more of the region's biodiversity. Conserving Melanesia's biodiversity begins in your home; by using less electricity or sourcing power from renewable sources, you can do something towards curbing global warming.

It's important that initiatives such as wildlife management areas (see opposite for details) gain support, as they are Melanesia's best chance to conserve its wildlife in the long term.

David Attenborough's BBC documentary *Attenborough in Paradise* is the definitive work on birds of paradise. You could spend years in the bush and not see some of the behaviours recorded there.

Food & Drink

PNG and the Solomon Islands are not destinations for the gourmet traveller. While wonderful seafood can be found on the coasts and islands, the rest of the traditional diet consists largely of bland, starchy vegetables that get boring fast. Which bland vegetable is served depends where you are; in the Highlands it will likely be *kaukau* (sweet potato), on the islands taro or yam. In some places you might be offered all three. With little to inspire them, locals generally take a 'food for fuel' attitude to eating, though this changes for celebrations so if you get an invite, don't turn it down.

There are no restaurants dedicated to traditional food and you really need to get into a village (or find a local friend in the city) to find it. Elsewhere, travellers can expect to eat reasonably well in hotels and resorts, and in the growing number of independent restaurants, mostly Asian.

These restaurants are a good bet for vegetarians. And there are plenty of vegetables in villages. However, in some places refusing food can be insulting, so vegetarians at pig feasts should sensitively suggest *before* the meal arrives that they don't dig swine. This might help avoid an embarrassing situation.

STAPLES & SPECIALITIES

The staple food is *saksak* (sago) in the Sepik and other swampy areas of PNG. *Saksak* is basically pure starch, but where it is too swampy to grow anything else, it is vital. On the Sepik, dry *saksak* is usually mixed with water and fried into a rubbery pancake, but it can also be boiled into a gluey porridge. Mixed with grated coconut it becomes quite palatable, but by itself it is almost tasteless. To make *saksak*, men cut down a sago palm, cut away the bark and pound out the pith, leaving a fibrous sawdust. Women then knead the pith in a bark funnel, draining water through the pith to dissolve the starch. The starch-laden water is collected (often in an old canoe) and the starch settles in an orange, glutinous mass at the bottom.). In the Highlands the staple is *kaukau*. In taste, it is virtually indistinguishable from staples elsewhere in the region, which include taro, yams and cooking bananas. The situation is sometimes a little more inspiring along the coast because there is

---

BUAI

Virtually everybody in PNG (barring expats) chews *buai* (betel nut), used to chew *buai* or will some day chew *buai*. The evidence is everywhere; great streams of bright-red saliva stain the streets and teeth of the nation. *Buai* is used as a little pick-me-up during the day, a bit like a midmorning cup of tea. The mild stimulant effect is created by the reaction of the nut, the *daka* (mustard stick) and the *cumbung* (crushed-coral lime). It tastes awful!

However, foreigners chewing *buai* tend to make friends fast, so it's worth having a go. Take the husked nut between your back teeth and crack it near the stem end. Dig out the kernel and chew it in the back of your mouth to one side. You'll suddenly be producing large amounts of colourless saliva but spit, don't swallow – that can be nauseating.

Once the nut is mashed take the *daka*, moisten an end with your mouth and dip it in the *cumbung* until a few millimetres are 'frosted'. Bite off the frosted part and chew and spit. Repeat this three or four times and keep chewing and spitting. Be careful, though, that red spit stains. It is also a form of traditional medicine (see p254 for more details).

excellent seafood and the cooking makes heavier use of coconut and, increasingly, spices like ginger. For recipes that reflect modern PNG cooking (such as chicken taro bake and yamm patties), check out www .michie.net/pnginfo/recipe.1.

Because of the limited animal life, protein deficiency has traditionally been a problem. In many regions, potential game (reptiles, birds, rodents and small marsupials) is scarce but hunting is still important. Apart from the fresh fish available on the coast and some rivers, pigs are the main source of meat protein, although they are generally saved for feasts (p42). Chicken is also quite popular.

Rice, instant noodles, tinned fish (usually mackerel) and bully beef (introduced during WWII) have also become staples.

You'll see plenty of coconut husks lying around, particularly in the island provinces of PNG and in the Solomons. The milk from a green coconut is drunk or used in cooking (such as in a *mumu*, p42), and the flesh is also used in preparing food.

DRINKS

Most of the coffee grown in the PNG Highlands is arabica and it's excellent (if you can get it). Many locals drink Nescafé. In coastal areas of PNG and throughout the Solomons young coconuts are a common source of liquid refreshment.

South Pacific Brewery in PNG produces two very good beers. SP Lager is the everyday drink and comes in a short brown bottle known as a 'brownie'. The more expensive version is South Pacific Export Lager, and comes in a clear bottle or white can. Australian wine and spirits are available in hotels and restaurants, though they are not cheap.

The local brew in the Solomons is Solbrew, which is a lager beer and Solbrew SB is stronger.

WHERE TO EAT & DRINK

Where you eat will depend on your budget, your sense of adventure and the size of the place you're in. In towns and cities the ubiquitous *kai* bar will probably lure you in for a snack at least once. *Kai* bars look and taste like Australian milk bars of the late 1970s; that is, they sell meat pies (K2 to K3), sausage rolls (K2), deep-fried dough balls (K0.50) and, probably your best bet, preprepared meals of indeterminable Asian origin (about K6). We haven't listed many *kai* bars – just look for people milling around.

The number of restaurants and their quality is rising, though in both PNG and the Solomons they're found only in larger centres and resorts. Chinese restaurants predominate, ranging from cheap and cheerful places with meals for about K10 to more elaborate affairs where you'll spend up to K40. There is also the odd Japanese, Korean or Thai place in Port Moresby where meals cost about K45 to K70. Hotels and resorts all have fairly good restaurants, with prices reflecting the quality of the establishment; expect to pay between K35 and K80 per meal. Tipping is not necessary, but most restaurants add 10% VAT to the bill.

Hours can vary considerably, but in general restaurants open for lunch from about 11.30am to 2.30pm and dinner from 6 or 7pm until 10pm, or whenever the last diner leaves. Where the price of a meal is listed in this book, we are referring to a main dish plus one other course (usually a salad or dessert) and a drink.

In villages you'll eat whatever the villagers eat (see opposite) and pay between K15 and K30. If you're lucky enough to be around for a *mumu*

DID YOU KNOW?

While it's unlikely you'll be offered spiders and cockroaches as often as other parts of Asia, there are some local faves that might have you hesitating. Skewered sago grubs (with or without the heads), roasted flying fox and python soup are good sources of protein, but the latter involves a protected species so it can't really be recommended.

DID YOU KNOW?

The yam is sacred in the Trobriand Islands but a growing population and limited food source has seen some locals dismiss their local yams in favour of the African yam, which is more 'flavoursome' and can grow up to 15 times more yams than a local one.

(traditional underground oven) the price will probably rise a bit to cover the cost of meat.

Self-catering is the cheapest way to eat and markets are the best and most interesting place to buy fresh produce. Outside towns you buy other ingredients from the small trade stores found in almost every village. The range will probably be limited to rice, instant noodles, tinned fish, bully beef, salt, beef crackers (aka Kundu crackers) and, if you're lucky, SP Lager. Anything more you'll need to take with you. Most large towns have a good-sized supermarket with a wide range of foods.

Formal drinking venues consist of hotels and resort bars, restaurants and the occasional nightclub. Otherwise, you could do worse than a village with beer, a beach and a tropical sunset.

Food Rules: Hunting, Sharing, and Tabooing Game in Papua New Guinea (2000) by Harriet Whitehead is an intriguing anthropological look at the central role of food in traditional PNG society, in this case the Seltaman people living in a highland rainforest.

HABITS & CUSTOMS

Food plays a vital role in many PNG and Solomon Island cultures. For some, pigs are the traditional measure of wealth and even today a pig is preferred to cash. A man's status is often measured by his skills as a gardener; how many yams he produces and how large they are, for example.

The most famous local cooking style is the *mumu*, a traditional underground oven in which fire-heated stones are placed in the bottom, meat and vegetables are wrapped in herbs and banana leaves on top, and then the pit is sealed with more heated stones, branches and leaves and left to steam. For feasts, the pits may be hundreds of metres long, and filled with hundreds of whole pigs. Such a feast might be held to celebrate the settlement of a tribal conflict.

Most people eat three times a day and meals are often big, especially in rural areas; don't be surprised if your trekking guide eats two or three times as much as you. Most people can't afford restaurants and will eat at home. They probably won't talk too much until the meal is finished, and women will often eat separately to men.

For travellers, it's best not to head out to dinner too late, especially if you're after a cheap feed. *Kai* bars close by 7pm.

Ethnographer Miriam Kahn's insightful book, *Always Hungry, Never Greedy: Food and the Expression of Gender in a Melanesian Society* (1996) shows how the Wamira people use food to objectify emotions, balance relationships and control their desires.

EAT YOUR WORDS
Useful Phrases

Most restaurants have menus in English only, but in smaller places these phrases might be handy:

Is the restaurant open/closed?	*Haus kaikai i op/pas?*
Do you have an English menu?	*Yu got menyu long Tok Inglis?*
Does this dish have meat?	*I gat abus long dispela kaikai?*
I don't eat beef/pork/chicken/	*Mi tambu long bulmakau/pik/kakaruk/*
dairy products	*susu samting*
I'd like...	*Mi laikim...*
The bill, please	*Mi laik peim kaikai bilong mi*
I enjoyed the meal	*Mi laikim tumas dispela kaikai*

Food Glossary

alcohol	*wiski*
beef	*bulmakau*
beer	*bia*
black coffee	*kopi i blak/ret*
breadfruit	*kapiak*
chicken	*kakaruk*
coconut, green/ripe	*kulau/kokonas*

TOP FIVE RESTAURANTS

■ **Asia Aromas** (Port Moresby, p53) The Chinese and Thai food is a perennial favourite and you're likely to be dining with a who's who of PNG's movers and shakers. Apart from great food, there's a friendly atmosphere, good service and fair prices.

■ **Madang Lodge** (Madang, p103) The Lodge boasts PNG's only French chef and an à la carte menu that will make your mouth water. The wonderfully intimate waterfront location tops it off.

■ **Zipolo Habu Resort** (Lola Island, Solomon Islands, p209) The restaurant here serves delicious food but it's the classic, island-paradise setting that is the clincher. Romantics, take note!

■ **Butia Lodge** (Trobriand Islands, p83) In an open-sided building supported by intricately carved posts, the satay mud crab is almost worth the trip alone. Add some of the islands' famous yams, fruit, fish and a cold SP and you'll be very content.

■ **Vanimo Beach Hotel** (Vanimo, p142) Don't be fooled by the simple dining room; the strong Asian flavour on the menu is a rich mix of Indonesian and Malay that is the perfect antidote to endless sago on the Sepik – the *tôm yam* soups, stir-fries and noodle dishes are all good.

crab	*kuka*
crayfish	*kindam*
egg	*kiau*
fish	*pis*
food	*kaikai*
fry/to fry	*prai/praiim*
ginger	*kawawar*
ice cream	*aiskrim*
meat	*abus*
milk	*susu*
pandanus	*karuka/marita*
pawpaw (papaya)	*popo*
prawn	*liklik kindam*
rice	*rais*
soft drink	*loli wara*
steam/to steam	*mumu/mumuim*
sweet potato	*kaukau*
to prepare a meal	*rediim kaikai*
to roast	*praiim*
vegetables	*sayor/kumu/kumis*
water	*wara*
white coffee	*kopi wantaim susu*

Port Moresby

Almost everyone who comes to Papua New Guinea will spend some time in Port Moresby. And while the sprawling capital couldn't be counted among the world's great metropolises, and it does have something of a law and order problem, it also has a few redeeming features that mean you shouldn't just spend the time sitting around in your hotel.

A visit to Parliament Haus, PNG's most impressive building, and the cultural displays at the National Museum are recommended – the mosaic façade of Parliament Haus will excite any photographer in the late afternoon. The National Botanical Gardens are a highlight, and when the orchid garden is bloomimg, it's perhaps the city's most pleasant spot. Outside town Varirata National Park will excite bird-watchers and the drive up there is quite something.

Relatively sophisticated infrastructure is another bonus, particularly if you've been wandering through villages for weeks. A meal at Asia Aromas, or one of several other good restaurants, will help you forget the dozens of sweet potatoes you've consumed…or serve as a welcome treat before heading bush.

But a visit to Port Moresby is really about being there rather than seeing anything mind-blowing. The city is a microcosm of PNG's future and it's fascinating to talk with the locals, expats and nationals alike, and get a feel for what it's like to live in a city rated one of the least liveable on earth. You'll likely hear that, as in many developing countries, people come from all over PNG seeking opportunities in 'the big smoke', attracted by the city's reputation for money, glamour and excitement. Unfortunately most fail to find fame or even a job, and frustration mounts when 'excitement' is all around you but you have no money with which to participate. As a result, a cultural melting pot of disillusioned migrants lives in squalid squatter settlements and contributes to Port Moresby's high crime rate.

And on that front you do need to be careful, but not paranoid. It's not as bad as reputation would have you believe.

HIGHLIGHTS

- Gazing up at the mosaic façade of **Parliament Haus** (p49), the Sepik-style *haus tambaran* (spirit house) and symbol of Papua New Guinean independence

- Looking at the kaleidoscope of colour in the orchid garden at the carefully maintained **National Botanical Gardens** (p51)

- Driving up the Sogeri Rd to **Varirata National Park** (p56), with its trails, birds of paradise and panoramic views

- Browsing through the monthly **Ela Beach Craft Market** (p54), where local artists sell crafts from around the country

- Enjoying the food at **Asia Aromas** (p53) or a few afternoon ales by the harbour at the **Royal Papua Yacht Club** (p53)

National Botanical Gardens ★
Varirata National Park ★
Parliament Haus ★
Royal Papua Yacht Club ★
★ Ela Beach Craft Market
Asia Aromas

 LAND AREA: 240 SQ KM

 POPULATION: 305,000

PORT MORESBY

HISTORY

While Port Moresby today has dozens of different tribal groups, only two can truly call it home: the Motu and Koitabu. The Motu are traditionally a sea-going people and they probably didn't arrive until relatively recently (perhaps less than 2000 years ago). Motu villages were built on stilts over

Moresby Harbour. Hanuabada (the Great Village) was the largest of their communities and still exists today.

The first European to visit was Captain John Moresby in 1873, after whom the harbour was named. Moresby explored extensively along the south coast and spent several days trading with villagers at Hanua-

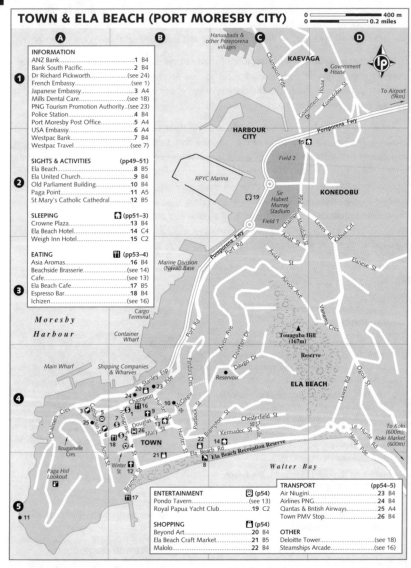

TOWN & ELA BEACH (PORT MORESBY CITY)

0 ————— 400 m
0 ————— 0.2 miles

INFORMATION
ANZ Bank.................................1 B4
Bank South Pacific....................2 B4
Dr Richard Pickworth...............(see 24)
French Embassy........................(see 1)
Japanese Embassy......................3 A4
Mills Dental Care.....................(see 18)
PNG Tourism Promotion Authority..(see 23)
Police Station............................4 B4
Port Moresby Post Office...............5 A4
USA Embassy..............................6 A4
Westpac Bank.............................7 B4
Westpac Travel...........................(see 7)

SIGHTS & ACTIVITIES (pp49-51)
Ela Beach...................................8 B5
Ela United Church.......................9 B4
Old Parliament Building................10 B4
Paga Point................................11 A5
St Mary's Catholic Cathedral..........12 B5

SLEEPING (pp51-3)
Crowne Plaza.............................13 B4
Ela Beach Hotel.........................14 C4
Weigh Inn Hotel........................15 C2

EATING (pp53-4)
Asia Aromas.............................16 B4
Beachside Brasserie...................(see 14)
Cafe......................................(see 13)
Ela Beach Cafe.........................17 B5
Espresso Bar............................18 B4
Ichizen..................................(see 16)

ENTERTAINMENT (p54)
Pondo Tavern............................(see 13)
Royal Papua Yacht Club................19 C2

SHOPPING (p54)
Beyond Art..............................20 B4
Ela Beach Craft Market.................21 B5
Malolo...................................22 B4

TRANSPORT (pp54-5)
Air Niugini..............................23 B4
Airlines PNG............................24 B4
Qantas & British Airways..............25 A4
Town PMV Stop..........................26 B4

OTHER
Deloitte Tower.........................(see 18)
Steamships Arcade......................(see 16)

bada. He was impressed with the people and their lifestyles, posing the rhetorical question in his diary, 'What have these people to gain from civilisation?' One year later, the London Missionary Society arrived and was soon followed by traders and 'blackbirders', who recruited indentured labourers and were little better than slave-dealers.

In 1888 Port Moresby became the capital of the newly declared British New Guinea. Under Sir William MacGregor's remarkable 10-year administration, the government in Port Moresby and a national police force were established.

Port Moresby was overshadowed by Lae and Rabaul until WWII, when the city became the staging post for Allied troops fighting along the Kokoda Track. Port Moresby remained in Australian hands throughout the war.

After the war, Papua and New Guinea were administered as one territory (see p200) with Port Moresby becoming the capital largely by default – more attractive alternatives such as Lae and Rabaul were now rubble.

ORIENTATION

Port Moresby sprawls around the coast and inland hills and can be a difficult place to get your bearings. The modest CBD is called Town, and perches on a spit of land that ends in Paga Hill, at the southwest end of the city. Town has the majority of Port Moresby's few older buildings, the shipping docks and wharves, and is bounded to the south by popular Ela Beach. Town has a couple of decent restaurants but few hotels.

The Poreporena Fwy runs from the Royal Papua Yacht Club, just north of Town, inland to Hohola, Gordons and the airport, about 11km away. It is also the best route to Waigani, home to Parliament, the National Museum & Art Gallery, and most government offices.

The potholed Hubert Murray Hwy, once the only road linking the airport with Town, is still the best route between Town and Boroko, the city's second centre of business with shops, banks, hotels and a few good restaurants.

To the south of Town, the main road runs alongside popular Ela Beach until you reach Koki, home to Koki Market and another stilt village.

A few kilometres past the airport the road divides, the left branch heading north then west toward Kerema and the right climbing east to Sogeri and the Kokoda Track.

Town and Boroko are the main PMV (Public Motor Vehicle) hubs (see p55).

MAPS

The best and most up-to-date maps of Port Moresby are found in the front of the Papua New Guinea Telephone Directory. Maps are also available at the **National Mapping Bureau** (Map p50; ☎ 327 6223; natmap@datec.com.pg; Melanesian Way, Waigani; 8.30am-3.30pm Mon-Fri). It has a huge two-part 1:10,000 street map of Port Moresby (2000), which is also available as a far more manageable book (K30).

INFORMATION
Bookshops

Sadly, there is only one decent bookstore in Port Moresby: the **UPNG Bookshop** (Map p50; ☎ 326 7375; UPNG, Waigani Dr, Waigani; 8.30am-4pm Mon-Fri). Top-end hotels have a few books on PNG at about twice the price you'd pay on Amazon.

Emergency
Ambulance (☎ 325 6822)
Fire (☎ 110; 321 3658)
Police (☎ 000)
Women's counselling (☎ 180 1991)

Internet Access

Top-end hotels offer (inconsistent) Internet access (see p52). Apart from hotels, Port Moresby has only two Internet cafés, both keeping short hours.
Datec (Map p50; ☎ 303 1333; www.datec.com.pg; Waigani Dr, Boroko; per hr K15; 8am-5pm Mon-Fri, 8am-noon Sat) The fastest connection.
E.Business Centre (Map p50; ☎ 325 6860; Angau Dr, Boroko; per hr K15; 8am-6.30pm Mon-Sat) Has XP for direct downloads of photos and Internet phone calls to most countries for K1 per minute.

Libraries
National Library & Archives (Map p50; ☎ 325 6200; Independence Dr, Waigani; 9am-4pm Mon-Fri, 9am-1pm Sat, 1-4pm Sun) An independence gift from Australia, this library houses a huge PNG collection.

Medical Services

Whatever the situation, it's probably worth calling one of the two clinics first. If they

can't help, they will probably refer you to the emergency department at the hospital.
Port Moresby General Hospital (Map p50; ☎ 324 8200; Taurama Rd, Korobosea)
Port Moresby Medical Centre (Map p50; ☎ 325 6633; info@pmms.net; cnr Vaivai Ave & Mavaru St, Boroko; ☼ 24hr) Best place in an emergency. Can arrange medivac and has a decompression chamber on site.
Private Hospital & Clinic (Map p50; ☎ 325 6022; Taurama Rd, Boroko; ☼ 24hr)

DENTISTS

Dr Richard Pickworth (Map p46; ☎ 321 1137, after hrs 321 1298; ground fl, Mogorn Motu Bldg, Champion Pde, Town) Good reputation.
Mills Dental Care (Map p46; ☎ 320 0600; 1st fl, Deloitte Tower, Douglas St, Town)

Money

ANZ and Westpac are more efficient than Bank South Pacific, where you'll likely grow old waiting to change your money. If you're changing cash or travellers cheques, ask for the international desk. See p228 for more on money.

TOWN

ANZ (Map p46; ☎ 180 1444; cnr Champion Pde & Musgrave St) ATMs are more reliable than Westpac and work with Visa and MasterCard.
Bank South Pacific (Map p46; ☎ 321 2444; cnr Musgrave & Douglas Sts) Agents for Western Union.
Westpac (Map p46; ☎ 322 0888; cnr Musgrave & Douglas Sts) Agent for American Express. In theory, ATMs work for Visa, MasterCard, Cirrus, Plus, Maestro. There's a charge of K20 to change cash.

BOROKO

ANZ (Map p50; ☎ 180 1444; Hubert Murray Hwy) Has ATMs.
Bank South Pacific (Map p50; ☎ 323 2288; cnr Nita St & Angau Dr)
Westpac (Map p50; ☎ 322 0888; Nita St)

Post

Boroko Post Office (Map p50; ☎ 300 3794; Tabari Pl, Boroko; ☼ 8am-4pm Mon-Fri, 8-11.30am Sat)
Port Moresby Post Office (Map p46; ☎ 300 3797; cnr Cuthbertson St & Champion Pde, Town; ☼ 8am-4pm Mon-Fri, 8-11.30am Sat)

Telephone

At least half of the phones at the airport and outside the post offices in Town and Boroko should be working.

Tourist Information

PNG Tourism Promotion Authority (TPA; Map p46; ☎ 320 0211; 5th fl, MMI Haus, Champion Pde, Town; ☼ 8.30am-4.30pm Mon-Fri) Provides limited information on accommodation but is mainly about marketing and promotion. Less adventurous than most independent travellers.

Travel Agencies

Dove Travel (Map p50; ☎ 325 9800; fax 325 1451; Angau Dr, Boroko; ☼ 8.30am-4.30pm Mon-Fri) Catholic-run agency is pretty well connected with all forms of transport in PNG plus international flights. Can also suggest cheap sleeping options if you're desperate.
Westpac Travel (Map p46; ☎ 322 0663; fax 322 0640; Douglas St, Town)

DANGERS & ANNOYANCES

Port Moresby can be a dangerous place, but it's not the hell-on-earth many who've

---

THE MILLENNIUM JOB

An attempted bank robbery in Port Moresby in 2000 illustrates the cockiness of some *raskol* (bandits) and the level of frustration felt by police. It began when a group of *raskol* sabotaged the only police helicopter and put it out of action. A month later they hijacked a commercial helicopter outside Port Moresby and instructed the pilot to head for the PNGBC Bank (now Bank South Pacific) building in the centre of Town. Dressed in army fatigues, the five thieves leapt from the helicopter onto the roof of the bank and raced downstairs.

Little did they know, however, that the police had been tipped off and were waiting with itchy trigger fingers in the street below. As the thieves returned to the roof all hell broke loose. Hundreds of shots were fired and despite one *raskol* being hit in the leg, the chopper took off down Musgrave St. The shooting continued and a rotor was hit. The helicopter lost control and the pilot did an amazing job to crash-land in an open lot opposite the wharves. Police, and hundreds of city workers, were soon on the scene; the police wanted to finish the job. The *raskol* probably knew they would be shown little mercy. Despite their best efforts (one tried to swim away in the harbour) the *raskol* were rounded up. Within hours all five were dead.

never been here make it out to be. The majority of visitors to Port Moresby leave unscathed, and if you use your common sense you should be fine (see p223 for more on trouble and how to avoid it).

There are no guarantees, and the situation can change quickly, so ask the locals when you arrive about what is safe, then make your own choice. The following advice, however, is worth taking. During daylight hours walking around Town and Boroko should be fine, but anywhere else you should walk with a local. Avoid secluded urban areas at any time – *raskols* (bandits) are not strictly nocturnal.

Walk up Paga Hill to look at the view by all means, but don't do it alone. Stay out of the settlements unless you are with one of the residents (that includes Hanuabada). Don't walk around Kila Kila, Sabama or Six Mile at any time. After dark, don't walk anywhere.

The most important thing is not to make yourself a target – it's just common sense.

SIGHTS
Most of Port Moresby's few sights are in Town and the government district of Waigani. Unless you have access to a boat the sights cupboard will be bare within a couple of days.

Port Moresby City   Map p46
There is little of historical interest remaining in Port Moresby's CBD, where office towers and neglect have steadily claimed much of the area. The oldest building still standing is the **Ela United Church** (☎ 321 7426; Douglas St), opened by the London Missionary Society in 1890. **St Mary's Catholic Cathedral** (Musgrave St, Town) is not so old but it does have an impressive entrance portal in the style of a Sepik *haus tambaran* (spirit house). The **Old Parliament Building** (McGregor St, Town) was never an architectural wonder, but its opening as the House of Assembly in 1964 was a significant milestone on PNG's road to independence. Sadly, the shell it has become is something of a metaphor for the country's steady decline in recent years.

Paga Point is the harbour headland adjacent to Town. It's worth walking to the top of Paga Hill for the fine views over the town, the harbour and the encircling reefs, though don't go alone. On the southern side of Town is the long, sandy stretch of **Ela Beach**. The beachfront promenade is a popular walk during the day, though the sands are seldom full of sunbathers these days as locals perceive even this area as potentially unsafe. If you do decide to swim here, the biggest threat is likely to be the shallow water, thick seaweed and black, spiny and painful sea urchins.

Hanuabada
Past the docks to the north lies Hanuabada, the original Motu village. Although it is still built out over the sea on stilts, the original wood and thatched houses were destroyed by fire during WWII. They were rebuilt in all-Australian building materials – corrugated iron and fibrocement – but it's still an interesting place and the people have retained many traditional Motu customs.

It is not acceptable to wander around the villages if you are not a guest or if you don't have a local guide. Your hotel should be able to suggest someone.

Koki
The picturesque stilt village of Koki, at the eastern end of Ela Beach, is worth visiting if you can find a local to take you. The best way to do that is by visiting the neighbouring **Koki Market**, one of the oldest and, after a vast improvement in security, safest markets in the city. Fresh produce and fish straight off the boat are sold here, but even if you're not buying the market offers a taste of how the majority of Papua New Guineans shop in relative safety. Having said that, you'd be stupid to flash around cash or expensive cameras if you're alone. If you go with a local (someone from your hotel, perhaps) then carrying a camera won't be a problem. PMVs stop outside the market.

Parliament Haus
The impressive **Parliament Haus** (Map p50; ☎ 327 7377; Independence Dr, Waigani; ☺ 8am-noon & 1-3pm Mon-Fri, or when sitting) was officially opened in 1984 with Prince Charles on hand. The main building is in the style of a Maprik, or Sepikstyle, *haus tambaran*, while the attached, circular cafeteria building follows Highland design principles. The façade is quite stunning, with a mosaic featuring unmistakably Papua New Guinean motifs; photographers with wide-angle lenses will be rewarded by being here as close to 4pm as possible.

PORT MORESBY

BOROKO & WAIGANI

0   800 m
0   0.5 miles

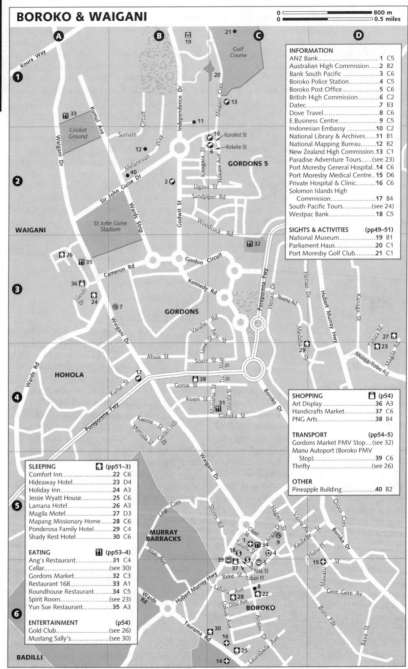

INFORMATION	
ANZ Bank	1 C5
Australian High Commission	2 B2
Bank South Pacific	3 C6
Boroko Police Station	4 C5
Boroko Post Office	5 C6
British High Commission	6 C2
Datec	7 B3
Dove Travel	8 C6
E.Business Centre	9 C5
Indonesian Embassy	10 C2
National Library & Archives	11 B1
National Mapping Bureau	12 B2
New Zealand High Commission	13 C1
Paradise Adventure Tours	(see 23)
Port Moresby General Hospital	14 C6
Port Moresby Medical Centre	15 D6
Private Hospital & Clinic	16 C6
Solomon Islands High Commission	17 B4
South Pacific Tours	(see 24)
Westpac Bank	18 C5

SIGHTS & ACTIVITIES	(pp49–51)
National Museum	19 B1
Parliament Haus	20 C1
Port Moresby Golf Club	21 C1

SHOPPING	(p54)
Art Display	36 A3
Handicrafts Market	37 C6
PNG Arts	38 B4

TRANSPORT	(pp54–5)
Gordons Market PMV Stop	(see 32)
Manu Autoport (Boroko PMV Stop)	39 C6
Thrifty	(see 26)

OTHER	
Pineapple Building	40 B2

SLEEPING	(pp51–3)
Comfort Inn	22 C6
Hideaway Hotel	23 D4
Holiday Inn	24 A3
Jessie Wyatt House	25 C6
Lamana Hotel	26 A3
Magila Motel	27 D3
Mapang Missionary Home	28 C6
Ponderosa Family Hotel	29 C4
Shady Rest Hotel	30 C6

EATING	(pp53–4)
Ang's Restaurant	31 C4
Cellar	(see 30)
Gordons Market	32 C3
Restaurant 168	33 A1
Roundhouse Restaurant	34 C5
Spirit Room	(see 23)
Yun Sue Restaurant	35 A3

ENTERTAINMENT	(p54)
Gold Club	(see 26)
Mustang Sally's	(see 30)

The cavernous lobby is entered through doors whose handles are stylised *kundu* drums (an hourglass-shaped drum with lizard skin). Inside, huge Sepik masks share space with several display cases full of fantastic butterflies, beetles and some very large stick insects; they're under the stairs.

It's possible to visit the chamber and sit in on parliament, if it is sitting itself (a rare phenomenon in 2004, as the government arbitrarily ended the session in an effort to avoid a no-confidence motion). A taxi from Boroko costs about K10, or K15 to K20 from Town. Alternatively, take a PMV along Waigani Dr, get out at the white, empty Pineapple Building, and walk about 2km northeast.

National Museum
Just beyond Parliament Haus, the **National Museum** (Map p50; Independence Dr, Waigani; admission K10; 8.30am-3.30pm Mon-Fri, 1-3.30pm Sun) looks like it needs a good dusting, but it's nonetheless worth spending an hour going through the displays covering the geography, fauna, culture, ethnography and history of PNG. There are superb examples of masks, shields and totems, a magnificent Milne Bay outrigger canoe decorated in cowrie shells, and a display showing how *bilums* (string bags) are made. Cameras are not allowed, but you can take pictures of the few birds, lizards and snakes living in the courtyard.

National Botanic Gardens
At the northern end of Waigani Dr, just beyond the University of Papua New Guinea, the **National Botanic Gardens** (Map pp56-7; 326 0248; www.ncbg.org.pg; Waigani Dr, Waigani; adult/child/student/family K8/3/5/10; 9am-4pm) are an island of serenity and beauty in the midst of an otherwise lacklustre city. Don't miss them! They have more than 2km of boardwalk threading under and through the jungle canopy; manicured lawns and gardens displaying both Papua New Guinean and exotic plant species; excellent wildlife displays and probably the best collection of native and hybrid orchids in PNG.

Islands, Beaches & Reefs
The wreck of the Burns Philp cargo ship **MV MacDhui** can be seen just breaking the surface in Moresby Harbour, off Hanuabada. It was sunk by Japanese aircraft in the early days of their WWII involvement. Its mast now stands in front of the Royal Papua Yacht Club.

Many expats have boats and the yacht club is busy on weekends. If you play your charm cards right, you might get asked out for the day. **Manubada (Local) Island** is used for weekend beach trips but beware – there is no shade. The **Bootless Bay** area (southeast of Port Moresby) and the other islands around the harbour are also popular; see p63.

Among the many places that you can reach if you can find a boat are **Basilisk Passage**, the deep, narrow entrance to the harbour of Port Moresby named by Captain Moresby after his ship, HMS *Basilisk*; the nearby **Nateara Reef** on which the SS *Pruth* was wrecked in 1924; the beautiful **Sinasi Reef** outside the passage; and the adjoining **Daugo Island**, also known as Fisherman's Island, with its white-sand beaches.

ACTIVITIES
The diving around Port Moresby is excellent. Loloata Island (p63) is popular, but for other places it's best to speak to the **Dive Centre** (Map pp56-7; 323 1355; www.divecentre.com .pg; poolside at Airways Hotel, Seven Mile). They offer PADI courses, equipment, air, and a wide range of diving and snorkelling tours. Very professional.

A round at the well-managed **Port Moresby Golf Club** (Map p50; 325 5367; Waigani) costs K80, plus K20 to hire clubs. The **restaurant** (meals K15-30; 7am-8pm) here is decent and is open to nonmembers.

TOURS
Paradise Adventure Tours (Map p50; 311 2130; daniel@paradisetours.com.pg; Hideaway Hotel, Tamara Rd, Six Mile) If you want to see birds of paradise (or any others) Daniel Wakra is your man. The trip to Varirata National Park (minimum two people, per person K80) is well worth it.
South Pacific Tours (Map p50; 323 6486; spt@global.net.pg; Holiday Inn, Islander Dr, Waigani) Several pricey but professional day trips, including full-day tours of Port Moresby Town (per person K220), Town and Varirata National Park (K242) and Taste of Kokoda Track (K264). Per-person prices fall as group size increases.

SLEEPING
Places to stay are scattered all over Port Moresby and are expensive in almost anyone's language. You'll find places near the airport, in Boroko, Waigani and Town,

with a few others inbetween. If you plan to use PMVs, Boroko is the most convenient location. All mid-range and top-end places have a free airport shuttle. For more on accommodation, see p215.

Budget

Most cheaper rooms are found around the Boroko area.

Jessie Wyatt House (Map p50; ☎ 325 3646; Taurama Rd, Boroko; s/tw per person K60/50) Run by the Country Women's Association, this clean, quiet and homely place has a kitchen, free tea and coffee, and a fridge in each room. A good place to meet Papua New Guineans. Rooms are few and you must check in between 8am and 4pm Monday to Friday and 8am and noon Saturday.

Mapang Missionary Home (Map p50; ☎ 325 5251; mapang@daltron.com.pg; Lahara Ave, Boroko; dm incl breakfast K60-75; 🏊) Mapang offers clean rooms, good food and interesting conversation. Rates depend on how many others are in your room.

Ponderosa Family Hotel (Map p50; ☎ 323 4888; Nuana Rd, Gordons; d/f K85/120) This former Air Niugini residence is simple but clean and friendly. It's in a quiet area and food here is cheap.

Magila Motel (Map p50; ☎ 325 0536; www.magila.com.pg; Magila St, Six Mile; d/tw K99/109; 🏊) This clean and fairly secure place has rooms with bathroom and satellite TV. The attached Magila Gorilla Club can be boisterous until late; ask for a room at the far end. It's in a bad area, but it's fair value.

Mid-Range

Comfort Inn (Map p50; ☎ 325 5091; comfortinn@daltron.com.pg; Mairi Pl, Boroko; d K120-180, apt K280-330; 🏊 🍴) In a quiet location two minutes' walk from central Boroko, and with friendly service and comfortable if not inspiring rooms, this is about the best value in the city. The garden and pool are a good place to come home to, and the meals (lunch and dinner K30 for guests, K50 for visitors) aren't bad.

Hideaway Hotel (Map p50; ☎ 323 6888; www.accommodationpng.com.pg; Tamara Rd, Six Mile; d/ste K145/310; 🏊 🍴) If it wasn't in Six Mile, which is not the safest suburb, this would be the best value. As it is, the compact but spotless standard rooms and vast suites are very cheap. The hotel minibus will chauffer

you wherever you want to go, making the location less of an issue. The attached **Spirit Room** (meals K35; ☽ 6am-10pm) restaurant has a good K27 set lunch.

Lamana Hotel (Map p50; ☎ 323 2333; www.lamanahotel.com.pg; off Waigani Dr, Waigani; d K181-198; 🍴) Rooms here are nice enough and service good, even if the numbering system doesn't make much sense. The K198 rooms are more like small apartments. If nightclubbing is your thing, the attached Gold Club (p54) will be attraction enough.

Gateway Hotel (Map pp56-7; ☎ 325 3855; www.coralseahotels.com.pg; Morea-Tobo Rd, Seven Mile; r K319-440, apt K281; 🏊 🍴) One minute from the airport, this member of the Coral Sea chain has comfortable if aging rooms and plenty of facilities. There are a couple of bars and restaurants, the pizzeria probably being the pick.

Ela Beach Hotel (Map p46; ☎ 321 2100; www.coralseahotels.com.pg; Ela Beach Rd, Ela Beach; r K215-320; 🏊 🍴) Recently bought by the Coral Sea group; the desperately needed renovations should be finished in 2005. The prime location notwithstanding, rooms are grossly overpriced, except on Fridays, Saturdays and Sundays when K143 buys you any room – be sure to look first. Some apartments are excellent value at K550 per week.

Also recommended:

Shady Rest Hotel (Map p50; ☎ 323 0000; www.shadyrest.com.pg; Taurama Rd, Boroko; d 145-181; 🏊) Restaurants, bars and decent rooms; a solid option.

Weigh Inn Hotel (Map p50; ☎ 321 7777; theweighinn@global.net.pg; Poreporena Fwy; r K130-160; 🏊) Fair-value rooms with TV, fridge and phone, behind a popular poker-machine palace.

Top End

All rooms in this bracket come with satellite TV and minibar. In-room Internet access can be arranged for about K75 for 10 hours, or you can use the hotel business centres for between K30 and K40 per hour. It's worth asking for any sort of corporate discount you can think of.

Airways Hotel & Apartments (Map pp56-7; ☎ 324 5200; www.airways.com.pg; Jacksons Pde, Seven Mile; r K385-700; 🏊 💻 🍴) The perfect place for the visitor who wants nothing to do with Port Moresby. Airways offers luxury rooms (ranging from standard rooms through to suites) and classy service two minutes from the airport, and the hotel is part of a complex with two restaurants, the wonderful **KC's Deli** (7am-7pm) and bars including the Dakota Lounge, inside an old DC-3.

Crowne Plaza (Map p46; ☎ 309 3000; cnr Douglas & Hunter Sts, Town; r K495-595;) In the heart of Town, the views from the Crowne Plaza are great and the rooms nearly as good, if not all that big. The larger executive rooms come with free use of the club lounge.

Holiday Inn (Map p50; ☎ 303 2000; www.holiday inn.com.au; Islander Dr, Waigani; r K594-670, ste K730-1050;) Not bad, but not worth the cash.

EATING & DRINKING

There are some good restaurants in Port Moresby, but little to fill the void between *kai* bars (takeaway food bars) and pricey restaurants. *Kai* bars close by about 7pm so at night hotels and restaurants are the go.

Restaurants

Cellar (Map p50; ☎ 323 0000; Taurama Rd, Boroko; meals K45-60; 6am-10pm;) This tastefully decorated, softly lit place at the Shady Rest Hotel serves a mix of food including steaks (K40), oysters (K35) and several Indian dishes. Fittingly, there's a wide selection of good wine.

Ichizen (Map p46; ☎ 320 3000; 1st fl, Steamships Arcade, Champion Pde, Town; meals K45-75; closed Sun;) The teppanyaki, sushi and sashimi are delicious, and the aerial delivery is as entertaining as you'd expect from a teppanyaki place.

Beachside Brasserie (Map p46; ☎ 321 2100; Ela Beach Rd, Ela Beach; meals K35-50; 6.30am-10.30pm;) The beachside ambience and tasty seafood here make for an enjoyable meal, especially at lunch.

Ang's Restaurant (Map p50; ☎ 323 0863; Munahu St, Gordons; meals K20-30; 7.30am-10pm;) It might look like Fort Knox from outside, and the area is none too inviting, but it's worth the trip for excellent Chinese food at reasonable prices. The hot-and-sour soup is special.

Roundhouse Restaurant (Map p50; ☎ 325 8899; Okari St, Boroko; meals K14-30; 10am-2pm & 5-10pm;) The Chinese food here is pretty good and the lunchtime deals (K14) are excellent value. The Sunday dim sum *(yum cha)* is popular.

Also recommended:

Rattle'n'Hum Pizzeria (Map pp56-7; ☎ 327 8162; Morea-Tobo Rd, Seven Mile; meals K30;) The best pizzas in town and a good atmosphere.

Restaurant 168 (Map p50; ☎ 325 1868; Waigani Dr, Waigani; meals K25-40;) Upstairs in the Port Moresby Country Club; the Malay and Indian food here is better than the dull surrounds might suggest. Try the seafood laksa (K16).

Coffee Shops

Espresso Bar (Map p46; ☎ 321 6600; ground fl, Deloitte Tower, Douglas St; 7.30am-5pm Mon-Fri, 8.30am-2pm Sat;) The coffee is good, as are the light meals (about K10).

Cafe (Map p46; ☎ 309 3000; Crowne Plaza Hotel, cnr Douglas & Hunter Sts; 6.30am-10pm;) The lunchtime buffet is not bad but meals aren't cheap.

Quick Eats

There are all manner of *kai* bars around, with Boroko being the *kai* capital. The better options are listed here.

Yun Sue Restaurant (Map p50; ☎ 325 6011; off Waigani Dr, Waigani; meals K10) Serves good, cheap and large Chinese lunches.

Ela Beach Cafe (Map p46; ☎ 685 3918; Bramell St, Ela Beach; meals K9-15; 8am-11.30pm) At the west end of Ela Beach, this rustic-looking eatery has coffee, beer and lunches of simple *kai*.

Self-Catering

Koki Market (Map pp56-7) is the place to head for a good range of fruit and veg, plus fresh seafood. The bustling Gordons Market (Map p50), one of the largest in the country, has an excellent selection of vegetables and fruit.

Yacht Club

Royal Papua Yacht Club (Map p46; ☎ 321 1700; Poreporena Fwy) This airy place is mainly about sitting on the decking, drinking cold beer and watching the harbour, but the food isn't bad and is reasonably priced. Theoretically you have to be signed in by a member, but a little charm should see you in.

ENTERTAINMENT

It's not New York, but Port Moresby has come some way from the entertainment black hole it was a few years ago. In the nightclub field, in particular, things are on the up. The *Post Courier* publishes the 'What's On' entertainment guide on Wednesday.

What little live music there is in Port Moresby will be found in a nightclub.

Gold Club (Map p50; ☎ 323 2333; www.lamana hotel.com.pg; off Waigani Dr, Waigani; admission K20; ⏰ 11am-5am) The open-air dance floor surrounded by layers of bars gives the impression that this could, actually, be in New York. The music is good and there's no riffraff here; if you play your cards right you might end up dancing with the prime minister's daughter. If not, you can still play cards in the upstairs casino. Good fun.

Pondo Tavern (Map p46; ☎ 309 3000; cnr Douglas & Hunter Sts, Town; ⏰ 11am-4.30am) Underneath the Crowne Plaza Hotel, this place is less consistent than the Gold Club, with more milling than dancing.

Mustang Sally's (Map p50; ☎ 323 0000; Taurama Rd, Boroko; ⏰ 9am-2am) Attached to the Shady Rest Hotel, this place offers a more 'genuine' PNG experience – raw and spirited. If you're offended by loud music, the odd swinging pool cue or women of the night, best to steer clear.

SHOPPING

Imelda Marcos probably never said: 'See you later, Ferdi, I'm off to Moresby for a weekend's shopping.' No shoes. Not much on the clothes front. And surprisingly little in the way of handicrafts.

Ela Beach Craft Market (Map p46; Ela Beach International School, Ela Beach Rd, Ela Beach; admission K1; ⏰ 7am-noon last Saturday of every month) This is the best market in PNG, with all the paintings, carvings, baskets, shells and weavings you can poke a *koteka* (penis gourd) at. Barbecued food and traditional dancers (about 10am) contribute to the carnival atmosphere.

PNG Arts (Map p50; ☎ 325 3976; Poreporena Fwy, Gordons; ⏰ 9am-4.30pm Mon-Sat, 10am-3pm Sun) The long-running PNG Arts warehouse is the next-best option to the Ela Beach Craft

Market. Artefacts come from all over PNG and prices are reasonable, credit cards accepted and freight and documentation can be organised.

Beyond Art (Map p46; ☎ 320 2257; Champion Pde; ⏰ 9am-5pm Mon-Fri, 8am-2pm Sat, 10am-1pm Sun) In Town, Beyond Art is small and pricey.

Art display (Map p50; Islander Dr, Waigani; ⏰ 7am-5pm) There is often a good display of handicrafts and contemporary art for sale at this display outside the Holiday Inn.

Handicrafts Market (Map p50; Tabari Pl, Boroko; ⏰ 8am-5pm) This display is in the dusty square in central Boroko.

Malolo (Map p46; ☎ 321 0098; Ela Beach Rd; ⏰ 8am-4pm Mon-Fri) In the City Mission building on Ela Beach is this inspirational project in which reformed *raskols* have been trained in the arts of designing and screen-printing. The T-shirts, throws and cushion-covers are attractive.

GETTING THERE & AWAY
Air

Flights link Port Moresby to virtually everywhere in PNG and anywhere Air Niugini flies internationally (p236). For routes and prices, see p237.

Airline offices in Port Moresby include:

Air Niugini (Map p46; ☎ 327 3444; www.airniugini .com.pg; ground fl, MMI House, Champion Pde, Town)

Airlines PNG (Map p46; ☎ 325 0555; Champion Pde, Town)

Airlink (Map pp56-7; ☎ 325 9555; www.airlink.com.pg; Jackson's Airport)

MAF (Mission Aviation Fellowship; Map pp56-7; ☎ 325 2668; www.maf.org.au; General Aviation section, Jackson's Airport)

Qantas & British Airways (Map p46; ☎ 321 1200; www.qantas.com.au; Cuthbertson St, Town)

Boat

There are no regular passenger boats sailing out of Port Moresby. Many freighters do have passenger facilities, but none of the shipping companies officially allow passengers. Asking around at the wharves might get you a berth. If you want to go to the gulf, ask around the smaller boats at the jetties north of the main wharf.

Heading east towards Milne Bay you could go to Kupiano and look for a small boat or canoe. A series of hops along the south coast could, after nights in villages and days waiting under palm trees, get you to Alotau.

Car

There are several companies renting cars and 4WDs in Port Moresby. See below for details.

PMV

Rural PMVs leave from Gordons Market (Map p50) and head west as far as Kerema (K35, five hours) and east along the Magi Hwy. PMVs also leave here for Bomana War Cemetery (No 16) and destinations along the Sogeri Rd.

GETTING AROUND
To/From the Airport

The easiest way to or from the airport is in a hotel minibus. All but the smallest establishments have one and if you contact them ahead, or call from the airport, you'll soon have a free ride. In the international terminal arrivals hall, go into the NCD Tourist office and you can use the phone for free. In the domestic terminal, buy a phone card (p231) from the shop beside the café.

Taxis wait outside both terminals and unless you spot a **Scarlet Taxi** (☎ 323 4266), which have meters, you'll need to negotiate the fare before you leave. A taxi to Waigani costs about K12, to Boroko K15, and to Town between K20 and K25.

The third option is to take a PMV, but you need to be very confident and/or desperately short of cash to do this if you don't know the city. PMVs leave from about 50m east of the international terminal and cost K0.50. Route 10 takes you to Town via Boroko.

Car & 4WD

The airport is full of companies renting cars and 4WDs, and the major names also have offices in several top-end hotels. Port Moresby can be a confusing place to navigate at first, so be sure to have a map and take out full insurance. Police check points are common after dark but shouldn't be a problem if you have your license. For more information, see p244.

Some rental companies and their central reservation numbers:

Avis (Map pp56-7; ☎ 324 9400; www.avis.com.pg) Offices at airport's domestic and international terminals.

Hertz (Map pp56-7; ☎ 302 6822; sales@leasemaster .com.pg) Desks at airport and Gateway Hotel.

Thrifty (Map pp56-7; ☎ 325 5550) Offices at the airport, Airways Hotel & Apartments and Lamana Hotel.

PMV

Port Moresby has an efficient PMV service, though you'll see very few white faces in the windows. Most expats will strongly advise against using PMVs, but if you stick to certain routes you should be fine.

PMVs run frequently from 6.30am to 6pm and cost K0.50 for any trip, near or far. The main interchange point is Manu Autoport in Boroko; look for the pedestrian overpass and crowds of people. In Town, the main stop is on Douglas St, and at Gordons it's near Gordons Market. PMVs get crowded at peak hours and especially on Friday evenings.

PMVs run set routes and have route numbers (and sometimes the destination itself) painted on the front. They go both ways. Some useful routes:

No 4 From Hanuabada, through Town, Koki and Boroko to Gordons Market.

No 7 A handy route between Boroko and Waigani.

No 10 From Hanuabada to Town, Boroko (Jessie Wyatt House; past the hospital and the CWA Hostel), and on to the airport. Avoid getting on or off in the Kila Kila and Sabama areas, which are relatively unsafe.

No 11 From Town to Two Mile Hill, Boroko, Waigani (not all stop at the government offices) and Morata.

No16 From Gordons Market out to Bomana Prison, past the War Cemetery.

For more on PMVs, see p246.

Taxi

Port Moresby has no shortage of taxis, and you'll usually be able to find one outside a hotel or the airport, or many in Boroko. Sample fares include: Town to Boroko, K10; Town to Waigani, K15; Town to the airport, K20. Chartering a taxi will cost about K30 per hour. For more on taxis, see p246.

The fast-growing number of **Scarlet Taxis** (☎ 323 4266) offer a far superior and cheaper alternative. Their clean, relatively new taxis have meters, radios and drivers in ironed shirts. But the clincher: betel nut and smoking are banned.

AROUND PORT MORESBY

Apart from Loloata Island (see p63), the most visited areas near Port Moresby are along or just off the Sogeri Rd, which veers right off the Hubert Murray Hwy a couple of kilometres past the airport. 'Most visited', however, is a relative term; other than Sunday you'll likely be the only people around. The reason is that the road has developed a reputation for trouble, with several serious incidents. Thankfully things seem less volatile than they were around 2000. If you make this trip, do it with a local.

It's only 46km to Sogeri but there is enough to see to make it a full-day trip. The first stop is the large and carefully tended **Bomana War Cemetery** (☽ 8am-4pm), where 4000 Australian and Papua New Guinean WWII soldiers are buried; American soldiers who died in PNG were generally shipped home for burial. It's a serene yet sobering place. The No 16 PMV from Gordons Market runs past the gate.

Continuing on, the road winds up the impressive **Laloki River gorge** and you're soon more than 600m above sea level. There are several viewing points looking into the gorge and up to the **Rouna Falls** and power station. Just beyond is a store where you can buy food and water, and a track leading to the rundown Kokoda Trail Motel (opposite).

Right after the store is the turn-off to **Varirata National Park** (☎ 325 0195 in Port Moresby, ask for Jim Onga; admission K5), the highlight of the Sogeri Rd. It's 8km from the turn-off and you'll find six clearly marked walking trails ranging from 45 minutes to three hours long, and some excellent lookouts back to Port Moresby and the coast. The birdwatching here can be quite rewarding, with

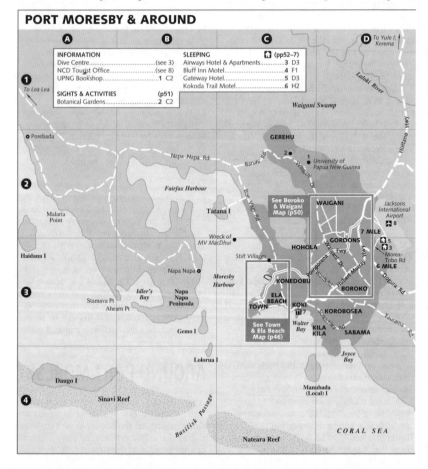

PORT MORESBY & AROUND

INFORMATION		
Dive Centre	....	(see 3)
NCD Tourist Office	....	(see 8)
UPNG Bookshop	....	1 C2

SIGHTS & ACTIVITIES	(p51)
Botanical Gardens	.... 2 C2

SLEEPING	⌂ (pp52–7)
Airways Hotel & Apartments	.... 3 D3
Bluff Inn Motel	.... 4 F1
Gateway Hotel	.... 5 D3
Kokoda Trail Motel	.... 6 H2

an array of kingfishers and Raggiana bird of paradise as highlights. It's possible to camp in the park and the best place is on the grass outside the disused lodge. There are toilet facilities (a long-drop) but the showers don't work. Speak to the ranger-in-charge.

There's nothing worth stopping in Sogeri for, but a couple of kilometres beyond along a diabolical dirt road the **Crystal Rapids** (admission per vehicle K7) make a pleasant swimming and picnic spot.

Sleeping & Eating

Apart from camping at Varirata National Park there are the following options.

Bluff Inn Motel (☎ 328 1223; fax 328 1311; Sogeri Rd; s/d K143/165; 🍴) This sprawling motel is by the river at 17 Mile. This is the only place worth staying out here and the rooms are fair value. The attached **Phoenix Bar** (meals K12-20; 🕑 10am-2pm & 5-10pm Mon-Fri, 10am-10pm Sat & Sun) is the best place to stop for lunch.

Kokoda Trail Motel (☎ 325 4403; fax 325 3322; r K60) Cheap but dirty and if you don't book ahead, there will be no food. Only if you are desperate.

Getting There & Away

PMVs leave from Gordons Market (K2.50) semiregularly. The road is surfaced to Sogeri and all the way down to the Varirata National Park, however the section from Sogeri to Owers' Corner – the beginning of the Kokoda Track – is for 4WDs only.

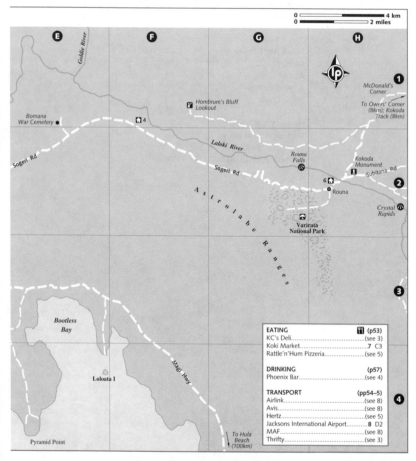

Central, Oro & Milne Bay Provinces

CENTRAL, ORO & MILNE BAY PROVINCES

CONTENTS

Central, Oro and Milne Bay Provinces are all about the outdoors. Whether it's trekking, diving, snorkelling, lazing on a beach or playing Trobriand Islands cricket, you're guaranteed to get the blood pumping.

The Kokoda Track is the highest profile trek anywhere in PNG and more Australians (plus the odd Japanese group) are making the often-painful pilgrimage across the Owen Stanley Range than they have since the end of WWII. Reliving, in part, the trials of the WWII soldiers who fought there can be deeply moving, as can spending a week with the carriers and villagers of the track.

While the Kokoda Track is important to Australians, it is the region's breathtaking snorkelling and diving opportunities that are world famous. You can swim close to a giant manta ray as it gets a thorough cleaning by a school of wrasses, dive on WWII planes and boat wrecks, marvel at the kaleidoscopic colours of the reefs, or muck dive (diving amid the critters that lurk at the sea floor and the detritus of history) under the pylons of the Samarai Island Wharf.

But perhaps the most surprising aspect of the region is that, despite everything on offer, you'll be one of very few tourists. No problems with human damage to reefs here, or hordes of people at the Milamala Festival in the famous Trobriand Islands – the sense of discovery is palpable and the locals are generally very friendly, even by PNG standards.

Alotau, the capital of Milne Bay Province, is one of the safest and most attractive towns in the country, and is populated by a community of locals who seem determined to attract tourists to a place worthy of your time.

HIGHLIGHTS

- Trekking across the rugged Owen Stanley Range on the infamous **Kokoda Track** (p64)
- Muck diving under the rotting wooden pylons of the wharf on **Samarai Island** (p79)
- Playing a unique brand of cricket on the **Trobriand Islands** (p81) and observing the rituals of the **Milamala Festival** (p81)
- Living in a seaside village among the amazing volcanic *rias*, or fjords, of **Tufi** (p72)
- Swimming among the giant manta rays at the **Manta Ray Cleaning Station** (p80) in the China Strait

■ LAND AREA: 67,940 SQ KM	■ POPULATION: 527,000

History

The coastal people and islanders of this region have traded for centuries in extensive barter networks, the most famous of which was the *kula* ring (see p74). The *hiri* trade between Motuans in Central Province and villages further around the gulf was conducted in huge two-masted *lakatois* (sailing boats).

In 1606 Spanish mariner Luis Vaéz de Torres, after whom the Louisiades were named, abducted 14 children and took them to Manila in the Philippines to be baptised. He was followed by an array of explorers, including the famous Frenchman Antoine Raymond Joseph de Bruni d'Entrecasteaux, who left his name on a large group of is-

lands. But it wasn't until 1847 that Europeans sought to settle the region. In that year, Marist missionaries arrived on Muyua (Woodlark) Island, but the locals, it seems, were unenthusiastic about Christianity and the Marists were gone within eight years. Apparently undeterred, the London Missionary Society (LMS), Catholics, Anglicans, Methodists and finally the Seventh-Day Adventists opened for business between the 1870s and 1908. Most notable among them was Reverend Charles W Abel, a dissident member of the LMS, who in 1891 founded the Kwato Extension Association on Kwato Island, near Samarai in the China Strait. This was the first church to provide skills training to the indigenous people of Milne Bay.

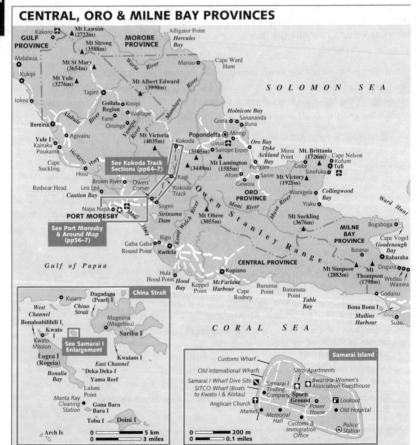

CENTRAL, ORO & MILNE BAY PROVINCES

Apart from men of God, the region attracted a less savoury crew of opportunists who forcibly removed local men to work in northern Australian sugar plantations. This loathsome practice was known as 'blackbirding' and continued well into the 20th century. Errol Flynn, who spent his formative years ducking and diving around New Guinea from 1927 to 1933, later wrote of the 'confidence' required to persuade local elders to allow their men to be carted off.

On the north coast early European contacts with the Orokaiva people were relatively peaceful, but when gold was discovered at Yodda and Kokoda in 1895, violence soon followed. A government station was established after an altercation between locals and miners, but the first government officer was killed shortly after he arrived. Eventually things quietened down and the mines were worked out. Then came the war (see boxed text, p62).

Milne Bay became a huge Allied naval base and a few American landing craft (p76) and several memorials can still be seen. The gardens and plantations inland from Buna and Gona had barely recovered from the war when Mt Lamington's 1951 eruption wiped out Higaturu, the district headquarters, and almost 3000 people. The new headquarters town of Popondetta was established at a safer distance from the volcano.

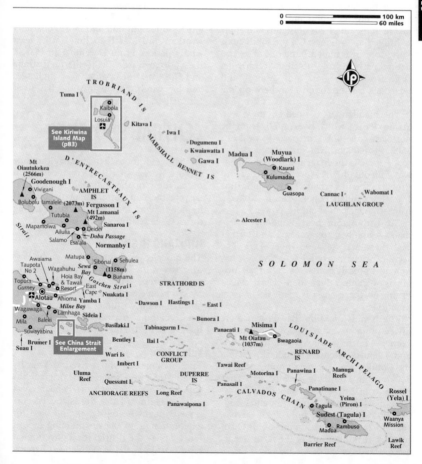

THE BATTLES OF MILNE BAY

The two major battles of Milne Bay are regarded as turning points of WWII in the Pacific. In the Battle of the Coral Sea (5–8 May 1942), the Japanese navy, intent on invading Port Moresby, was repelled by the Allies. It is regarded as a classic naval battle, but the warships did not come within 300km of each other; the fighting was confined to the air, with some of the heaviest dogfights above the Louisiades. There were heavy losses on both sides, but the crippled Japanese navy would no longer be a significant threat in the Pacific.

And yet the Japanese resolve to capture PNG saw them land troops at Buna and Gona, in Oro Province, in July 1942 and move south along the Kokoda Track. In August they attempted to capture Milne Bay, but after 12 days of heavy fighting in the Alotau area Australian troops secured the first Allied land victory in the Pacific. See www.diggerhistory.info/pages-battles/ww2/milne_bay.htm for more on the battle.

Geography & Climate

The region stretches down the 'dragon's tail' at the eastern end of mainland PNG and out into the Coral and Solomon seas, taking in the hundreds of islands and atolls of Milne Bay Province. On the south coast Port Moresby is built around one of several natural harbours and sits in the centre of a large area of dry grasslands; swamps and tidal flats can be found elsewhere on the coast.

The mainland is divided by the Owen Stanley Range, which rises rapidly from the northern and southern coasts to peaks of 3500m to 4000m. Not surprisingly, major roads are few: the Magi and Hiritano highways run out of Port Moresby, while in Oro Province the only road of any length runs from the capital, Popondetta, to Kokoda, from where it's all about leg power.

Mt Lamington, near Popondetta, remains a mildly active volcano and further east there are volcanoes near Tufi. The section of coast around Cape Nelson has unique tropical 'fjords', or *rias*; their origin is volcanic rather than glacial. Much of this northern coast is made up of coral limestone.

The islands of Milne Bay Province are divided into six main groups: the Samarai group; D'Entrecasteaux group; the Trobriand Islands; Muyua (Woodlark) Island; the Conflict and Engineer groups; and the 300km-long Louisiade Archipelago. They range from tiny dots to mountainous islands like Fergusson, Normanby and Goodenough which, while only 26km across, soars to 2566m at the summit of Mt Oiautukekea, making it one of the most steeply sided islands on earth.

Weather patterns are unpredictable, particularly in the east where rainstorms can be spontaneous and heavy. In Milne Bay Province November to January generally has the optimum and most consistent weather, and March to June is the least windy period. From December to March, the cyclone season in northern Australia and the Coral Sea can trigger high seas and big winds, although Milne Bay itself is usually calm.

CENTRAL PROVINCE

Stretching for more than 500km either side of Port Moresby, Central Province lives in the shadow of the national capital. And despite the concentration of people and money in Port Moresby, the surrounding districts see relatively few visitors.

HIRITANO HIGHWAY

The unsealed Hiritano Hwy connects Port Moresby with Kerema, far to the west in Gulf Province. This area is home to the Mekeo people, who are noted for their colourful dancing costumes and face painting. On ceremonial occasions the men paint their faces in striking geometric designs.

Yule Island

The missionaries who arrived at Yule Island in 1885 were some of the original European visitors to reach the Papuan coast of New Guinea. Later the island became a government headquarters and base for explorations into the surrounding mountains. Today the district local government headquarters is on the mainland at Bereina but the island remains a pleasant place to visit. The **Carmelite convent** on Yule Island is empty but intact – you can stay here but you'll need to bring everything. There are no phones on the island though the mission can usually be contacted through the **Diocese of Bereina** (☎ 325 6102) office in Port Moresby.

One of France's top WWI air aces, M Bourgade, was an early mission worker and you can see his grave on Yule Island.

GETTING THERE & AWAY

Turn off the Hiritano Hwy about 38km past Agivairu. From the turn-off, travel another 20km to Poukama, where there is a car park, and a canoe or dinghy will take you to the island. Poukama is about 160km (a three-hour drive) from Port Moresby. It's about 4½ hours by PMV (public motor vehicle). A PMV leaves Gordons Market early, most days.

MAGI HIGHWAY

This highway runs east from Port Moresby, circling round Bootless Bay to the small marina (Tahira Boating Centre) from which the ferry crosses to Loloata Island, easily the main attraction on this route. It continues in varying states past many fine beaches, the pick being **Hula Beach**, about 100km from the capital. Hula gets windsurfers especially excited; you can stay at the church guesthouse. The road has seen a lot of *raskols* (bandit) activity in recent years and is best undertaken in a group. Ditto for Hula Beach.

Loloata Island

About 20km east of Port Moresby, Loloata Island in Bootless Bay is a popular weekend escape – midweek is even better. The attraction is the **Loloata Island Resort** (☎ 325 8590; www .loloata.com; s/d US$170/250 incl all meals; 🏊), where snorkelling, fishing, sailboarding and diving equipment are for hire. There are dozens of dive sites (see www.loloata.com/DiveSites), including a Boston Havoc bomber. Or you could just laze around. Ask about weekend rates or day-trip specials. Diving costs US$45 for one or US$100 for three dives (including equipment).

To get there, drive out on the Rigo Rd (which meets the airport road in Six Mile) to the Tahira Boating Centre on Bootless Bay. The resort's ferry makes regular trips to the island. Alternatively, call ahead and the resort bus will collect you from the airport or a hotel.

GOILALA REGION

If you want to look at the high country behind the coastal strip, experience heart-in-mouth airstrips or try lesser-known but interesting walks, the mountain villages of the Goilala region are well worth a visit. The hiking up here is wonderful, with steep mountains, often covered in bush, and the pretty villages of **Woitape**, **Tapini**, **Ononge** and **Fane**, ranging from about 930m to 1764m high.

The Catholic fathers bequeathed the area an excellent network of well-graded tracks that once took mule-trains. June to October are the walking months; June to August are best.

The village airstrips are some of the most exhilarating in PNG. At Tapini, the strip is carved into a hillside, running steeply uphill and ending in a sheer face so you can only come in one way. Almost worth the trip alone.

Sleeping & Eating

There is a government station at Tapini and Catholic missions at Fane, Ononge, Kosipi and Woitape, and if you turn up you'll be able to find a bed, a village meal and a guide without problem. Prices are negotiable, but low. Alternatively, the comfortable **Woitape Lodge** (☎ 325 2011 in Port Moresby; all-inclusive r per person K130), run by Airlines PNG, is a great place to end a long day's trekking, with its open fire, bar and rustic atmosphere. They can arrange guides and cook up some tasty food, but you need to let them know that you're coming.

Getting There & Away

Airlines PNG flies from Port Moresby to Woitape (K205, four weekly), Tapini (K233, twice weekly), Fane (K206, twice weekly) and Ononge (K189, weekly), but you'll need to book ahead and check right up until the last minute – these flights are often cancelled. All flights are short, but how long it takes to get to your destination depends on how many stops there are along the way.

There is no road access.

CENTRAL, ORO & MILNE BAY PROVINCES

KOKODA TRACK

One day on the Kokoda Track is enough to understand why it has become synonymous with Australia's self-image of never-say-die and the mateship that rises from shared ordeals. Every one of the steep, slippery steps you take on this 96km natural rollercoaster requires concentration. Imagine how tough it must have been carrying a pack, rifle and ammunition, constantly ill with dysentery and waiting to be ambushed by the Japanese.

By 2004 the challenge of the track had seen the annual number of trekkers making this painful pilgrimage rise past 1100 and that number is expected to grow. The majority walk as part of an organised group, and that is the recommended way of doing the trek. Only the most experienced trekkers should consider walking independently (see Warning opposite).

Apart from the wartime history, relationships built with today's residents of the track, and particularly the guides and carriers who trek with you, are equally rewarding. They serve as a reminder that the Kokoda Track is about people not just a distant but heroic military campaign.

This section should be used as a guide to planning, but not walking, the track. For full details Clive Baker's *The Kokoda Trek* is a must; see Books & Maps on p66.

PLANNING

All trekkers must pay a K200 trekking fee to the Kokoda Track Authority (KTA). If you're on an organised trek, the company will deal with the fee. But if you're going solo, you need to obtain your own permit by emailing the **Kokoda Track Authority** (kokoda trackauthority@global.net.pg) for an application form and details on transferring the fee to their bank account. The **PNG Tourism Promotion Authority** (☎ 320 0211; 5th fl, MMI Haus, Champion Pde, Town) in Port Moresby can take over-the-counter payments.

There are basic 'resthouses' in most villages plus various shelters and campsites along the track. Some of the resthouses (usually about K10 to K15 per person) and shelters are small, so if you meet another

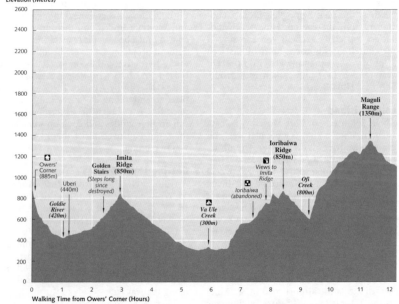

KOKODA TRACK – SOUTH

Elevation (Metres)

- Owers' Corner (885m)
- Uberi (440m)
- Goldie River (420m)
- Golden Stairs (Steps long since destroyed)
- Imita Ridge (850m)
- Va Ule Creek (300m)
- Ioribaiwa (abandoned)
- Ioribaiwa Ridge (850m)
- Views to Imita Ridge
- Ofi Creek (800m)
- Maguli Range (1350m)

Walking Time from Owers' Corner (Hours)

party you might have to camp in the village. On most treks you'll spend some nights in villages and some in the forest. Note that if a large group is in the village, and you have no tent, you might need to move to the next village.

Organised treks supply the bulk of your food, which accompanies you on the backs of local carriers. It's replenished about halfway along via a chartered flight as there are no trade stores on the track – only at Sogeri and Kokoda. Bring any comfort food yourself and keep it light. And don't forget sachets of rehydration salts – maintaining your fluid and carbohydrate levels is critical. See p253.

When to Trek

Most trekking companies operate between March and October, but the coolest, driest and best months to trek are from May to September. It could rain at any time of year, but between November and February it will rain, and most companies don't operate because it is too dangerous and uncomfortable.

WARNING

The Kokoda Track is not PNG's most difficult trek, but it's no walk in the park. You must be pretty fit and, if in doubt, aim to do it in nine days, not six. Be sure to use local guides and carriers and never walk with less than four people. If there is an accident two can get help and one can stay with the injured. Most trekking companies carry a satellite phone or a two-way radio; if you don't have one and there's a problem, no-one will hear the screams. Most villages have radios but it could be a long walk to the nearest one. Conflicts among traditional landowners have led to the track's closure in the past, but in recent years the situation has been fairly calm. Still, it's worth keeping an ear open.

What to Bring

You can't go without a comfortable pair of boots or running shoes with good grip. You'll also need a tent with fly (some tour companies provide these); a water bottle or a water bladder, to be refilled from streams

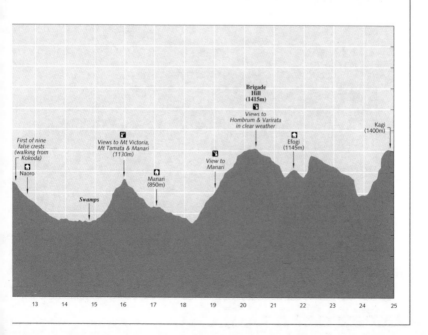

CENTRAL, ORO & MILNE
BAY PROVINCES

as you go; a light sleeping bag; and wet-weather gear (even in the dry season) – a poncho is a good, multipurpose option. Prepare yourself with a comprehensive medical kit (see p248). The total weight of your pack should not exceed 15kg. Local fruits and vegetables are available in villages, but you or your carriers will need to carry the rest.

Information Sources

Apart from the books mentioned below, the best information is available from the trek operators' websites; see Organised Treks opposite. At the time of research, the Kokoda Track Authority's website was forthcoming.

Books & Maps

There is an ever-growing number of books about the Kokoda campaign, though only one that is worth carrying with you. Clive Baker's *The Kokoda Trek* has a full description of the trek. Baker's book, and almost any other on the subject, can be bought from the on-line mail order shop: www

.warbooks.com.au. They also have plans for a Kokoda news item page for the latest stories that emerge.

A lighter but most valuable companion is definitely the *Kokoda Trail Diary & Guide* (www.kokodatrail.com.au/forums/index .php?showtopic=78), which has a decent history, maps and pictures. Be sure to bring zip-lock bags for any paper, lest you sweat it to death.

Maps of varying vintage are available in Port Moresby from the **National Mapping Bureau** (NMB; ☎ 327 6223; natmap@datec.com.pg; Melanesian Way, Waigani), though they're more interesting than necessary. In Australia, Map World (www.mapworld.com.au) stocks the 1:100,000 topographic maps for Popondetta, Kokoda, Efogi and Port Moresby (A$10 each) and the most recent *LongitudinalCross-Section of the Kokoda Trail* (1995), which has useful descriptive notes and detailed sections of tricky areas.

There is a reasonable choice of publications about Kokoda and a number of these titles are generally available second-hand. Some recommendations:

KOKODA TRACK – NORTH

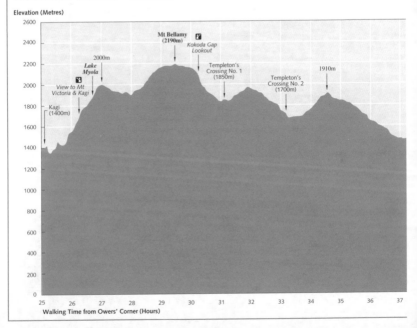

Elevation (Metres)

Walking Time from Owers' Corner (Hours)

Kokoda (2004) by Paul Ham
Those Ragged Bloody Heroes (1992) by Peter Brune
The Kokoda Trail: a History (2003) by Stuart Hawthorne
Kokoda (2004) by Peter Fitzsimons
Blood and Iron (1991) by Lex McAuley

Guides & Carriers

If you're trekking independently, don't do it without a good guide. A personal recommendation is best – you could try asking the kokodatrackauthority@global.net.pg or asking other trekkers on the www.kokoda trail.com.pg web forum. There are dozens of guides and carriers working on the track and most are freelancers. In Kokoda you will find someone to go with you, but from the Sogeri end it could be a problem: the KTA office is at Sogeri so email them for information.

On your own or in a group, having a carrier might mean the difference between finishing the trek or giving up along the way. One carrier between two or three is a good idea. If the weight becomes too much, you can employ a carrier in most villages along the track, but they are getting busier as the route becomes more popular. Pay guides about K60 per day and carriers about K40 per day, plus K5 per day for food; you'll also need to pay their airfares back home (about K200).

Organised Treks

You can choose to walk the track with one of about 10 companies, which takes most of the hassle out of the preparation, leaving you to focus on getting fit. Your choice will depend on your budget, interest in the military campaign, the company's safety record and how it deals with emergencies, and what sort of relationship you want with the carriers. Costs depend on length of the trek, whether it includes airfares from Australia, what equipment is provided and whether you employ a carrier or not. See the websites for full details and make sure you are comparing like with like. The following are some of the options:

Kokoda Trekking (www.kokoda.com.au; A$1450) This PNG-owned company has no expert guides, which makes their trips cheaper and often encourages greater interaction with local guides and carriers. Good feedback, but historical knowledge is limited.

CENTRAL, ORO & MILNE BAY PROVINCES

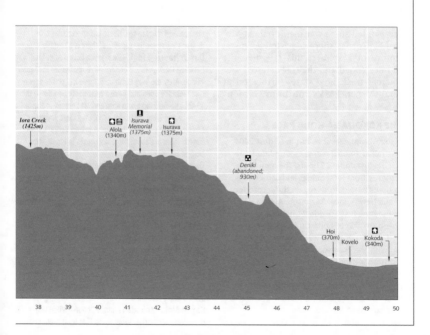

Kokoda Treks & Tours (www.arach.net.au/~kokoda/ index2.htm; A$2700) When it comes to knowledge of the campaign, Frank Taylor is hard to beat. Treks are organised with military precision and include a trip to Buna and Gona. Fair value.

Executive Excellence (www.executiveexcellence .au; $A5500) Known by some as the 'men in tights', this Brisbane-based operation employs ex-soldiers and includes a full predeparture training programme.

Adventure Kokoda (www.adventurekokodatreks.com; A$4450) High-profile and well-organised treks, though some critics question the tendency to walk at night. You can do better, for less cash.

Koiari Treks & Tours Ltd (sogent@global.net.pg) & **Elai Guide & Tour Services** (☎ /fax 329 7335 in Kokoda) Cheaper, locally-operated outfits.

Several of PNG's larger tour operators also run treks, including: **Eco-Melanesia** (www.em .com.pg), **South Pacific Tours** (spt@global.net.pg) and **Niugini Tours** (www.nghols.com). Otherwise, the forthcoming KTA website is expected to list all operators.

GETTING TO & FROM THE TREK

The Kokoda Track runs between Owers' Corner in Central Province and Kokoda in Oro Province. At the southern end you'll need a 4WD to reach Owers' Corner, taking the turn-off just before Sogeri – look for a white-painted stone war memorial. At Mc-Donald's Corner there is a strange metal sculpture of a soldier; this is where the road once ended and the track started, but the actual track now starts further on at Owers' Corner. PMVs run from Gordons

Market in Port Moresby to Sogeri early in the morning. From there, you'll need to wait and hope for a lift to Owers' Corner or start walking the 16km. Note: due to the rutty and slippery surface, the road is often impassable to any vehicles, so be prepared to walk at least part of it if required. See also Short Cuts, opposite.

THE TREK

Depending on how fit you are, it takes between six and 11 days to traverse the track. The itinerary shown here starts at Owers' Corner, but just as many people walk the other way, which involves about 550m more climbing. By taking a longer trip, you have more time for side-trips, exploring the battlefields and actually experiencing village life. The average trekker walks about 50 hours from beginning to end. No itinerary is set in stone and this one is indicative only.

Day 1: Owers' Corner–Va Ule Creek campsites (10km, six hours) The campsites are about one to 1½ hours past Imita Ridge. Watch for the extensive weapon pits on the northern face of Imita Ridge, where the Australian's made their last stand in 1942.

Day 2: Va Ule Creek campsites–Naoro (17km, eight hours) The track follows the original wartime route over Ioribaiwa Ridge. A memorial is being installed on the ridge and on the slopes there are many interesting weapons pits, bunkers and relics to see. Naoro has spectacular 270-degree views over the valley and there is a large resthouse.

Day 3: Naoro–Efogi (19km, seven hours) About halfway between these points there are three resthouses in Manari village. After the long climb up Brigade Hill you suddenly come into the open and have a wide panorama down the 1942 battlefield, across to Kagi and Mt Bellamy in the distance and Efogi, just below you. On a clear day you can see all the way back to Hombrum and Varirata, near Sogeri. There are about three resthouses in Efogi – the biggest village on the track.

Day 4: Efogi–Kagi–Mt Bellamy (12km, seven hours) An hour of climbing and descending past Efogi is Kagi, another spectacular village site. From here, the track climbs to its highest point at Mt Bellamy. You can side-trip to Myola in three to four hours return. Along the way, and just off the track, is the huge crater where a WWII bomber blew up and scattered aircraft parts in all directions. Your guide/carrier should know the place.

Day 5: Mt Bellamy–Alola (17km, 11 hours) After a long down and up section, the track passes Templeton's Crossing, followed by another up, down and up to Alola – quite a tiring section.

Day 6: Alola–Kokoda (19km, 10 hours) When you reach the Isurava Memorial; allow yourself at least an hour at

---

THE KOKODA 24-HOUR RACE

It sounds unbelievable, but in August 2004 Australian Brian Freeman completed the track in just under 25 hours. The immediate response from local guides and carriers was to go into training to regain the record for Papua New Guinea. As a result, August 2005 will see the first Kokoda 24-hour race, from Kokoda to Owers' Corner. It has been organised by the people at www.kokodatrail.com .pg with the corresponding aim of attracting attention for the track both at home and abroad. If successful, it could become an annual event. At the time of writing plenty of local and a few crazy international runners had expressed interest.

THE KOKODA TRACK'S ROLE IN WWII

Following the bombing of Pearl Harbor in December 1941, the Japanese made a rapid thrust down the Malayan peninsula and across Southeast Asia to New Guinea. Defeat at the Battle of the Coral Sea, while on their way to invade Port Moresby, caused a reassessment of Japanese strategy.

They decided to attack Port Moresby via a totally unexpected back door assault. The plan was to land on the north coast in the Gona–Buna area, travel south to Kokoda and then march up and over the central range to Sogeri and down to Port Moresby.

They made one serious miscalculation: the Kokoda Track was not a rough track that could be upgraded for vehicles. It was a switchback footpath through some of the most rugged country in the world, endlessly rising and falling and hopelessly muddy when it rained.

The Japanese landed on 21 July 1942 and stormed down the track, battling an increasingly desperate Australian opposition. At that stage the only troops available to garrison Port Moresby were poorly trained and poorly equipped militia. It was not until they were reinforced by battle-hardened veterans from the Middle East conflict that the tide started to turn.

The Japanese came to within 48km of Port Moresby before the Australians were able to halt their advance and start the slow, bloody battle back up the Kokoda Track. It wasn't just about Australians, however. Papua New Guineans supplied invaluable labour to the Australian forces, most notably carrying wounded soldiers back along the track from the battle zones. Their efforts won the respect of Australian soldiers and the public alike, and they become known affectionately as Fuzzy Wuzzy Angels.

As the Japanese commander General Horii withdrew, lines of defence were drawn at Templeton's Crossing, Eora Creek and at Oivi, on the road from Kokoda to Buna. The Australians took each position after drawn-out and desperate fighting. Horii drowned while attempting to escape cross the Kumusi River. Finally, the campaign to dislodge the Japanese from Buna on the north coast resulted in the most bitter fighting of the Pacific War, with disease and starvation taking as high a toll as actual combat.

the old battle site. It's a most impressive and moving place. After the memorial there is an optional two-hour detour to a wrecked Japanese aircraft with its paintwork still clearly visible. It is a steep climb and you will need a guide.

Short Cuts

Not everybody is up for the full trek – there are ways of having the Kokoda experience without taking on the full challenge.

You could take a PMV from Port Moresby to the village of Madilogo, which avoids two hard days' walk from Owers' Corner to Naoro. It takes about two hours to reach the track from Madilogo; from there it's one to 1½ hours to Naoro.

If you want a little taste of the track, you can walk down to the Goldie River from Owers' Corner in just an hour or so.

If you have the energy, struggle up what was once the Golden Staircase to Imita Ridge.

Another option would be to fly in to Kagi, Efogi or Manari, walk a section and fly out. Flying to Kagi and walking to Manari (one day) would be interesting. All these strips are serviced only by expensive charter flights.

Cheaper would be to get to Kokoda and walk to the Isurava Memorial and back; a two-day trip, stopping in the Isurava Memorial trekkers hut.

KOKODA

The Owen Stanley Range rises almost sheer as a cliff face behind the Oro Province village of Kokoda, where the northern end of the track terminates. It's a sleepy place and the grassed area in the centre of town houses a small museum with photos and descriptions of the campaign. Ask around to have it opened. **Grace Eroro** (☎ 329 7536) is the postal agent and Airlines PNG representative in Kokoda and is great for a conversation and very helpful with information. She can assist with just about anything and is talking of setting up a resthouse of her own, near Rusty's Place.

Sleeping & Eating

There are a couple of resthouses in Kokoda. The **Kokoda Mountain View Lodge** (all-inclusive per person K70), which is behind the trade store that sells beer (you'll soon find it), has a couple of local-style huts and plans for more.

About 2.5km along the road to Popondetta is **Rusty's Place** (☎ 325 4423, 323 6650; KTL 1 on radio; all-inclusive per person K40), run by Russell Eroro (who operates Kokoda Trekking Tours, the on-the-ground part of the www .kokodatrail.com.pg operation) and his extended family. It's a friendly place, the food is good and there's a small *stoa* (store). Accommodation is simple (but there are showers!) or you can camp on their lawn.

The **Kokoda Memorial Hospital** (per person K60) has some dormitories with toilets, showers, gas stoves and kitchen utensils. Money goes towards much-needed medical supplies.

Limited food and, mercifully, beer is usually available from Kokoda's **trade stores**; send a runner ahead to organise ice.

Getting There & Away
Most people fly into or out of Kokoda on a flight chartered by their tour company. Airlines PNG flies to and from Port Moresby (K187) several times a week, with a flight going via Tufi (K305, one weekly) most of the year.

Some people get to Kokoda via Popondetta (see opposite). PMVs (K8, 3½ hours) leave Popondetta between about 10am and noon, returning during the ungodly hours of midnight to 2am (so that locals can get at the front of the bank queue). Rusty's Place has a colourful new PMV (K12) leaving Kokoda at 3am and returning at 1am; charter it for K700 per day.

ORO PROVINCE

Oro Province (often called Northern Province) is sandwiched between the Solomon Sea and the Owen Stanley Range. It is a physically beautiful area but an uninspiring capital and poor transport connections mean few travellers make it.

Oro Province is the home of the world's largest butterfly, the Queen Alexandra's Birdwing. You might think that you've seen some big butterflies in PNG, but these are monsters, with wingspans of nearly 30cm. The first specimen collected by a European was brought down by a shotgun! That butterfly, a little damaged, is still in the British Museum. The Queen Alexandra's Birdwing

is now a threatened species. It lays its eggs on a particular species of vine which is poisonous to most birds and animals; the butterfly is poisonous as well.

POPONDETTA
Popondetta, which is the provincial capital, is spread along the Oro Bay Hwy a few kilometres from the old administrative capital of Higaturu. Popondetta exists because the previous two provincial headquarters were ill-fated: the one on the coast was invaded by the Japanese and destroyed, and the other – moved safely inland after the war – was destroyed by the eruption of Mt Lamington.

It's not a pretty place, with dust, litter and idle people seeming to predominate. Most of those who come here do so to see the area's WWII history – Buna and Gona are an easy day trip – or as part of a slow boat trip along the coast. Popondetta itself has an Australian war memorial with an interesting map of nearby battle sites and an adjoining memorial to the victims of the Mt Lamington eruption. That's it.

Popondetta is not a place to be wandering around alone at night.

Information
EMERGENCY
Ambulance (☎ 329 7066)
Fire (☎ 329 7172, 329 7144)
Police (☎ 329 7333)

MONEY
Bank South Pacific (☎ 329 7171)

Sights & Activities
Popondetta is a good base for visiting Mt Lamington, and Buna and Gona.

MT LAMINGTON
The 1585m peak of Mt Lamington is clearly visible from Popondetta (there's a good view on the road to the airport). Mt Lamington still shakes and puffs a little and local residents paid no attention to a slight increase in activity in 1951. However when the mountainside suddenly blew out and a cloud of super-heated gases rushed down, about 3000 people died and 8000 were left homeless. It is estimated the temperature stood near 200°C for about 90 seconds, and the gas cloud rolled down at over 300km/h.

Mt Lamington has been fairly calm since and keen bushwalkers can climb it today. The Oro and Birdwing Butterfly guesthouses can provide information and arrange guides.

Ecotourism Melanesia (www.em.com.pg) has trekking tours around Mt Lamington.

BUNA & GONA

The villages of Buna and Gona became Japanese bases during WWII and were the scene of some of the most desperate fighting of the war. At Giropa Plantation, on the Buna Rd, a Japanese plaque commemorates the country's dead.

Most of what remains of the bases is covered with overgrowth and a guide is necessary to work out what went on where. Basil Tindeba, from Buna, knows his way around the area pretty well; ask for him at the Oro Guesthouse and try to give a few days' notice. Another recommended guide is Maclaren Hiari MBE, who runs the **Kokoda Buna Historical Foundation** (☎ 329 7627). He lives two doors east of the Oro Guesthouse. These guys charge about K90 for their guiding and will generally arrange to take you by PMV and boat to both sites, which is important because without a boat you can't get from one to the other without returning to Popondetta. You could go by PMV to Gona for K2. Another good option is Pol Toki at the Birdwing Butterfly Lodge, who supplies a truck and his guiding to Gona for K80 and also takes in the village of Seremi, the scene of George Silk's famous photograph of Fuzzy Wuzzy Angel Raphael Oimbari leading blinded Australia soldier Dick Whittington.

Sleeping & Eating

Lamington Lodge (☎ 329 7222; www.coralseahotels .com.pg; tw K180-230; ❄) Part of the Coral Sea chain, this is the best hotel in town but easily the worst in the chain. Lack of competition means it's overpriced, but it does have the only bar and **restaurant** (meals K35; ❄ lunch & dinner) in town; the dishes, including steak, pasta, curries and fish, are reasonably good.

Birdwing Butterfly Lodge (☎ 329 7477; per person/plus 2 meals K80/110) This friendly place, 1.5km northeast of town on the road to Gona, has simple, clean rooms with share kitchens. Owner Pol Toki is a good guy who can arrange stays in **Seremi village** (all-inclusive per person K40).

Oro Guesthouse (☎ 329 7127; fax 329 7246; s/d incl 2 meals K148/216) There is a range of rooms and prices here that need some decoding. Ask about discounted prices for students with ID (per person K63), backpackers and those who've walked the Kokoda Track. The rooms are simple, and those with share bathrooms are cheaper (single/double including two meals K124/192). The food includes plenty of local vegetables. Alcohol is banned.

Bendoroda Fishing Lodge (☎ 7 3216 7700 in Brisbane; www.pngblackbass.com; all-inclusive per person per day fishing trips/ecotourism A$600/375) At the mouth of the Bendoroda River, south of Popondetta, this is an environmentally friendly lodge in a truly remote part of the country. The area is known for its fishing (black bass is the current favourite among fishers); it is a genuine PNG experience. The accommodation is simple, with six rooms and a single share bathroom. The fishing is strictly tag and release, but each group is allowed one of the famous black bass for tasting purposes. Ecotourism programmes can also be arranged.

Getting There & Away
AIR

Girua airport is 15km from town and one of several wartime strips in the area. From the air, you'll notice the area around the airstrip is scattered with horseshoe mounds – the remains of WWII gun emplacements. **Air Niugini** (☎ 329 7022, next to the post office) has flights to and from Port Moresby (K193, 40 minutes, daily), while Airlines PNG has a milk-run that begins in Port Moresby on Sunday and stops at (among others) Popondetta, Tufi, Wanigela, Alotau and Rabaraba, before flying back from Tufi to Port Moresby via Popondetta on Monday.

BOAT

All boats leave from Oro Bay, see p72.

PMV

PMVs for Buna (K3, about 9am, 45 minutes) and Kokoda (K8, about 11am, 3½ hours) leave from beneath the large trees outside Oro Motors in the centre of town. For Oro Bay (K4, 40 minutes) and the airport it's one block south. Ask at your hotel for times, which vary, but PMV runs are usually in the morning.

Getting Around

Popondetta is small enough to walk around. PMVs on the Oro Bay to Popondetta highway pass the airport, though they're not that frequent, especially on Sunday. Your best bet is to get a lift with a local or one of your fellow passengers. Otherwise, use Lamington Lodge's airport shuttle (K27.50 per person) or, if you're on the early flight, a lift with the Air Niugini staff from behind their town office – be there about 5.30am.

ORO BAY

Oro Bay is the province's main port. It became a major American base after the Japanese had been prised out of Buna and Gona, though the bustle of those days is long gone. Today it's a quiet place with occasional banana-boat traffic up and down the coast, and two larger boats travelling weekly to Lae.

If your ship doesn't come in, it's not a bad place to hang out. The **Oro Bay Guesthouse** (all-inclusive per person K50) is on the water near the wharf, but it's a 30-minute walk around the bay to the PMV boats.

The **Edna Resort Centre** (all-inclusive per person K80) has a few simple two-room bungalows.

THE PT BOATS OF TUFI

Tufi wharf, just in front of the resort, was used as a forward base for American PT boats, two of which now rest about 40m down, at the bottom of the ria (fjord). It was a widely held view that these boats had been sunk by Japanese bombs, but Russ Hamachek, who served as a PT boat captain at Tufi, wrote to Lonely Planet with the real story: 'Two of our boats were refuelling at the dock and the red flag of Baker was properly hoisted to warn passers-by of the need for caution. That took care of the US personnel, but was meaningless to a curious native. He was a smoker and unknowingly tossed a lighted cigarette butt into the adjacent water, which had just been the recipient of a 100 octane gasoline spill, resulting in the loss of two highly valuable PTs.'

Divers can still see torpedoes and a machine gun on the bottom, and other relics are around the bar at the Tufi Dive Resort. Hot, Straight & True is Hamachek's recently published novel about PT boat operations in New Guinea.

Contact the Birdwing Butterfly Lodge (p71) for bookings.

Rabaul Shipping (Star Ships) has a boat to Lae (K81/101, 18 hours) at 3pm Sunday, while Luship's Rita or Mamose Express leave for Lae at 4pm Sunday for about the same price. Buy your tickets on the wharf.

Banana boats to Tufi (K65) run if the winds aren't too high and usually leave midmorning.

TUFI

Carefree and far away from the world, Tufi is one of PNG's best-kept secrets. On the stunningly beautiful Cape Nelson, where steep-sided rias penetrate the land like the fingers of a grasping hand, this picturesque spot has a more relaxed atmosphere than any city in the country. Once home to fishing and rubber industries, the settlement now heavily relies on tourists drawn to the excellent Tufi Dive Resort.

The area, however, is much more than the resort. Several villages within two hours of Tufi welcome guests to their bush-material guesthouses, some of them set under swaying palm trees beside sandy beaches –a truly idyllic way to spend a few days. If you're there around July to September you might catch the Tufi Cultural Festival (admission K100 for three days), a relatively intimate sing-sing (celebratory dance/festival) with groups mainly from Oro Province. Check www.tufi dive.com for dates.

The cape was formed by ancient eruptions of its three volcanoes and the lava which flowed down into the sea creating the ria, for which the cape is now famous.

Sights & Activities

Diving is one of Tufi's great attractions; there is consistent 30m-plus visibility and one diver we met said 'there are more fish than water out there'. Maloway, Cyclone Reef and Marion Reef are memorable, and the muck diving under Tufi wharf is exceptional. Nearby are some WWII ships easily accessible in shallow water, while the famous B17 'Black Jack' bomber is down the coast. For a full list of dives, with pictures, see www.tufi dive.com/diving.html. Tufi Dive Resort has dive boats and a fully equipped dive shop. The dive season is from September to May. From June to August high winds make diving difficult.

Local villages can provide outrigger canoes (the standard form of transport) if you want to go fishing, and the dive resort's dive boat also does fishing trips.

There is a network of tracks in the area ideal for trekking. Many follow the *ria* around the coast and others can be quite difficult; you must be fit. Tufi Dive Resort can arrange a guide and village stays, or you could take your chances and ask around yourself. The villages and the resort can arrange boats to pick you up at various locations at the end of your walk.

Sleeping & Eating

Tufi Dive Resort (☎ /fax 329 6000, in Port Moresby 320 1484; www.tufidive.com; all-inclusive r per person K225-370) A short walk from the grassy airstrip, this upmarket resort is wonderfully appropriate to the area – it's quiet, has comfortable chairs, a friendly bar and a very relaxed atmosphere. There is a broad-ranging library, video collection and a great cliffside barbecue area with spectacular views across the *ria*. The rooms are all comfortable, but if you're in the budget range ask for Room 3. The food is delicious. Diving is the main attraction and reliable equipment is available for K50/100 per half/full day. There is a fun *ria* tour by boat and kayak (K45), and fishing, windsurfing and trekking can be arranged. The resort encourages people to get into the local villages and can connect you with whichever you choose; see Around Tufi.

Getting There & Around

Airlines PNG flies to and from Port Moresby (K351, four weekly), some via Popondetta (K240). Sunday's flight continues from Tufi to Wanigela (K136), Vivigani (K227), Salamo (K316) and Alotau (K320). All prices are one-way from Tufi.

See opposite for information on small boats to and from Oro Bay. Between Tufi and Wanigela you can hire a banana boat (K90, 30 minutes). Getting to the villages around Tufi is usually done on foot or by outrigger canoe; you'll be expected to help with the paddling.

Rabaul Shipping (Star Ships) boats from Alotau stop here a couple of times per month, and Lutheran Shipping has one slow service between Lae and Alotau per month.

AROUND TUFI

Village guesthouses dot the coastline either side of Tufi and you could spend weeks wending your way along the coast this way. The accommodation is basic, with mosquito nets and local food (the seafood is tasty) for about K75 per person. Boat transfers are extra. They can also arrange fishing and snorkelling; bring your own gear. It's best, though not essential, to contact them ahead, and this is done through the Tufi Dive Resort.

Most of the villages offer treks, birdwatching, snorkelling, fishing and participation in *singsings*. Some of the better options include:

Kofure Guesthouse (30 minutes by outrigger canoe north of Tufi) White sands, palm trees and the best food of any of the villages.

Kamoa Beach Guesthouse (15 minutes outrigger canoe ride to the mouth of Tufi Fjord) Pretty beach.

Jebo Guesthouse (one hour by dinghy south of Tufi) Located on a white-sand beach in Sinofuka village. Sinofuka literally means 'pig and dog'! There's a waterfall where you can swim, and birds of paradise can be seen.

Bauwame Guesthouse (30 minutes by dinghy south of Tufi) Standing on a coral reef, it offers great access to impressive sites for snorkelling and bird-watching.

MILNE BAY PROVINCE

At the eastern end of mainland PNG, the Owen Stanley Range plunges into the sea and islands are scattered across the ocean for hundreds of kilometres further out. This is the start of the Pacific proper – tiny atolls, coral reefs, volcanic islands, swaying palms and white beaches. It's safe, secluded and unfailingly friendly.

More than 435 islands give the province 2120km of coastline, but poor transport infrastructure and limited arable land have hindered the region's development.

CULTURE

The church is central to the lives of Milne Bay people, but the confluence of traditional beliefs and contemporary church teachings can be confusing to the uninitiated. Witchcraft is widely respected and still practised, especially on the islands. Contract killings can still be arranged with witch doctors, who sometimes employ the spiritual powers of cyanide from disused mining operations.

In most island societies landownership and family rights are passed down through the mother. Clan leaders and the paramount chief are still men, but behind the scenes women wield considerable power.

In many of the region's cultures people were traditionally buried standing up, with their heads poking out of the ground and covered by clay pots. When the heads eventually separated from the bodies, the pots were removed and the skulls were placed in a skull cave. These caves are common in the area and clay pots are a traditional regional artefact.

ALOTAU

Alotau is a sleepy little town built on the hillsides of the northern shore of Milne Bay. It became the provincial capital in 1968 when administrators were moved from overcrowded Samarai Island.

Alotau and the coastal strip either side was the scene of the WWII Battle of Milne Bay (see p62) and there are several memorials and relics around. Apart from that, the market, harbour and a lookout near the hospital might soak up some time, after which you can just soak up the atmosphere in what is one of the most laid-back, secure and enjoyable towns in the country. The locals – nationals, expats and a red wine–loving cuscus alike – are welcoming and a lot of fun. Spend a night drinking with them and you'll soon know what's going on and who's going where.

Information

EMERGENCY
Ambulance (☎ 641 1200)
Fire (☎ 641 1055, 641 1014)
Police (☎ 641 1222, 641 1253)

INTERNET ACCESS
Bayside Internet Cafe (☎ 641 1490; Masurina Business Centre, Charles Abel Hwy; per hr K22; ✆ 8am-4.30pm Mon-Fri & 8am-12.30pm Sat)

MONEY
Most banks, shops and other services are in a couple of short streets in the centre of town.
ANZ (☎ 180 4444)
Bank South Pacific (☎ 641 1024)
Westpac (☎ 641 1003)

POST
Post Office (☎ 641 1207; in the town centre)

TOURIST INFORMATION
The warm and efficient **Milne Bay Tourist Bureau** (☎ 641 1503; www.milnebaytourism.gov.pg; Masurina Business Centre) can arrange village and town accommodation, give transport advice and is a great historical and cultural source; check the website. Even more helpful is **Gretta Kwasnicka-Todurawai** at Napatana Lodge , who as a veteran traveller knows what independent travellers need. Her *wantok* (clanspeople) network is extensive and she can contact just about anyone. Gretta is very honest – she'll call a spade a fucking shovel – and a great PNG character.

KULA RING

Extending around the islands of Milne Bay Province is an invisible circle, or *kula* ring, that binds the islands together in a system of ritual exchange. The ring encompasses the Trobriand, Muyua (Woodlark), Louisiade, Samarai and D'Entrecasteaux islands. Things have changed now, but in the past, the *kula* ring involved the trade of red-shell necklaces, called *bagi* or *soulava*, in a clockwise direction and white shell armlets, *mwali*, in an anticlockwise direction. Each trader had a *kula* partner on their nearest neighbouring island in each direction. Once a year, the trader and a delegation from his clan journeyed to the island of his *kula* partner to receive gifts in elaborate public ceremonies. On a separate significant date he would be visited by another *kula* partner who would be presented with the prized gifts. Accompanying these voyages were other ceremonial objects and surplus fish and yams to be exchanged with neighbouring islands. Since the *bagis* and *mwalis* rarely left the circle, this system ensured a distribution of wealth among the islanders.

The exchange mostly occurred between traditional families of high status and thus helped to reinforce clan-based hierarchies. Today some people are required to journey to the island home of a traditional *kula* partner bearing ritual gifts in a banana boat rather than the traditional sailing canoe.

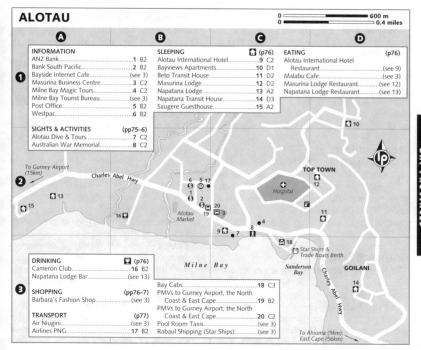

ALOTAU

0 _____ 600 m
0 _____ 0.4 miles

To Gurney Airport (15km)

Charles Abel Hwy

TOP TOWN

Hospital

Alotau Market

Milne Bay

Star Ships & Trade Boats Berth

Sanderson Bay

GOILANI

Charles Abel Hwy

To Ahioma (9km); East Cape (56km)

CENTRAL, ORO & MILNE BAY PROVINCES

Sights & Activities

The **harbour** is the most colourful part of town and it's worth exploring. There are one-man canoes, brightly painted island boats, chartered dive boats and passenger boats. The busy harbour activity attests to it being the province's main cargo hub. For a bird's-eye view of the harbour, walk up the steps in town to the hospital, take the right fork and keep going for a couple of hundred metres.

Back on the foreshore, the recently commissioned **Australian War Memorial** has a detailed description of the Battle of Milne Bay. There's a service here on 26 August every year, commemorating the beginning of the Battle of Milne Bay.

There are several good **black-sand swimming beaches** to the east of town towards Ahioma, although they're not obvious from the road. PMVs run past and it's dead easy to hitch a ride along this stretch of road, though women should obviously be more cautious.

The well-organised **Milne Bay Game Fishing Club** can advise on boats and is happy to find some gear for you, particularly during one of the regular competitions or the annual Milne

Bay Classic, which takes place on the first weekend of December. For information, contact Tim Seeto (aealotau@online.net.pg).

After all that, a **Joyce Hiskins massage** (upper body/full body with oil/aromatherapy K60/80/100) can be very welcome indeed. Contact her through Napatana Lodge.

DIVING

Alotau is the launch pad for some incredible diving. Along the north coast, within the bay and around the islands, it won't take long to fully appreciate the underwater wonders available, but it would take years to see them all. The best way to access dive sites near and far is by dive boat, and several are based here.

Among those is **Marlin I** (www.marlin1charters .com.au) which is not the most luxurious dive boat around, but owners Wayne and Lee Thompson mean it's up there for friendliness. Rob Van de Loos has been around these parts for years and his **MV Chertan** (www .chertan.com) can sleep 12 passengers. The 10-berth **Telita** (www.telitadive.com) is another excellent option operated by one of the authors of Lonely Planet's excellent (seriously!) *Diving & Snorkelling Papua New Guinea*. In Alotau the Japanese-run **Alotau Dive & Tours** (☎ 641 0300; www.png-japan.co.jp, in Japanese) at the Alotau International Hotel has regular day trips to popular dive sites, and day trips to Tawali Resort (p78) can be arranged through Napatana Lodge or the Milne Bay Tourism Bureau. For more on diving see p218.

Organised Tours

Milne Bay Magic Tours (☎ 641 0711; www.toursmilne bay-png.com; Charles Abel Hwy) offers a range of professionally run tours, including a WWII tour of the Battle of Milne Bay sites and a creek bed filled with abandoned landing craft; a trip to Samarai and Kwato Islands and some diving trips. They're good value.

Festivals & Events

The **Milne Bay Kenu Festival** (first weekend in November) made a successful debut in 2004 and is definitely worth seeing. Apart from being fun and a great photo opportunity, it is helping to save the ancient arts of canoe building and sailing that have almost gone with the advent of outboard motors. For details see www.milnebaytourism.gov.pg.

The colourful **Cameron Cultural Show** (July to August) involves students from Cameron High School and other local artists.

Sleeping, Eating & Drinking

Apart from a couple of places, the hotels and guesthouses are the only food and drink options.

Napatana Lodge (☎ 641 1209; www.napatanalodge .com; Charles Abel Hwy; bungalows s/d/tr K143/187/231) Napatana is not the most luxurious place in Alotau, but it's definitely the pick. The drawcards are a combination of attractive and comfortable bungalows not far from the water, a great bar in a traditional-style building, and probably the widest range of information about the province. The **Napatana bar** (meals K25-35; 🕙 7am-late) is the place to meet expats and nationals. The food is both appetising and a little exotic (the crab is sublime). There are various rates depending on the inclusion of meals, plus hefty discounts for backpackers and weekend stays. The **Napatana Transit House** (☎ 641 1209) in Goilanai also has top-value rooms aimed at volunteers and long-stay aid workers.

Alotau International Hotel (☎ 641 0300; www .airways.com.pg; Charles Abel Hwy; r K286; 🔲 🖳 🖳) For size and facilities these rooms, each with a balcony and bay view, are Alotau's best. They are, however, more comfortable than characterful. Babysitters can be arranged, and there's **Internet access** (per 10 min K20). The **restaurant** (meals K30-50) is reasonably good but not exactly earth-shaking.

Masurina Lodge (☎ 641 1212; www.masurina .com; s/d with breakfast/apt K198-225/210/150; 🔲 🖳) The large, ageing rooms and apartments are comfortable enough and have a distinct feel of Australia circa 1963. Rates include laundry and airport transfers. The **restaurant** (meals K35; 🕙 7-9am, noon-1.30pm & 7-9pm) serves a mix of tasty dishes and every second Friday the barbecue buffet (K20) out by the poolside bar is excellent value.

Bayviews Apartments (☎ 641 0401; bayviewspng@ daltron.com.pg; r K75-160) The welcome here is warm and the small but comfortable rooms, especially those upstairs, are great value; 'Pitow' has the best view. Food is available to anyone at very reasonable prices, and every second Thursday draws locals to the traditional **mumu** (traditional oven; per person K20); a fun night and amazingly cheap!

Beto Transit House (☎ 641 0520; s/tr per person K40/60; 🔲) If there were enough backpackers in Alotau, this place in from Sanderson Bay would be their lodge; it's pokey and has a lived-in feel. Food is served on request, or use the kitchen.

Saugere Guesthouse (☎ /fax 641 0165; per person without/with food K25/70) On the waterfront west of Napatana, this is a simple place with (as yet) no electricity but a genuine, casual and hospitable PNG atmosphere.

Apart from the hotels mentioned here, the **Malabu Cafe** (meals K8; 🕙 8am-4.30pm Mon-Fri, 8am-1.30pm Sat) in the Masurina Business Centre is the best *kai* bar in town, and the owners Rod and Serah Clark are the people to talk with if you're heading to the Trobriand Islands. The **Cameron Club** (☎ 641 1087; 🕙 5pm-midnight), near the waterfront west of the centre is a good local drinking hole.

Shopping

Trobriand Islanders come to Alotau to sell their carvings and they'll find you around town; some carvings are quite good. There is a small handicrafts shop at Napatana Lodge, and **Barbara's Fashion Shop** (☎ 641 1540;

Masurina Business Centre, Charles Abel Hwy, Gurney) has some gaudy shirts and a small range of interesting and reasonably priced artefacts.

Getting There & Away

AIR

There were no international flights to Alotau at the time of research, but this will likely change. **Air Niugini** (☎ 641 1100, 641 0158 for Gurney airport office, Masurina Business Centre, Charles Abel Hwy; Gurney) has one or two flights daily between Port Moresby and Gurney (K383, 50 minutes). **Airlines PNG** (☎ 641 1591, Gurney 641 0013) flies from Gurney to Misima (K329), then returns to Gurney, then flies to Losuia (K355) and then to Port Moresby (K378) on Sunday and Tuesday. They also fly on Sunday from Gurney to Rabaraba (K184), and to Tufi (K320) via Salamo (on Fergusson Island, K203), Wanigela (K309) and Popondetta (K450). The duration of these flights depend on the routes, which vary.

BOAT

In 2004 **Rabaul Shipping** (Star Ships; ☎ 641 0012; mona@pngbd.com; Masurina Business Centre; Charles Abel Hwy, Gurney) began scheduled services throughout Milne Bay Province, allowing for planned boat travel in the province for the first time in decades.

Schedules were still being fine-tuned at the time of writing, but boats will generally sail to the destinations below at least once a week. Prices are for adults, one-way. Children travel for half-price and students get a 20% discount.

North Coast Dogura (K40), Rabaraba (K44), Cape Vogel (K54), Tufi (K66)

D'Entrecasteaux & Trobriand Islands Nuakata (K20), Esa'ala (K36), Salamo (K36), Mapamoiwa (K36), Sanaroa (K40), Bolubolu (K44), Amphlet (K52), Losuia (K68)

China Strait & South Coast Samarai Island (K16), Suau (K30)

Apart from the Star Ships, work boats service the trade stores on the islands and offer uncomfortable, slow and irregular trips to anywhere with a *stoa*. Getting a ride can in-mean waiting around wharves, asking about destinations and usually adding a few hours to the alleged departure times. But once you're on the open water sitting atop a load of SP Lager, Kundu Crackers and margarine you'll be feeling the province's charm – until you start feeling very uncomfortable.

Apart from hanging around the harbour, ask around the trade stores to see when they might have a boat departing. Work boats to Esa'ala and Salamo cost K25, to Losuia it's K60.

PMV

PMVs run along the coast to East Cape (K7, twice daily) and on to the north coast.

Getting Around

Alotau's airport is at Gurney, 15km from town, and was named after Bob Gurney, an Australian who began flying for Guinea Airways in 1929 and was killed in action with the RAAF in 1942. Taxis to town cost K30, but most hotels provide transfers for K20 to K25, or for free. PMVs run to town from the nearby main road (K3), but they're infrequent. PMVs to the airport leave from near the Bank South Pacific. The best way into town is by simply asking someone for a lift.

Alotau is well-served by taxis. **Bay Cabs** (☎ 641 1093) is the main taxi company and sometimes provides car hire. Others include **Pool Room Taxis** (☎ 641 0448; pool room of the Masurina Business Centre, Charles Abel Hwy, Gurney); **Gramp's Taxi** (☎ 641 1557) and **HT Taxis** (☎ 641 9087).

AROUND ALOTAU
East Cape

East Cape is at the very eastern end of mainland New Guinea. It's a quiet but picturesque village, where banana boats come and go for Normanby Island and others, including nearby Yamba Island with it's famous 13-trunk coconut palm; there is a K10 photo fee. There's terrific snorkelling and diving in this area, and a skull cave is about an hour's walk away.

Bernhard's Guesthouse (per person K25) is opposite the Dulia Stoa (tell the PMV to stop here) and has a pleasant veranda on the water. Meals can be arranged for K10. The rustic **Oima Guesthouse** (per person K30), beside the market, has a couple of very basic rooms; BYO everything.

PMVs to and from Alotau cost K7 and run a couple of times daily, less on Sunday. It's about 1½ hours each way along a newly sealed road, where you pass many pretty villages and black-sand beaches. Times vary, but one usually leaves East Cape at 7 or 8am.

Wagawaga

On the southern shore of Milne Bay, this tiny settlement in a cove often called Discovery Bay sits below the steeply rising mountains of the southern peninsula. It's a popular day trip for divers and snorkellers, who swim around the mostly submerged *Muscoota*, a WWII coal transport ship that sprang a leak and sank here in 1946.

From Wagawaga there is a steep one-hour walk to Moon Rock (Da'a Nawalahi), which bears markings thought to have been made by Europeans as a navigational aid. On the way up you'll pass a skull reputed to greet you with a grin; one, two or even a full set of teeth depending on how much it likes you. Take a guide (K10) for the trip; ask around for Mr Deka or Mr Bondi. Lone women should think about finding a partner in climb.

About a 20-minute tough walk, or a short trip in a 4WD, uphill from Wagawaga is **Ulumani Treetops Lodge** (☎ /fax 641 0916; beds per person K50-150), with stunning views over the bay and wonderful bird-watching opportunities. Accommodation is in two buildings: the upper is in the treetops, sleeps eight (four comfortably), and has the balcony for bird-watchers. Down the hill is a traditional-style building with simple rooms (per person K50). Both have kitchens and bathrooms.

From Alotau, Ulumani will collect you in a dinghy (K75 per person). Cheaper is the PMV boat (K5, 30 minutes), which leaves Wagawaga about 7am daily (except Sunday) and returns in the early afternoon. You can drive from Alotau in about an hour.

Baleki

A few kilometres along a rough road east of Wagawaga is the tiny village of Baleki, perched on a steep hill that becomes, as it drops into Milne Bay, first a reef and then a sheer 50m drop. This unlikely venue is home to **Penari Place** (☎ 641 1209, contact through Napatana Lodge; per person K50), operated by an Australian and his family; it's the closest thing to a traditional backpacker retreat we saw in PNG. The bungalows, hammocks and food (K10 per meal, free vegies) are good, and activities include snorkelling and diving (muck divers will enjoy the WWII surplus dump), trekking and wildlife spotlighting. Napatana can arrange transport.

NORTH COAST

The north coast is a string of villages, beaches and reefs that reward those prepared to get off the beaten track. There are several appealing walks, and with time you could quite easily travel by foot, PMV and dinghy all the way from East Cape to Tufi. A growing number of villages have simple accommodation, including, from east to west: Boianai, Wagahuhu, Awaiama (Mahimahi Plantation Guesthouse; just outside the village), Wedau and Bogaboga at Cape Vogel.

You can walk from Rabaraba or Wedau to Alotau partly on the coast road that takes PMVs depending on the season. There are many villages enroute so finding a bed is easy. Rabaraba to Wedau takes two days, and from Wedau to the tiny Taupota No 2 settlement takes three easy days or two longer ones. Then you can reach Alotau in a day by going south across a low range, but it's best to take a local village guide. There are some other good routes across the range. For an account of the walk from Alotau to Wamira (near Wedau), see www .michie.net/pnginfo/wamira.html.   Speak with Gretta at **Napatana Lodge** (☎ 641 1209) or the Milne Bay Tourism Bureau to contact the villages and any guides required.

Airlines PNG flies between Rabaraba and Gurney (K184) on Sunday. PMVs operate from Alotau as far as Topura, from where you need to walk or take dinghies if you want to go further west.

Tawali Resort

On a headland overlooking Hoia Bay, newly opened **Tawali Resort** (www.tawali.com; all-inclusive s/d US$200/240; 🟦) is one of the best in PNG. It's almost completely hidden from the sea, but the views from the main building and rooms are exceptional. Tasteful decorations include a wonderful display of bottles recovered from the seabed around Samarai Island, and the 10 rooms are luxurious. The main attraction is diving, with several famous reefs within a short boat ride. The dive shop is excellent and there is a decompression chamber (originally part of a US nuclear submarine) on site. This place is highly recommended. Otherwise, day dives can be arranged from Alotau. Transfers from Gurney Airport cost US$25/40 one-way/return. Or take a PMV and tell the driver you want to go to Tawali Resort. You should be dropped by a lone tree atop a hill, and follow the right dirt track five minutes down to the coast, from where a boat will collect you (if they know you're coming). Tawali is not accessible by road.

SAMARAI ISLAND

The tiny island of Samarai, just 24 hectares in area, is a must-see. In the China Strait (so named by Captain John Moresby because he thought it would be the most direct route from the east coast of Australia to China), at the southern tip of the Milne Bay mainland, Samarai has a faded-glory feel about it from the colonial days, when it was said to be one of the most beautiful places in the Pacific.

Samarai predates Port Moresby and was the provincial headquarters until 1968; it's been in decline ever since. Before WWII it was the second-largest town in PNG, but in 1942 the Australian administration destroyed almost every building in anticipation of a Japanese invasion that never came. Its postwar reincarnation was built in Australian country-town style.

Just about all communications to Samarai are made through the **Samarai Island Trading Company** (SITCO; ☎ 642 1008; sitco@daltron.com.pg), which has a well-stocked store opposite the wharf. Owner Philip Taudevin is both knowledgeable and helpful, and can arrange Internet access at the shop. Wallace Andrew, in the house southwest of the Christopher Robinson memorial (which you must read), is another good source of local information. He's a Kwato old boy, grandson of a cannibal, local identity and fascinating character to listen to (you won't do much talking).

Sights & Activities

The main thing to do on Samarai Island is just wander around. From the wharf, head toward the hill and, at the northeast corner of the sports ground, you'll pass the memorial to Christopher Robinson, the one-time administrator who committed suicide in 1904. Near the southeast corner of the ground a road leads up to the abandoned hospital and, just north of here, a small hill with great views of the island and China Strait. The customs and immigration people are on the south shore, near the sports ground, and south of the wharf is Samarai's oldest-surviving building, the Anglican church.

Even if you don't climb the hill, you simply must go snorkelling or diving around the rotting piers of the **Samarai Island Wharf**, which has become a world-famous muck-diving site. The marine life is incredible and as you drift carefully between the piers you'll be surrounded by schools of brightly coloured fish. Below them, pipefish and various odd nudibranches can be seen. The bottom is also littered with the detritus of history, but don't be tempted to 'rescue' anything more than the rubbish. The easiest place to enter is just north of the Samarai Island Trading Company wharf. Be sure to bring a snorkel and mask.

Sleeping & Eating

There are only two places to stay, and the **SITCO Apartments** (☎ 642 1008; sitco@daltron.com.pg; all-inclusive per person K45) is easily the pick. Just east of the Christopher Robinson memorial, this spacious two-storey house has a TV, kitchen, large living area and two bedrooms. Email ahead or speak to staff at the store.

At the top of the stairs leading up from the north side of the sports ground, **Bwanasa Women's Association Guesthouse** (☎ 642 1121, contact Mr Enoka at the district office; s/tw per person K50; ☺ 7.45am-4pm Mon-Fri) has simple rooms and shared cold-water bathrooms. BYO food.

Getting There & Away

The *Kavieng Queen* motors between Alotau and Samarai (K16, 1½ hours, daily). Much slower and less predictable are the work boats; ask at the Morobe Tourism Bureau in Alotau, or at SITCO on Samarai Island.

NEAR SAMARAI ISLAND

China Strait and the surrounding islands have a reputation for witchcraft and, despite the influence of missionaries, superstitions linger. Strange lights, ghost ships and sirens (the singing kind) all crop up.

On **Kwato Island**, about 3km west of Samarai, the Reverend Charles Abel and his wife, Beatrice, founded a nonhierarchical church in 1891. Kwato Mission functioned as a successful educational and boat-building centre, although it wasn't until the 1930s that the last of the nearby cannibal tribes was 'saved'. People brought up on Kwato are disproportionately represented in the upper echelons of PNG business. The Kwato Church suffered a decline in the 1970s and today the island can be eerily quiet. The impressive stone church dates from 1937. Boats to Kwato are easy to catch from Samarai Island Wharf.

At **Doini Island**, a privately owned and stunningly beautiful place about 10km southeast of Samarai, overnight stays are possible with Milne Bay Magic Tours (p76).

Not far west of Doini Island is Gona Bara Bara Island, and just off the northwest shore is a dive site known as the **Manta Ray Cleaning Station**. Just a few metres below the surface, there is an isolated bommie (a natural spire, covered in coral, rising from the sea floor). Around the bommie is where giant, graceful mantas (some with wingspans of up to 5m) are cleaned by tiny wrasses – it is one of the best places on earth to see this happening. Watching them take turns to approach the bommie and then 'standing' up to be cleaned is unforgettable, as is the close proximity allowed to courteous divers. Snorkelling is also possible, though high winds make it (and diving) difficult between June and September. To arrange a dive here, speak to Alotau Dive & Tours or one of the charter boat operators (see p75).

It should be possible to stay in villages on many of the islands in the area, including Logea Island (Rogeia) and Sariba.

D'ENTRECASTEAUX ISLANDS

Scattered across a narrow strait from the PNG mainland, the D'Entrecasteaux group were named by French explorer Antoine Raymond Joseph de Bruni d'Entrecasteaux, who sailed through in 1793. The islands are extremely mountainous and covered by dense jungle. Whales, dolphins and dugongs move through the area; off-the-beaten-track Milne Bay at its best.

It can be difficult to contact anyone on the islands because the phones rarely work. Try the Milne Bay Tourism Bureau instead.

Getting There & Away

Airlines PNG flies to Normanby, Fergusson and Goodenough from Gurney on Sunday; see p77 for details. Rabaul Shipping (Star Ships) also services these three islands, see p77. Work boats run frequently but not regularly from Alotau to Salamo on Fergusson or Esa'ala on Normanby, and dinghies run early most afternoons from East Cape across to Sibonai, in Sewa Bay, for K20.

Normanby Island

Esa'ala, the district headquarters, is at the entrance to the spectacular Dobu Passage. It's a tiny place, with a couple of stores, a market and a trade store. A reef just offshore offers excellent snorkelling.

The friendly **Esa'ala Guesthouse** (call the district office ☎ 641 1217; all-inclusive r per person K75) is on the beach near the main wharf, and **Tom Inman B&B Esa'ala** (☎ 641 1209) is a pleasant place run by Tom's son David. Ask for either and you'll soon be pointed in the right direction. The airstrip is about one hour's drive away.

Sewa Bay on the southwest coast was used by Allied warships during WWII. It's a beautiful place surrounded by mangroves and rosewood forests, which have attracted the attention of Malay loggers. In **Sibonai village**, in the southwest corner of the bay, local activist Mombi Onesimo is encouraging tourism as an alternative to logging. Snorkelling, fishing from a canoe and occasionally hunting pigs can be done for about K20 per day. A bed in the village costs K40 per person, with food. BYO mosquito net. Contact Mombi through Napatana Lodge in Alotau. It's possible to walk to Esa'ala from Sibonai.

Fergusson Island

Fergusson is the largest island in the group and the highest peak is 2073m, with two other lower ranges from which the island's many rivers and streams flow. It is notable for its hot springs, bubbling mud pools, spouting geysers and extinct volcanoes. The hike from Warluma to the caldera of **Mt Lamanai** takes about 1½ hours and affords fantastic views over an immense crater. Take a local guide (ask around to arrange for one). Thermal springs can be found at Deidei, opposite the main town of **Salamo**.

The **Salamo United Church Women's Guesthouse** (all-inclusive per person K50) has recently been renovated. If they don't know you're coming, bring some supplies.

Goodenough Island

The most northwesterly of the group, Goodenough is one of the most steeply sided islands on earth, with Mt Oiautukekea reaching 2566m at the summit. There are fertile coastal plains flanking the mountain range and a road runs around the northeast coast through **Vivigani**, site of the major airstrip in the group. **Bolubolu** is the main settlement, about 10km south of Vivigani. In the centre of the island there is a large stone, covered in mysterious black-and-white paintings, which is said to have power over the yam crops. The **Bolubolu Guesthouse** charges K50 per person with meals.

TROBRIAND ISLANDS

Ever since Bronislaw Malinowski was exiled to the Trobriand Islands for the duration of WWI, this small group has been seen as one of the most exotic places on earth. Despite the dozens of anthropologists who followed Malinowski, in many ways the Trobriands remain one of the most culturally intact exotic places you could possibly find.

Known locally as the Trobes, the islands lie to the north of the D'Entrecasteaux group in the Solomon Sea. They take their name from Denis de Trobriand, an officer on d'Entrecasteaux's expedition. The Trobriands are low-lying coral islands, in contrast to their mountainous southern neighbours. There are some very good beaches and it's possible to stay in villages.

The Trobriand Islanders have fiercely resisted western culture and it is the survival of its traditional culture that is much of the attraction (see p82). A strict hierarchical social system, enormous and highly decorated yam houses, exquisite carvings and the colourful festival of clan prestige and free love that accompanies the yam harvest will keep your head turning.

Trobriand Islanders have a distinct Polynesian appearance and there are scattered remains of stone temples that resemble those of Polynesia. Trade between the islands had strong cultural and economic importance and the pre-European traders crossed vast distances of open sea in canoes, exchanging fish, vegetables, pigs, stone axes, a rare jadelike stone from Muyua (Woodlark) Island and volcanic glass from Fergusson Island. The *kula* ring (p74) is the most famous of these trade routes.

It's good manners to let the paramount chief know you have arrived. If you are there for reasons other than tourism, you should request an audience with him to explain why you've come. It's enough to ask almost anyone to pass on the message to the chief; it will reach him.

Tok Pisin is not spoken in the Trobes and with most islanders having little English, *dim dims* (white people) can find communication difficult.

Festivals

The **Milamala Festival** is usually held around the second week of July to celebrate the yam harvest. It is easily the most colourful time to come, as there's much ritual associated with the yam harvest. The spirit of free love is at its most heightened at this time.

However, before you get too excited, it's worth noting that visitors with boiling loins usually have to make their own entertainment because, while yams are considered objects of great beauty, *dim dims* are not. For exact dates, see www.milnebaytourism .gov.pg at the start of the year.

Kiriwina Island

The largest of the Trobriand Islands is Kiriwina, which is home to the district capital of **Losuia** and the airstrip. Kiriwina is relatively flat, although there is a rim of low hills (uplifted coral reefs) along the eastern shore. The central plain is intensely cultivated and with the island's population growing fast, there are concerns that cutting trees to plant gardens will devastate the island.

The airport is in the north, where the US Air Force had two bases during WWII. South of here, on the west coast, Losuia is the only real town and is generally known as 'the station'. It has a wharf, police station, health centre, two trade stores and that's about it. It's more like a sprawling village than a town. The telephone network is highly unreliable. There is no bank, but the Konki Enterprises Store can change Australian and US dollars.

AROUND THE ISLAND

Going north from Losuia is 'inland' to the locals. This area has most of the island's roads and villages. **Omarakana**, about halfway between Losuia and Kaibola, is where the island's paramount chief resides. You'll know you're there by the large, intricate, painted yam house. The paramount chief presides over the island's oral traditions and magic and strictly maintains his political and economic power. He oversees the important yam festival and *kula* rituals.

Megaliths made of a coral composite have linked the Trobriands to possible early

YAMS, SEX & CRICKET: TROBRIAND ISLAND CUSTOMS

Bronislaw Malinowski's celebrated books – *Argonauts of the Western Pacific*, *Coral Gardens and Their Magic* and *The Sexual Life of Savages in North-Western Melanesia* – were published after WWI, and revealed much about the intricate trading rituals (see p74), yam cults and sexual practices of the Trobriand Islands. Malinowski found a matrilineal society, in which the chief's sons belong to his wife's clan and he is succeeded by one of his oldest sister's sons. The society is strictly hierarchical, with distinctions between hereditary classes and demarcations in the kind of work each person can perform.

Yams

Yams are far more than a staple food in the Trobriands – they're a sign of prestige and expertise, and a tie between villages and clans. The quality and size of your yams is important. Many hours are spent discussing yam cultivation, and to be known as a *tokwaibagula* (good gardener) is a mark of great prestige.

The yam cult climaxes at the harvest time, which is usually July or August. The yams are first dug up in the gardens then displayed, studied and admired. At the appropriate time, the men carry the yams back to the village, with the women guarding the procession.

In the villages, the yams are again displayed before being packed into the highly decorated yam houses. Each man has a yam house for each of his wives and it is his brother-in-law's responsibility (in other words, his wife's clan's obligation) to fill his yam house. The chief's yam house is always the biggest, most elaborate and first to be filled.

Sex

Malinowski's tomes on the Trobriand Islanders' customs led to Kiriwina being given the misleading title of the 'Island of Love'. It is not surprising that such a label was applied by inhibited Europeans when they first met Trobriand women, with their free and easy manners, good looks and short grass skirts, but it led to the inaccurate idea that the Trobriands were some sort of sexual paradise. The sexual customs are different to many other places, but are not without their own complicated social strictures.

Teenagers are encouraged to have as many sexual partners as they choose until marriage, when they settle down with the partner who is chosen as suitable and compatible. Males leave home when they reach puberty and move into the village *bukumatula* (bachelor house). Here, they are free to bring their partners back at any time, although they usually opt for somewhere more private. Even married couples, subject to mutual agreement, are allowed to have a fling or two when the celebrations for the yam harvest are in full swing.

Aside from all this activity, it's said that few children are born to women without permanent partners. The people do not believe there is a connection between intercourse and pregnancy – a child's spirit, which floats through the air or on top of the sea, chooses to enter a woman, often through her head.

All this apparent freedom has negligible impact on visitors. Freedom of choice is the bedrock of Trobriand Islands life, so why would any islander choose some unattractive, pale *dim dims* who can't speak like a civilised human, doesn't understand the most fundamental laws and will probably be gone tomorrow?

Cricket

Trobriands Islands cricket developed after missionaries introduced cricket as a way of taking the islanders' minds off less-healthy activities. It's since developed its own style, which is quite unlike anything the MCC ever had in mind. There is no limit to the number of players, meaning you can wait days for a bat. Women's cricket is played in little more than a grass skirt, making it rather difficult to concentrate on line and length. If there's a game scheduled while you're there, don't miss it!

Polynesian migrations. You can see them, but not without a guide – speak with Bweka Village Resort or Butia Lodge.

At **Kaibola** village, at the northern tip of Kiriwina, you can swim and snorkel at the picture-postcard beach, though much coral has died recently. About 1½ hours' walk from Kaibola is **Kalopa Cave**, near Matawa village. There are several deep limestone caves housing burial antiquities and skeletal remains. Stories are told of Dokanikani, a giant whose bones are said to be buried with those of his victims in one of the caves. PMVs run from Losuia to Kaibola (K2, one hour, several times daily).

The road south of Losuia is dotted with villages but seldom sees motorised transport. **Wawela** is on a beautiful, curving sand beach edging a cool, deep, protected lagoon. On a falling tide, beware of the channel out to sea from the bay: the current can be very strong. To get here you'll need to rent a bike from Butia Lodge or charter a PMV for a few hours (over K70).

War relics, including the scattered remains of a couple of planes, can be seen near Butia Lodge; ask the gatekeeper to show you around.

Of the islands off Kiriwina, **Kaileuna** is the easiest and cheapest to access as boats carrying *buai* (betel nut) travel from Losuia most days (K7). The villages of **Kaisiga**, in the south, and **Tawema** to the north have beautiful white-sand beaches and predictably relaxed locals. Ask around the wharf from about 10am to see if a boat is going.

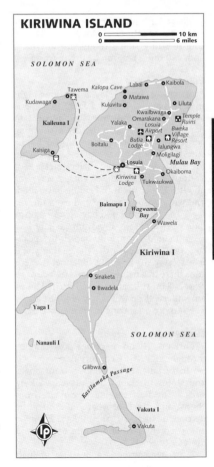

SLEEPING & EATING
Formal Lodgings

Butia Lodge (☎ 643 9003; malabu@online.net.pg; all-inclusive s/d K154/198) Located near the airport, on either side of an abandoned WWII-era airstrip, Butia Lodge is the best option. It's new, clean, comfortable, well priced and as inviting as you'd expect a Pacific island to be, but it's a 20-minute hike to the beach. The **restaurant and bar** (meals K20; ☺ breakfast, lunch & dinner) are in an attractive, open-sided building supported by 18 posts, each carved with a Trobriand legend. The food is superb, mixing traditional vegetables (yes, yams), fish, and masses of mouth-watering mud crabs. Highly recommended.

Bweka Village Resort (malabu@online.net.pg; s/d incl 2 meals K65/95) Bweka doesn't take too many

tourists anymore, but owners John Kasaipwalova and his Malaysian wife, Mary, are great conversation and Mary is a wonderful cook. It's walking distance to Butia Lodge and there's a sacred cave where you can swim. A great place for lunch; let them know you're coming.

Cindarella's (book through Konki Enterprises, ☎ 643 9033; malabu@online.net.pg; per person incl 2 meals K55) Opposite the cricket field (to the west), big-smiling widow Cindy opens her home to visitors, which can sleep three or four. It's a small, typical local home, and the home-baked bread goes off! It's excellent.

Kiriwina Lodge (☎ 641 1326; s/d incl 2 meals K165/231; ☒) Overpriced, decaying and altogether uninviting.

Village Birth Attendant Centre (VBA; call the district office ☎ 641 1502; s without/with meals K40/70) The five tiny single rooms are ultrabasic and, without a fan, can be pretty warm.

Villages

Most visitors opt to stay at least one night in a village and find it a fantastic experience. Certainly you must be prepared to pay for what you use (hardly a shocking concept for good capitalist tourists), but be sure to establish what you're (not) paying for in advance with the village chief.

Butia Lodge arranges village stays for about K25 per night, including basic food, and will transport you to and from the village. The transport and having an English-language speaker is an advantage here.

You could arrange it yourself by speaking with the chief of the village that you'd like to stay in. Friendly Emanuel Tosieru runs three **traditional-style rooms** (all-inclusive per person K40) on stilts at Kaibola Beach. Almost any other village will take you – just ask.

For more on staying in villages, see p217.

SHOPPING

Trobriand Island carvings are famous throughout PNG. Certain villages specialise in certain styles, ranging from bowls and stools to elaborately carved walking sticks. The best carvings are made from ebony, and much of what you see will be decorated with pearl-shell inlays. Ebony is an extremely hard and brittle timber, and difficult to work.

A master carver is a position of high prestige in the Trobriands and, like dancers, singers and many other roles, is a role bestowed upon people at birth. A carver cannot fell his own timber, as this role belongs to another, and must purchase it from the landowner where it is grown. Watching him work, and then buying direct from the master, is a memorable experience. Look closely at the carvings and expect to pay for what you get – a master carver's work will be immaculately finished in all the recesses and details, with pearl-shell inlays, and a good walking stick might cost K200 to K300 or more.

Butia Lodge has a small range of high-quality carvings, all priced very fairly. Check it out before you head out to get an idea of price and quality.

Other than carvings, you can get shell money and expensive *bagis*. *Doba* (leaf money) is also still used by some women as negotiable currency; it's a bundle of banana leaves with each leaf incised with patterns.

GETTING THERE & AWAY

Airlines PNG flies between both Losuia and Gurney (Alotau, K355) and Port Moresby (K541) on Sunday and Tuesday. These flights are often late or cancelled.

Star Ships sails the *Atolls Queen* from Alotau to Losuia (K68, 19 hours) and back via Esa'ala (K36, eight hours), departing Friday and returning the same way on Sunday morning.

The two main trade stores in Losuia run work boats to Alotau every fortnight or so; ask at **Konki Enterprises** (☎ 643 9033). They charge about K60 for the trip, which takes two days (stopping in the D'Entrecasteaux Islands for the night). Bring your own food and water.

GETTING AROUND

Most of Kiriwina's main roads are in fairly good condition and, if Butia Lodge have got their bikes sorted, cycling is a great way to see the island.

The island's few PMVs are cheap but infrequent. Almost all private vehicles (there aren't many) operate as de facto PMVs.

LOUISADE ARCHIPELAGO

This archipelago received its name after Louis Vaéz de Torres' 1606 visit, but was probably known to Chinese and Malay sailors much earlier. **Rossel (Yela) Island** is the most westerly inhabited island. The **Calvados chain** and **Conflict group** are a long chain of islets and reefs between **Sudest** and the mainland and make navigation through the province an exacting and often dangerous operation.

Mountainous **Misima Island** is the most important in the group, with the district headquarters at Bwagoia. A major gold and silver mine was recently decommissioned. Misima has about half of the total population of the archipelago, and the **Misima Guesthouse** (☎ 643 7443) and **Jeb's Guesthouse** (☎ 643 7443) have rooms at Bwagoia.

Airlines PNG flies to and from Port Moresby (K571, three hours) via Gurney (K371, 40 minutes) on Sunday and Tuesday. This takes in the various stops along the way.

Morobe & Madang Provinces

Morobe and Madang rise from the beaches and bays of Papua New Guinea's northern coast into a series of imposing mountain ranges and ultimately the Highlands. The region has much to offer the traveller. The coastline is quite stunning, with thickly forested hills above pristine beaches, from where, especially in and around Madang, the diving on reefs and wrecks is awe-inspiring. Madang is often described as the 'prettiest town in the Pacific', and it has a relaxed resort feel that will have you shifting down the mental gears in no time. It also has some fine accommodation and the best tourist infrastructure in the country.

By contrast, the Morobe capital Lae is PNG's second-largest city and the country's industrial heart. It can be an intense place where you'll need to be alert, but it is still a fairly attractive town and the nearby Rainforest Habitat is a must-see for anyone remotely interested in PNG's spectacular wildlife. Where else can you see several species of bird of paradise, both types of cassowary and all manner of other bird and mammal life in the one place? Lae is also the best-connected place in PNG, with road, sea and air links to just about everywhere else. Banana-boat hopping your way along the coast via Salamaua, Lababia and Bau, staying in village-run guesthouses along the way, is a great way to lose a few days.

From a historical point of view, Wau and Salamaua were the centres of the gold boom in the 1920s and a few years later they, and Lae, Finschhafen and Madang, were all WWII battlegrounds. Wrecked planes and sunken ships still attract visitors, as do important war cemeteries.

The islands off the coast reward anyone who makes it out there, with soaring volcanoes – on Manam, Karkar and Long Islands – and impressive bird life.

MOROBE & MADANG PROVINCES

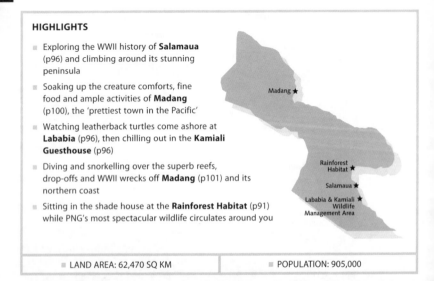

HIGHLIGHTS

- Exploring the WWII history of **Salamaua** (p96) and climbing around its stunning peninsula
- Soaking up the creature comforts, fine food and ample activities of **Madang** (p100), the 'prettiest town in the Pacific'
- Watching leatherback turtles come ashore at **Lababia** (p96), then chilling out in the **Kamiali Guesthouse** (p96)
- Diving and snorkelling over the superb reefs, drop-offs and WWII wrecks off **Madang** (p101) and its northern coast
- Sitting in the shade house at the **Rainforest Habitat** (p91) while PNG's most spectacular wildlife circulates around you

Madang ★

Rainforest Habitat ★

Salamaua ★

Lababia & Kamiali ★ Wildlife Management Area

| ▪ LAND AREA: 62,470 SQ KM | ▪ POPULATION: 905,000 |

History

Ancient axe heads that have been found suggest people have been living in this part of PNG for about 40,000 years. Simbai settlements date back 15,000 years. Bilbil and Yabob people in Madang Province are famous for their pots, which they've been trading with Morobe peoples and Highlanders for eons.

The first European to spend any length of time on the PNG mainland was Russian biologist Nicolai Miklouho-Maclay. He arrived at Astrolabe Bay, south of the present site of Madang, in 1871 and stayed for 15 months before leaving to regain his health, which was badly affected by malaria. He came on two more visits. Maclay's relations with local people were remarkably good and his studies make fascinating reading.

Arguably the most rapid change, however, began when the German New Guinea Company established a settlement at Finschhafen in 1885. It was a disaster, with malaria, boredom and alcohol all taking a heavy toll. The company moved north, first to Bogadjim on Astrolabe Bay, and then on to Madang, before finally conceding defeat to the mosquitoes and decamping for the relative comforts of New Britain. The Lutheran Mission arrived during this time and Finschhafen remains a Lutheran base.

The legendary prospector 'Sharkeye' Park is credited with discovering gold near Wau in 1921. By the mid-1920s the gold hunters were flooding in, arriving at Salamaua and struggling for eight days up the steep and slippery Black Cat Track (p98) to Wau, a mere 50km away. Malaria, the track itself and unhappy tribesmen claimed many.

In 1926 a richer field was discovered at Edie Creek, high in the hills above Wau. To squeeze the most out of these gold-rich streams the miners turned to aircraft (p242) and within a few years more air freight was being lifted in PNG than the rest of the world put together. The goldfields continued to be productive until after WWII. Today, local people still work the fields but it's nothing more than a cottage industry.

Lae was a tiny mission station before the gold rush but soon became a thriving community clustered, in true PNG fashion, around its central airstrip. It was from here that, in 1937, pioneer aviator Amelia Earhart took off on one of the final legs of a round-the-world flight and disappeared without trace.

Volcanic eruptions at Rabaul in 1937 prompted a decision to move the capital of New Guinea to Lae, but WWII intervened and instead Lae, Salamaua and Rabaul became major Japanese bases. The Japanese also took Madang.

In early 1943 the Japanese, reeling from defeats at Milne Bay and the Kokoda Track, attempted to take Port Moresby by attacking towards Wau, marching over the mountains from Salamaua. The Battle of Wau was fought hand-to-hand after the ammunition ran out, with villagers watching in much the same way that foreign researchers (with an advanced knowledge of clan disputes) and voyeurs watch Highlands battles today.

In September 1943 Allied troops took Salamaua, Nadzab and finally Lae. Many Japanese escaped into the mountain wilderness of the Huon Peninsula and started on an incredible retreat that saw them fight their way over the Finisterre Range towards Madang, and eventually all the way to Wewak. Today, groups of Australian military-history buffs occasionally walk the route over Shaggy Ridge, scene of some of the most desperate fighting of the campaign. Lae, Wau, Bulolo and Salamaua were badly damaged during the war and Salamaua was never rebuilt. Madang was demolished and completely rebuilt.

Postwar, Lae became a major transport hub for goods shipped to and from the Highlands. The road between Wau and Lae had been built during the war and work on the Highlands Hwy was made a priority so it could service the fast-growing coffee and tea industries. The Highlands mineral boom of the 1980s and '90s, with its need for massive heavy cargo shipments, resulted in Lae becoming the main port and industrial centre of PNG.

Geography & Climate

The Huon Peninsula is the hump in the New Guinea 'dragon's back', an area of steep ranges leading down to northern coastal grasslands and swamps. The Finisterre, Sarawaget and Rawlinson Ranges form a rib along the Huon Peninsula, with the lower slopes blanketed in one of the most tangled and impenetrable rainforests

MOROBE & MADANG PROVINCES

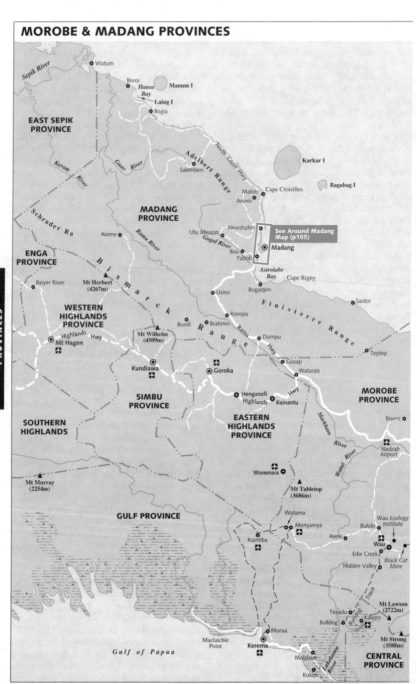

in PNG. Further north, Madang Province rises from the coast into the Schrader and Bismarck Range and the highest peaks in the country; Mt Wilhelm (4509m) stands near the border with Simbu Province.

Both provinces have river valleys that are important cattle and sugar cane farming areas; in Morobe it's the valley astride the 190km-long Markham River, while Madang has the Ramu Valley. There are 45 islands off the coast of Madang Province, three of which are active volcanoes. Morobe also has a number of volcanic islands between the Huon Peninsula and New Britain.

The climate in this part of PNG can be confusing. The Lae-Finschhafen area's rainy period is from May to October and it has only a slight seasonal variation in temperature. But while it can rain every day for weeks in Lae, just a couple of hours down the coast by boat it is sunny most days. Madang is dry between June and September.

Culture

Even today, the Anga people from the highland areas of Morobe Province are renowned throughout PNG as fierce warriors. Traditionally they lived a nomadic existence interspersed with violent raids on lowland villages – or upon each other. Despite the bitter climate in their mountain homeland, they wore only tiny grass skirts and cloaks made of beaten bark, known as *mal*.

JK McCarthy, who made some of the first contact with these people between the wars, described in his book *Patrol Into Yesterday* the Angas' first sight of an aircraft, when men crawled beneath the plane in search of its genitals, apparently unsure whether it was male or female.

MOROBE PROVINCE

Morobe Province is the industrial heart of PNG and gateway to the Highlands. The coast is beautiful and a string of village guesthouses are a great way to pass some time.

LAE

Lae is PNG's second-largest city and, despite having a sizable industrial base, it is vastly more attractive than Port Moresby. The city is laid out around the Botanical Gardens, not unlike Manhattan and Central Park (OK, so comparing Lae to New York might be drawing a *slightly* long bow). On its outskirts Lae boasts the wonderful Rainforest Habitat, probably the best place in PNG for seeing the country's fantastic wildlife without having to mount a months-long expedition to do so.

Orientation

Lae is built on a flat-topped headland that ironically gets almost no benefit of a view over the beautiful Huon Gulf. The old airstrip lies at the foot of the steep hill to the west and runs up beside the Botanical Gardens. It was, for many years, Lae's main airport, but today the city is served by Nadzab Airport, the wartime airstrip 40km northwest of Lae.

Huon Rd is the main through street, running in from the Highlands Hwy, past the Eriku PMV stop and through the city centre (still sometimes known as Top Town). It connects with Markham Rd, another major thoroughfare, which leads down past the old airport and Voco Point.

Most passenger boats, from banana boats to passenger ships, leave from Voco Point, southeast of the town centre. The shipping companies have their offices nearby. Another wharf, off Bumbu Rd beside Lae's main container terminal, deals with banana boats heading south to Labu villages and is the Rabaul Shipping terminal. It's not, however, a place to be wandering with anything you really don't want to lose.

MAPS
Recent city maps are available in the front of the phone book. Otherwise, see the **Department of Surveying & Land Studies** (☎ 473 4951; enquiries@survey.unitech.ac.pg; Unitech).

Information
EMERGENCY
Ambulance (☎ 479 1068)
Fire (☎ 472 4333)
Police (☎ 473 2100; Coronation Dr)

INTERNET ACCESS
Destiny Internet Cafe (☎ 479 3193; 4th St; per hr K25; ⏰ 8am-4.30pm Mon-Fri, 8am-2pm Sat) On the ground floor of the big blue building; prepare for a slow connection and recently downloaded Memphis-style gospel music.

MEDICAL SERVICES
Chemcare (☎ 472 4141; 4th St; ⏰ 8am-5pm Mon-Fri, 8am-2.30pm Sat, 9am-1pm Sun) One of several pharmacies.

Masalohan Medical Services (☎ 479 1222; 7th St; ⏰ 8am-5pm) Reported to be good, especially for broken bones.
Tusa Private Hospital (☎ 472 4688; cnr Huon Rd & Coronation Dr; ⏰ 24hr) For emergencies.

MONEY
ANZ (☎ 180 4444; ANZ Haus, Central Ave) ATMs (with security guard) take MasterCard, Visa, Cirrus and Maestro. Best option.
Bank South Pacific (BSP; ☎ 472 2244; cnr Coronation Dr & 7th St)
Westpac (☎ 472 1066; Central Ave) Credit-card advances over the counter. K30 charge on travellers cheques.

POST
Post office (cnr 2nd & 3rd Sts)

TOURIST INFORMATION
Lae Explorers' Club (☎ 472 5900) Club members organise occasional 4WD expeditions into the interior. Ask for Fred Rosée.
Morobe Tourism Bureau (☎ 472 7823; www .tourismmorobe.org.pg; 1st fl, IPI Bldg, 2nd St) One of the better information offices in PNG; staff here are helpful and have some handy contacts and information.
Village Development Trust (VDT; ☎ 472 1666; www.global.net.pg/vdt; Trist Ave, Eriku) These guys help manage a series of village guesthouses along the Huon Gulf coast and are a must-see if you're heading that way.

UNIVERSITIES
Unitech (☎ 473 4999; www.unitech.ac.pg; Independence Dr, Taraka) About 8km out of town, and located in some nicely landscaped parks and gardens. The Matheson Library is impressive, as are Duncanson Hall's 36 Sepik-style carved pillars. From the city centre, take PMV No 11A or 11B.

Dangers & Annoyances
Lae has a reputation for danger and it pays to be more cautious than normal while you're here. Having said that, there's no reason why you can't walk around most parts of town during the day, though keep valuables to a minimum and as inconspicuous as possible (see p223). The quiet Botanical Gardens, however, are not suitable for lone travellers.

PMVs are safe to use but, if possible, women should choose buses with other women on board. There are no taxis in Lae, which can be a problem after dark. However, hotels will usually run you the short distance to, say, the Yacht Club, or pick you up before 8pm, and you'll soon be offered a lift home by someone from the local expat community.

The road to Nadzab Airport has been resealed and hold-ups have declined dramatically; it's a lot tougher to stop a vehicle travelling at 130km/h (drivers don't spare the horses on the airport run) than one slowing to 10km/h to negotiate potholes.

Sights
RAINFOREST HABITAT
Next to Unitech (opposite), visiting the **Rainforest Habitat** (☎ 475 7839; www.habitat.org.pg; adult/child K10/5; ☻ 10am-4pm) is like stepping into a microcosm of PNG's most exotic flora and fauna; it shouldn't be missed. It comprises about 3000 sq metres of reconstructed rainforest inside a covered shade house, which incorporates a lake, raised walkways and an abundance of plants and birds. The many birds include several species of bird of paradise, and there is also an impressive orchid garden. Outside is a mini-zoo with *cuscuses* (possums), tree kangaroos and cassowaries. There are simple accommodation facilities in the nearby Rainforest Habitat Guesthouse (p92). To get there, take PMV No 11B or 11C from Top Town or Eriku and ask to be let off at Unitech Gate 2, not the main gate.

BOTANICAL GARDENS
The **Botanical gardens** (☎ 472 4188; Milford Haven Rd; admission K1; ☻ 6am-7pm Sat & Sun) offer a pleasant stroll through a small patch of rainforest and grassland in the centre of Lae. The huge, vine-covered trees host colourful birds and butterflies, and the gardens have an exotic orchid collection. Officially, it's closed on weekdays but the guards at either the main northern gate (near the RAAF DC-3) or the southern gate (near Lae War Cemetery) usually let you in. Try to avoid coming here alone.

LAE WAR CEMETERY
The manicured lawns of the **Lae War Cemetery** (Memorial Ave; ☻ 7am-4pm) are just south of the Botanical Gardens. There are 2808 graves here, 2363 of which are Australian and most of the rest, Indian and British. If the war seems rather distant and unreal, pay a visit and read some of the headstones; the tributes can be quite moving. There are security guards and it's quite safe to visit.

MT LUNAMAN
To the southeast of town **Mt Lunaman** or, more correctly, Lo' Wamung (First Hill), was used by the Germans and Japanese as a lookout point. The Japanese riddled it with caves and tunnels, though none of these are open today. Don't go here alone.

Activities
If golf is your game, the **Lae Golf Club** (☎ 472 1353; Bumbu Rd) is one of the best in PNG and has a fine clubhouse. Fishers should contact the **Lae Game Fishing Club** (www.laegamefishing.org.pg).

Tours
Morobe Tours (☎ 472 3647; gjfinall@global.net.pg; Air Corps Rd) operates air-con bus and boat trips around Lae and the province. A tour of Lae is K210 for one person, a two-day 4WD trip to Menyamya and the smoked bodies is K1800. It has a 35ft luxury cruiser for charter (K5000 per day).

Festivals & Events
The **Morobe Show** (www.morobeshow.org.pg; admission K3) has become arguably the best-organised cultural show in PNG. It's usually on the full-moon weekend in late October. It's 16–17 October 2005 and 4–5 November 2006. There are no tourist prices here, though photographers can gain access to the performance field (and the shaded members stands) by purchasing a show pass for K35. The *singsing* (celebratory festival/dance) is held on the second day.

The **Unitech Show** (admission K4) is held on even years in the university grounds. It's next scheduled for April 2006; check www .tourismmorobe.org.pg for dates.

Sleeping
Most sleeping options are in Top Town or Eriku, and the majority can provide dinner, meaning you don't have to venture out after dark.

BUDGET
Klinkii Lodge (☎ 472 6040; Klinkii St, Eriku; tw/tr K74/96) Everything about Klinkii is pretty basic, but it's cheap and cheery. Rooms have shared bathroom, except two that also have air-con (K108). Local-style meals are K13 to K15.

YWCA (☎ 472 4191; 7th St; dm/r K10/25) This women-only place is very cheap. There's beds in twin rooms with bathroom and kitchen, or a room by yourself (a transit room). It gets really cheap by the fortnight, just K98!

Lutheran Guesthouse (☎ 472 2556; Busu Rd, Ampo; dm K40) In attractive surrounds in Ampo (pronounced 'umpo'), the homely, colonial-style guesthouse buildings are 200m off the main road. They contain clean shared rooms (two to five beds) and bath-rooms; rates include breakfast. The gates close from 11pm to 5am. It's too far to walk; take the 13A PMV to Butibum.

Rainforest Habitat Guesthouse (☎ /fax 475 7839; Unitech; dm K75) Bunk beds and shared bathrooms and kitchen will appeal to those wanting to be near to nature, and far from everything else. Ring first.

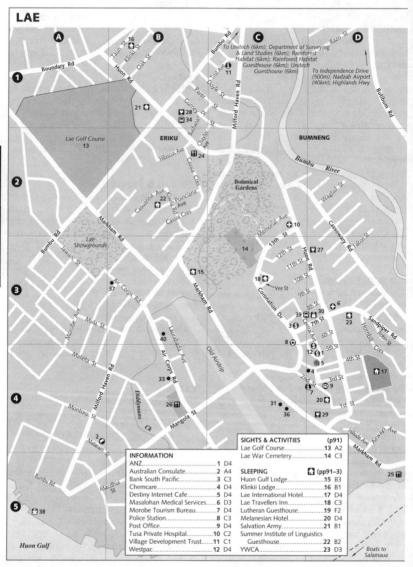

LAE

MID-RANGE

Lae Travellers Inn (☎ 479 0411; Vee St; tw/d K93.50/176;
🞫) Clean, quiet, professional and centrally
located, this is the pick of Lae's mid-range
options. Standard rooms have satellite TV
and kettle, while budget twins have fan, TV,
desk and share a bathroom. The **restaurant**
(meals K25-35; ☯ 6am-10pm) serves tasty meals.

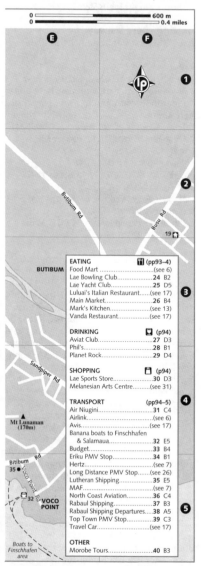

EATING	🔟 (pp93–4)
Food Mart	(see 6)
Lae Bowling Club	24 B2
Lae Yacht Club	25 D5
Luluai's Italian Restaurant	(see 17)
Main Market	26 B4
Mark's Kitchen	(see 13)
Vanda Restaurant	(see 17)

DRINKING	🍺 (p94)
Aviat Club	27 D3
Phil's	28 B1
Planet Rock	29 D4

SHOPPING	🛍 (p94)
Lae Sports Store	30 D3
Melanesian Arts Centre	(see 31)

TRANSPORT	(pp94–5)
Air Niugini	31 D3
Airlink	(see 6)
Avis	(see 17)
Banana boats to Finschhafen & Salamaua	32 E5
Budget	33 B4
Eriku PMV Stop	34 B1
Hertz	(see 7)
Long Distance PMV Stop	(see 26)
Lutheran Shipping	35 B3
MAF	(see 7)
North Coast Aviation	36 C4
Rabaul Shipping	37 B3
Rabaul Shipping Departures	38 A5
Top Town PMV Stop	39 C3
Travel Car	(see 17)

OTHER	
Morobe Tours	40 B3

Unitech Guesthouse (☎ 473 4488; s/d/tw/tr K80/
106/106/120) If you're prepared to stay out at
Unitech, this is the best value in Lae. It's
a pleasant house with a few clean rooms
and share bathrooms. Breakfast is K14,
lunch K20 and dinner K27, or use the
well-equipped kitchen. From the university entrance, follow the signs to the vice
chancellor's residence; it's opposite.

Huon Gulf Lodge (☎ 472 4844; www.coralsea
hotels.com.pg; Markham Rd; d K168-205; 🞫 🞫) Not
the jewel in the Coral Sea Hotels' crown.
Rooms in the newer wing are better, but
you're better off in the Travellers Inn.

Salvation Army (☎ 472 2487; Huon Rd, Eriku; tw/tr
K110/143; 🞫) Near the shops and PMVs at
Eriku, the self-contained motel-style units
have kitchenettes and are clean, if a little aged.
The staff are very friendly. Good value.

Summer Institute of Linguistics Guesthouse (SIL;
☎ 472 2939; sillaeguesthouse@datec.com.pg; Poinciana
Ave, Eriku; s K65-85, d K85-115; 🞫 🞫) The clean,
quiet mission guesthouse has good-value
rooms with kitchenette, fan and shared
bathroom, and bigger apartments with
several beds and a bathroom.

TOP END

Lae International Hotel (☎ 472 2000; www.laehotel
.com.pg; 4th St; d K290-320, ste K415; 🞫 🖥 🞫) The
spacious, secluded and secure Lae Inter is
the best in town. Set amid tropical gardens,
it boasts a sports bar and three restaurants
serving good food (see p94). Some rooms
have Internet access.

Melanesian Hotel (☎ 472 3744; www.coralseahotels
.com.pg; 2nd St; d K226-319, ste K440; 🞫 🖥 🞫) The
'Mello' has three grades of room, all the
same size but with varying degrees of comfort. Service can be especially good.

Eating

Ask your hotel to drop you somewhere
different for dinner. Don't, however, be
tempted to walk at night.

RESTAURANTS

Lae Yacht Club (☎ 472 4091; Butibum Rd; ☯ 8am-
midnight) The airy, informal 'Yachty' is in a
prime position on the harbour and is good
for both drinking and eating. Its Tuesday and
Friday night barbecues are excellent value
(your choice of steak plus chips and myriad
salads for K28, or just salads for K9.50) and
the best place to meet people in Lae, both

expats and nationals. The lunchtime menu has a variety of burgers for K7.50.

Vanda Restaurant (☎ 472 2000; Lae International Hotel, 4th St; meals K50-75; ⏰ 6.30-10pm Mon-Sat) The classiest place in Lae, the Vanda serves a mix of well-prepared international dishes, including pumpkin and potato gnocchi, coconut curry crocodile and double-chocolate pudding. All good!

Mark's Kitchen (☎ 472 1353; Lae Golf Club, Bumbu Rd; meals K20-30; ⏰ noon-2pm & 6-10pm Tue-Fri) A local favourite because of its consistently good Chinese fare; the lunchtime salt-and-pepper squid (K8) is hard to beat.

Luluai's Italian Restaurant (☎ 472 2000; Lae International Hotel, 4th St; pizzas K25) Possibly the best pizzas in PNG. Can't say the same for the pasta.

QUICK EATS

Lae Bowling Club (☎ 472 0823; Hibiscus Ave, Eriku; meals K7-10; ⏰ 8am-9pm) Filipina Nana serves a few cheap, tasty dishes in informal surrounds.

There are lots of *kai* bars (takeaway food bars), the best being in Food Mart.

SELF-CATERING

There are several well-stocked supermarkets in the centre of Lae and at Eriku, but the local markets are more fun for fresh food. The **main market** (Air Corps Rd; ⏰ 7am-4pm Mon-Fri, 7am-noon Sat), just west of the old airstrip, has food and a few local curios.

Entertainment

Lae has a small but vibrant nightlife. Lone women should find a friend before heading to any of these places.

Planet Rock (Markham Rd; ⏰ 7pm-3am) A big nightclub opposite the old airfield where the music is deafening and security both inside and out is necessarily tight.

Phil's (Eriku; ⏰ 7pm-3am) Off Huon Rd; has a loyal following of both nationals and expats and a better reputation.

Aviat Club (☎ 472 3565; Huon Rd; ⏰ 11am-3am) Serves the cheapest beer and is a very local scene; there's a band most Wednesdays. The main bar is members-only but the nightclub is not.

Shopping

Beside the old airstrip, the **Melanesian Arts Centre** (☎ 472 1604; quinn.lae@global.net.pg; Markham Rd) has a good collection of artefacts, mostly from

the East Sepik but also Tami Island bowls and Trobriand Islands carvings. Prices are reasonable and shipping can be arranged.

Footpaths in the city centre, especially outside Chemcare, are a good place to look for baskets and especially *bilums* (string bags), which are quite cheap.

Masks, flippers, snorkels and T-shirts can be bought in **Lae Sports Store** (☎ 472 1396; 7th St).

Getting There & Away

Lae is the best-connected city in PNG.

AIR

Several airlines fly scheduled services out of Lae's Nadzab Airport, and most have offices both at the airport and in town. Fares listed here are one-way full-fare; only Air Niugini offers discounts on return tickets (see p241).

Air Niugini Town (☎ 472 1892; Markham Rd) Nadzab (☎ 475 3055)

Airlines PNG Nadzab (☎ 472 5747)

Airlink Town (☎ 472 0771; 7th St) Nadzab (☎ 475 3189) Doesn't fly Sundays.

MAF Town (Mission Aviation Fellowship; ☎ 472 1555; INI Bldg, 2nd St) Nadzab (☎ 472 3804)

North Coast Aviation Town (☎ 472 1755; Markham Rd) Nadzab (☎ 475 3006)

Air Niugini has direct flights from Lae to Port Moresby (K363, 45 minutes) several times daily, and to Madang (K210, 35 minutes) three times a week. To the islands, it flies to Manus (K445, one hour) once a week and Hoskins (for Kimbe, K353, 55 minutes), Rabaul (K502, two hours) and Kavieng (K546, three hours) two or three times per week. For all other destinations you'll have to go to Port Moresby first.

Airlink has a Monday-to-Saturday milk run beginning in Lae and flying to Madang (K200, 45 minutes), Wewak (K369, two hours), Aitape (K551, three hours) and Vanimo (K579, four hours), before returning the same way. Airlink also flies most days to Port Moresby (K281, one hour 10 minutes), Goroka (K186, 35 minutes) and Mt Hagen (K254, one hour 20 minutes).

Airlines PNG has less-frequent services to Port Moresby (K338, 50 minutes), Goroka, Mt Hagen and Tabubil.

For flights around Morobe Province speak with North Coast Aviation or MAF. Both have (loose) schedules; see the relevant towns later in this chapter for details.

PMV

PMVs to Bulolo (K8, two to three hours) and Wau (K10, three to four hours) leave Lae's **long-distance PMV stop** (main market) between about 2pm and 3pm; for Goroka (K20, four hours) and Madang (K30, four hours) they leave between 8am and 9am. There are fewer on weekends.

The road to Wau is not sealed but is generally good, with spectacular scenery as the road skirts the Bulolo River.

PMVs to Goroka follow the Highlands Hwy (see p113).

If you're heading for Madang, the PMV trip costs about the same as a transfer to Nadzab Airport; it compares very well with flying.

SEA

As the busiest port in the country, Lae is the best place in PNG from which to sail off into the sunset. Banana boats run northeast as far as Finschhafen and south as far as Bau; for details see the boxed text on p97.

Lutheran Shipping (Luship; ☎ 472 2066; fax 472 5806; Butibum Rd, Voco Point) has a fleet of boats servicing the coast plus some islands north of Lae. Luship publishes a schedule at the beginning of each month. All prices listed here are one way for deck/cabin class.

Lutheran Shipping has a weekly boat to Rabaul (K175/290, 36 hours) via Kimbe (K100/160, 24 hours), usually leaving Lae on Monday. **Rabaul Shipping** (Star Ships; ☎ 472 5699; Butibum Rd, Voco Point) also sails to Rabaul weekly, for the same price.

A Luship boat sails to Lorengau (K100/160, 48 hours) once a week (often on Friday), and there should be one boat a week to Madang (K33/39, 24 hours). Virtually all the Madang-bound boats call at Finschhafen but the fastest and most comfortable journey is on the passenger-only *Gejemsao*.

The ultimate coast-hopping slow trip is on the freighter *Nagada*, which runs via Oro Bay, Tufi, Cape Vogel and all stops in between to Alotau (K166, three long days) once a month. Take a couple of books.

Luship's *Rita* or *Mamose Express* run to Oro Bay (K81/101, 12 hours) every Saturday night at 9pm, returning the following day.

Getting Around

There are no taxis in Lae, but **Bas A Nova** (☎ 472 7300) will run you around if you call.

TO/FROM THE AIRPORT

Most visitors use one of the airport bus services, which collect you from your hotel and complete the journey at alarming speed – usually only 20 minutes. The **Balus Bus** (☎ 472 7350) and Bas A Nova are popular for K20 a trip, while the security on **Guard Dog Security** (☎ 475 1069; K55) would make Rambo look under-equipped.

Local PMVs (K3, 45 minutes) leave from the main market, but with no taxis, getting to or from the market can be a hassle.

The aforementioned buses usually meet any arriving flights. Alternatively, cadge a lift with a local.

CAR

There's no shortage of choice if you want a hire car:

Avis Town (☎ 472 4644; Lae International Hotel; 4th St) Nadzab (☎ 472 4929)

Budget Town (☎ 472 3230; Boroko Motors, Milfordhaven Rd) Nadzab (☎ 472 4889)

Hertz Town (☎ 472 5982; IPI Bldg, 2nd St) Nadzab (☎ 475 3150)

Travel Car Town (☎ 472 2840; Lae International Hotel, 4th St) Nadzab (☎ 475 3186)

PMV

PMVs around Lae cost K0.50. The local PMV stop in Eriku is on Huon Rd. The other local PMV stop (known as Top Town) is on 7th St. There are route numbers painted on urban PMVs but these can be fairly vague.

DOWN THE HUON GULF COAST

The Huon Gulf coast is a ray of sunlight on a dreary day as you hop your way east – all for a relatively small amount of money. This beautiful coastal stretch is home to a series of village guesthouses that allow you to while away a few days (or weeks). To describe the way of life down here as laid-back is an understatement, like saying Errol Flynn, who once made his way to these parts, had just a bit of luck with the ladies.

Being ultrarelaxed can have its drawbacks. Transport is a touch on the inconsistent side and little things like electricity don't always work. But, hey, this really is off-the-beaten-track PNG at its best, so trash the calendar and hop in a boat.

The following towns are listed in a southeasterly direction from Lae. Before leaving you should speak with the **Village Development**

Trust (☎ 472 1666; www.global.net.pg/vdt; Trist Ave, Eriku), which will book accommodation by radio and give you the lowdown on what boats are running. VDT can also give you details of the guesthouses, most of which offer basic accommodation in a dorm or multibed room; prices are usually about K30 to K40 for the bed plus a similar amount for two or three meals of local food per day. For transport details, see the boxed text on p97.

About 50 minutes from Lae by banana boat, **Busama** is a village on the beach near **Labu Tali**. This area is known for the leatherback turtles (below) who use the beaches as a nesting area. It is an attractive area in itself, and an easy 20-minute walk inland from Busama brings you to **Gwado** and the Bula Falls Guesthouse, run by the villagers with the help of VDT.

The picturesque peninsula protruding from the coast an hour south of Lae marks **Salamaua**. There is little to suggest that the tranquil village you find today played such a significant part in the development of Wau and Bulolo in the gold-rush days, or a pivotal role in the course of the Pacific war (see p19). You can walk to, or dive on, a few interesting war relics and it's a great escape from Lae. Follow the steep trail to

LEATHERBACK TURTLES

The beaches around Busama and Labu Tali villages are an important breeding site for leatherback turtles, incredible reptiles that can live to a great age, weigh up to 500kg and measure up to 2m in length. From November until February they come ashore, dig deep nests and lay as many as 100 eggs, which hatch about two months later. It is a truly extraordinary sight.

Traditionally the eggs are gathered by local villagers, but over the years demand for eggs has increased to the point where the turtle is in danger of dying out. To save the turtle and improve the villagers' basic living standards, sections of the beach have been set aside for conservation.

The beaches north of Lababia are also a favourite with the turtles. A US-backed monitoring programme here links villagers by radio, and means you can be called when the turtles arrive, rather than just sitting on an empty beach all night for nothing.

four Japanese gun emplacements and what remains of the original town cemetery in the peninsula's hills. The trail begins in the northwest corner of the school oval. Near the start of the path is the now-blocked entrance to a Japanese tunnel.

If you want a full day's walk, Mt Tambu has spectacular views and a huge battlefield where the Australians met the Japanese as they advanced towards Wau. Local guides are available for about K35 a day.

The Black Cat Track starts and ends at Salamaua; see p98 for details.

In Salamaua the **Haus Kibung** (bungalows per person K22) has bungalows with share bathrooms plus a couple of larger family rooms (K60). Bring your own food and use the well-equipped kitchen. The village store sells rice, noodles and SP Lager (Haus Kibung has a fridge!). The other option is the **Salamaua High School** (Education Dept in Lae ☎ 472 3001; tw per person K20), which has a few simple but clean rooms. Washing is by bucket and there are no fans, but the atmosphere is expectedly communal and good fun.

A further 30km south of Salamaua is **Lababia**, a village of about 750 people in a sandy cove. The attraction here is the 69,000-hectare **Kamiali Wildlife Management Area**. The area comprises forests, mangroves, sandy beaches, coral reefs, waterfalls, rivers and lakes, and includes the steep **David Suzuki Trail** through some pristine forest – the view from the top is well worth an early rise. At night, if the season is right, you can see leatherback turtles laying their eggs.

Kamiali Guesthouse (per person K35, incl 3 meals K75) is located here. It is comfortable and serves good traditional food. BYO snacks, water, torch and snorkelling gear.

The next **guesthouse** (all-inclusive per person K50) is a big hop down the coast to **Saigara**, one of many villages dotted along the Waria River as it winds inland. You can take a boat up-river to **Pema**, where there's an interesting arts-and-craft centre and another VDT **guesthouse** (all-inclusive per person K50). A better way is to walk, following a shaded riverside path through the villages. A guide will lead you for a small fee, but it's not essential.

From Pema you can walk back along the Waria River, cross over and finish in **Bau**, not far from the border with Oro Province. The **Tulip Guesthouse** (all-inclusive per person K45) here is run by the Tulip Women's Club.

DOWN THE COAST BY BOAT & FOOT

Trips down the coast from Lae start at Voco Point and your conveyance is almost always a PMV banana boat. There's no schedule, but a general rule is that the further the destination, the less frequently it runs. Very few boats operate on Sundays. Banana boats along this stretch of coast usually come from the village early in the morning, bringing people to market. They return about noon, with the same people they brought. *Nothing* is guaranteed, but it's worth checking the day before for approximate departure times.

Most days there are several boats between Lae and Salamaua (K20, one hour), which will also stop at Busama if requested. Alternatively, you could disembark at Busama and walk along the beach to Salamaua in about five hours. You could walk along the beach all the way from Lae to Salamaua in about two days. Two major rivers must be crossed: the Markham and the Buang. You can wade across the second but you must definitely get a boat across the first.

Boats run between Lae and Lababia (K40, two to three hours) about three times a week, and from Salamaua to Lababia (K20, one hour) whenever they feel like it. Tell one of the boatmen who leaves Salamaua for Lae to pass on a message that you want a ride south. Or walk; it takes at least a day.

Occasional boats head south from Lababia to Saigara or Bau (K85 to K100, four to five hours), but if you don't want to wait for days, your best bet is to pass a message through a boatman. If you get desperate, pay a local boatman to take you out to Lababia Island, then ambush the PMV boat as it goes past. It should be able to squeeze you in.

You can charter a boat, but it will very nearly break the bank. Multiply the prices here by five or six, then double it (you have to pay for a return trip). If you walk, stick to the flatter paths just back from the beach, as walking on the steep sand will have your back feeling like a bag of chips by days' end.

FINSCHHAFEN AREA

The town of Finschhafen was the German New Guinea Company's first attempt at colonising New Guinea (see p87). Finschhafen was moved from its original location after WWII, and today is a series of peaceful coastal towns, the centre of which is Gagidu Station.

Towards the end of WWII the area was used as a staging post for US troops and vast numbers of GIs passed through. The war's abrupt end left millions of dollars worth of aircraft and equipment redundant, so the whole lot was bulldozed into a huge hole; ask at Dregerhafen High School, about 4km south of Gagidu Station, for directions. There are a number of well-preserved sunken ships and aircraft offshore.

Malasiga, a village just south of Dregerhafen, was settled by Tami Islanders. It is possible to buy the famous Tami Island bowls here, or better, to take a boat to the **Tami Islands** themselves (K10 each way as a passenger or K120 return in a chartered banana boat). Ask around Dregerhafen for boat departure times. Unless you charter you'll have to stay the night; there are two village guesthouses on the islands.

Sleeping & Eating

Huon Peninsula Lodge (☎ 474 7073; hplodge@global .net.pg; Gagidu Station; tw K72-165; ⊠) Set in a well-kept garden on the coast, fan rooms and air-con rooms share a bathroom and kitchen; there's one self-contained room. Go fishing in the lodge outrigger (gear is provided) and barbecue your catch in the *haus win* (open-air structure like a gazebo). The lodge is opposite the municipal headquarters, about 700m north of Gagidu market.

Dreger Lodge (☎ 474 7050; Dregerhafen; r K50-60; ⊠) In a stunning position overlooking the sea, this lodge is run by Dregerhafen Provincial High School, 4km south of Gagidu. It's not Club Med, but this is a great place to chill out for a couple of days, hang out with the teachers, do some guest teaching and be led around the area's beaches (BYO snorkelling gear), villages and WWII junk. Rooms are clean enough, but when we visited the bathroom was pretty grim. There is a simple kitchen; bring food from Lae or buy a limited range in Gagidu.

Getting There & Around

Nearly all Madang-bound boats call at Finschhafen. Lutheran Shipping's comfortable

Gejamsao (pronounced 'gem-sow') passenger catamaran runs between Lae and Finschhafen (K35, three hours) four times a week. It leaves Lae at 9am and returns from Maneba Wharf, which is 45 minutes north along a diabolical road from Gagidu Station, between 12.30pm and 1.30pm. Tough-as-nails PMVs run between Gagidu and Maneba for K3.

Rabaul Shipping (☎ 472 5699; Butibum Rd, Lae) has a slower boat (K25, six hours) departing Lae at 10am Thursday and Sunday and Buki Wharf, which is 500m north of Dregerhafen High School, at 10am on Friday and Monday.

Alternatively, banana boats (K35, two to three hours) leave from Buki Wharf and Lae when they're full – usually in the morning. They won't run in bad weather, which is frequent between June and September.

WAU & BULOLO

In the 1920s and '30s New Guinea's gold rush made the mining towns of Wau (pronounced 'wow') and Bulolo thriving centres of industry (see p87). Not anymore. The nicest thing about these towns today is the welcome change from the stifling heat and humidity of the coast. At an altitude of about 1300m, the abundant pines give a refreshing slant on equatorial vegetation.

Unemployment is sky-high and local people still work small claims in the area. Gold traders advertise with signs saying: *'Salim Gol Long Hia'* (Gold Sold Here). Only one old dredge remains from the glory days, rusting in the creek bed downstream from town. Everything else has long been scrapped.

A new gold mine at nearby Hidden Valley is bringing some hope to the area. This is im-

IN THE FOOTSTEPS OF HISTORY

Two of the most historic and famous tracks in PNG still attract a few trekkers. They require experience, planning and stamina, and don't even think about attempting them without a local guide. Speak with the **Morobe Tourism Bureau** (www.tourismmorobe.org.pg), which can help find you a guide and offer up-to-date information on the condition of the tracks.

Black Cat Track

This track was used by miners in the 1920s (p87) and its difficulty lies in the no-matter-what route straight from Salamaua to its objective – the Black Cat mine, northeast of Wau. The miners took eight days to cover the 50km, and parts of the track were later used by Australian soldiers during WWII.

These days the middle sections of the Black Cat are seldom used by anyone, and the trail itself is often overgrown or obstructed by landslips and fallen trees. It will take three to five days to walk depending on which end you start (the climb is 1800m) and how fit you are. Note that this track shouldn't be attempted by inexperienced walkers. A couple we met in Salamaua, one a former member of the British SAS, rated the Black Cat an eight out of 10 for difficulty, compared with a five for the Kokoda Track. There is a series of traverses with loose footing and long drops below, plus several crossings of the Bitoi River.

For a fuller description see http://richard.stanaway.net/blackcat.htm. Be sure to wear long pants and boots with an edge and heel for grip on the traverses.

Bulldog Track

The WWII Bulldog Track, intended to link Wau with the south coast, winds its way from Edie Creek to Bulldog, from where you had to travel by river. When completed in 1943 the track was actually a road capable of bearing large trucks. It has deteriorated since and been cut by landslides and jungle. Depending on how much of it you want to walk, the Bulldog Track takes from three to nine days and passes through a stunning array of landscapes and villages, little changed in centuries. You'll pass through cool moss forests, tracts of pine-covered hills and villages where grass skirts remain common.

The longer trip is a bona fide adventure; see Richard Stanaway's excellent description at http://richard.stanaway.net/bulldog.htm. The shorter trip requires as much planning, and requires a charter flight to meet you at Kakoro. Don't be late.

portant, as right now Wau and Bulolo have a reputation as dangerous 'cowboy towns'. It's hard to say exactly how accurate this assessment is, but it has affected visitor numbers to the extent that Wau no longer has a hotel.

If you make it up here, your best bet is to contact long-time resident **Donna Harvey-Hall** (☎ 474 6298; dharveyhall@global.net.pg) in Wau, preferably before you arrive. Donna is a mine of information and is good for at least a cup of coffee. She can be found at **Donna's Stoa** (☎ 474 6210; Wau), where the PMVs stop in the centre of town.

Sights
There are several places around Wau and Bulolo of interest to walkers and nature lovers, particularly those with a thing for insects. The **Wau Ecology Institute** (WEI; ☎ 474 6431) seems to be steadily running down, but its laboratory, library, museum, lecture theatre, large insect collection and accommodation (below) are due for a cash injection in 2005. Its aim is to research grass-roots ecology and save PNG's rainforests and biodiversity.

Perhaps the most viable of the WEI's activities is its **Butterfly Ranch** (☎ /fax 474 6212). It supplies collectors around the world with examples of PNG's astounding variety of insects. The philosophy is that villagers earn money by collecting and selling butterflies, beetles and other insects that have usually already laid their eggs, thereby ensuring the procreation of their species. While earning an income, villagers also interact more closely with their environment (and become less tempted to cut down trees for a fast buck). Similar is the **Insect Farming & Trading Agency** (☎ 474 5285; www.ifta.com.pg; Godwin St) in Bulolo, uphill and to the left from the post office.

Eating & Sleeping
There aren't many options in Wau and Bulolo. The only official place to stay in Wau is the **Wau Ecology Institute** (WEI; ☎ 474 6431), a couple of hilly kilometres west of town; call ahead for a pick-up. Its basic twin rooms and shared bathrooms need some work. There's a kitchen; bring your food.

In Bulolo, **Pine Lodge** (☎ 474 5220; fax 474 5284) has passable rooms and food. The cheaper option is the **Bulolo Vocational Center** (☎ 474 5223; fax 474 5471), but you'll need to bring your own food.

Getting There & Away
North Coast Aviation flies between Lae and Wau (K222, 40 minutes) on Tuesday and (usually) Thursday. Wau's airstrip is one of the steepest in PNG, falling 91m in its 1km length; one of many exhilarating landings in these parts.

PMVs to Lae (K10, three hours) via Bulolo (K7, two hours) leave Wau between 6am and 7am most days, though they're fewer on Sunday.

In Wau, PMVs stop near the market. They return from Lae in the early afternoon.

MENYAMYA & ASEKI
Menyamya, in the heart of Anga country, is truly remote. Those who make the significant effort to get here usually come to see the **smoked bodies** at Aseki or Watama, nearer to Menyamya. The Anga used to smoke their dead and leave the mummified bodies in burial caves. These days they practise Christian burials, though a very small number choose the traditional death rites.

The best place to view a smoked body is at Watama, a village within an easy walk of Menyamya. Ask at the Menyamya provincial authority, which will contact the relevant village elders.

Sleeping & Eating
The **Anga Development Authority** (☎ 474 0211) has a guesthouse but food is not always available. Alternatively, ask around and you'll soon find someone to spend the night with.

Getting There & Away
AIR
North Coast Aviation should have regular flights to both Menyamya and Aseki. MAF flies on request (K228 per person one way, minimum four).

PMV
A road runs from Bulolo up to Aseki then on to Menyamya through some extremely rough and absolutely spectacular country. PMVs run most days; Bulolo to Menyamya costs about K10. In Bulolo, PMVs usually leave from the **Wabu Trade Store** (☎ 474 5352). The road actually bypasses Aseki, so if you're going there make sure the driver knows so he can take you into the village.

MADANG PROVINCE

Madang Province is PNG in miniature. It has coastal people, islanders, mountain people and river dwellers. The fertile coastal strip is backed by some of the most rugged mountains in PNG – the Adelbert and Schrader Range to the north, and the Finisterre Range to the south. Attractions include active volcanic islands just offshore and lovely Madang itself.

MADANG

'Prettiest town in the Pacific' is often applied to Madang. It's perched on a peninsula sprinkled with parks, ponds and waterways decked in water lilies. The warm, wet climate and fertile soil produce luxuriant growth, and there are many huge trees, particularly casuarinas, towering over the Madang streets. These house huge colonies of giant bats. There's a scattering of picturesque islands around the town's deep-water harbour. Following WWII, Madang was demolished and completely rebuilt.

Madang is PNG's most tourist-oriented city and provides a range of facilities and there are some excellent places to stay in all price brackets.

Orientation

Madang is built on a peninsula surrounded by harbours, bays and nearby islands. The main road is Modilon Rd, which runs vaguely north-south and connects the town centre to the hotels, schools and hospital in Madang's south. Coronation Dr follows the coast past Madang's affluent neighbourhood, the golf course and the Coastwatchers' Memorial to the Madang Resort Hotel on the peninsula's northern point. The airport is 7km out of town.

MAPS

The Madang Visitors & Cultural bureau (right) has a free visitors' map, and the phone book has some excellent maps in its front pages.

Information

EMERGENCY
Ambulance (☎ 852 2002)
Fire (☎ 852 2777/2245)
Police (☎ 852 3233/43; Yamauan St)

INTERNET ACCESS
The major hotels offer Internet access at about K30 per 30 minutes, or sometimes free for guests.
InfoTech (☎ 852 3899; Kasagten Rd; per min K0.60) Clean and friendly; offers printing and scanning services.

MEDICAL SERVICES
Pharmacies are well represented.
Madang General Hospital (☎ 852 2022; Modilon Rd) At the southern end of town, with a casualty ward.

MONEY
All major hotels change travellers cheques, often at a rate that's competitive with the banks. There can be long queues at the banks. Major credit cards are widely accepted.
ANZ (☎ 180 1444; Coastwatchers Ave) Opposite BSP and has ATMs.
Bank South Pacific (BSP; ☎ 852 2477; Coastwatchers Ave) Charges a flat K50 to change travellers cheques. It has an ATM lobby in the Beckslea Plaza on Nanulon St.
Westpac (☎ 852 2213; Nuna St) No ATMs. It charges 1% of the face value to change travellers cheques.

POST
Post Office (☎ 852 2006; Nuna St)

TELEPHONE
Telekom (Nuna St) Next to the post office. It has public phones outside.

TOURIST INFORMATION
Madang Visitors & Cultural Bureau (☎ 852 3302; www.madangtourism.com; Modilon Rd; ☷ 8.30am-5pm) Has good information on the province and its attractions, as well as accommodation in nearby villages. There's a small museum that displays local artefacts and historical photographs. This is one of the few useful tourist offices in the country, and well worth a visit. It coordinates a clutch of nature-based tourism projects, bush guesthouses and tours. Near the Coronation Dr intersection.
Melanesian Tourist Services (MTS; ☎ 852 2766; www.mtspng.com; Madang Resort Hotel, Coastwatchers Ave) Runs the live-aboard *Melanesian Discoverer* as well as tours and resorts. It has a travel agency and good tourist information.

Sights & Activities
CEMETERY
On an overgrown grassy mound in the centre of town is the old **cemetery**. Tombstones have fallen over and become illegible with time, but it's an interesting reminder of the German and Australian colonial days.

COASTWATCHERS' MEMORIAL

This 30m-high **beacon** is visible 25km out to sea, a reminder of those who stayed behind enemy lines during WWII to report on Japanese troop and ship movements. It's rather an ugly concrete memorial, but the 3km beach-front road south of the memorial is the most pleasant walk in Madang,

fringed by palm trees and poincianas and backed by the golf course with fine views across Astrolabe Bay.

DIVING & SNORKELLING

Excellent visibility, stunning tropical coral and fish life and countless WWII wrecks make the diving and snorkelling around

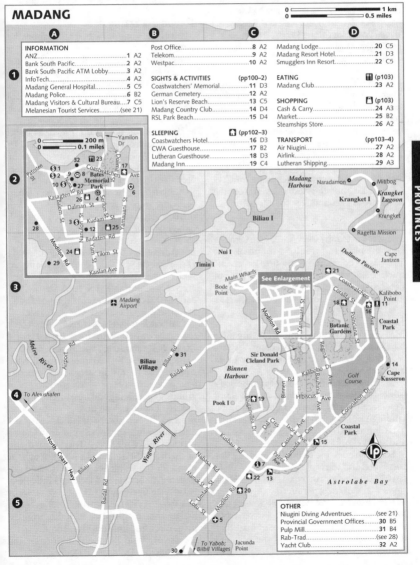

MADANG

0 |———————| 1 km
0 |———————| 0.5 miles

INFORMATION
ANZ..1 A2
Bank South Pacific.......................2 A2
Bank South Pacific ATM Lobby.........3 A2
InfoTech.....................................4 A2
Madang General Hospital................5 C5
Madang Police.............................6 B2
Madang Visitors & Cultural Bureau...7 C5
Melanesian Tourist Services..........(see 21)

Post Office..................................8 A2
Telekom.....................................9 A2
Westpac...................................10 A2

SIGHTS & ACTIVITIES (pp100–2)
Coastwatchers' Memorial..............11 D3
German Cemetery.......................12 A2
Lion's Reserve Beach...................13 C5
Madang Country Club...................14 D4
RSL Park Beach..........................15 D4

SLEEPING (pp102–3)
Coastwatchers Hotel....................16 D3
CWA Guesthouse........................17 B2
Lutheran Guesthouse...................18 D3
Madang Inn...............................19 C4

Madang Lodge............................20 C5
Madang Resort Hotel...................21 D3
Smugglers Inn Resort..................22 C5

EATING (p103)
Madang Club.............................23 A2

SHOPPING (p103)
Cash & Carry.............................24 A3
Market.....................................25 B2
Steamships Store.......................26 A2

TRANSPORT (pp103–4)
Air Niugini................................27 A2
Airlink.....................................28 A2
Lutheran Shipping......................29 A3

OTHER
Niugini Diving Adventrues.............(see 21)
Provincial Government Offices........30 B5
Pulp Mill..................................31 B4
Rab-Trad.................................(see 28)
Yacht Club................................32 A2

MOROBE & MADANG PROVINCES

Madang world famous. There are many dive sites around the Madang waters and on the nearby northern coast. There are several dive operators in Madang:

Aquaventures PNG (☎ 852 2023; www.aquaventures -png.com.pg) Based at Jais Aben Resort, 30km north of Madang, Aquaventures offers full instruction, diving trips and the live-aboard MV *Kamai*.

Blue Sea Charters (☎ 852 2300; www.blueseacharters .com; Modilon Rd) Operating the live-aboard MV *Moon-lighting*, Blue Sea Charters visits all the local dive sites.

Niugini Diving Adventures (☎ 852 2766; www .pngdiving.com; Madang Resort Hotel, Coastwatchers Ave) Operates various boats and offers night dives.

You can hire gear from all of the dive shops. There's good snorkelling just off Lion's Reserve Beach and off the rocks at Madang Lodge and Smugglers Inn Resort, but watch the swell and the tides because the rocks, coral and sea urchins can be hazardous.

SWIMMING
Some small swimming beaches are on Coronation Dr, but the best ones are on the nearby Krangket and Siar Islands (p104).

GOLF
The **Madang Country Club** (☎ 852 2181; Coronation Dr) is the place to organise a round of golf. The beach-side nine-hole course is very attractive and well maintained. Thousands of bats hang from the nearby trees. The clubhouse is a great place for a beer or snack.

Tours
Madang's resorts and hotels can organise harbour cruises, and the Madang Visitors & Cultural Bureau (p100) offers day tours and excursions.

Madang Resort Hotel's **harbour cruise** (half-/full-day K60/110) departs every day at 9am. You'll see the rusting wreckage of Japanese landing craft, view fish and coral through glass-bottomed boxes at Krangket Island and snorkel off Siar Island.

Several places, including the Madang Resort Hotel and the Malolo Plantation Lodge (p107) on the north coast, offer villages tours that can incorporate *singsings*.

MTS Discoverer (☎ 852 3543; www.mtspng.com; Madang Resort Hotel, Coastwatchers Ave; per person US$1050) is a luxurious live-aboard boat that does a four-day tour around the Madang Islands.

Festivals & Events
The four-day **Mabarosa Festival** is held annually in August or September, and features *singsing* groups from all over the country. There's a canoe race from Krangket Island to Madang, parades and live bands.

The **Madang Provincial Government Day** is celebrated in early August, and **Independence Day** on 16 September is celebrated with gusto.

Sleeping & Eating
Madang has some of the best accommodation options in the country, from budget stays to plush resorts. The overall standard for restaurant dining in Madang is probably PNG's best, due to the resort-town atmosphere and a local economy pitched towards tourism. The hotels have good restaurants but there are almost no independent restaurants.

Madang Resort Hotel (☎ 852 2655; www.madang resort.com; Coastwatchers Ave; s K210-405, d K230-425; 🍴 🖳 🐊) 'Madang Resort', as it's often truncated, is the best hotel in Madang and probably the whole of PNG. It's enormous, and its waterfront grounds take in a pool, some brilliant orchid gardens, various wildlife menageries, a carvers' workshop, pool-side bars and restaurants, a conference centre, gift shop, travel agent, hairdresser, Niugini Diving Adventures and the berth for the MTS *Discoverer* (see p102). The fancy rooms are pretty flash, and even the standard rooms are very comfortable. The **Janek Aben Restaurant** (meals K32-65) has an excellent international menu, and Japanese is served at Rukaen.

Coastwatchers Hotel (☎ 852 2684; coastwatchers@ coralseahotels.com.pg; Coastwatchers Ave; r K195-260; 🍴 🖳 🐊) A modern, tasteful place adjacent to the Coastwatchers' Memorial and the golf course. The rooms are large and some are split over two storeys – ideal for families or groups. There's a good restaurant and all the facilities of a plush hotel. Coastwatchers is owned by the Coral Sea Hotels chain and offers discounts and loyalty points to Qantas Frequent Flyer members. There's good dining in the **restaurant** (meals K25-60), although the menu for the Coral Sea Hotels is standardised, big on buffets and lacking a little flare.

Lutheran Guesthouse (☎ 852 2589; Coralita St; s/d/f K66/77/98; self-contained units K132) A good budget choice, this place includes breakfast in the tariff, and lunch (K8) and dinner (K12) are also available. It's clean and friendly and offers kitchen facilities.

Smugglers Inn Resort (☎ 852 2744; smugglers@daltron.com.pg; Modilon Rd; s K110-165, d K130-198; 🔃 🖳 🐍) This place has a spectacular waterfront setting, and a lovely *haus win* (gazebo-like structure) dining area and bar. It was once a great place to stay, but has become run-down and needs updating. The room rates include breakfast and theAsian-influenced **restaurant** (meals K22-45; ⊙ 11am-11pm) is still one of the best in town.

Madang Inn (☎ 852 3496; madinn@global.net.pg; Bougainvillea Dr; s K88-132, d K110-143; 🔃 🐍) The rooms are clean and comfy, if a little plain, but the location lets it down. It's on a poorly lit street in a dodgy part of town. Rates include breakfast and the best rooms have TV. Good meals are served in the dining area.

CWA Guesthouse (☎ 852 2216; Coastwatchers Ave; s/d/f K40/80/170) Conveniently located on the waterfront near the town centre, this is an excellent budget option. Bathroom facilities are shared except in the self-contained family room. Meals aren't served but there's a communal kitchen. It's clean and cheery.

Madang Club (☎ 852 2885; Coastwatchers Ave; meals K18-32; ⊙ 11.30am-3pm & 6-10.30pm) Popular for lunch or dinner, there's good pub-style food and pizza. NGOs, volunteers and expats catch up here and lunch on the harbour-side veranda.

Madang Country Club (☎ 852 2181; Coronation Dr; meals K20-40; ⊙ 11.30am-3pm & 6-10.30pm) The clubhouse is between the golf course and the sea, and serves cold beer and light meals. It's a nice spot to watch the ocean.

The market sells excellent fresh fruit and vegetables, peanuts, bread and smoked fish. There are a few big supermarkets.

Shopping

Madang is a good place to get artefacts. Bilbil clay pots are a local speciality, Highlanders come down with some *bilums* and hats, and you'll see Bukaware and items from the Sepik. Have a look through the market and in the carvers' huts attached to Madang Lodge and Madang Resort Hotel. All the hotels have gift shops.

The market has fruit and vegetables as well as some clothing, *bilums* and local shell jewellery.

The large Cash & Carry and Steamships trade stores carry pretty much everything you might need, including bush knives, kerosene lamps, food and clothing.

Getting There & Around
TO/FROM THE AIRPORT

The airport is 7km out from Madang. Most of the hotels and guesthouses have complimentary airport transfers and will meet your flight. PMVs run along Independence Dr and into town (K2).

AIR

Madang is well serviced by domestic flights. Between them, **Air Niugini** (☎ 852 2699; fax 852 2849; Nuna St) and **Airlink** (☎ 852 2933; fax 852 2725; Modilon Rd) have flights into Madang every day from all over the country. One-way full fares include Port Moresby (K397, one hour), Goroka (K212, 30 minutes), Wewak (K276, 40 minutes) and Rabaul (K611, 2½ hours), which flies via Port Moresby.

BOAT

Lutheran Shipping (☎ 852 2577; luship.madang@global.net.pg) connects Madang to all the other ports in the country at least weekly. It's predominantly a cargo carrier, but some of its ships carry passengers also.

PMV

On the north coast the road is sealed to Malolo and continues to Bogia. PMVs travel to Siar village (K1), Riwo/Jais Aben (K1) and Malolo (K3, one hour).

Heading south along Madang's main thoroughfare, the road becomes the Ramu

Hwy and rises over the tortuous Finisterre Range into the vast Ramu Valley on its way to Lae; and via the Highlands Hwy, deep into the central mountains. This is very spectacular driving and the only 'interstate' in the country.

Wet seasons wash out bridges in the Ramu Valley and cause occasional landslides in the Highlands, but the road is mostly sealed and in good condition.

Be aware that PMV travel on the highways has an element of risk, no matter how small. Very occasionally there are buses and vehicles held up for robbery, but this has been almost exclusively confined to the Southern Highlands regions of Mendi and its environs. PMVs aren't comfortable, but they're cheap and the road is amazing.

Buses gather around the market at 8am and the door-guys yell out their destinations 'LaeLaeLaeLae' and 'HagenHagenHagen' with a great sense of theatre. Once full they head off. The fare to Lae is K30 (four hours), to Goroka K30 (six hours) and to Mt Hagen K50 (eight hours).

AROUND MADANG
Krangket Island
Krangket Island, across Dallman Passage from Madang, is a large island with several villages and a beautiful lagoon. Krangket has an idyllic setting where you can swim, snorkel and get around in an outrigger canoe. There's a popular picnic spot, which was a former rest area for wounded Australian soldiers in the days following the Japanese surrender in WWII. Krangket is a lovely spot and worth at least a day trip.

SLEEPING
Krangket Island Lodge (c/o Madang Visitors & Cultural Bureau ☎ 852 3302 or Madang Resort Hotel ☎ 852 2655; s K60) is operated by the Dum clan (pronounced 'doom'). It consists of a few comfortable bush cottages tucked away from the village. They're rustic but come with kitchenette, private bathroom, shower and septic toilet. The kitchenette has a gas stove, kerosene fridge and utensils. There's fresh linen, but you need to take your own provisions.

GETTING THERE & AWAY
Small boats run to Krangket from Madang (K1.50, 15 minutes) from an inlet behind the CWA Guesthouse, hourly or so from

7am to 5.30pm. On Krangket they drop passengers about 45 minutes' walk from the lodge, though you should be able to negotiate passage to the lodge end of the island. Madang Resort Hotel (p102) or Madang Visitors & Cultural Bureau (p100) can arrange a boat for about K15.

Biliau Island
There are three wrecked Japanese freighters and a landing barge on Biliau Island, the large island right in the middle of Madang Harbour. More barges are nearby. You can reach the island by canoe while staying at Siar village.

Siar Island
Siar is another pretty island with beautiful white-sand beaches, great snorkelling and village guesthouse accommodation. Siar is a short boat ride from Madang and has lots of WWII aircraft wreckage. People come on the weekend to picnic here. Take a mask and snorkel.

Sair Island Guesthouse (☎ 852 3302; s K50) is another established grass-roots guesthouse in the Madang region; this is village living in a stilt house. The guesthouse can provide local meals but bring some food as well in case you tire of tinned fish, rice and sweet potato. Simon can arrange transport from Madang, or enquire with the Madang Visitors & Cultural Bureau (p100).

Yabob
Take the main Modilon Rd south out of Madang and you'll come to the Yabob road forking left just after the hospital. It passes a lookout and a Japanese memorial on it's way down to Yabob village. There's a little island offshore, which you can reach by canoe.

Before Europeans came, Yabob was famous for fine clay pots that were traded along the coast, but not nowadays.

Bilbil
This attractive village still produces pottery. Take the first road left after the Gum River, off the Ramu Hwy; this loops back to the highway. Get a PMV from Madang (K1).

Balek Wildlife Sanctuary
This wildlife management area is 10km south of Madang. It's featured in scenes from the 1996 film production of *Robinson Crusoe*

with Pierce Brosnan. There's a sulphur creek that flows from a huge limestone formation. Spirits inhabit the site and the water has curative properties. The water is incredibly clear and you can feed eels and turtles with bananas and fresh meat. It's a lovely spot. Catch a 15A PMV from town (K1.50).

Ohu

The **Ohu Butterfly Habitat** (☎ 852 2303; person/family K10/15; ☼ 7am-3pm), 15km southwest of Madang, is a community conservation and research project where butterflies, including PNG's famous birdwing varieties, feed on the nectar of the flowering *aristolochia*. Catch a 13B PMV from Madang.

NORTH COAST HIGHWAY

The road runs a long way north of Madang and people say that it eventually reaches Wewak. The bitumen stops at Malolo, but the road continues.

The whole north coast offers excellent beaches, diving and snorkelling, and some great hills and rivers to explore. You can hire banana boats in the bigger villages or organise a tour with the Malolo Plantation Lodge (p107).

Nobonob & Nagada Harbour

Beyond the Siar village turn-off on the North Coast Hwy, 17km from Madang, there are two turn-offs. The right leads to the Lutheran Mission on Nagada Harbour. The left leads to Nobonob Mission outstation, used as a Japanese lookout during WWII. It's about a 20-minute drive. There is a pretty park here with a fine view over the north coast, Madang and the harbour; below the park is one of few remaining virgin rainforests near Madang.

Local guides can show you around; contact the Madang Visitors & Cultural Bureau (p100). A guided walk can take in nearby Guntabag village and spectacular Tamolalakud lookout.

Jais Aben Area

Divers rave about the north coast sites, such as the US freighter *Henry Leith* in 20m of water near Jais Aben Resort, and the nearby minesweeper *Boston*. The 'waterhole' is an enclosed lagoon connected to the open sea by a large underwater tunnel and offers dramatic snorkelling.

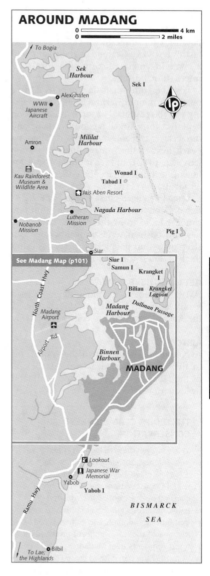

Jais Aben Resort (☎ 852 3311; jaisaben@global .net.pg; s K100-160, d K140-205; ❄ ▢ ☒) is 20km from Madang, off the main road. It's a pretty place on its own little peninsula, with beaches and lawns. The rooms, in semi-detached bungalows, are large and very comfortable and they have a lovely seafront outlook, TV and verandas; some have kitchens. There's a beach-front bar and a fine **restaurant** (meals K20-46) and guests can pay for a full three meals (K70) or breakfast only (K15). Seafood is the theme and a changing menu incorporates local and international dishes.

Jais Aben offers half-day tours (K45) to a nearby barramundi farm at Dylup, bushwalking and village visits. The surrounding lagoon is perfect for snorkelling and kayaking, and hire gear is available at the resort. There's a beach next to the Aquaventures dive-shop jetty (see p102), and it's a popular spot for lunchtime burgers. Jais Aben does town and airport transfers (K15).

Damon Gesengan Guest Village (☎ 852 2370; kennedys@global.net.pg; s/d K80/100) is a 10-minute canoe paddle from the resort. This place has four bush-material bungalows that can sleep up to four people. It's pretty basic, but the location is nice and it's run by locals.

GETTING THERE & AWAY
PMVs 3A and 3C run along the main road from Madang (K2). Alternatively, you can get the Aquaventures boat to collect you (K15).

Amron
A couple of kilometres further north, off to the left of the road, is Amron, the site of the Japanese WWII strategic command headquarters.

THE DIDIPA CLAN & FOREST CONSERVATION

In 1963, when the PNG logging industry was in its infancy, one clan, the Didipa clan, set aside over 300 hectares of its forest as a wildlife conservation area. Since then the clan, led by prescient *bigman* (leader) Kiatik Batet, has protected the area from gardening, burning, logging and hunting. Today, it is one of the last significant undisturbed forest remnants near Madang.

In 1992 the clan refused to sign an agreement with a Japanese company to log the area, despite pressure from the PNG government. A handful of Madang paradise birdwing butterflies, insects previously considered extinct, was discovered during an environmental impact study.

There's a small museum that seeks to retain and display traditional knowledge.

Kau Rainforest Museum & Wildlife Area
On the west side of the main coast road, not far from the turn-off to the Jais Aben Resort, is a rough track leading to the Kau Rainforest Museum & Wildlife Area, operated by the Didipa clan (see the boxed text, left). You can learn about traditional uses for plants for food and medicine – sticky sap of the breadfruit tree can be used as glue, and two local vines can be used as contraceptives.

Alexishafen
Alexishafen Catholic Mission is off the road to the right, 23km north of Madang. Like so much of the area, it was damaged during the war but the graveyard stands as a reminder of the early missionary period.

Beyond the mission you can see the old overgrown mission airstrip. The WWII Japanese airstrip is a little off the road to the left, between the mission airstrip and Alexishafen. Jungle has almost reclaimed it; only bomb craters and the odd aircraft wreck hint at the saturation bombing that destroyed the base. The wreckage of a Japanese bomber is next to the bomb crater that destroyed it. Nearer to the road is the fuselage of an early Junkers mission aircraft.

Malolo to Hansa Bay
The road continues north to the old Malolo (pronounced '*mah*-lollo') plantation, 42km up the coast, site of the Malolo Plantation Lodge. The **black-sand beaches** along the coast are indicative of volcanic activity on Karkar and Manam Islands. There's good swimming, but watch the currents. The 1996 film production of *Robinson Crusoe* was shot on the north coast of Madang.

About 20km on from Malolo, there's a Catholic mission at **Magiya**. Beyond here is a road leading inland about 5km to **Aronis**. A kilometre from the main village is an aid post, near which is **Manubyai Cave**, home to a colony of horseshoe bats.

Salemben is a small village about a three-hour drive from Madang inland over rough roads from Malolo. At 900m above sea level, the area is home to many birds of paradise and a nice guesthouse (opposite).

Bogia is 200km northwest of Madang and the departure point for Manam Island. The road peters out a short distance before the mighty Ramu River. At Bogia Bay, a Japanese

Zero fighter lies upside down in water a few hundred metres out from the jetty.

Hansa Bay is a popular diving spot past Bogia, where the wreckage of 35 Japanese freighters and US aircraft lie in a shallow harbour. The upper deck of the 6000-ton *Shishi Maru* lies in just 6m of water, two anti-aircraft guns on the bow point upwards and brass shell castings litter the deck. Two fire engines are sitting in the hold, just before the bridge, where they were waiting to be unloaded.

Hansa Bay also has some spectacular wreck dives. A Japanese freighter has one davit projecting from the water (known as the Davit Wreck); it was sunk in 1943 by US bombers. You can swim through the wreck, which makes this an exciting dive in only 12m of water. Nearby, in 10m of water, is the Mast Wreck, with its mast protruding from the water; there is a gun on the bow, ammunition on the deck and a field artillery piece in the hold. The Madang dive shops organise dives to Hansa Bay and other north-coast sites. See p101 for diving operators.

There's some marine biology research happening on **Laing Island** in Hansa Bay, a beautiful island with white beaches and good snorkelling.

SLEEPING
Malolo Plantation Lodge (☎ 852 1662; www.png tours.com/lodge3.html; r US$176, all-inclusive per person s/d US$380/290; In lovely surrounds and fronting a long black-sand beach, the lodge operated by **Trans Niugini Tours** (☎ 542 1438; Mt Hagen) was once a plantation house. The grounds are planted with orchids and stag-horn ferns, and birds abound, including a tame kokomo featured in *Robinson Crusoe*. Malolo is sometimes empty, catering as it does mostly for inbound package tourists who spend a few days each in Trans Niugini Tours' hotels around PNG.

Tours are available to nearby hills, villages and islands. A full-day tour costs US$119 per person. Madang transfers cost US$22. There's a dive shop and kayaks are available for hire. It's a very nice place, but it's way overpriced for a walk-up punter.

There is plenty of bird life in the area and the resort can take you to some good bird-watching places. Malolo also offers river rafting and mountain climbing.

Keki Mountain Lodge (c/- Madang Visitors & Cultural Bureau ☎ 852 3302; Salembin; s K30) Perched high on a ridge, two traditional bungalows have double rooms and cooking facilities. Meals can be provided with notice. Bird-watching can be organised (K50 per person) and other tours are offered (from K22).

GETTING THERE & AWAY
PMVs from Madang to Malolo cost K5. It's more than three hours drive to Bogia and PMVs travel up daily (K10). It should be possible to get from Bogia to the Sepik – you can get a bus to Boroi, take a canoe to Watam and another up the Sepik to Angoram.

INLAND
There are some isolated and interesting places in central Madang Province – remote Bundi is wedged between Mt Wilhelm and Mt Herbert in some of the roughest country in PNG. Some people from the area are small and sometimes called pygmies. The Ramu is one of PNG's great rivers and the people also produce good woodcarvings. The river's broad valley – sugar cane and cattle country – is a major fault zone prone to earthquakes and wet-season floods.

Ramu Sugar Refinery
This is a major industrial development designed to make PNG self-sufficient in sugar. There's accommodation at the refinery and sporting facilities. Contact the **administration office** (☎ 474 3299).

Bundi & Brahmin
Bundi is a six-hour walk from Brahmin Mission, and Brahmin is about 25km from the Lae-Madang road. PMVs travel from Madang to Brahmin (K10, two hours). There are some simple bungalows in Bundi at **Mt Sinai Centre** (c/- Madang Visitors & Cultural Bureau ☎ 852 3302; s K30). This is midway on the walk down to Madang from the Highlands, and about the only place to stay in the region.

Teptep
Almost 2000m up in the Finisterre Range, Teptep is a small, isolated village on the border with Morobe Province, and is a good base for trekking in the area. Guides are necessary and cost K20 a day. The **Teptep Guesthouse** (c/- MAF in Madang ☎ 852 2229; s K30) is

simple, but the region is rugged and beautiful. Evenings are cool, like the Highlands, so come prepared.

MAF flies to Teptep a few times each week from both Madang and Lae. Prices vary depending on duration. You can walk in from Saidor on the Madang Rae Coast.

ISLANDS
Long Island
The largest of the volcanic islands, Long is 48km off the coast. It has two active craters, one of which contains a lake surrounded by crater walls that rise to 250m. There are only a few hundred people on the island and it's renowned for prolific birdlife and the many fish that swarm around its reefs. Turtles come ashore to lay their eggs at certain times of the year. Getting there isn't easy – you can hire a banana boat or catch a lift with a boat supplying a trade store.

Karkar Island
English pirate/explorer William Dampier made an early landing on this island. Later, Lutheran missionaries had a hard time from malaria and the fierce inhabitants. The island's population is 30,000 and it has a high school and 20 community schools. It's one of the most fertile places in the country.

Karkar has both Catholic and Lutheran missions as well as some of the most productive copra plantations in the world. The volcanic cone rises to 1831m. The volcano erupted violently in 1974 and again in 1979, killing two vulcanologists.

It takes all day to climb the crater. Seek permission from the villagers because the crater has religious importance.

A road encircles the island and it takes four hours to drive around. You can also walk around, but treat the river crossings

with caution. When it rains on the mountain, water comes down the rivers like a wall – there have been deaths crossing rivers on Karkar. Karkar also has good beaches and snorkelling.

The high school and the airstrip are at the government station at Kinim.

SLEEPING
Kevasob Guesthouse (☎ 852 1636; s K30) is a rustic place that can accommodate nine people in its three-bedroom house. There's a gas stove, kerosene lamps and clean drinking water, but guests must bring their own bed linen and nets.

Kaviak Guesthouse (☎ 853 7477; s K35) is another simple place to stay.

GETTING THERE & AWAY
A boat runs to Karkar daily from Madang's Rab-Trad wharf, stopping at Biabi (K10) and at Kulili (K12). Kulili is 15km from the Kinim government station.

Manam Island
Manam is 15km offshore from Bogia. It's almost a perfect volcanic cone, rising to 1829m. The soil is extremely fertile and very productive, but the volcano has blown 23 times in the last 100 years. It erupted in 1996 and 1997, killing 30 people and wiping out villages. At night the crater glows and spurts orange trailers into the sky. There is a seismological observatory on the side of the cone. Manam erupted twice again in late 2004 causing the rapid evacuation of the island's 9000 people. It remains one of the world's most active volcanoes.

Manam is 193km from Madang and not easy to get to. Government and private boats leave Bogia for Manam most days, although there is no schedule.

The Highlands

CONTENTS

THE HIGHLANDS

This was the last part of the country to be explored by Europeans – and not until the 1930s. The prevailing theory was that Papua New Guinea's centre was a tangle of largely unpopulated mountains, and it was quite a shock when the populated valleys, stretching across the country, were discovered. It was a shock too for the Highlanders, who thought that the white-skinned people were returning spirits of dead ancestors. It was not until the 1950s and '60s that the Highlands really started to open up.

Today, the region is a dynamic part of PNG and a unique part of Melanesia. Its people's lives are changing quickly, but many aspects of their traditional cultures remain, particularly their social organisation. Clan and tribal loyalties are still very strong. It's possible to see *singsings* (celebratory dance/festival) where warriors dance wearing ostentatious traditional dress, but mostly, especially in towns, the people wear Western clothes – commonly *sekonhan klos* (second-hand clothes). Highlanders are proud people with a strong sense of style and walk with a strut. They are perhaps the most recently 'modernised' people in the world.

The Highlands – dramatic and beautiful, with wide, fertile valleys, streams and rivers, and seemingly endless, saw-toothed mountains – is the most densely populated and agriculturally productive region of PNG. It's divided into five provinces – Eastern Highlands (around Goroka), Simbu (pronounced *chim*-bu, around Kundiawa), Western Highlands (around Mt Hagen), Enga (around Wabag) and Southern Highlands (around Mendi).

The region has the county's most extensive road system, half-a-dozen major towns and a growing cash economy based on coffee and tea. Gold and copper mining has brought wealth to some areas, as well as rapid change to the traditional lifestyles of some very remote people. But, as elsewhere, pigs and gardening remain the two most important things in life. Tribal fighting is a popular pastime.

HIGHLIGHTS

- Travelling along the stunning **Highlands Hwy** (p113)
- Climbing **Mt Wilhelm** (p119) and seeing the north and south coasts
- Experiencing thousands of performers singing and dancing at the **Goroka Show** (p116)
- Meeting **Huli wigmen** (p130) in the Tari Basin area and **Asaro mud men** (p117) near Goroka
- Visiting magnificent **Lake Kutubu** (p127) and the **Wasi Falls** (p129), PNG's highest

▦ LAND AREA: 62,500 SQ KM	▦ POPULATION: 1,971,400

History

Kuk Swamp, in the Wahgi Valley (Western Highlands Province), has evidence of 20,000 years of human habitation. Gardening began 9000 years ago, which makes Papua New Guineans among the world's first farmers.

In 1930 Mick Leahy and Mick Dwyer came to the Highlands searching for gold, after gold rushes in Wau and Bulolo. To their surprise they walked into the previously undiscovered Eastern Highlands.

In 1933 Leahy returned with his brother Dan and they stumbled upon the huge, fertile and heavily populated Wahgi Valley. After aerial reconnaissance, they walked in with a large, well-supplied patrol.

Missionaries followed and government stations near present-day Mt Hagen and in the Simbu Valley, near present-day Kundiawa were built. The first patrol built an airstrip at Mt Hagen. However, gold was never found in great quantities.

The documentary *First Contact* includes original footage by Mick Leahy and is a priceless record of the first interaction between Highlanders and Europeans (see p28).

Not until the 1950s were changes felt and many areas remained largely unaffected until the 1960s and '70s. The construction of the Highlands Hwy had a huge impact, as did the introduction of cash crops, particularly coffee. The Highlanders had long been traders and skilful gardeners, and adapted to the cash economy with remarkable speed.

The dense population and cultural differences have caused some problems, however. Ritual warfare was an integral part of Highlands life and to this day payback feuds and land disputes can erupt into major conflicts – Highlanders are volatile and passionate people.

Geography & Climate

The Highlands are made up of a series of valleys and rugged intervening mountains that form the watershed for some of the world's largest rivers (the Ramu, Sepik, Strickland, Fly and Purari). The mountains are a central spine running the length of the island. Several Highlands mountains exceed 4000m in height, and Mt Wilhelm, PNG's highest, is 4509m.

Nights can be darn cold, particularly at altitude, but daytime temperatures are very pleasant, about 24° to 28°C – 'perpetual

MOGAS

The most vivid demonstrations of wealth and status are the *moga* ceremonies near Mendi (*tee* ceremonies in Enga Province). *Mogas* are movable feasts – during some, hundreds of pigs are slaughtered and cooked. Each clan attempts to surpass its neighbours by feasting on as many pigs as possible. A big pig is worth K500 to K1000.

These ceremonies flow from village to village, with one group displaying its wealth and handing the *moga* ceremony on to the next village. Even enemies are invited.

There are ceremonial grounds where these feasts are held along the road past Mendi – fenced quadrangles, sometimes covering half a hectare, surrounded by long houses (guest quarters) and long pits in straight lines filled with cooking stones.

springtime', as it is said. In the mountains, late-afternoon mists can drift in and billowing clouds can suddenly advance and envelope everything – it's quite wonderful. The dry season is May to November for this region, and rains can be very heavy in the wet season.

Culture

Wealth is essential in establishing status, and *bigmen* (leaders) are invariably affluent. Ceremonial life in the Highlands is centred around ostentatious displays of wealth, which is part of a wide circle of exchange and interclan relationships, where gifts cement a relationship with the receiver, who then has obligations. Obligation and pay back are deadly serious in Highlands culture.

Pay back is common and disputes over women, land and pigs are often settled by financial negotiations. Pay back can be levied against a clan for crimes done by an individual – the clan is responsible for its people – so if a murder is committed, someone from the murderer's clan might be killed in revenge. Even today when negotiations break down the clans start fighting.

Try to see a Highlands *singsing* – the costumes alone rival Rio de Janeiro at Carnivale time and the bedecked marchers of Sydney's Gay and Lesbian Mardi Gras. *Singsings* can happen for all sorts of reasons and they are always spectacular. Highlanders in traditional costume and face paint dancing in formation and playing their *kundu* drums (an hourglass-shaped drum with lizard skin) are really quite a sight. The Goroka and Hagen shows are annual events that bring together thousands of performers. The Highlands shows wax and wane a bit, but bring about 500 tourists and thousands and thousands of bedecked Highlanders and performers from all over PNG.

Highlands people are skilled farmers and take pride in their decorative gardens. They grow sweet potato in neat mounds about 1.5m in diameter. The mounds are fertilised with ashes and are very productive.

Body art and personal decoration in the Highlands are particularly refined and incredible to look at. In PNG this is called *bilas,* and where Sepiks and others developed powerful carved arts and artefact manufacture, the Highlanders turned their creative energies mostly on themselves.

The Highlands is a 'dry region', that is alcohol cannot be purchased outside licensed premises – hotels, clubs and resorts. However, there's a booming black market in beer and all of PNG has a problem with wickedly strong home-brewed alcohol and violence.

Dangers & Annoyances

Parts of the PNG Highlands are genuinely high. You should give yourself a few days acclimatisation at lower altitudes before taking on any serious mountain climbing or anything else that's too physical. This is truer the higher you go. If you're planning on climbing Mt Wilhelm or trekking to bird-watching sights in the mountains there is detailed information about mountain sickness, or AMS, on p252.

Bus travel through the Highlands is not nearly as dangerous as the expat community will lead you to believe, but there is an element of risk. Very occasionally there are hold-ups, buses are ambushed and the passengers are robbed. Buses travelling west of Mt Hagen towards Mendi have had the most recent incidents. Seek advice from locals (hotel staff) in each town before heading off to the next in a PMV.

HIGHLANDS PROVINCES

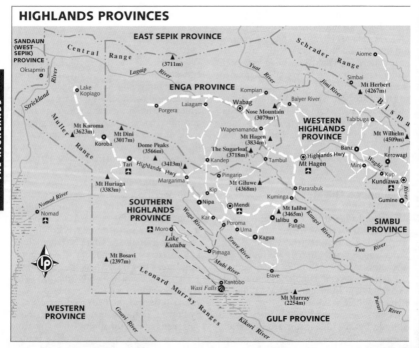

Getting There & Around
AIR
Air Niugini and Airlink have regular connections between Goroka, Mt Hagen, Wewak, Madang, Lae and Port Moresby. MAF (Mission Aviation Fellowship), based in Mt Hagen, has very interesting connections all over the Highlands – the Baiyer River and Jimi Valley areas, and Telefomin and Kawito.

ROAD TRAVEL
The most important road in PNG starts in Lae and runs up into the central Highlands. Where the highway ends depends on your definition. As a decent road, it now continues to Tari, in rougher condition to Koroba and in still rougher condition to Lake Kopiago. The highway is sealed as far as Mt Hagen and, in parts, between Mt Hagen, Mendi and Wabag. New branches off the main road are being developed, although their condition varies widely.

The road up from Madang joins the Highlands Hwy just east of Watarais. Past Goroka the road continues through the

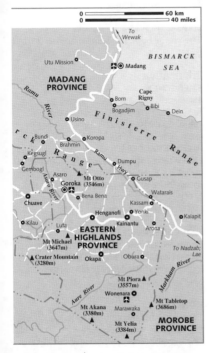

> **DARTS**
>
> Darts is serious business in the Highlands and great fortunes are won and lost on a single throw. Men play darts at roadside 'clubs' where a dozen dartboards are fixed to posts sticking out of the ground. The rules are more or less the same as for regular darts, but you stand a lot further away – Highlands darts is something between regular darts and javelin throwing. Sometimes you can see men in traditional costume playing at village darts clubs.

valley to Asaro, then climbs steeply to the high Daulo Pass (2450m), about 25km from Goroka. It continues twisting and turning to Kundiawa, the midpoint between Goroka and Mt Hagen.

Then the road descends into the Wahgi Valley and to Mt Hagen. Between Mt Hagen and Mendi the road is spectacular; you skirt Mt Giluwe, PNG's second-highest mountain at 4368m, and go through some beautiful valleys. After Mendi you pass ceremonial grounds, a suspension bridge over the Lai River and travel through the stunning Poroma Valley. After Poroma you climb the 2900m pass overlooking the wide and fertile Tari Basin. The road deteriorates after Tari.

A fork in the road after Mt Hagen goes to Wabag, and this stretch has some incredibly jagged mountains and fierce rivers. A reasonable road runs north from Mt Hagen through the spectacular Baiyer Gorge to Baiyer River and a good road branches off the Mendi road and continues on to Wabag and Porgera. From Wabag, there's a loop through Laiagam to Kandep and down to Mendi. It may not be passable because of washed-out bridges and slides. There's a breathtakingly precarious road north from Kundiawa to Kegsugl on the way to Mt Wilhelm.

Car
You can drive yourself, but you'll pay a premium for a hire car and it will have to be a 4WD. Rental firms often have restrictions on remote-area use, which particularly applies to the Highlands. The same risks apply to car travel as to bus travel – at least in a bus you're with other people.

THE HIGHLANDS

PMV

PMVs travel from the coast as far as Goroka and Mt Hagen is safe, easy and cheap. It's also incredible country to drive through. Buses don't go anywhere unless they're packed to the brim, so expect a squeeze.

PMVs only run in daylight hours and it's best to get an early one so you're not wandering around the Highlands towns at night looking for accommodation. Catch buses at the main market area and normally they drop you at the market area of the next town, although the driver will often take you to your place of stay if you ask politely.

WALKING

You can walk into the Highlands from Madang, although it's easier to walk downhill from the Highlands to Madang. You need to take a guide and be well prepared and provisioned. There's a vast network of tracks through the Highlands, but the trekking can be hard. For guides, contact **Madang Visitors & Cultural Bureau** (☎ 852 3302; fax 852 3540; Modilon Rd, Madang), or **Trans Niugini Tours** (☎ 675-542 1438; www.pngtours.com; Mt Hagen).

EASTERN HIGHLANDS PROVINCE

Eastern Highlands Province has had longer contact with the West than other part of the Highlands, and its people have abandoned traditional dress for day-to-day use. Although the province is heavily populated, the Eastern Highlanders are a less cohesive group than people in other parts of the Highlands.

Villages have neat clusters of low-walled round huts. The design includes two peaks to the roof, each with a tuft of grass, one from the owner's area and the other from a neighbouring area. These tufts talk to each other in the night, so you can hear your neighbour's secrets.

The mountains of this province form the headwaters for two of PNG's most important river systems: the Ramu River, which runs parallel to the coast to the northwest, and the Wahgi and Aure Rivers, which run south and enter the Gulf of Papua as the Purari River. The province's highest point is Mt Michael at 3647m. Most of the population lives at altitudes between 1500m and 2300m.

GOROKA

Goroka has grown from a small outpost in the mid-1950s to being a major commercial centre, and the main town in Eastern Highlands Province. It's still a typical PNG town, clustered around the airstrip, but it's also one of the country's most attractive – a green, shady, well-organised place with decent shopping, transport and facilities. Goroka is the centre of PNG's coffee industry.

The town is small enough to walk around and it's more relaxed than Mt Hagen. There are a few old colonial houses with spacious verandas and gardens on McNicholl St.

At an altitude of 1600m, Goroka's climate is springtime (warm days and cool nights). Temperatures can be 10°C at night, usually in the May–November dry season.

Orientation

Most of Goroka's places of interest are clustered around the northern end of the airport, although there are a few places to stay and a tiny museum in the streets on the airport's western flank. Town PMVs run up and down the stretch of main road, Edwards Rd (Highlands Hwy).

MAPS

The phone book has some maps in its front pages.

Information

EMERGENCY

Ambulance (☎ 732 1166)
Fire (☎ 732 1111/3) Near the airport terminal.
Police (☎ 732 1443; Elizabeth St)

INTERNET ACCESS

Hotels have Internet-enabled computers for about K30 per 30 minutes.
Harma Office Supplies (☎ 732 1966; Fox St; per 15 min K10.50) There's just one machine and modem connections are slow in PNG. Located above Westpac.

MEDICAL SERVICES

There are several pharmacies in town.
Goroka Hospital (☎ 731 2100; Leigh Vial St) Goroka's hospital is one of the best in the country and houses the PNG Institute of Medical Research.

MONEY

Travellers cheques can be cashed at the bigger hotels as well as banks – compare rates. The bigger hotels accept major credit cards.

ANZ (☎ 732 2021; Elizabeth St) ANZ has ATMs.
Bank South Pacific (☎ 732 1633; Parer St) There are ATMs in a booth and a foreign-exchange desk inside.
Westpac (☎ 732 1140; Fox St) Doesn't have ATMs.

POST
Post Office (☎ 732 2470; Elizabeth St; ⏱ 8.30am-5pm)

TELEPHONE
There are Telikad prepaid public phones near the post office and at hotel foyers.

Sights
RAUN RAUN THEATRE
Raun Raun Theatre is Goroka's acclaimed theatre group, and has toured nationally and internationally. The **theatre** (☎ 732 1116; Wisdom St) is a superb building, which blends traditional materials and modern architecture. It's located on parkland about 500m due north of the post office. Performances are irregular, but you might get lucky. The building is used annually for the Goroka Show.

JK MCCARTHY MUSEUM
JK McCarthy was one of PNG's legendary patrol officers and wrote one of the classic books on New Guinea patrolling – *Patrol into Yesterday*. The **museum** (admission by donation; ⏱ 8am-noon & 1-4pm Mon-Fri, 2-4pm Sat, 10am-noon Sun) is not far from the National Sports Institute, near the corner of Makinono and Morchhauser Sts, but a long walk from the town centre. It's small but worth visiting.

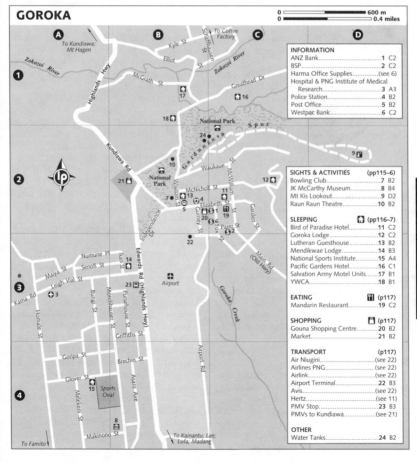

GOROKA

0 ─────── 600 m
0 ─────── 0.4 miles

THE HIGHLANDS

Among the exhibits are pottery, weapons, clothes and musical instruments, even some grisly jewellery – necklaces of human fingers! There's a fascinating collection of photos, many taken by Mick Leahy when he first reached the area in 1933. There are WWII relics, including a P-39 Aircobra.

MT KIS LOOKOUT

Wisdom St, beside the post office, leads to a track that climbs to an excellent lookout, Mt Kis, so-called because it's the lovers' leap of Goroka. It's a long, steep walk. There are two large water tanks halfway there, and a ladder you can climb to catch spectacular views of the distant valleys through the pine trees and the Highlands mist. It's well worth the effort.

Tours

Samuel Lulu of **PNG High Country Tours** (☎ 732 1682; fax 732 1394) runs tours and treks around the jungles and caves of the Eastern Highlands and out towards Chimbu. He offers village accommodation in the Namasaro Unggai district west of Goroka.

Festivals & Events

The **Goroka Show** (adult per day/3 days K100/200, child aged 10-16 per day/3 days K50/100, child aged under 10 free), the best of the Highlands shows, is held over the Independence Day weekend (mid-September) annually. It attracts more *singsing* groups than Mt Hagen's show and there are also bands and other cultural activities, as well as some elements of an agricultural show. It's an extraordinary event and attracts more international visitors to PNG than any other – Goroka Show is the glamour event on the social calendar for performers from all over the country. The show runs over three days.

The **PNG Coffee Festival** (adult/child K4/free) is usually held over the first weekend in May and features *singsing* groups, contemporary music, art exhibitions, a trade fair and formal coffee ball at the Raun Raun Theatre.

Sleeping & Eating

There's a good range of accommodation options, from budget rooms to high-end suites. Eating options outside the hotels are few.

Accommodation in Goroka becomes very scarce around show time and prices go way up – expect them to double during the show. Make your arrangements early. Many places are booked out months in advance. Local people offer rooms in their houses during show time for around K90 per night – contact **Norman Carver** (☎ 732 1602; png.gold@global.net .pg) at PNG Highland Tours for more information about billeted accommodation.

National Sports Institute (☎ 732 2391; natspo in@daltron.com.pg; Glover St, s/d K39/77) This is a good budget option, although it's out of the way. There are 92 single rooms and six doubles. Bathroom and kitchen facilities are shared. It's like a university dorm and has a gym, cafeteria and conference facilities – rates are cheaper for sporting groups, church affiliates, students and volunteers.

Lutheran Guesthouse (☎ 732 1516; McNicholl St; s incl breakfast K50) Right in the centre of town behind the post office. Clean and straight, the two-storey house has shared rooms and facilities.

Salvation Army Motel Units (☎ 732 1218; Mc-Grath St; s/d K70/90) The units are a bit run-down, but they're OK, each with a stove, fridge and attached bathroom. The bigger rooms sleep four.

Goroka Lodge (☎ 732 2411; McNicholl St; s K80-147, d K107-173) At the foot of Mt Kis, it's a bit grungy, but the better self-contained rooms are OK. The cheapest rooms have shared facilities and meals are available.

Mendikwae Lodge (☎ 732 3466; Ikani St; up to 4 guests K150) In west Goroka, with self-contained units with two rooms, a double bed in one, two singles in the other, kitchen with utensils and TV. Good choice for a group or family.

Pacific Gardens Hotel (☎ 732 3418; Mokara St; s K130-170, d K150-230; 🖳) In the grounds of an expats' residential estate, 10 minutes' walk from town. The vast, hilly property has lovely lawns and a river runs through it, and the rooms, though small, are comfortable. Highly recommended. There are meals-inclusive rates or you can pay for meals separately – the food's OK but not great.

Bird of Paradise Hotel (☎ 731 3100; www.coral seahotels.com.pg; Elizabeth St; s & d K205-400; 🖳 📠) 'The Bird', as it's known, is pretty swanky, and part of the Coral Sea chain in the centre of town. All the rooms are large, comfortable and the Bird has first-class facilities, including bars and a gym. The **restaurant** (meals K22-45; ✾ 6.30am-midnight) is the best place to eat in town with à la carte and shifting buffet menus.

Mandarin Restaurant (☎ 732 2999; Elizabeth St; meals K20-40; ⏰ 11am-11pm) Opposite the Bird, the Mandarin serves good Chinese food.

The market sells an array of fresh fruit and vegetables, peanuts and probably a *cuscus* (possum) or two.

Shopping

There are several supermarkets and stores in town.

Goroka has very good artefacts – Bukaware, spears, bows and arrows, masks, and, naturally, hats and *bilums* (string bags). The market sells some, but most sellers congregate around the Bird and the provisional government building on Elizabeth St.

The **market** (⏰ closed Sun) is interesting to walk through. It's very busy on Saturday, but colourful any day and you'll see piles of potatoes and exotic leafy greens as well as more familiar tomatoes, capsicums and avocados. *Bilums* and Highland hats are sold, as are spools of intensely colourful twines and strings used in *bilum* manufacture. Watch for pickpockets.

Getting There & Around

AIR

Goroka airport has daily services to destinations all over the country. **Air Niugini** (☎ 732 1444), **Airlink** (☎ 732 2879) and **Airlines PNG** (☎ 732 2879) are represented at the airport. Sample one-way full fares include Port Moresby (K352), Madang (K648) and Lae (K545).

CAR & PMV

The highway is in good condition around Goroka and it's an easy trip to Mt Hagen and beyond to the west, and down to Kainantu, Lae and Madang to the east.

Hire cars are available from **Hertz** (☎ 732 1710; Bird of Paradise Hotel, Elizabeth St) and **Avis** (☎ 732 1084; Goroka airport), but you'll pay a fortune for one.

PMVs heading west gather at the market area early in the morning, but more leave as the day wears on.

AROUND GOROKA
Famito

The beautiful Famito Valley is 10km south of Goroka. A rough road leads in through pretty villages and coffee plantations. There is a nine-hole golf course and the clubhouse has panoramic views.

Mt Gahavisuka Provincial Park

This 80-hectare area is set in beautiful mountain surrounds. Eleven kilometres from Goroka and 1000m higher, the **park** (admission free) is reached by 4WD and includes a botanical sanctuary, walking tracks and a lookout at 2450m with incredible views. There are picnic shelters, two orchid houses and an information centre.

Crater Mountain Wildlife Management Area

In the tri-border area, where the Eastern Highlands, Simbu and Gulf provincial borders meet, is the Crater Mountain Wildlife Management Area. This is one of the best places in PNG to experience the spectacular countryside, the wildlife and the village culture.

The area encompasses 2700 sq km ranging from lowland rainforests on the Purari River to forests on the slopes of Crater Mountain. You can hike between the various villages, but it's serious trekking. There are three villages with basic **guesthouses** (c/- Research & Conservation Foundation ☎ 732 3211; per person K11) that provide beds (bring your own linen) and kerosene stoves. You must bring your own food. The Research & Conservation Foundation in Goroka can radio each village and make arrangements, and help you organise a charter flight with **MAF** (☎ 732 1080) or **Pacific Helicopters** (☎ 732 1833). Flight costs vary depending on routes and number of passengers. Guides can be hired for K30 per day.

Daulo Pass

The road out to Mt Hagen is fairly flat through Asaro, but it then hairpins its way up to 2450m Daulo Pass. The pass is cold and damp but the views are spectacular.

ASARO MUD MEN

Asaro village, northwest of Goroka, is famous for its mud men – warriors who traditionally covered themselves in grey mud and wore huge mud masks before heading off on raids. It's a very striking image, and the Asaro men recreate the scene for tourists, but it's often rather contrived. Mud-men tours can be arranged by tour operators in the region.

KAINANTU

The major town between Lae and Goroka, Kainantu is an important cattle and coffee-production region. Work has started on a major gold mine in the area. The small town, 210km from Lae and 80km from Goroka, is strung along the highway. At 1600m, evenings can be cool. Telephone services to Kainantu can be unreliable.

There's a **cultural centre** (8am-4.30pm Mon-Fri, 9am-4pm Sat & Sun) on the highway, and it's worth visiting. It sells traditional pottery, hand-woven rugs, silk-screen prints and flutes, and there's a small museum.

Kainantu Lodge (☎ 737 1020; mobilekkb@global.net.pg; s with shared facilities K80, s & d K180-200; 🖳 🕾) is on a hill overlooking town. A 20-minute walk from the PMV stop, the lodge is signposted and a very nice place to stay with a bar and à la carte **restaurant** (meals K24-30), and a crackling log fire at night. There's also a tennis court. It's peaceful and pleasant and offers a free shuttle to/from Goroka airport (two-hour drive).

PMVs from Lae to Kainantu cost K15 and take three hours; from Kainantu to Goroka they cost K10 and take about two hours.

KURU

Kuru was a disease unique to the Fore area southwest of Kainantu. Attacking the central nervous system, the disease persisted in the body for a year before causing death. Dubbed 'the laughing disease', its victims died with a peculiar smile on their faces. It only affected one language group and was limited to women and children. It is known to have existed since the early 1900s, but reached epidemic proportions in the 1950s when over 200 cases were reported. Years of epidemiological research by Goroka's PNG Institute of Medical Research finally solved the riddle of the disease's cause.

Kuru was linked to diet and feasting behaviour; specifically it was caused by the ritualised cannibalism of the brain tissue of dead clan members by women and children. Kuru is said to be linked to mad cow disease.

Due to changed dietary and ritual behaviour, there's only been a handful of cases in recent years, the last reported in 1997.

AROUND KAINANTU
Ukarumpa

Ukarumpa is the PNG headquarters of the American-founded Summer Institute of Linguistics (see the boxed text, opposite). It's in the Aiyura Valley, about 30 minutes by PMV from Kainantu and is worth visiting to see 'little America' in the midst of PNG.

Yonki & the Upper Ramu Project

Yonki, 23km from Kainantu, is the support town for the Upper Ramu hydro-electric project. Commissioned in 1979, the project was financed by a K23 million World Bank loan and powers Lae, Madang and the Highlands.

SIMBU PROVINCE

West of Goroka, Simbu's mountains are much more rugged and steep, and the valleys are smaller and less accessible. Some of PNG's highest mountains are in this region, including Mt Wilhelm, at 4509m the highest of them all. There are vast limestone caves near Kundiawa and Chuave.

Simbu (pronounced '*chim*-bu', and sometimes spelt that way) derived its name when the first patrol officers gave steel axes and knives to the tribespeople, who replied 'simbu' – very pleased. Despite its rugged terrain it's the second most heavily populated region in PNG. The people have turned their steep country into a patchwork of gardens spreading up every available hillside. Population pressures are pushing them to even higher ground, threatening remaining forests and bird of paradise habitats. As in Enga Province, most people speak a similar language – Simbu dialects make up the PNG's second-largest language group.

Simbus are said to be avid capitalists who watch their coffee profits, and strong believers in pay back – minor warfare is still common around Simbu and there's a pervading eye-for-an-eye ethos. Kundiawa has a painted signboard at the police station that depicts a tribal battle.

KUNDIAWA

Kundiawa was the site of the Highlands' first government station, but has been left behind by Goroka and Mt Hagen. Although it's the provincial capital, Kundiawa is pretty small. There's a bank, post office, limited shopping, and that's about it. Most people go straight through to Mt Wilhelm, Goroka or Mt Hagen.

There's spectacular rafting on the Wahgi River near Kundiawa, but no operators are currently offering it, due, as usual, to land disputes. The scenery is excellent – the river goes through deep chasms, under rope bridges and there are rapids and waterfalls.

Caves around Kundiawa were used as burial places. At the time of research, it wasn't clear whether a local guide could take you there. Don't visit the caves without consulting local advice as it might be *tambu* (taboo). Other large caves, suitable for caving, are close to Kundiawa, while the **Keu Caves** are very close to the main road near Chuave. The **Nambaiyufa Amphitheatre**, near Chuave, has rock paintings.

Sleeping & Eating
Kundiawa Hotel (☎ 735 1399; fax 735 1103; s K170) The hotel doesn't have much competition. It's expensive, a bit run-down, although the tariff includes breakfast and dinner, free laundry and airport transfers.

Simbu Premier Motel (☎ 735 1002; s K110) Might be a better alternative.

Haus Kai Bilong ol Meri is the best place to eat for lunch – it has good food and a shady place to sit.

Getting There & Away
AIR
The airport is quite spectacular, on a sloping ridge surrounded by mountains. **Air Niugini** (☎ 735 1273) has flights to/from Port Moresby (K375) on Tuesday and Saturday.

PMV
The fare to Goroka is K10, to Mt Hagen K8 and Kegsugl (for Mt Wilhelm) K10; each of these sectors can take two hours. The Kegsugl road might be closed for a day or two each week in the wet season (October to March) for road clearing, for which locals can charge road users a 'levy'. PMVs for Kegsugl leave from the Shell station, others stop on the highway near the police station.

MT WILHELM
For many, climbing to the 4509m summit of Mt Wilhelm is the highlight of their visit to PNG. On a clear day, you can see both

SUMMER INSTITUTE OF LINGUISTICS (SIL)

The SIL is a missionary organisation that aims to translate the Bible into every language in the world. Given the extraordinary number of languages in PNG – 867 distinct languages at last count – SIL has a lot of work to do here.

Whatever the motive, the fact is that SIL has made an incredible record of PNG languages, their distribution, numbers of speakers and the like. This is particularly important, as some languages are dying out.

SIL's translator-missionaries, who are usually husband-and-wife teams, typically spend 15 to 20 years in a remote village, learning the language, developing a written alphabet and translating the Bible. The institute is working on 185 languages and has completed translations for 94.

SIL publishes Ethnologue (www.ethnologue.com) which is a comprehensive worldwide languages standard.

the north and south coasts of PNG. Even if you don't intend to tackle the summit, the region around the base offers fantastic walking and dramatic landscapes.

Niglguma and **Gembogl**, both traditional high-altitude villages, are worth visiting – you can walk to Gembogl from Kegsugl in a couple of hours and, on the way, you pass through half-a-dozen villages, including Niglguma.

Climbing the Mountain
PLANNING
While not technically difficult, this popular climb is hard work. Preparation is important and the dangers should not be underestimated. Climbers in this region have died. Don't try to climb the mountain on your own no matter how fit you are – a guide is essential. The final ascent starts in the black of early morning to see the dawn and both coasts before the clouds roll in, and the tracks are not visible in the dark.

If the weather is fine, the climb takes three or four days, but frequently the weather is too bad so take a book to read in the huts. The April–October dry season for this area is the best time to climb and there are several ways to do it. **PNG Highland**

Tours (☎ 732 1602) and **Trans Niugini Tours** (☎ 542 1438; Mt Hagen) can organise guides, porters, equipment and food. Or you can hire your own guide in Kegsugl or from Betty's Place (below).

If you've just come up from the coast, allow yourself time to acclimatise to the altitude before climbing (see p252).

It can get very cold on top and can easily become fogbound, and even snow. Sunburn and hypothermia are also hazards. You need sufficient food, equipment and warm clothing, water containers (there's no water past the lakes), a torch, gloves and candles. Cooking gear might be useful – check in Kegsugl whether there are still utensils at the lake huts.

THE CLIMB
The climb goes up to the Pindaunde Lakes from the high school and disused airstrip at Kegsugl. The lakes sit at 3500m and it can get very cold here, but the views are incredible. There are National Parks Board huts at the lakes. You might be offered strawberries, as a kind gesture by locals, on the first stretch of the walk. European fruits and vegetables – strawberries, cabbages, cauliflower and broccoli – grow year-round in the constant spring conditions of these climes.

From the Pindaunde Lakes, it's a long, hard walk to the summit – about five hours. Some say it's better to spend a day acclimatising at the lake huts and exploring the area before attempting the summit – this is wise. It can become very cold, wet, windy and foggy at the top. Clouds roll in after dawn so summit climbers start out as early as 1am. The descent back to the huts at the lakes takes about three hours, but some people go all the way back to Kegsugl, a further 2½ hours from the lakes.

Sleeping
Betty's Place (radio ☎ 0561145 112037; fax 0561145 212037; s with/without meals K90/K60) Also known as Lake Pindi Yaundo Lodge, this is about 1km from Kegsugl, near the start of the trail. It's a lovely place situated on a ridge with superb views out over the valley. Electricity is provided by generator, but it's surprisingly comfortable, with hot showers and amazing surrounds. There's a trout farm and commercial vegetable gardens, and the meals at Betty's are splendid.

Getting There & Away
Kegsugl is 57km from Kundiawa along a razorback road that has to be seen to be believed. PMVs from Kundiawa cost K10 and take a couple of hours. They leave from the Shell service station. If you leave Goroka or Mt Hagen early in the morning, you can reach Pindaunde Lakes in one day, spend an extra day acclimatising and avoid overnighting in Kundiawa. Alternatively, stay at Betty's Place. There's an airstrip at Kegsugl, which can only cater for smaller charter aircraft like the MAF fleet, although it routinely falls into disrepair.

WALKING TO MADANG
You can walk to Madang, but it's unwise to go without a guide. The turn-off for the Bundi road and the trek to Brahmin (and Madang) is between Gembogl and Kegsugl. You can walk right down to Madang – but most people catch a PMV at Brahmin. A relatively easy route goes through **Pandambai** and **Bundikara** to **Bundi**, where there's a guesthouse called the Mt Sinai Centre (see p107). From Bundi the route goes to the **Brahmin Mission**, from where a PMV to Madang costs K10 and takes 1½ hours. The whole route takes three or four days. To arrange for a guide, contact **PNG Highland Tours** (☎ 732 1602) or **Trans Niugini Tours** (☎ 542 1438; Mt Hagen).

WESTERN HIGHLANDS PROVINCE

West of Simbu Province is the 80km-long Wahgi Valley, one of the most productive agricultural areas in the country. Mt Hagen, the capital, really is the frontier of a group of wild and undeveloped regions further to its west. Across the province the terrain varies between swamps in the lower Jimi Valley (370m) and high peaks, including Mt Hagen (3834m). Forest only remains on the steepest slopes, while the valleys and lower hills are grassland – bare from slash-and-burn cultivation. Gardens and stands of casuarinas are scattered through the hills and large coffee plantations dominate the most fertile valley floors.

Men are usually bearded and their traditional clothing includes a wide belt of beaten bark with a drape of strings in front and a rear covered by a bunch of leaves attached to a belt. The leaves are known collectively as *tanket* or *arsegras*. Women are traditionally dressed in string skirts and cuscus fur hanging around their necks. Today, in major towns, such attire is now reserved for *singsings* and political rallies, and Western dress is preferred for everyday wear. However, traditional dress is still common in more remote towns and villages. At *singsings* men and women are bedecked in beautiful headdresses with bird of paradise plumes. Highlanders have a keen sense of style.

Wahgi people tend vegetable gardens and neat villages, paths with decoratively planted flowers, parks, groves of trees and memorials to deceased *bigmen*. *Singsings* are still an integral part of life – make every effort to see one.

MT HAGEN

Despite its environs, Mt Hagen is not nearly as attractive as Goroka. It's PNG's third biggest city, lying 445km from Lae and 115km from Goroka. 'Hagen', as it's often called, was a patrol station before WWII, and has boomed in the last 30 years, as Enga and the Southern Highlands have opened up. Now it's an unruly city with major squatter settlements and many itinerant people. As in Lae and Port Moresby, Hagen's streets are packed with people.

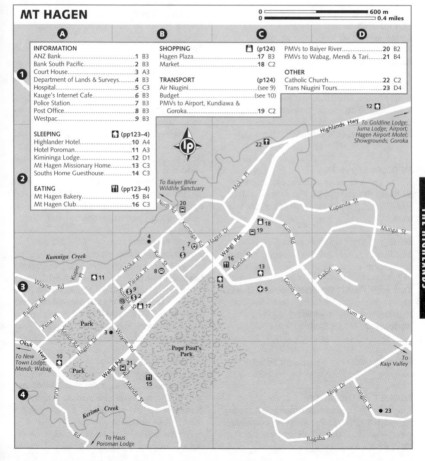

MT HAGEN

0 — 600 m
0 — 0.4 miles

INFORMATION		
ANZ Bank	1	B3
Bank South Pacific	2	B3
Court House	3	A3
Department of Lands & Surveys	4	B3
Hospital	5	C3
Kauge's Internet Cafe	6	B3
Police Station	7	B3
Post Office	8	B3
Westpac	9	B3

SLEEPING	(pp123–4)	
Highlander Hotel	10	A4
Hotel Poroman	11	A3
Kimininga Lodge	12	D1
Mt Hagen Missionary Home	13	C3
Souths Home Guesthouse	14	C3

EATING	(pp123–4)	
Mt Hagen Bakery	15	B4
Mt Hagen Club	16	C3

SHOPPING	(p124)	
Hagen Plaza	17	B3
Market	18	C2

TRANSPORT	(p124)	
Air Niugini	(see 9)	
Budget	(see 10)	
PMVs to Airport, Kundiawa & Goroka	19	C2

PMVs to Baiyer River	20	B2
PMVs to Wabag, Mendi & Tari	21	B4

OTHER		
Catholic Church	22	C2
Trans Niugini Tours	23	D4

THE HIGHLANDS

The city's ambience can vary from the usual PNG relaxed vibe to periods of heavy tension during elections or interclan disputes – there's a 'wild west' feel.

Mt Hagen's main blocks are built around three parallel streets: Moka Pl, Hagen Dr and Wahgi Pde. The Highlander, Hagen's flash hotel, is at one end, and the market is at the other. There are a few parks and large residential neighbourhoods outside the centre.

Maps

The phone directory has an excellent Mt Hagen map in its front pages. The **Department of Lands & Surveys** (Kuri St) can supply town maps and some regional maps.

Information

EMERGENCY
Ambulance (☎ 542 1166)
Fire (☎ 542 1311/5)
Police (☎ 542 1233; Kumniga St)

INTERNET ACCESS
Major hotels have Internet access for about K30 per 30 minutes (sometimes free for guests).
Kauge's Internet Cafe (Romba St; per 15 min K12) Opposite the two banks.

MEDICAL SERVICES
There are several pharmacies in town.
Mt Hagen Hospital (☎ 542 1166; Kumniga Rd) The *haus sik* (hospital) borders Pope Paul's Park near the town centre.

MONEY
The bigger hotels change travellers cheques and accept most major credit cards.
ANZ (☎ 542 1220; Hagen Dr) Has an ATM lobby.
Bank South Pacific (☎ 542 1877; Romba St) Changes travellers cheques for a K50 flat fee. It has an ATM lobby across the street behind Hagen Plaza.
Westpac (☎ 542 1056; Romba St) No ATMs.

POST
Post office (☎ 542 1270; Hagen Dr) In the middle of town.

TOURIST INFORMATION
There's no formal tourist office in Mt Hagen, although it's home to several tour companies (see right), and the hotels and guesthouses can provide good local information.

Dangers & Annoyances

Aside from *raskols* (bandits), tribal warfare can break out over coffee production, land disputes, pigs or gardens. Clan warfare never embroils outsiders, confining itself to the protagonists, but it can make things unstable and unpredictable. During the day, Mt Hagen is perfectly safe. Nobody hassles or asks for money, but the town is thronged with security guards and dogs around banks and shops. Walking the streets and exploring the shops is quite safe. It's not, however, safe at night and the market area is rife with cons and pickpockets. Although the Highlands are a 'dry' region, home-brew alcohol is increasingly a problem. Crime can be quite brazen in Mt Hagen but if you're mindful of your belongings and personal safety you'll be fine – Hagen is no more dangerous than Los Angeles or Amsterdam.

Tours

The best parts of Mt Hagen are its surrounds and all the Hagen-based tour companies and hotels offer half- and full-day tours.

Trans Niugini Tours (☎ 542 1438; Kongin St; www.pngtours.com) is one of the main inbound tour companies in PNG, and organises tours and activities across the country. It's well organised, professional and rather expensive, but good value for what it offers.

Paradise Adventure Tours (☎ 542 1696; www.paradisetours.com.pg) is another Hagen-based operation (locally owned) that offers tours, trekking and activities around the Wahgi Valley area.

Haus Poroman Lodge (☎ 542 2250; www.hausporoman.com.pg) offers a range of local tours, village visits and activities, such as **trekking tours** (per person K24) which cost less with more numbers in the group, **half-day vehicle tours** (per person for 2-3 person groups K144), **full-day tours** (per person for 2/3/4 people K419/352/270) with lunch, Asaro mudmen show, musicians and Oma Masalai group included.

Festivals & Events

It's not as big as the Goroka Show, but the **Mt Hagen Show** (adult day/3 days K100/200, child aged 10-16 day/3 days K50/100, child aged under 10 free) is definitely a must-see. It's held annually, on the third weekend of August.

Arrive before 8am to see groups dressing and impromptu performances for those that can't afford a ticket into the main arena. These vigorous performances are powerful, even ribald, compared to the formal stuff dished up in the arena. Contrary to what you might fear, there's not general bird of paradise slaughter just before show time – the feather headdresses and costumes are extremely valuable and rarefied heirlooms, held in village safe houses.

The showground is out of town, beyond the airport.

Many of the tour companies (see opposite) offer packages that include the Mt Hagen Show as part of a broader itinerary.

Sleeping & Eating

Mt Hagen has lots of places to stay suitable for all budgets. Eating options are largely confined to the hotels and guesthouses. Consider also Kumul Adventure Resort Hotel (p126), which is in Enga Province, but closer to Mt Hagen (40 minutes) than Wabag. Be aware that accommodation is scarce and expensive around show time, sometimes booked a year in advance.

Souths Home Guesthouse (☎ 542 2338; Kumniga Rd; s/d K60/80) The double room upstairs has its own kitchen, while singles downstairs might be asked to share.

Mt Hagen Missionary Home (☎ 542 1041; Kumniga Rd; s K70-85) Opposite the hospital, this is friendly and clean. Bathroom and kitchen facilities are shared.

New Town Lodge (☎ 542 2870; Highlands Hwy; s incl transfers K55-75) Slightly out of town towards Mendi, New Town Lodge is about 1km past the Highlander Hotel. A good budget option, there are large self-contained rooms and shared kitchen facilities.

Juma Lodge (☎ 545 1310; fax 545 1368; Highlands Hwy; s/d K70/100) Juma has 10 rooms in a large house, as well as a bar and restaurant. The better rooms are those that are self-contained and are a triple room. It's on the highway out towards the airport.

Goldline Lodge (☎ 542 3333; fax 542 2000; Highlands Hwy; s/d incl breakfast K90/180) Has a bar and restaurant, and a pokies venue and disco on-site. The self-contained rooms are comfortable with TV and minibar. Discounts are offered for stays of three days.

Hagen Airport Motel (☎ 545 1647; mmakap@online .net.pg; Highlands Hwy; s & d K132) This place, near the airport, has 20 rooms all with en suite and TV. It's a very clean and friendly place

with a **restaurant** (meals K20-35). It's also an 'alcohol-free zone'.

Hotel Poroman (☎ 542 1388; hausporoman@glo bal.net.pg; Moka Pl; s & d incl breakfast K96-175; 💻) Formerly Hagen Park Hotel, this is now managed by the Haus Poroman people and has been tastefully refurbished. The comfortable budget rooms have no TV; deluxe rooms have TV and fridge. There's a bar and excellent **restaurant** (meals K20-40), and tariffs include airport transfers.

Kimininga Lodge (☎ 542 2399; www.wampnga .com.pg/kimininga/INDEX.HTM; Highlands Hwy; s K110-180, d K120-190; 🅱 💻) Run by the local government, Kimininga is towards the airport on the Goroka side of town. Most of its 37 rooms are self-contained with TV and IDD telephone. It's comfortable, if a little plain. There's a licensed **restaurant** (meals K22-46) and offers free airport transfers.

Highlander Hotel (☎ 542 1355; www.coralsea hotels.com.pg; Okuk Hwy; s & d K205-400; 🅱 💻 🅡) The Highlander, part of the Coral Sea chain, is the top address in Mt Hagen, and has all the amenities you'd expect from a first-class hotel, including pool-side restaurants, bars, tennis and volleyball courts and 24-hour foreign-exchange desk. The 60 rooms are all self-contained with satellite TV, phone and fridge. The **Palmuri Restaurant** (meals K25-50) offers fish, chicken and beef dishes, as well as pizzas and burgers, and an all-you-can-eat buffet several nights a week.

Hagen Club (☎ 542 1537; Kuniga Rd) Serves cold beer, good pub-style burgers and light meals.

Shopping

There are some supermarkets and stores. The market is the best place to buy *bilums* and Highland hats, and there are artefacts for sale at hotel gift shops. Years ago, men would come to the market in traditional dress, but not anymore. Hagen's market is one of PNG's biggest and most varied (Saturday is the big day). It's busy each day and thieves work the crowd. They're mostly kids working in tandem – one might distract you while another snatches a bag or wallet.

It's unwise to photograph anyone without asking first and being prepared to pay. If you buy something the seller will happily pose for a photo, but don't thrust cameras into people's faces. The atmosphere in the market can be edgy, and the best way to make friends is to buy stuff.

A vast range of fresh produce is on sale and *bilums* and Highlands hats are cheaper here than anywhere in the country. You'll also see cuscus, pigs and birds trussed up on poles or in enclosures.

The village behind Haus Poroman Lodge has a small gift store that opens on request, and contains excellent *bilums,* hats and traditional costumes and valuables.

Getting There & Around

AIR

The airport is at Kagamuga, about 10km from town. Between them, **Air Niugini** (☎ 542 1444; Romba St) and **Airlink** (☎ 545 1407; Romba St) have flights that connect Mt Hagen to most destinations daily. **MAF** (☎ 545 1506; airport) offers interesting connections from Mt Hagen to all sorts of remote destinations. Sample one-way full fares include Port Moresby (K406), Lae (K600) and Madang (K703).

CAR

Hertz (☎ 545 1522; airport), **Budget** (☎ 542 1355; Highlander Hotel) and **Avis** (☎ 324 9400; airport) are among the hirers in Mt Hagen.

PMV

At the time of research, roads heading west from Mt Hagen towards Mendi were considered unsafe due to bandits and ambushes.

Travel to Wabag by PMV was thought to be relatively safe. Seek advice from your place of accommodation before jumping on a west-bound bus from Mt Hagen.

PMVs going east, to Kundiawa and Goroka, leave from the market. PMVs going west, to Wabag, Mendi and Tari, leave from the highway near the Dunlop building.

PMVs to Wabag cost K10 and take four hours; to Mendi it's K10 and three hours. In the other direction, buses to Kundiawa cost K8 and take two hours; and to Goroka they're K20 and take four hours.

BAIYER RIVER

The 120-hectare Baiyer River wildlife sanctuary is 55km north of Mt Hagen is now quite run-down and unsafe because of *raskol* activity. The sanctuary houses one of the world's largest collection of birds of paradise.

ENGA PROVINCE

Enga is PNG's highest province and its least developed. Despite the extraordinary ruggedness of its terrain, Enga is densely populated. Even other Highlanders refer to Engans as 'mountain people' and many live traditional subsistence lifestyles on incredibly sheer mountainsides.

Porgera, the giant gold and copper mine in the far west, has brought about rapid change for some, but most people still grow cash crops – coffee, pyrethrum and cool-weather European vegetables. Porgera is all but spent, but other nearby mineral finds mean that the mining town will be there a long while yet.

Even in the 1960s, Enga was still largely independent of government control; tribal warfare still occurs today. You might see circular, fenced areas filled with green-and-purple tanget bushes. These are the burial places of victims of tribal fighting.

Wabag is the provincial capital but it's more of an outlying town to Mt Hagen than a major centre. People live in small clans, but the Enga language group – the largest in PNG – covers most of the province. Alcohol is prohibited in Enga and can't even be bought in hotels. Vehicles coming from Mt Hagen are often stopped and searched by police for alcohol and firearms.

Trekking around Enga is superb – Lake Rau is a crater lake at 3000m above sea level.

Laiagam in the west has botanical gardens with more than 100 native orchid species and various types of rhododendrons.

It can get very cold in Enga, so come prepared.

WABAG

People tend to sit around a lot in Wabag – outside houses, by the road, wherever. Life in general is slow in PNG but it is even slower in Wabag. The stores have all the main necessities, but the cost of transport makes things a little expensive.

The town itself has little to attract tourists, except a cultural centre and the mighty Lai River barrelling through town, but the hills around Wabag are stunning – jagged mountains, gushing rivers and picturesque villages nestled in the mountains.

Wabag has a large **cultural centre** (☎ 547 1128; ☻ 8am-4pm theoretically), art gallery, museum and workshop where you can see young artists making sand paintings, the principal work on display. The museum has shields, wigs and masks from many parts of PNG, including Enga Province.

The annual **Enga Festival**, a smaller version of the Mt Hagen and Goroka Shows, is held in August at the sports ground.

Wabag's water and electricity supplies are erratic. The Kaiap village area, high in the hills behind Wabag, is spectacular, with villages and gardens on steep slopes that seem suitable only for mountain goats. Getting up there is hard now that the road has deteriorated and no longer carries PMVs, but it's navigable by 4WD.

Sleeping

Wabag Guesthouse (☎ 547 1210; s/d K85/120) The guesthouse has several single and double rooms with shared facilities. The kitchen is clean and well equipped.

Dae Won Wabag Hotel (☎ 547 1140; fax 547 1033; Highlands Hwy; s K124-180, d K124-240) Wabag's only formal hotel. It's on the Mt Hagen side of town and there's a communal lounge area and kitchen, as well as a restaurant.

Kaiap Orchid Lodge (☎ 547 1281) Although this fantastic place – one of the best in the Highlands – closed in 2002, it has done so before and reopened again. It's listed here because we hope it does reopen. Its position, on a razorback ridge, is incredible and the food and home-grown coffee are fantastic.

Getting There & Away
AIR
Although the Wabag airstrip is closed, you can fly to Wapenamenda (call sign WBM), an hour's drive away on the highway towards Mt Hagen. This airstrip is serviced by the third-level airlines.

PMV
The PMV trip from Mt Hagen takes four hours and costs K10. The road to Porgera and the mine is in good service, but PMVs rarely go there. You can get to Mendi via Laiagam and Kandep over a very rough road with frequently washed-out bridges, and a few PMVs do go this way (see p127 for a discussion about safety in and around Mendi).

AROUND WABAG
Laiagam & Rau
Laiagam has a **botanic garden** with a huge range of orchids and a research centre. **Lake Rau** is a crater lake at nearly 3000m in Enga Province's centre. It's a day's walk from Pumas, above Laiagam, and you will need a guide, which you can arrange in Mt Hagen.

PORGERA

This is a mining company town 3½ hours west of Wabag. The mine itself, a massive open-cut dig, is nearly exhausted, having been the biggest gold producer in the country, but nearby gold discoveries will keep the mining town operating. The environmental impact of the mine, run by and majority owned by Placer Dome (10% owned by the Engan Provincial Government and landowners), has been devastating to the Strickland River where waste (tailings containing mercury and arsenic) has been dumped since 1992. The practice is illegal in most countries. Concerns raised by international environmental watchdogs led to the Porgera Environmental Advisory Komity (PEAK) being formed. It included local people, NGOs, the mining company and environmental experts. Yati Bun, PEAK chairperson, later quit after Placer Dome did nothing to clean up the river. As elsewhere in the developing world, the big multinational mining companies have got away with whatever they could, poisoning rivers and leaving environmental ruin.

THE HIGHLANDS

Kumul Adventure Resort Hotel

Kumul Lodge, as **Kumul Adventure Resort Hotel** (☎ 542 1615; kumul-lodge@global.net.pg; s K120-140, d K140-160) is known, is 40 minutes from Mt Hagen, and closer to Hagen or Wapenamenda airstrip than to Wabag. It is in Enga, but just at the border with Western Highlands Province. Kumul Lodge is a wonderful place, owned and managed by the local community and, although geared towards bird-watchers, is a lovely place for a few days' holiday. The bungalows, built from bush materials, are comfortable, self-contained and have large windows and balconies overlooking the surrounding forest. It's at the base of Mt Hagen and offers guided walks up the mountain and to nearby caves. You can see birds of paradise in the grounds of the lodge. Transfers from Hagen are K65, from Wabag, K78.

Mountain Lodge (☎ 547 9357; s K100) is Porgera's only formal accommodation outside the mine's own facilities.

SOUTHERN HIGHLANDS PROVINCE

Southern Highlands Province is made up of lush, high valleys between towering limestone peaks. This region is particularly beautiful and traditional cultures thrive, especially in the Tari Basin where many people retain their traditional ways and dress. The headwaters of some mighty rivers, including the Kikori, Erave and Strickland, cross the province, and 4368m Mt Giluwe is the second-highest mountain in PNG.

The most remote province of the Highlands, the Southern Highlands is still relatively undeveloped, although the establishment of oilfields near Lake Kutubu and an alluvial gold mine at Mt Kare are rapidly opening up the region. Some of PNG's most remote areas are in the Southern Highlands Province. In pre-European times it was at the end of the trade route from the Gulf of Papua into the Highlands.

Beyond the Wahgi-Mt Hagen area, to the southwest past Mendi and northwest around Wabag, is the country of the wigmen – these are the Huli (see p130), the Duna and other tribes whose men are famous for the intricately decorated wigs they wear. The proud Huli men of the Tari Basin, in particular, still wear their impressive traditional decorations.

The Mendi area is the most developed region of the Southern Highlands (although Tari has more attractions and services for travellers), but it was not explored by Europeans until 1935. It was 1950 when the first airstrip was constructed and 1952 before tribal warfare was prohibited. The Mendi tribes then focused their attention on attacking government patrols and were still fighting them in the mid-1950s. The discovery of the beautiful Lavani Valley in 1954 triggered newspaper journalists to write elaborate stories about the discovery of a lost Shangri-la.

The limestone hills and high rainfall are ideal for the formation of caves. Some caves of enormous depth and length have already been explored and it is a distinct possibility that some of the deepest caves in the world await discovery in this region.

MENDI

Despite being the provincial capital, Mendi is a relatively small town, built around an airport. It shelters in a long green valley, surrounded by beautiful limestone peaks. There is not much to keep you hanging around in Mendi – it's really just the starting point for a trip into the Tari Basin or Lake Kutubu. Friday and Saturday, when tribespeople crowd into town, can get pretty rowdy. The situation in Mendi was volatile at the time of research.

There's an artefacts shop near Mendi Motors that sells hand-loomed products, baskets and weapons. Mendi dolls make a good buy, although they are now rarely in the traditional designs, which had religious significance.

From the town centre there's a shortcut down to the market and the main road on a steep dirt path, but it's slippery and almost impossible to walk with a pack after rain.

Information

Mendi's **police station** (☎ 549 1333) is open, although the **Mendi Hospital** (☎ 549 1166) is currently closed and the banks have suspended their operations in town due to tribal fighting. The **post office** (☎ 549 1016) is in the middle of town.

Sleeping

Pentecostal Guesthouse (☎ 549 1174; s K30) There are only a few rooms in the Pentecostal Guesthouse, not far from the airport. The rooms are small but clean and there are cooking facilities and hot showers.

UCWF Guesthouse (☎ 549 1062; s/tw K30/50) The United Church Women's Fellowship has a guesthouse 20 minutes' walk from town. The twin room has an attached bathroom. To get there, walk out onto the old Mt Hagen road past Mendi Motors, take the left fork after the bridge, pass the turn-off to the large Menduli Trade Store and it's further up the hill on your right, near the hospital.

Muruk Lodge (☎ 549 1188) Has been closed since May 2001. It might reopen.

Kiburu Lodge (☎ 549 1077; fax 549 1350; s K120) Kiburu is a few kilometres south of town, on the Highlands Hwy, just beyond the turn-off into Mendi. It has six chalets with 12 rooms in quasi-traditional style and pleasant grounds and views. It's on the bank of the Mendi River and owned by the Kiburu people. It has a restaurant, lounge and bar. Tours of the area are available.

Getting There & Away

AIR

The Mendi airstrip is often unserviceable, mostly in the mornings, because of fog. **Air Niugini** (☎ 549 1233) has daily flights to/from Port Moresby (one-way full fare K451), sometimes direct and at times via Wapenamanda (for Wabag) or Tari. The Mendi–Tari leg costs K163. **Airlines PNG** (☎ 549 1060) has links to Mendi, as does **MAF** (☎ 549 1091).

Moro, a 20-minute flight away (try MAF or possibly Airlines PNG), is an hour's walk from the west end of Lake Kutubu. From there you can catch a boat to Tage Point (at the other end of the lake).

PMV

PMVs run back and forth between Mt Hagen and Mendi with reasonable regularity, taking three hours or so and costing about K10. The road to Tari goes via Nipa and is a spectacular four-hour drive costing K12. There's a road to Pimaga and on to Moro.

IALIBU

Halfway between Mendi and Mt Hagen, Ialibu is the home of the Imbong'gu people, who also wear wigs. It is a major area for

> **WARNING**
>
> The Southern Highlands region has become beset with lawlessness and tribal fighting. Mendi's hospital has closed and the banks have pulled out. Normally tribal fighting is confined to those involved, but it can make travelling through the region unpredictable and dangerous nonetheless. There's been talk in parliament about suspending the provincial government and imposing a state of emergency, and the Australian deployment of federal police, part of the Enhanced Cooperation Program treaty, will have its hands full restoring law and order in a widespread culture of guns, violence and corruption.
>
> Seek advice before travelling to the Southern Highlands Province. Travelling by PMV makes you vulnerable to bandits and ambushes, and there have been several incidents near Mendi. Air travel is safer. Tari is much quieter and the resorts there are secure and safe.

the production of sawn timber, and basket-making is a common village industry. Nearby is Mt Ialibu (3465m). The local people have built a cultural centre and museum made of river stones and local timber in the old style, with exposed posts and beams and woven walls. There are good walking trails nearby.

LAKE KUTUBU

The Lake Kutubu area has one of just five national parks in PNG. South of Mendi, Lake Kutubu has some of the Highlands' most beautiful scenery. According to legend, the lake was formed when a fig tree was cut down by a woman looking for water. The story goes that whatever the tree touched turned to water – hence the lake.

The lake is beautiful, and the surrounding country is home to friendly people living a largely traditional life. Butterflies and birds of paradise are common. You can swim in the lake and visit local villages or walk and appreciate the beauty and peace. Kutubu is the Highlands' second-largest lake, and, at 800m above sea level, PNG's highest substantial body of water (although the Mt Wilhelm's crater lakes are higher). It has a remarkable level of fish endemicity –

10 of the 14 species of fish are found only in this lake.

The big oil project near Lake Kutubu has changed the Mendi area, and local people are used to dealing with oil workers with fat wallets and expense accounts. Prices asked to cross a bridge or walk across land can be outrageous.

Oil began flowing through the pipeline down to the Gulf of Papua in 1992. Chevron Niugini has a good reputation, fulfilling its agreements with the local landowners, the Foi and Fasu people. There's a road from Mendi to Pimaga and on to Moro and the company headquarters near the northwest end of Lake Kutubu.

Sleeping

Tubo Eco-Tourism Lodge (☎ 327 3286, 323 9681; ctaukuro@airniugini.com.pg; s K60) Tubo is based on

---

SOUTHERN HIGHLANDS CULTURE

The Huli are one of the biggest clans and their homelands are among PNG's most remote and undeveloped regions. Most Huli have had little more than a single generation of contact with the outside world. Though not typical of all Highlanders, the Huli make an interesting case study (for more information, see p130).

Black Brides

Mendi brides wear black for their wedding – they're rubbed down in black tigaso tree oil and soot, and they wear this body colouring for a month after the wedding. The tigaso tree oil is very valuable. It comes from Lake Kutubu and is traded all over the area. During this time neither bride nor groom work, nor is the marriage consummated. This gives the bride time to become acquainted with her husband's family and for the groom to learn 'antiwoman' spells to protect himself from his wife.

Throughout the Highlands, women are traditionally distrusted by men, who go to extraordinary lengths to protect themselves and maintain their status. Sexual relations are not undertaken lightly – contact with women is believed to cause sickness and men usually live in separate houses and prefer to cook their own food. Boys can be removed from their mothers' houses at a very young age. Women travellers should bear these customs in mind because in many places they are still strictly upheld. Violence against PNG women is widespread.

Blue Widows

A dead man's wife, daughters, mother, sisters and sisters-in-law coat themselves with bluish-grey clay while in mourning. The wife carries vast numbers of strings of the seeds known as 'Job's tears'. One string a day is removed until eventually, with the removal of the last string, the widow can wash herself of her clay coating and remarry – about nine months after the death.

Long Houses

Long houses, known as *haus lains*, are built along the sides of Mendi ceremonial grounds and used as guesthouses at *singsings* and pig kills. They can be up to 150m long, although 70m is the usual length, and they are built beside stone-filled pits where the pigs are cooked.

Warfare

Land ownership, particularly in the Highlands, is highly complex and very important – disputes over land are often at the root of conflicts. People can inherit land, not just from their parents, but from any known ancestor. All descendants of a woman who planted a tree have rights to its fruit, and people have rights to widely scattered pieces of land.

Fighting arrows are carved from black palm and are traditionally tipped with human bone. The tips are traditionally made from the forearm of a male ancestor so that his spirit can guide the arrow to an enemy. The men are fine bowmen and can shoot arrows over long distances. They also carry bone daggers carved from the leg bone of a cassowary. Tribal warfare is serious – fighting is still common and increasingly guns are being used.

an island in the lake – access is by canoe and a 300-step climb. It's community owned and run, built from bush materials and affords commanding views across the magnificent lake. The grounds have butterflies, orchids and birds of paradise. The remoteness of the area adds to the experience; it's very lovely.

Getting There & Away

Airlines PNG (☎ 549 1060) flies into Moro, as does **MAF** (☎ 549 1091). Some PMVs from Tari and Mendi come this way.

It's possible to walk into the Lake Kutubu region. You should take a guide – contact **PNG Highland Tours** (☎ 732 1602) or **Trans Niugini Tours** (☎ 542 1438; Mt Hagen) to arrange a guide, or talk to the folks at Tubo Lodge.

KANTOBO

Kantobo village is on the banks of the Mubi River, near the eastern end of Lake Kutubu. It is home to the Muti clan of the Foimeana people. This is virgin rainforest, rich in bird and animal life. A 700-hectare wildlife management area has been created around the nearby Wasi Falls with the help of the WWF. **Wasi Falls** is the local name for a series of waterfalls that includes the Bisi Falls, the largest in PNG, which plummet over 100m into a limestone basin. Also in the management area are the Maskimu Falls and Geagosusu Falls. There are many caves in this area, including some that were used for ancient burials, and some with a unique blind cave-fish species.

TARI

Tari is the only town for the Huli wigmen and the centre for the beautiful Tari Basin. The main attractions are the people and the surrounding countryside. The town really is just the airfield plus a handful of buildings. There is a post office, a few large but basic stores and a hospital. Tari is one of the few towns in PNG where some people still wear traditional dress.

There's a tiny museum in a stockaded compound and most of the items in the small display are for sale. The place is a sort of old men's home and a couple of older fellows show you around and accept your donation. The covered structure in the compound is the grave of a former provincial premier, and you'll see similar (but usually smaller) structures all around the Tari area – people live under thatch roofs, but when they die they get corrugated iron to keep the rain off.

Saturday is the main market day but there are smaller markets between Wednesday and Saturday.

Sleeping & Eating

Despite the small size of the town, the Tari area boasts some excellent accommodation.

Warili Lodge (c/- MAF in Tari ☎ 540 8014; www .papua-warili-lodge.com; s K60) This is another fantastic example of bush-material accommodation. Warili is on the edge of a rainforest at 2100m, among orchids and rhododendrons. The forest is spectacular and home to birds of paradise. The huts are very comfortable, with separate dining areas, running water, flushing toilet and generator electricity. Meals are available and tours are offered.

Ambua Lodge (☎ 542 1438; www.pngtours.com; per person all-inclusive s/d/tr US$444/360/324) Run by Trans Niugini Tours, Ambua is a very upmarket and plush resort 45 minutes by road from Tari. The showpiece of the Trans Niugini Tours operation, the lodge offers commanding views across the Tari Basin and Huli homelands. In 2001 it was listed as one of the 10 best ecotourism facilities worldwide by *National Geographic Adventure* magazine, and Sir David Attenborough is a regular patron. At 2100m, the lodge enjoys a refreshing mountain climate and attracts many bird-watchers and orchid enthusiasts. You can relax for hours in the lounge-bar just watching the clouds roll by. There's also an outdoor spa.

Guests are accommodated in individual, luxury, bush-material huts. The huts have a great 180-degree view and are surrounded by flower gardens with a backdrop of mossy forest. Grand opulence in such rugged circumstances is certainly impressive.

Ambua is beyond the means of many travellers, although most guests come on a package deal that includes a stay at other Trans Niugini resorts and a spell on the live-aboard MV *Sepik Spirit*.

Getting There & Away

AIR

Air Niugini (☎ 540 8023) flies from Port Moresby to Tari on Monday, Wednesday, Friday and Sunday via Mendi (one-way full fare K506). The Mendi–Tari leg costs K163.

THE HIGHLANDS

HULI WIGMEN

The Huli are the largest ethnic group in the Southern Highlands, with a population of around 55,000 and territory exceeding 2500 sq km. Huli don't live in villages, but in scattered homesteads dispersed through immaculately and intensively cultivated valleys. The gardens are delineated by trenches and mud walls up to 3m high, broken by brightly painted gateways made of stakes. These trenches mark boundaries, control the movement of pigs and also hide troops of warriors in times of war. As usual, the women do most of the work, while men concentrate on displaying their finery and plotting war with each other.

Traditional Huli culture is highly developed and strikingly executed in dress and personal decoration. Body decoration is high art. Flutes similar to panpipes are a popular form of entertainment and bamboo jew's-harps are played.

Huli men wear striking decorative woven wigs of human hair. The hair is usually the wigman's own, supplemented by hair donated by wives and children, who are thus short-haired. Designs are indicative of a wigman's tribe.

The Huli cultivate yellow everlasting daisies used to decorate their wigs and they also use feathers and *cuscus* (possum) fur. There's a band of snakeskin across the forehead, and usually a cassowary quill through the nasal septa. Their faces are decorated with yellow and red ochre. Kina shells are worn around the neck, decorative belt and *bilum* (string bag) -cloth covering the privates and an *arsegras* (tanket leaves stuck into a belt) up back.

Airlines PNG (☎ 545 1407), **MAF** (☎ 545 1477) and **Airlink** (☎ 540 8023) fly interesting routes between Tari and several other smaller airstrips.

PMV

While PMVs can take a while to collect enough passengers to leave Tari, it's best to get to the market early in the morning if you're heading in the Mendi direction. PMVs to Mendi cost K20 and take four hours. PMVs also run from Tari to Koroba for around K8.

KOPIAGO TO OKSAPMIN

From Lake Kopiago, you can walk to Oksapmin in West Sepik Province in four or five days. There's a mission guesthouse about 3km from Kopiago and a more basic council guesthouse in town.

Kopiago to Oksapmin is a hard and potentially dangerous walk, so don't undertake it unless you are pretty fit and you've hired a guide. If you are really keen, you can continue walking to Tekin, Bak, Bimin and down to Olsobip in Western Province, or to Telefomin.

The Sepik

The Sepik is one of the great rivers of the world, and is to Papua New Guinea as the Congo is to Africa and the Amazon to South America. However, the Sepik is more than just a river – it's also a densely populated repository of complex cultures and produces the most potent art in the Pacific. Travelling up the river is the adventure of a lifetime.

The population, as in other parts of PNG, is clustered into different language groups and clans. Violence between these groups used to be commonplace and rivalries remain. Today, most of these languages are spoken by fewer than 2000 people. The main Sepik language group is Ndu, including its subgroups Abelam, spoken mostly around Maprik, and Passam, which is found mainly around Wewak. As in many parts of the country, Tok Ples is being replaced by Tok Pisin and clan languages are being eroded.

There are very few roads in the region and the river carries traffic from simple kids' dugouts and huge outboard-powered canoes, to luxury live-aboard touring vessels like the MV *Sepik Spirit* and the MTS *Discoverer*. Although tourists prefer to travel up the river by motor-canoe, locals prefer outboard-powered dinghies which are faster and more man-oeuvrable, but beyond the means of most villagers. While cruising on the river you still see naked kids poling dugout canoes, woven fish traps and the towering façades of *haus tambarans* (spirit houses).

The Sepik region also takes in the sleepy provincial capitals of Wewak and Vanimo, two beachside towns that boast vast stretches of white sand, excellent diving and seasonal surf. Aitape, between Wewak and Vanimo, was the area devastated by the tsunami in July 1998. This chapter first looks at the two provinces through which the river flows and later, the river itself, its tributaries and the riverside towns and villages.

HIGHLIGHTS

- Cruising the **Sepik River** (p145) in a giant canoe, and seeing birdlife and crocodiles
- Staying around **Chambri Lakes** (p152), experiencing the lifestyle and culture
- Buying a carving from a master carver in **Tambanum** (p150)
- Swimming and surfing off the white-sand beaches of **Vanimo** (p141) and **Wewak** (p137)
- Examining the architecture of *haus tambarans* (spirit houses) and stilt houses around **Mapik Area** (p140)

| LAND AREA: 79,100 SQ KM | POPULATION: 528,000 |

THE SEPIK

History

The Sepik's first contact with the outside world was probably with Malay bird-of-paradise hunters – the feathers from these beautiful birds were popular in Asia long before fashionable European millinery incorporated them into late 19th-century women's headwear.

The first European contact came in 1885, with the arrival of the German New Guinea Company. Dr Otto Finsch named the river the Kaiserin Augusta, after the wife of the German emperor. Dr Finsch, after whom the Germans' first station – Finschhafen – was named, rowed about 50km upstream from the mouth.

The Germans established a station at Aitape on the coast in 1906, and in 1912 and 1913 sent a huge scientific expedition to explore the river and its vast, low-lying basin. They collected insects, studied local tribes and produced maps of such accuracy that they're still referred to today. Angoram, the major station in the lower Sepik, was established at this time.

The early 1930s saw gold rushes in the hills behind Wewak and around Maprik, but development and exploration ceased when WWII started.

The Japanese held the Sepik region for most of the war. Australian forces pushed along the coast from Lae and Madang, and the Japanese withdrew to the west. In early 1944 the Americans seized Aitape and the Australians moved west from there. When a huge American force captured Hollandia (now Jayapura in West Papua) in April, the Japanese in Wewak were completely isolated. A year later, in May 1945, Wewak fell and the remaining Japanese withdrew into the hills. Finally, with the war in its last days, General Adachi surrendered near Yangoru. The formal surrender took place a few days later on 13 September 1945 at Wom Point near Wewak. Of 100,000 Japanese troops, only 13,000 survived.

The region has been volatile since the Indonesian takeover of Dutch New Guinea (now West Papua). The border was jointly mapped and marked in 1968. On several occasions large numbers of Papuan refugees have fled into PNG. In 1984 more than 100 Indonesian soldiers deserted to the OPM (*Organisasi Papua Merdeka*, or Free West Papua Movement), sparking a major Indonesian operation which in turn drove 12,000 Papuans into PNG. Some of these refugees were settled permanently in PNG in camps close to the border at Blackwater, near Vanimo, and Green River, near the Sepik River. Since then, following brutal Indonesian crackdowns on West Papuan separatist activity even more West Papuans have fled over the border to PNG.

In March 2001 PNG police beat some asylum seekers at the Blackwater camp in an attempt to coerce them and others back across the border. The PNG government has been fickle about recognising the West Papuans as refugees and negotiated the repatriation of some with Indonesia in early 2002. In late 2004 about 400 border crossers, mostly women and children who had fled West Papua in 2000, were finally granted refugee status within PNG after sustained pressure on the government from the Catholic church and the UNHCR. The refugees were transferred to East Arwin camp in Western Province. The situation remains unstable.

Geography & Climate

The Sepik River is 1126km long and is navigable for almost its entire length. It starts up in the central mountains, close to the source of PNG's other major river, the Fly, which flows south. The Sepik flows in a loop, first west across the West Papua border, then north, before returning east across the border. It then runs through two PNG provinces – Sandaun (West Sepik) and East Sepik.

At its exit from West Papua, the Sepik is only 85m above sea level and from there it winds gradually down to the sea – a huge, brown, coiling serpent. It has often changed its course, leaving dead-ends, lagoons, oxbow lakes or huge swampy expanses that turn into lakes or dry up to become grasslands in the dry season.

As an indication of its age and changing course, there are no stones or rocks within 50km of the river's banks. Villages have 'sacred stones' that have been carried in from far away and placed in front of village *haus tambarans*.

The inexorable force of the river tears great chunks of mud and vegetation out of the riverbanks and these drift downstream as floating islands. There is no delta and the river stains the sea brown for 50km or more from the shore.

For much of its length, the Sepik is bordered by huge expanses of swamp or *pitpit* (wild sugar cane). There are hills further inland and eventually the Sepik climbs into wild mountain country near its source. Between the river and the coastal plain, the Bewani and Torricelli mountains rise to over 1000m. There are no natural harbours on the Sepik region's 450km of coastline.

June to October is the driest time in most of the Sepik, but microclimates vary significantly. Average annual rainfalls lie between 2000mm around Wewak and Maprik, and a stunning 5200mm at Amboin. You can expect drenching rain at any time on the river, but the wet season is from December to April.

Most rain falls in January and February and the river level starts to drop after April. Temperatures and humidity can be high, but it's usually pleasant on the river, where you catch the breeze.

Early in the dry season is the best time to visit – the mosquitoes are less numerous and there's plenty of water in the river system. By August the level drops significantly emptying some tributaries and *barets* (artificial channels cut as shortcuts across loops in the river), and this makes travel times much longer.

In the dry season the Chambri Lakes can get very smelly – they shrink, fish die and weed rots.

Culture

The Sepik region is the best-known part of PNG outside the country, and Sepik artefacts (carvings and pottery) are displayed in many of the world's great museums. Traditional art was closely linked to spiritual beliefs. Sepik carvings were usually an attempt to make a spirit visible and concrete, although decorations were also applied to practical, everyday items, like pots and paddles.

Carving is rarely traditional – it's now more a mixture of long-established motifs, imagination and commercial tastes. Some villages still retain their own signature styles – Kambot makes the famous storyboards. Even these are not traditional – storyboards were originally painted on large pieces of bark, and now they're carved in relief from timber. Sepik storyboards are one of the very few narrative art forms in the whole Pacific. These days a generic 'Sepik style' is emerging.

Carving is a vital part of the river's economy. In some villages, carving is the only significant source of cash. Coffee is grown in the Maprik region, but on the river there are no cash crops, no paid employment and rarely any agricultural surplus.

Sepik people invest great spiritual power in crocodiles. People around Korogo village in the Middle Sepik perform an initiation rite where young men are cut with thousands of incisions on the back, chest and buttocks which are packed with ash. Once healed, this extraordinary scarificial technique represents the teeth marks of a crocodile. This initiation rite can take months to complete while initiates are kept in seclusion. Korogo people believe that ancestral crocodiles established human populations.

SALVINIA & WATER HYACINTH

The water weed *Salvinia molesta* once threatened ecological disaster for the Sepik River system. *Salvinia* originated in Brazil, has small, fleshy fan-like leaves and can double in size in two days.

When it was introduced to the Sepik, it went wild. In the early 1980s it covered 60% of the Lower and Middle Sepik's lakes, lagoons and *barets* (artificial channels), often forming a mat too thick for canoes to penetrate, isolating villages and preventing fishing.

A weevil was introduced; the adult feeds on *Salvinia* buds and the larvae burrow through the plant which dies, becomes water-logged and sinks. Wide distribution of the weevil began in 1983. The results were dramatic and within months the spread of the weed had been reversed.

Another major environmental problem on the Sepik is the water hyacinth. Although attractive, this is one of the world's worst aquatic weeds.

Since 1993 three insects which will kill the water hyacinth, but not other plants, have been released. Over 180,000 water hyacinth weevils were released at various locations in PNG; two other insects, a moth and bug, are also being tested.

Dangers & Annoyances

Natnat is Tok Pisin for mosquito, and Sepik mosquitoes aren't particularly big but they can be numerous and pretty vicious. They're not a problem while you're on the river, but on the banks they can descend in hordes. They can be bad in the late afternoons and evenings. For information on malaria see p251.

There are far fewer mosquitoes in the June-to-October dry season, and they are less of a problem once you get up the tributaries, to higher altitudes and cooler weather.

EAST SEPIK PROVINCE

East Sepik Province is much more developed than Sandaun Province and includes the most-visited and heavily populated sections of the Sepik, as well as several large tributaries.

Vanilla underpins a booming cash-crop economy and, while prices remain high, many small landholders are making good profits. Prices are often better in Jayapura in West Papua – you might end up sitting in a small plane heading west beside a villager with a large consignment of vanilla beans.

WEWAK

This provincial capital, is a thriving commercial centre, separated from the Sepik Basin by the Prince Alexander Range. Wewak is an attractive town. Apart from good shopping and accommodation options, there's an attraction that is rare for PNG coastal cities – golden sand, backed by swaying palm trees, right next door to town. Beautiful beaches stretch all along the coast.

Wewak is built at the foot of a high headland that overlooks the coast and nearby islands of Kairiru and Muschu. The hills behind the town climb steeply.

All the major banks and airlines are represented in Wewak. This is the spot to stock up with cash and food for a Sepik expedition.

Orientation

The headland overlooking Wewak is a largely residential area with some nice houses. The Paradise New Wewak Hotel and the Seaview Motel are up here. The main commercial area is at the bottom of the hill behind the beach. The rest of town stretches eastward

towards the airport, about 8km away. Wewak is spread out, but fortunately there's an excellent bus system around town.

The intersection of Boram Rd with the road leading down to the main wharves and the provincial government offices is called 'Caltex', despite the fact that the service station is a BP outlet.

There's a wharf for local fishing boats and canoes next to Wewak town, and a longer one for ships east of the Windjammer Hotel, along the bay formed by Wewak Point and Cape Boram.

MAPS

The **Christian Bookshop** (☎ 856 2126) in town has some simple tourist maps.

Information

EMERGENCY

Police (☎ 856 2633)
Ambulance (☎ 856 2166)

INTERNET ACCESS

The better hotels have Internet-enabled computers for about K30 per half-hour.
Help Resources (☎ 856 1453; help@global.net.pg; per 30 min K15) Right on top of the headland; a community education centre. It has a state-of-the-art Internet café.
Windjammer Hotel (☎ 856 2388; Boram Rd; per 15 min K12) Has an Internet café in its foyer.

MEDICAL SERVICES

Hospital (☎ 856 2166) On the point at Cape Boram.

MONEY

Major credit cards are accepted at Wewak's hotels, and the bigger ones will also change travellers cheques.
Bank South Pacific (☎ 856 2344; The Centre) In the middle of town; charges a flat K50 to change travellers cheques. It also has ATMs.
Westpac (☎ 856 2113; The Centre) Opposite Bank South Pacific but has no ATMs. It charges 1% of face value to change travellers cheques.

POST

Post Office (☎ 856 2290; cnr The Centre & Boram Rd)

TOURIST INFORMATION

Tour companies are a good source of information. See p240 and p247 for details.
East Sepik Cultural & Tourism Bureau (☎ 856 2005; Boram Rd; ☾ 9.30am-4pm) Like so many of PNG's

tourist offices, this is dreadfully under-resourced. It's worth visiting just in case there's a local event happening that they can tell you about, but otherwise it's pretty useless.

Ralf Stüttgen (☎ 856 2395) Ralf is an amazing man, quite eccentric. He is a former German missionary who's been in the Sepik region since 1968. He doesn't run tours but he offers advice and expects to be paid. Alternatively, you can buy some artefacts (p138) and get some free advice. He also offers accommodation (p137).

Sights & Activities
MISSION POINT TO CAPE BORAM
Near the main wharf lies the rusting remains of **MV Busama**. Further down at Kreer, on the road to the airport, there's the wooden hulk of a Taiwanese fishing junk. On the beach between Kreer Market and the hospital are some rusting Japanese landing barges, which are rapidly disappearing. The **Japanese War Memorial** marks the mass grave of many troops. The soldier's bodies were later exhumed and returned to Japan.

JAPANESE MEMORIAL PEACE PARK
This park contains a memorial and a fish pond. Tok Pisin doesn't have a word for peace; 'Peace' sounds like *pis*, which means fish. Thus, most locals refer to the park as *pis park*, which is perhaps appropriate given the fish pond and the general ambivalence that many modern Papua New Guineans have towards WWII. Ironically, the peace park is enclosed by a wire fence.

SANDAUN & EAST SEPIK PROVINCES

SWIMMING & SNORKELLING
Wewak's beaches are excellent – long stretches of white sand that fall away gently under the water. The water is clean and clear, warm and very inviting.

There's excellent snorkelling around the Wewak headland, over the outer reef and off the nearby islands. Like many coastal places in PNG, the diving conditions around Wewak are sensational – reefs, wrecks, tropical fish – but there's no organised diving industry in Wewak.

SURFING
Between mid-October and late April monsoon swells bring waves between 3ft and 8ft to PNG's northern coast, and there are several good breaks around Wewak (and Vanimo). Some of the hotels have surfboards, but they're pretty battered – surfers usually bring their own.

GOLF
There's an 18-hole golf course behind the Windjammer, near the Japanese Memorial Peace Park. It has a pleasant clubhouse.

Tours
Wewak is the main departure point for trips up the Sepik River and there are a few Wewak-based companies that specialise in tours. They can arrange land and river transport, village accommodation on the river and guides. They can also arrange tours around Wewak and out to the off-shore islands of Mushu and Kairiru; see p240 and p247.

Festivals & Events
Wewak's **Garamut & Flute Festival** is usually held on the first weekend of September, and features song and dance as well as yam-planting ceremonies.

Sleeping & Eating
There are good accommodation options among Wewak's hotels and guesthouses. You can stay in town at a couple of decent hotels, but there's no reason not to stay along the beach a few kilometres away from town towards the airport. Daytime buses from here to town are frequent and cheap, and the beach is brilliant.

Eating options, beyond daytime *kai* bars, are confined to the hotels and yacht club.

Windjammer Hotel (☎ 856 2388; fax 856 2701; s 135-250, d 185-320; ✷ 🖳) The Windjammer is the top place to stay in Wewak (although it needs a bit of maintenance). It's halfway between the town and the airport, right on the beach. It's worth visiting just to see the carvings incorporated into the interior, including a magnificent crocodile bar, and carved stools and furniture. The beachside *haus win* (gazebo-like in structure) makes the Windjammer a nice place for dinner or lunch even if you're not staying there. The **restaurant** (meals K30-50) serves some of the best food in Wewak, including excellent seafood, burgers and salads. There a nightclub attached which can get noisy (and very rough) and an artefacts shop and Internet café in the

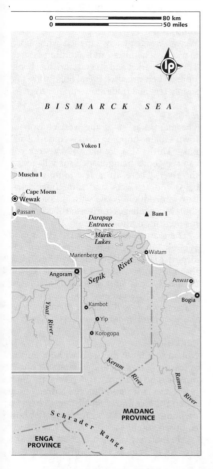

BISMARCK SEA

Vokeo I

Muschu I

Cape Moem
Wewak
Passam
Darapap Entrance
Bam I
Murik Lakes
Marienberg
Watam
Angoram
Sepik River
Anwar
Bogia
Yuat River
Kambot
Yip
Korogopa
Keram River
Ramu River
Schrader Range
MADANG PROVINCE
ENGA PROVINCE

0   80 km
0   50 miles

THE SEPIK

foyer. In 2004 fire gutted most of the rooms in the Windjammer's beachfront wing.

Airport Lodge (☎ 856 2373; marg@online.com.pg; s/d/f K154/165/308; ✄ ⌨) This is probably the pick of Wewak's accommodation if you're not staying at the Windjammer Hotel. It has a great location on the beach next to the airport. The lodge is comprised of bungalows and suites, all self-contained. It is well maintained and clean. It has a separate **restaurant** (set menu K40) and a great beachside bar where you can get lunch. It's also very popular and often full – you'll need to book.

Sepik Surfsite Lodge (☎ 856 2525; adventurepng@datec.net.pg; r K105-156; ✄) This is an interesting place, reminiscent of a beachside surfer's shack – fibro cement, simple drapes and fixtures. It has a rather basic charm to it and there's a great *haus win* with cold beer and reasonable meals. The cheaper rooms are fan-cooled and share facilities. There's only hot water in the air-con rooms. The manager, Alois Mateos, is another great Sepik expert and tour operator. He also has a lodge at Ambunti on the Sepik River (p147).

Seaview Hotel (☎ 856 1131; fax 856 2694; s/d/f K175/180/255; ✄) The Seaview has had incarnations as a hotel and police barracks, but it's a hotel again now, and a comfortable place to stay. It's halfway up Wewak hill opposite a park. There are excellent views, a bar, à la carte **restaurant** (meals K25-35) and a *haus win*. The rooms are self-contained and there are also some VIP rooms (K287 to K336), but these are overpriced.

Paradise New Wewak Hotel (☎ 856 2155; fax 856 3411; Hill St; s/d/f K110/132/154; ✄) In town, this is an old hotel with large rooms, fans, fridges, phone, air-con and private facilities. Though well equipped, the rooms are in need of a coat of paint. This location, on a hilltop overlooking the sea, is very good – it has spectacular views and is 10 minutes' walk uphill from town. There's a bar, set-menu meals area and plenty of poker machines.

Wewak Yacht Club (☎ 856 2708; meals K22-40; ✿ 4-11pm) The yacht club overlooks a nice part of the harbour. There aren't too many yachts tied up, and the patrons are mostly Wewak locals and expats who come for drinks and simple pub-style food.

SIL Guesthouse (☎ 856 2176/2416; s/d K70/90) The SIL Guesthouse is in Kreer Heights, and it's clean, secure and comfortable. It's also often full. There are several furnished two-bedroom flats with kitchens, bathrooms and TV. This is a good place for a group, but book well ahead. To get there, take bus Nos 13, 16, or 19 to Kreer Heights and then ask for directions.

Ralf Stüttgen's Place (☎ 856 2395; s K40) Ralf is a local legend and provides basic accommodation in two very simple rooms. The house is overflowing with dogs, storage boxes, carvings, books, WWII memorabilia and other stuff. Ralf doesn't get many hardcore backpackers any more so he's diversified into Sepik art dealing and he's a great authority on the Sepik (p136). Ralf's place is on a 400m ridge overlooking the coast at Tower (there's a radio mast) 15km inland from Wewak. Take bus Nos 14, 16 or 19 to Kreer Heights then a bus to Tower.

Shopping

Wewak is adequately supplied with supermarkets, chemists and clothing stores. There's a market and several Christian bookstores. There are also several bulk stores that supply regional trade stores up the river.

MARKET

The main market, at the west end of the town's main shopping strip is colourful and busy. This is also the main PMV stop; you can see goods being loaded for villages up the river. There are a few *bilums* (string bags) and artefacts, and sometimes a live baby crocodile for sale with its snout tied shut. Many villages upriver farm crocodiles for their meat and skins.

There are several other markets around Wewak, of which Kreer market, on the airport road just before it turns inland, is the most interesting. Chambri market on Boram Rd sells *buai* (betel nut) and a few artefacts. There are also Dagua and Nuigo markets which sell *buai*, *pitpit* and sometimes woven pandanus satchels.

CARVINGS

Nobody comes to the Sepik without buying at least one carving and buying just one is often a good strategy. Sepik pieces are often heavy and large, and they are a drag to lug around the country. Small flyers charge a premium on excess baggage no matter how empty the flight is.

Alternatively, there are good Sepik arts brokers in Wewak who will look after all

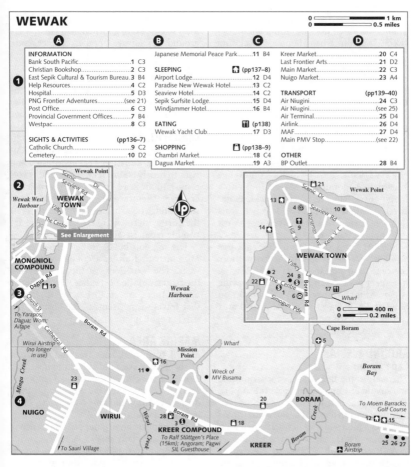

WEWAK

0 ————————— 1 km
0 ————————— 0.5 miles

INFORMATION		Japanese Memorial Peace Park........11 B4	Kreer Market...............................20 C4
Bank South Pacific............................1 C3			Last Frontier Arts..........................21 D2
Christian Bookshop...........................2 C3		SLEEPING (pp137–8)	Main Market................................22 C3
East Sepik Cultural & Tourism Bureau..3 B4		Airport Lodge................................12 D4	Nuigo Market...............................23 A4
Help Resources..................................4 C2		Paradise New Wewak Hotel...........13 C2	
Hospital...5 D3		Seaview Hotel...............................14 C2	TRANSPORT (pp139–40)
PNG Frontier Adventures...............(see 21)		Sepik Surfside Lodge....................15 D4	Air Niugini....................................24 C3
Post Office..6 C3		Windjammer Hotel........................16 B4	Air Niugini...............................(see 25)
Provincial Government Offices..........7 B4			Air Terminal..................................25 D4
Westpac..8 C3		EATING (p138)	Airlink...26 D4
		Wewak Yacht Club........................17 D3	MAF...27 D4
SIGHTS & ACTIVITIES (pp136–7)			Main PMV Stop.........................(see 22)
Catholic Church................................9 C2		SHOPPING (pp138–9)	
Cemetery...10 D2		Chambri Market............................18 C4	OTHER
		Dagua Market...............................19 A3	BP Outlet......................................28 B4

400 m
0.2 miles

your shipping needs for you – you can fill
up a box if you want. It'll be expensive.

Ralf Stüttgen (☎ 856 2395) He has a vast
array of Sepik carvings collected over a lifetime with pieces from 50 different villagers.
His artefacts are for sale, or he can tell you
where to buy particular pieces on the river.

Last Frontier Arts (☎ 856 1400; www.lastfrontier
arts.com.pg) This is the arts brokerage business
of PNG Frontier Adventures (p247). It has
a vast collection; some pieces are commissioned and bought over the Internet. Far
from profiteering from local people's artistic
work, this small business is keen to preserve
and encourage it. It's been very successful
and the best carvers are regularly fetching
K800 for large commissioned pieces.

Getting There & Around
AIR

Wewak is a major hub for air transport
around the Sepik and has frequent connections to Madang, Vanimo (K266) and the
Highlands. **Air Niugini** (☎ 856 2433) is in town
and flights include Port Moresby (K553), Lae
(K385) and Madang (K276). **Airlink** (☎ 856
3404) and **MAF** (Mission Aviation Fellowship; ☎ 856
2500) are represented at the airport.

BOAT
Lutheran Shipping (Luship; ☎ 852 2577; luship
.madang@global.net.pg) connects Wewak to
all the other ports in the country at least
weekly. It's predominantly a cargo carrier,
but some of its ships also carry passengers.

THE SEPIK

The Wuvulu–Aua community own MV *Thompson* which does a trading circuit between Wuvulu, Aua, Manus, Wewak and Madang, but there's no schedule.

Boats for Kairiru and Muschu Islands (K20, one way) leave from the wharf in town.

CAR & PMV
There are roads running west along the coast as far as Aitape, through the Torricelli Mountains and into the Sepik Basin, but they're very rough. Roads to Pagwi and Timbunke are impassable in the wet.

PMVs work mostly major routes like Wewak to Angoram and Maprik (both K30, four hours). They're mostly trucks, either covered with a tarpaulin with bench seats down each side, or a plain open tray. Most pull into Wewak's market area.

Starting times for PMVs in the Sepik area is often very early, although this is more the case returning to Wewak than leaving it. Expect to be on the road at 3am leaving Angoram for Wewak. PMVs don't run on Sunday. PMV travel on roads in this area can be *very* hard on your rear end, so buy a pillow to sit on.

AROUND WEWAK
Cape Moem
There are some fine beaches for swimming and diving at Cape Moem, past the airport. The cape is an army base, however, so seek permission from the **commanding officer** (☎ 856 2060). Get a bus to Moem Barracks, then walk 1km along a dirt road to the right.

At Brandi High School, to the east of Cape Moem, there's a collection of Japanese war relics.

Cape Wom
Fourteen kilometres west of Wewak, **Cape Wom International Memorial Park** (admission K1-2; ☯ 7am-6.30pm) is the site of a wartime airstrip and where the Japanese surrender took place. There's a war memorial flanked by flagpoles on the spot where Japanese Lieutenant General Adachi signed the surrender documents and handed his sword to Australian Major General Robertson on 13 September 1945. On the west side of the cape there's a good reef for snorkelling and a nice stretch of sand for swimming. It's a pleasant place for picnics and has good views across to the islands.

Cape Wom has had *raskol* (bandit) problems so it's best to go when many people are around. It's always popular on weekends. There's no transport that reaches there – you could catch a PMV bound for Dagua (a village further west) at the Wewak main market and get off at the turn-off to the cape at Suara. From the turn-off it is a hot 3km walk. There's a ranger at the gates.

Coastal Islands
Just off Wewak's coast are Muschu and Kairiru Islands. Kairiru is heavily forested and rises to nearly 800m. Its western end is volcanic and the sea has broken into an active crater at Victoria Bay where there's good snorkelling, hot springs and waterfalls. At the northeastern end of the island, there are two big Japanese guns.

The mission boats go between Wewak, Muschu and Kairiru a couple of times a week. The boat docks at the wharf across the road from the post office. On the beach nearby there are small boats and canoes that travel to the islands. The cost for the trip is negotiable.

MAPRIK AREA
Maprik town itself isn't great, but the area, in the Prince Alexander Mountains overlooking the vast Sepik Basin, is very interesting. It's noted for the Abelam people's distinctive *haus tambarans*, yam cults, carvings and decorations.

The population around Maprik is dense and there are many small villages, each with a striking, forward-leaning *haus tambaran*, an architectural style echoed in such modern buildings as Parliament House in Port Moresby. The front façade of the Maprik *haus tambarans* are brightly painted in browns, ochres, whites and blacks and in some cases they reach 30m high.

Yams are a staple food in this region. Harvesting entails considerable ritual and you may see yam festivals during the July or August harvest time. Woven fibre masks are used in ceremonies where yams are decorated to resemble people.

Interesting back roads connect villages between Maprik and Lumi, some with spectacular *haus tambarans* and good carvings. You can walk between these villages. Ask permission before entering a village and then see the *bigman* (local leader); also ask before taking photos. Traditionally *haus tambarans* were exclusively an initiated man's domain, but these days the rules are sometimes bent for Western travellers.

Sleeping

Maprik Waken Hotel (☎ 858 1315) is said to be still operating but only on request; you must ask for the accommodation section to be opened.

There may also be some local accommodation available. Just ask around.

Getting There & Away

From Wewak, the road climbs up and over the Prince Alexander Mountains, then goes 132km to Maprik. Maprik is 8km off the Wewak–Pagwi road. The junction is called Hayfields; there's a petrol station, trade stores and an airfield. A PMV from Wewak to Maprik costs K20, Maprik to Pagwi K10. The last stretch to Pagwi reaches the Sepik floodplain and is hard-going in the wet.

Roads will eventually link Lumi with Aitape. A road already continues from Maprik to Lumi, although missing bridges and deep rivers can make it hazardous.

SANDAUN PROVINCE

Sandaun (pronounced 'sundown') Province is so named because it's in the northwest of PNG – where the sun goes down. Formerly called West Sepik Province, it's largely undeveloped, but agricultural activity around Telefomin and timber development near Vanimo have brought rapid change. Gold is mined inland. There are opportunities to surf and enjoy the beaches here but it is a very remote part of PNG.

Sandaun Province is most notable to outsiders because of the devastating tsunami in the region near Aitape in 1998 (p143). As in East Sepik Province, cash-crop farmers are making good profits on vanilla beans which are often traded over the border into Indonesian West Papua.

VANIMO

This is on a harbour formed around a scenic hill – almost an island – joined to the coastline by an isthmus that proved ideal for an airstrip. Its topography, with its peninsula and hill, is reminiscent of Wewak and,

likewise, there are beautiful beaches on both sides of town. Vanimo, however, is much smaller and quieter, with generous and hospitable people. The town's Indonesian influence is quite marked in the goods for sale in the stores as much as the fabrics hanging up in the market. This gives Vanimo a slightly different feel to other PNG provincial capitals – on the upside the hotel-only eating options offer some good Asian-style food, but the Indonesian and Malaysian business people have a disdain for local service workers that is quite palpable and uncomfortable.

Malaysian logging company **Vanimo Forest Products** (www.vanimoforestproducts.com.pg) is logging the province and there are business opportunities with cross-border trade. Hopes are high for development, but Vanimo is still a tiny outpost on the western edge of the country.

The town has all the essentials – banks, a post office, and several supermarkets and places to stay. There's also an Indonesian Consulate in Vanimo, and most travellers who get this far go onto Jayapura.

Sights & Activities

There's a pleasant two-hour walk around the headland, but carry water and some sun protection. People in the villages there don't get a lot of tourists or even a lot of local passers-by so be respectful as you enter an area and seek approval before moving on. There's good snorkelling offshore and the beaches are sensational, but ask before stripping down and plunging in.

Another good walk is west along the beach from the airport. After 40 minutes you come to a limestone headland draped with vines – wade around it to the beautiful beach on the other side. There's a rusting Japanese landing barge just offshore.

Narimo Island can be seen offshore from the Vanimo Beach Hotel. This is an excellent place for picnics and swimming. The hotel may be able to arrange a boat to take you there or else ask about boat hire at West Deco village near the main wharf on the other side of the peninsula. Banana-boat hire for a full day can cost K80 to K100.

SURFING

One claim to fame that Vanimo does have is the best surf in PNG, and it's one of the primary reasons why people come to Vanimo.

THE SEPIK

The surf is strictly seasonal, from October through April, when monsoon swells bring waves between 3ft and 6ft. Vanimo and around has excellent point breaks and beach breaks with consistently good surf. There's a local bunch of surfers known as the Lido Surf Club – an informal collective who show visiting surfers around in a banana boat out to the nearby island breaks. They can even arrange accommodation in local villages. There's no surf-rage in PNG and the scene is just in its infancy. BYO boards.

Sleeping & Eating
Accommodation in Vanimo is a bit expensive, but the rooms are pretty good by PNG standards.

Varmoneh Lodge (☎ 857 1218; fax 857 1273; s/d/tr K90/120/160; ✖) This is a steep walk from town at East Tower and a good cheaper choice. It's clean and friendly where single rooms share facilities and the largest is self-contained with kitchenette. Meals are available and feature yams, sago, banana and fresh fish. Alcohol is not allowed and airport transfers are included in the tariff.

Sandaun Motel (☎ 857 1000; reception@sandaun motel.com.pg; r K168-196; ✖ 🖳) The motel is a nice place – a series of large airy bungalows, each with overhead fan, TV and fridge. The rooms are all self-contained and can sleep three. The motel is modest but well run with a bar and a good **restaurant** (meals K25-40) where à la carte options include chicken Kiev and steaks, and various Asian offerings like nasi goreng and *tôm yam* soup.

Vanimo Beach Hotel (☎ 857 1102/1310; s/d from K94/138) Owned by Ralat Indah Ltd, this hotel has a range of rooms and bungalow suites, including the most comfortable rooms in town. It's pitching itself at surfers too, offering packages at www.worldsurfaris.com. There are various room types with self-contained amenities and kitchen facilities, though the standard singles share facilities. There's a comfortable bar area, a good **restaurant** (meals K27-38) and poker machines for those inclined.

Shopping
There are several supermarkets and chemists in Vanimo all spread apart. There are markets located on a few green stretches around town selling fruit and vegetables, clothing and Indonesian cigarettes.

Getting There & Away
AIR
Between them **Air Niugini** (☎ 857 1014), **Airlink** (☎ 857 1584) and **MAF** (☎ 857 1091) service Vanimo most days of the week from Wewak (K266 one way, 50 minutes), although Air Niugini only flies in on Sunday, Monday and Wednesday. MAF has flights to Amanab, Green River, Telefomin, Tabubil and Oksapmin.

Air Niugini operates a weekly service to Jayapura.

BOAT
The MV *Libby II* does a weekly run between Vanimo and Jayapura (K70 one way). It departs on Friday at 4am, arriving in Jayapura at 7.30am, and caters mainly to Vanimo residents weekend-shopping in Jayapura. The return trip is on Sunday morning. Book through the Vanimo Beach Hotel.

CAR & PMV
The road from Vanimo to Jayapura is finally finished and travel to Indonesia by land is simple (see p239). The road from Vanimo stops at the border whereupon you cross to a line of waiting rickshaw drivers. You need to have a visa, which you can get from the Indonesian Consulate (p225), but other than that what used to be complicated is now very easy.

Getting Around
Vanimo itself is easy to get around by foot, although there are a couple of taxis. PMVs run along the beach roads. Banana boats ferry people around the coast – it costs K20 to Lido.

AROUND VANIMO
The coast between Vanimo and the Indonesian border has many superb beaches, waterholes and lagoons, pretty creeks and picturesque villages. There are panoramic views up and down the coast and locals will direct you to several fine waterfalls.

Lido village has a worthwhile surf beach and a village guesthouse. Outside every house at **Waramo**, there are smaller and well-constructed houses stacked meticulously with cut firewood. This variety of traditional wealth is presented to newly married couples.

AITAPE

Aitape is a tiny coastal town west of Vanimo towards Wewak. In 1998 a giant tsunami (right) devastated the area to Aitape's west – Sissano, Arop and Warapu – and this has put enormous stress on the Aitape area.

Aitape bears little evidence of its long colonial history. The Germans established a station here in 1905 and the jail they built in 1906 still stands above the town. It was used by the Japanese during WWII.

An Australian division relieved American units at Aitape in November 1944 and moved inland, against considerable Japanese opposition, to establish a base in the Torricelli Mountains. From there, they pushed the Japanese eastward until Wewak fell on 22 May 1945. A B24 bomber sits outside Aitape High School between Tadji airstrip and the town. There's a Japanese war memorial between the town and the Santa Anna Mission.

Tumleo and Seleo islands, 5km offshore, are rarely visited but worth seeing if you can arrange a boat.

Getting There & Away

There are two airstrips: Tadji and Aitape. Tadji airstrip, where most flights land, is 10km out of town. There's nothing at the grass strip except a windsock and guy with a two-way radio, and even he goes away between flights. The airstrip was the scene of much activity during WWII when the Australian Air Force flew Bristol Beaufort bombers from it – the original tarmac can still be seen in places through the vegetation. It is a bumpy landing on the grass but the strip is longer than the Aitape airstrip which, although close to town, can only handle small aircrafts.

The road between Wewak and Aitape is very rough and closed during the occasional bad wet season.

TELEFOMIN & OKSAPMIN

The remote stations of Telefomin and Oksapmin were only established in 1948 and 1962 respectively. They are among the most isolated settlements in the country, where missionaries are very active and traditional ways are dying out.

There are some dramatic **caves** in the Oksapmin Valley – you'll need a guide. Oksapmin is the main town in the area

---

TSUNAMI

On 17 July 1998, 30 minutes after a moderate earthquake shook the Aitape area, a 10m tsunami struck a 14km stretch of coastline and swallowed everything within 500m from the shoreline. More than 2200 people were killed and another 1000 suffered terrible injuries. Help didn't arrive for 16 hours and it was three days before most of the injured were admitted into hospitals at Vanimo and Wewak.

Ten thousand people became homeless in an instant. Many NGO and aid groups moved into Aitape to help with their relocation to higher grounds, but in the years since, land disputes (between *wantoks*, or fellow clanspeople!) have hampered much of the progress. There are still many people living in temporary accommodation.

---

where Southern Highlands Province meets Western and Sandaun Provinces. This is a beautiful region with the Om and Strickland Rivers and their spectacular valleys. The climb from the valley floor to the ridges is as high as 3000m in some places.

This area is driest in November and December but can be very wet any time. The region's name derives from its two main clans, the Ok and the Min.

Sleeping

Trabulok Guesthouse (s K40) A basic but well-equipped place to stay 1km southwest of Telefomin. It has shared bathroom and cooking facilities.

Getting There & Away

There are frequent flights from Port Moresby to Tari (K506, one way), as well as from other destinations. From Tari, MAF has many connections to remote airstrips.

The area is significant to the Ok Tedi mine at Tabubil as a source of fresh food and labour, so there are frequent flights. MAF has flights from Vanimo to Telefomin, Tabubil and Oksapmin at least twice a week.

AROUND OKSAPMIN

This district is important for the vegetables it grows and supplies to the Ok Tedi mine (p158). This was a protein-deficient area;

THE SEPIK

even spiders, grubs and beetles were eaten before *tinfis* (tinned fish) was introduced. In the evenings you can sometimes see torchlight around the valleys as women search for frogs, mice and snakes.

An interesting circular walk can be made through the villages around Oksapmin to the west and back along the Ariga River. North of Oksapmin, there are very few people, but around the town and to the south in the five high valleys of Bimin, Bak, Tekin, Teranap and Gaua there are over 10,000 people. For the most part their homes and gardens are at about 2000m. There's a sub-district office in the Teranap Valley.

THE SEPIK & ITS TRIBUTARIES

The mighty Sepik is the most famous feature of PNG, not just because fine art is produced in the area, but it has captured the collective imagination of adventure travellers. It represents to outsiders something quintessentially primitive, and an embodiment of ideas portrayed in Conrad's *Heart of Darkness* – a vast, densely populated river region home to isolated people (Conrad was a friend of Malinowski).

The scale of the river, the impressive architecture of *haus tambarans*, the beautiful stilt villages, the long canoes with crocodile-head prows, the birdlife, flower-clogged lakes, misty dawns and spectacular sunsets make a visit unforgettable.

The Middle Sepik is one of the most frequently visited parts of the country, but it is not crowded with tourists – you're unlikely to bump into other travellers. The river carries traders and missionaries, but that's about it. While photos of Sepik villages look idyllic, they don't show the heat and humidity, the mosquitoes or the basic village food. Nor do they indicate the meditative nature of travelling hours every day in a motor-canoe watching ibis take to the sky as you round a bend, or the rewards of experiencing these rich and fascinating cultures. Don't expect a lot of privacy when you're on the river.

The river has few exploitable natural resources and has attracted little development, despite the density of the population. Despite changes and Western influences, the people on the river are living much the same way as their ancestors – people cook in Western pots and drive motor-powered boats and canoes, they wear Western clothes, but they still practise many traditions.

Carving, though rarely traditional in form, is still an important part of river economies, and a master carver is still regarded with considerable prestige – Sepik art is alive, vigorous and unique.

The most artistic villages are concentrated on the Middle Sepik and the most spectacular scenery is on the lakes or tributaries. If you want to see a reasonable amount of the river at not too considerable a cost, Angoram or Pagwi are the best bases to use, but Timbunke and Ambunti are also worth considering.

Christianity, as elsewhere in PNG, is blended with many traditional beliefs. Although most Sepik people would claim to be Christian (they go to church every Sunday) it's a very localised interpretation. The religious world is also inhabited with the spirits of ancestors and crocodiles.

The Sepik is too big to cover, so pick a section and give yourself plenty of time to relax in the villages in between legs on the river – don't try and do too much. Two or three Middle Sepik villages are enough for most people, and some enjoy it more when they get off the main river.

The Upper Sepik extends from the river's source to just below Ambunti, the Middle Sepik covers from Ambunti to Tambanum and the Lower Sepik is the final section from Tambanum to the coast.

What to Bring

Only take to the Sepik what you need on the Sepik – leave your luggage with someone you trust in Wewak. A daypack is plenty for your time on the river.

The biggest issue on the Sepik is mosquitoes (*natnats*, p135) and you'll need to cover up when they start biting – long sleeves and trousers in lightweight fabrics are ideal. Loose-fitting clothes are better for the humidity. The *natnats* will bite right through looser weaves and fine cottons. Covered footwear is essential as is a broad-brimmed hat.

If you're travelling on a plush cruise boat you won't need much beyond some sensible clothes, but for everyone else preparation is important. You will probably be sleeping rough (although some river guesthouses provide mattresses and linen) and an inflatable hiker's mattress is perfect combined with a box-style mosquito net secured at four corners (the umbrella type are crap). You can buy good mosquito nets in Wewak. A sleeping sheet is ideal – silk is lighter and less bulky, cotton is a little cooler. A torch (flashlight) is essential and Sepik people have a voracious appetite for D-size batteries, so stow some to give away.

You bathe in the river, but never nude – bring some swimmers or a *laplap* (sarong) and a towel. Bring sunscreen, sunglasses, industrial-strength insect repellent, toilet paper, a spoon and a bowl. Rain water is collected and is fine to drink, but you might want to carry bottled water to be sure. Take a basic first-aid kit (see p248), and an umbrella might be worthwhile protection from the sun.

In Wewak or Vanimo you must stock up on food and cash. Of the former pack two-minute noodles, *Kundu* crackers (beef crackers), rice and *tinfis* (tinned fish). Take some cooking oil as well as that's precious in the Sepik. Any spare food you have remaining you can give away and it's gratefully received. Of the latter get plenty in small bills – figure on K100 per day for a motor-canoe and pilot, about K100 per day (or more) in fuel and K25 to K50 per night in a village guesthouse. A guide costs K50 per day and you'll need to pay your guide's PMV fares and accommodation costs in the villages.

Buy your fuel in Angoram or Pagwi because it costs a lot more on the river. Bring money for carvings, but remember that a 10kg carving might cost less than K100 but excess-baggage costs might be twice that if you're doing a lot more flying around the country.

A few days on the Sepik is enough for many people, and you'll get filthy so don't bring your tuxedo.

Getting There & Away

Getting to the Sepik can be challenge in itself – the PMV trips from Wewak to Angoram and Pagwi are long and uncomfortable, but you can arrange a hire car. The river is only accessible by road at three points – Angoram on the Lower Sepik (except after heavy rain)

GOIN' ALONE?

While it's possible to travel on the Sepik independently without a guide, very few people do and maybe this adds to the risks. To get the most out of the experience it helps to have a local person explain the everyday happenings, cultures and languages. There are some *raskols* upriver and a guide is honour-bound to get you onto the river and back again safely – once on the water you are days away from the nearest medical help.

If you really want to go alone talk to Ralf Stüttgen (p136) in Wewak before leaving. You'll need to have plenty of time to catch passing boats on the river and be well prepared and provisioned.

Most people pre-arrange their Sepik itinerary with either an inbound tour operator, or one of the smaller Wewak-based tour companies (see p247). This latter option is perhaps the best way to go, but give them a few weeks to make arrangements.

---

and Timbunke and Pagwi on the Middle Sepik. There are airstrips at Amboin on the Karawari River and Ambunti, further west.

Travel on the Sepik

Although travellers prefer the long dugout motor-canoes (pronounced *car*-noo), locals prefer the faster, more manoeuvrable motorboats, but these are expensive and fairly rare on the river.

There's nothing quite like cruising along the river sitting below the waterline in the bottom of a 20m dugout. It takes hours getting anywhere and the experience is quite calming and meditative. Once you've accepted that the canoe won't tip over rounding a corner you'll find the ride very relaxing. Even the buzz of the outboard motor seems to fade after a while.

There are several ways you can get about in the Sepik.

MOTOR-CANOES

You can hire motor-canoes in Ambunti, Pagwi and Angoram, and this is the best way to get around. Costs are a factor, and if you can spread the cost across a group of people, it will help. There are a few rogues who will try to rip you off or take you where they

THE SEPIK

DOS & DON'TS

There's probably too much hang-up about appropriate behaviour in the Sepik area. Good manners go a long way and locals usually forgive transgressions of local rules – you won't know you've done something wrong. Rules might be different for men and women. Try and remember the following:

- Don't wear your hat and shoes into a *haus tambaran*.
- Dress and act conservatively.
- Ask where you may wash.
- Ask before taking photographs of anybody or anything – *haus tambarans* are taboo.
- 'Best price?' Don't bargain, but objects sometimes have two prices. It's OK to ask and leave it at that.
- Don't be aloof. Meet with people, relate with them and demonstrate that you respect their culture.
- Be discrete about displaying your cash.
- Alcohol can be a very sensitive thing in villages – it's probably better not to have any.
- The gender politics can be a bit confusing; it's better that men mingle with the men and women with women. There can be awkwardness if Western women are allowed into sacred *haus tambarans* when local women aren't. Couples should not overtly show affection.

think you want to go. So it's better to plan an itinerary and bring a guide along from Wewak. The guide will know how much fuel to buy and what is a reasonable price.

If you charter a canoe you also have to pay for the driver to return to his base, whether you go or not. It's cheaper to travel downstream as the petrol (also known as *benzin*) consumption is reduced. Petrol will be the largest single cost – it's K4 or more per litre. At a leisurely pace you could travel from Ambunti to Angoram in five days and the cost could vary between K500 and K700.

Bearing in mind that various factors can have an influence, travelling downstream in a large canoe takes about 1½ hours from Ambunti to Pagwi, about six hours from Pagwi to Timbunke, and five hours from Timbunke to Angoram. Add at least 30% going upstream. A motorboat is twice as fast.

Canoes aren't superbly comfortable but the biggest drawback is uncertainty – you can arrive at the river and find there are no canoes available for days. It's much better to arrange all this in Wewak before you leave, or better still before you come to PNG.

VILLAGE CANOES & TRADERS

The river traffic is reasonably constant, and if you've got a pretty open-ended schedule and a lot of time you can catch rides in locals' boats and with traders moving up and down the river. This is the cheapest way to go – about K10 per hour – but you might be stuck somewhere for a few days before you can get a lift. There is very little traffic on the weekend and this is a very unpredictable way to get around.

PADDLING YOURSELF

You can purchase a small dugout for about K150 and paddle yourself. However, this is probably insane – the distances are vast and you can only paddle downstream. You might be able to buy a canoe in Ambunti or Pagwi; it may take a while to find one. Make sure it's suitably river-worthy. It takes a solid week of paddling to get from Ambunti to Angoram. This option should not be taken lightly and we don't recommend it, but die-hards should be well prepared and very well informed – talk to Ralf Stüttgen (p136) or Alois Mateos (p138) in Wewak.

Guides

There are plenty of people with motor-canoes who can take you on a Sepik tour. It seems as if everyone in Wewak is a part-time guide and you'll need a couple of days in Wewak to find a reliable guide or driver. Talk to locals to get recommendations, and get advice about how long a journey will take and how many

THE SEPIK

litres of petrol will be used. The going rate is K50 per day for a guide. If you get your guide in Wewak before leaving then he's responsible for getting you there and back as well, although you can get guides in Angoram, Ambunti and Pagwi as you go.

Tours

There are several ways you can pre-arrange a Sepik itinerary and this is the best way to see the region. The costs involved are not necessarily much more than what they'd be if you went independently. There are some very good options with touring cruise boats, but many travellers find the costs of the MTS *Discoverer* and *Sepik Spirit* prohibitive. Several companies organise travel in large motorcanoes, although prices vary considerably.

For information on major tour operators see p240.

There are a couple of Wewak-based operations that are generally much more modest and get you much closer to the village experience; see p247. Give these companies a couple of weeks to get things arranged – it's best to contact them before you come to PNG.

UPPER SEPIK

Above Ambunti, the villages are smaller and more spread out. The people are friendly and hospitable and have had less contact with Western tourists. Many villagers have no real understanding of the value of money, so prices can be erratic.

There's not the same concentration of artistic skills that you find on the Middle Sepik, but nature lovers will find this the most exciting part of the river. From Ambunti the river narrows and the land it flows through becomes hilly with denser vegetation. In many areas, trees grow right down to the water's edge.

There are few villages after Yessan and there is a long uninhabited stretch between Tipas and Mowi. The Upper Sepik is more isolated than the Middle Sepik, because there are no roads, so a visit requires detailed planning. Villages around here tend to move and there are lots of deserted settlements.

Green River

This is a subdistrict station, close to the Sepik River in Sandaun (West Sepik) Province, due south of Vanimo and very close to the West Papuan border. It's about a three-hour walk to the river but there is a road and you may get a lift. There are also links to Telefomin and Oksapmin.

Swagup

Well off the main stream, east of the April River, Swagup is the home of the insect cult people. Their unique art usually incorporates the figure of a dragonfly, sago beetle, praying mantis or other insects. The ferocious reputation these people earned in former times continues.

Maio & Yessan

The people here have a yam cult but they have been heavily influenced by missionaries. This area is quite swampy and marshy.

Maliwai

This village is on a small lake off the river. The people invest spiritual power in cassowaries and these flightless birds are carved into most things, regardless of function. It used to be customary in this village to cut off a finger joint when there was a death in the family.

Yambon

Not far from Ambunti, Yambon has good art and an interesting *haus tambaran*.

Ambunti

Ambunti is an administrative centre of no great interest but there is an airstrip and a couple of reliable people who hire motorcanoes, so this is one of the best places to start a trip.

SLEEPING

Because Ambunti gets a trickle of visitors there are various people prepared to accommodate you in their houses – you'll be expected to pay. There's also a guesthouse known as the **Ambunti Akedemi** (☎ 858 5929) as well as the SSEC guesthouse, in a house once used by missionaries.

Ambunti Lodge (☎ 856 2525; www.ambuntilodge -sepiktour.com.pg; s/d K65/98) has seven double rooms and two common bathrooms, but the lodge is being upgraded to include three additional self-contained rooms with aircon. Meals are available, as are half- and full-day tours. Mattresses, sheets and nets are provided. In the lounge area, there are numerous Sepik artefacts on the wall.

It's best to take a charter flight into Ambunti by MAF from Wewak or Mt Hagen.

Pagwi is a four- or five-hour trip over an arduous road from Wewak. There have been land disputes and security problems on the road to Pagwi – seek advice about whether it's safe. From Pagwi, Ambunti is a two-hour canoe trip upstream.

MIDDLE SEPIK
This region starts just below Ambunti and finishes at Tambanum. This area is regarded as the 'cultural treasure house' of PNG. Almost every village had a distinct artistic style, but these styles are now merging. The whole Middle Sepik region is interesting but the largest concentration of villages is just below Pagwi and it's possible to visit several ones on day trips.

Pagwi
Down the road from Hayfield, Pagwi is the most important access point to the Middle Sepik, although there is also a road to Timbunke. There is little of interest in Pagwi,

and despite its vital role it's rather an ugly little place – some rundown government buildings and trade stores where you can buy basic supplies.

You can hire motor-canoes here but be mindful that there are some rogues. Get advice in Wewak. Steven Buku from Yenchenmangua, 30 minutes away, is one of the Sepik's best guides, and you can contact him via the Windjammer Hotel (p137) in Wewak. Aldonus Mana, upstream at Japandai, is also a well-regarded local. Kowspi Marek is another recommended guide and boatman. He can be reached through the Ambunti Akedemi (p147).

Day trips can be made to Korogo. Aibom, Palambei, Yentchen and Kanganaman are all interesting and within reach. It's six hours to Timbunke and another five to Angoram. At a leisurely pace, stopping and taking side trips, you could take five or six days to get down to Angoram where you can get a PMV back to Wewak.

People have paid outrageous prices for canoes and tours at Pagwi – it's better to organise things in Wewak beforehand.

MIDDLE & LOWER SEPIK

GETTING THERE & AWAY
Pagwi is a four- or five-hour trip from Wewak. The rough 53km road from Maprik to Pagwi is impassable in the wet, and there have been land disputes that may make the road unsafe – seek advice in Wewak. There are passenger canoes running between Pagwi and Ambunti, two hours away upstream, most days.

Korogo
Korogo has a very impressive *haus tambaran* and there is a pleasant two-hour walk to an interesting inland village. There's an unsupervised guesthouse at Korogo, but in the past travellers have experienced thefts there – if you can't get someone to stay there with you, move on.

Korogo is half an hour by motorboat from Pagwi, half a day paddling.

Suapmeri
Variously spelt as Swatmeri and Sotmeri, Suapmeri is famous for its mosquitoes. There are few carvings for sale, although the village was famed for its orator's stools.

Despite this, it's an attractive village and the entrance to the Chambri Lakes. You may be able to stay with the family of James Yesinduma. James knows everyone who lives on the river and speaks English.

James can arrange a guide through the Chambri Lakes and along the weed-filled *barets* – you can take a shortcut to Kaminabit if the water isn't too low. Suapmeri is half an hour from Korogo by motor-canoe. To Aibom in the Chambri Lakes it's 1½ hours by motor-canoe.

Indabu
This is a good place to buy carvings and *bilums* and you can stay with local people, notably Steven Buku and his uncle Lawrence (contact the Windjammer Hotel, p137).

Yentchen
An hour by motor-canoe from Suapmeri, Yentchen is also a good place to stay. There is a big, clean *haus tambaran* for around K25. You bring a sleeping sheet, woven pandanus floor mat and mosquito net to sleep in these. The upper floor of a *haus tambaran* resembles a huge mezzanine structure that's open to the breeze.

The two-storey *haus tambaran* was copied from photographs taken at the turn of the century by German explorers of the building standing at that time. The top floor is only for initiates, who climb upstairs between the legs of a female fertility symbol and are blessed in the process.

Yentchen is noted for its wickerwork dancing costumes – figures of crocodiles, pigs, cassowaries and two-headed men.

Palambei
You can't see Palambei village proper from the river and it's easy to miss – there are a few huts and there may be some canoes on the bank. It's a hot 20-minute walk along a *baret* (empty in the dry season), but it is worth the effort because the village is beautiful. Built around several small lagoons full of flowering water lilies, the village has two impressive *haus tambarans* at either end of a ceremonial green.

Stones, which must have been carried many kilometres, have been set up in the glade. Locals are great *garamut* (drum made from a hollow log) drummers and you might see some beating out their powerful and complex rhythms. The village women make the best *bilums* on the river.

Palambei is 1½ hours from Suapmeri by motor-canoe.

Kanganaman

A brief walk from the river, this village is famous for the oldest *haus tambaran* on the river. Declared a building of national cultural importance, it's been renovated with help from the National Museum. It is a huge building with enormous carved posts. There's a new village guesthouse at Kanganaman, which was close to opening at the time of research.

Kaminabit

Kaminabit is not a particularly attractive village, not least because of the large lodge. There are, however, some good carvings. The lodge is used by a number of tour groups, including Trans Niugini, and is usually opened only for them. Local families offer accommodation – ask for James Minja or Anton Bob. Dominic and Francesca and their families have also been recommended.

From Aibom it takes one hour to get here by motor-canoe, and from Palambei it's 1½ hours by motor-canoe.

Mindimbit

The village is near the junction of the Karawari and Korosameri rivers. The Korosameri leads to the beautiful Blackwater Lakes region. Mindimbit is entirely dependent on carving and there is some nice work, though there is no proper *haus tambaran*. You can stay with a friendly family – ask for Peter Bai.

Timbunke

This is a large village with a big Catholic mission, a hospital and a number of other Western-style buildings. There are also some impressive houses.

Trans Niugini's *Sepik Spirit* calls in here which is why there's a good range of artefacts and carvings for sale. People have had problems trying to find somewhere to stay in Timbunke though, and the mission is not helpful. Ask a local about accommodation options.

Tambanum

This is the largest village on the Middle Sepik and fine, large houses are strung along the bank for quite a distance. The people here are renowned carvers. American anthropologist Margaret Mead lived here for an extended time. From Timbunke, Tambanum takes about 30 minutes by motor-canoe.

New Tambanum Lodge (contact Alois Mateos in Wewak ☎ 856 2525; per person K36) is an excellent bush guesthouse, which is situated 600m from the bank. There are six double rooms with shared kitchen and bathroom facilities and a separate septic toilet. Meals can be provided and tours can be organised. It's likely you'll stay here if you arrange a tour in Wewak.

LOWER SEPIK

The Lower Sepik starts at Tambanum and runs down to the coast. Angoram is the most important town on the Sepik. The Marienberg Mission station, which has been operated by the Catholics for many years, is about two hours downstream.

HAUS TAMBARAN

Tambaran is a spirit, so the *haus tambaran* is the house where spirits live, inhabiting sacred carvings and taboo objects. *Haus tambarans* are often referred to as 'spirit houses' or 'men's houses' because only initiated men (and tourists) are allowed to enter. Although Western women are usually allowed inside, times have not changed for village women (see p146).

Every clan has a spirit house and they are still very much the centre of local life. Men lounge around in the shade underneath the building, carving, talking or sleeping. Across the Sepik area young male initiates remain up to nine months in the upstairs section of the *haus tambaran* while they prepare for (and often recuperate from) initiation rites, and in this period they often cannot look at a woman until they are reborn as men. The *haus tambaran* is universally a female symbol – its entrance is sometimes vaginal in shape – yet everything about *haus tambarans* and what goes on in them is secret men's business and taboo to women.

Haus tambarans vary in style but can be up to 50m long, 30m high and extremely intricate.

Near the mouth of the river, the Murik Lakes are vast semiflooded swamplands, narrowly separated from the coast. Villages along this part of the Sepik are smaller, poorer and generally have had less Western contact than many in the Middle Sepik.

The vast volume of water and silt coming down means that the landscape around the mouth of the Sepik changes rapidly. Many villages here are only a few generations old, built on new land.

Angoram

This is the oldest and largest Sepik station. It was established by the Germans before WWII and now is a sleepy administrative centre for the Lower and Middle Sepik regions. Now, Angoram's population is falling and it's a town in decline – there has been no mains power in Angoram for 15 years despite the presence of power poles and cables. There used to be banks and businesses, a hospital and airstrip. Apparently this used to be a pretty swinging place in the colonial days with dances and parties – it's hard to imagine now.

The town centres around the marketplace and a large grassy area which was once a golf course.

If you haven't got a lot of time to spend but you want to see some of the Sepik, Angoram is the place to come to. It's accessible by road from Wewak and there are beautiful and interesting places just a few hours away by motor-canoe.

SLEEPING

There are a couple of reputable guides near Angoram. Elijah Saun and Cletus Maiban both offer accommodation and motor-canoe trips. They can be contacted at the Service Camp, a little upstream from Angoram.

Elijah's house adjoins his carving workshop on the riverbank. Mattresses, pillows, linen and mosquito nets can be provided. Cletus's house is a bit further upstream. There are various other people in nearby Angoram who will provide travellers with informal accommodation.

Angoram Hotel (☎ 858 3011; s K100; ✴) Owned by Joe Kenni, a local *bigman* and politician, the Angoram is in a pretty bad way, run down and closed a lot of the time – very few people stay here. The rooms have air-con but

only when the generator is running. Joe also runs tours and can recommend guides.

GETTING THERE & AWAY

Scheduled flights no longer call at Angoram. The airstrip is overgrown and not in use.

The road from Wewak to Angoram is the shortest access route to the Sepik. It branches off the Maprik road 19km out of Wewak. The 113km, all-weather road is good by Sepik standards but it's still extremely uncomfortable in the back of a PMV truck. Take a trade-store pillow to sit on. The traffic is reasonably frequent, but if you're returning to Wewak you start very early (around 3am). PMVs cost K20 and the trip takes three to four hours.

Around Angoram

A good day trip is to go south on the Keram River to **Kambot**, stopping at either **Magendo** or **Chimondo** on the way (about K200). These villages produce fantastic art – Kambot is the home to the Sepik storyboards. The river is narrow and winding, and the banks are crowded with luxuriant growth and ibis. There's informal accommodation at the culture house in Kambot. Further south on the Keram is **Yip**, and a beautiful rainforest with plenty of birds.

Another day trip from Angoram goes to **Moim** and **Kambaramba** and some beautiful lagoons. Further south on a tributary is **Wom**. The **Murik Lakes** are about four hours away and there's accommodation in **Mendam**.

TRIBUTARIES & LAKES

The Sepik River becomes monotonous as it winds through its vast, flat plain, with *pitpit* up to the water's edge. The most spectacular scenery is on the tributaries and the villages are generally smaller, friendlier and less visited. There are three main accessible tributaries in the Lower Sepik – the **Keram**, the **Yuat** and the smaller **Nagam**.

May (Iwa) River

This is a small town more than halfway from Ambunti to the West Papuan border. There's an airstrip and a mission settlement. It's possible to begin a river trip at this point. Villages in this area are very rarely visited and there are unresolved hostilities between clans. Seek advice before heading off from May River.

April (Wara) River & Wogamush River Area

Life on these tributaries continues in a more traditional manner, with initiation rites and various social taboos and systems still intact. Both areas are good for bird-watching. There are villages at regular intervals.

Wasui Lagoon

Also known as Wagu Lagoon, this is a beautiful place, with many birds. The Hunstein Range is behind Wagu and there is beautiful rainforest. There may be informal accommodation at the Wagu aid post.

Chambri Lakes

The Chambri Lakes are a vast and beautiful expanse of shallow water. They partially empty in the dry season, things get smelly and the water is unfit for drinking unless treated. It's difficult to find your way in, as floating islands can block the entrances – you'll need a guide. Rather than backtracking via Suapmeri, you can continue east and come back out on the river just above Kaminabit, if the water is deep enough.

Indagu is one of the three villages that make up Chambri region. There is a *haus tambaran* here with a huge collection of carvings in the polished Chambri style, as well as ornamental spears. **Aibom**, another village on the lakes, is famous for its fine pottery.

From Pagwi, the shortest way into Chambri is via Kandangai, but you can't get through if the water level is low.

From Suapmeri to Aibom, it takes 1½ hours by motor-canoe. From Aibom to Kaminabit it takes another hour by motor-canoe. There are village boats to Kandangai from Pagwi most days.

Karawari River

The Karawari runs into the Korosameri (which drains the Blackwater Lakes) and then into the Sepik just near Mindimbit. Initially the banks are crowded with *pitpit*. But jungle soon takes over and the river becomes more interesting, with abundant birdlife and attractive villages.

Amboin

Amboin is usually reached by air and from there it's a short distance up the river to the luxurious Karawari Lodge. The lodge river trucks will take you to nearby villages like Maraba, Marvwak and Simbut where traditional Sepik-style tree houses are still used. There are also tours that utilise the lodge at Kaminabit (p150) and some that stay in the villages. *Singsings* (celebratory dance/festivals) and re-enactments of the Mangamai skin-cutting ceremonies are all part of the deal. Special tours for bird-watchers to the Yimas Lakes can be organised.

SLEEPING

Karawari Lodge (☎ 542 1438; www.pngtours.com/lodge2.html; all inclusive per person s/d/tr US$444/360/324; 🞡) This is a luxury base, operated by Trans Niugini Tours, for exploring the Sepik near Amboin. Built with bush materials, the lodge has dramatic views across the Karawari River and a vast sea of jungle. There are 20 twin rooms, all with panoramic views. Trans Niugini Tours offers various packages based on one or two nights stay at Karawari. Sometimes tours with stays at nearby villages are also offered (far less luxurious). Like all of Trans Niugini operations it's cheaper to come to Karawari Lodge on a package.

Mameri

About 40 minutes by motor-canoe from Mindimbit and just before the turn-off to the Blackwater Lakes, Mameri is known for it's accomplished and dramatic carving.

Blackwater Lakes

To enter the Blackwater Lakes is to enter a vast water world where villages are often built on stilts and the people pole their canoes through shallow, reed-clogged lakes. The birdlife is incredible.

As you get higher, away from the Sepik, the climate is cooler and the scenery becomes more spectacular.

Govermas

A place of 'dream-like beauty', Govermas also has one of the most impressive *haus tambarans* in the region and some excellent carving. It's about one hour by motor-canoe from Mameri. If you get as far as this, it's worth going onto see Lake Govermas and the village of **Anganmai**, on top of a hill. **Lake Govermas** is covered in water lilies and surrounded by low hills, mountains, dense forest and three beautiful villages. On a tributary at the very south of Lake Govermas is **Mariama** which has a good *haus tambaran*.

Gulf & Western Provinces

CONTENTS

Gulf and Western Provinces are the wild west of Papua New Guinea. Vast, remote and sparsely populated, there is barely a sealed road to be found, and roads of any description are rare. Instead, locals hardy enough to survive the thriving population of malarial mosquitoes and endless meals of sago get around by foot, canoe and small plane.

The coastline arches around the Gulf of Papua and is broken by a series of river deltas, while mangrove swamps sweep inland before rising to the foothills and mountains of the Highlands. In the far west, the border with Indonesia runs north through the seasonally flooded grassland. Two of the country's greatest rivers, the Fly and the Strickland, run almost their entire length through Western Province.

Home to head-hunters and warring clans, these provinces have traditionally attracted adventurers, missionaries and prospectors. A few tough missionaries remain, and most other visitors come to the Ok Tedi mine, near Tabubil in the remote northwest corner of Western Province.

Few travellers reach the area and even fewer do so independently. Kerema and Daru are sleepy provincial capitals. But a growing number of nature enthusiasts are making the trip by air, especially to Kiunga and Tabubil. Their reward is the dizzying array of birds that thrive in the surrounding wetlands and mountains. And wet it certainly is – there's rarely a dry day in Kiunga, which receives more than 8m of rain per year.

HIGHLIGHTS

- Hooking up with Samuel Kapuknai in **Kiunga** (p159) and heading upriver for a couple of days of bird-watching
- Canoeing to **Kaintiba** (p157) and seeing traditional villages by foot
- Watching birds and fishing for barramundi at **Bensbach** (p159), one of the most remote places in the country
- Eating the fantastic mud crab in **Kerema** (p155) or **Daru** (p157)

- LAND AREA 133,800 SQ KM
- POPULATION 240,000

History

The coastal people of the Gulf traded their sago for the pottery brought by Motuans from the Port Moresby area for centuries. Less harmonious relations existed with the fierce Anga people, who live in the hills behind the coastal swampland. The Anga had a taste for human flesh (see right) but haven't pursued head-hunting seriously since the last major raid at Ipisi, near Kerema, just before WWII. Their proximity to the sea also made the coastal people prime targets of the 'soul hunters' of the London Missionary Society, who arrived in the early 1880s.

In 1842 Frenchman Dumont d'Urville charted the western side of the Gulf of Papua in HMS *Fly*, discovering the Fly River. In 1876 ruthless Italian explorer Luigi d'Albertis steamed over 900km up the Fly, terrifying any dangerous-looking villagers with fireworks and returning with a huge collection of botanical specimens, insects, artefacts and even painted skulls from village *haus tambarans* (spirit houses).

In 1901 the Scottish Reverend James Chalmers and 12 companions had their skulls crushed with stone clubs when they attempted to bring the word of God to Goaribari Island on the Gulf of Papua. Chalmers & co might have seemed like a gift from the gods to the protein-starved villagers, but 24 of them soon paid the price when they were killed by the crew of the *Merrie England,* sent from Port Moresby in the name of justice.

Charles Karius and Ivan Champion set out to travel up the Fly River from Daru in 1927, cross the central mountains and go down the Sepik to the north coast. Their first attempt failed, but a year later they completed the journey.

Geography

The Fly River starts high in the mountains and turns southeast towards the sea and a huge, island-filled delta. The Strickland River joins the Fly about 240km from the coast. Villages are usually some distance from the river to avoid flooding, and the Fly flows through 250,000 sq km of wetland where countless mosquitoes are the only welcoming party.

From the mouth of the Fly east to the Purari River, the Gulf of Papua is a succession of river deltas, backed by mangrove swamps running up to 60km inland.

Culture

Villages were traditionally centred around the *dobu*, a longhouse in which weapons, important artefacts, ceremonial objects and the skulls of enemies were stored. While men slept inside, women slept in smaller individual huts outside.

The *dobus* were veritable museums of traditional art, and seven distinct artistic styles have been categorised from the mouth of the Fly around to Kerema. There are no 'fully furnished' spirit houses left, but you can find figures, bullroarers, *kovaves* (conical ceremonial masks), headrests, masks, headrests, skull racks (every home should have one) and gope boards, which are elliptical in shape, rather like a shield, and incised with brightly coloured abstract patterns or stylised figures. Warriors were entitled to have a gope board for each act of bravery or to celebrate each successful conflict.

The Gulf people have been bombarded with Christianity for nearly a century and many traditions have been lost, including cannibalism, which had ritual and religious importance, but it is also possible that it was provoked by endemic protein deficiency in the area. The main food is sago: the tasteless, starchy food from the pith of the sago palm. There is no shortage of sago, so nobody starves, but severe protein deficiencies remain a problem.

Getting There & Around

Apart from the road to Kerema, most alternative transport is by air. Fares (p237) are astronomical.

GULF PROVINCE

Gulf is the country's least-visited province, which in many ways is its most appealing aspect. There is virtually zero tourist infrastructure and it is impossible to avoid the 'real' PNG. Getting around is an endurance test in itself and there's little respite at the end of the day; village or mission food and accommodation are pretty much it. There is, though, the mouth-watering mud crab.

KEREMA

Kerema was primarily chosen as the provincial capital because of its climate – it is comparatively drier than elsewhere in the province. Apart from its friendly people, there is little else to recommend it. As a stop on a journey into the interior, however, it does have a useful couple of trade stores, including **Ning's Trading** (☎ 648 1061), and a **Bank South Pacific** (☎ 648 1025) branch.

The **Hotel Kerema** (☎ 648 1396; fax 648 1397) should be able to rustle up one of the region's famous mud crabs. Perhaps a better option is the **Catholic mission** (☎ 648 1012, ask for Bishop Paul Marx) near the market, which has simple rooms and can provide invaluable information on the surrounding areas; it can also contact other Catholic lodges and link you with locals who can act as guides. Alternatively, try the **Salvation Army** (☎ 648 1384) or the **Missions of Charity** (☎ 648 1089).

Getting There & Around

Airlines PNG (☎ 648 1251) flies between Port Moresby and Kerema daily except Sunday. Flights continue to Baimuru (twice per week), Kikori (daily except Sunday), Balimo (three per week), Daru (twice per week) and Mt Hagen (weekly). **North Coast Aviation** (☎ 648 1230) flies three times a week from Kerema to Lae via Kaintiba and Kanabea and Menyamya.

The Hiritano Highway runs between Port Moresby and Kerema and PMVs (public motor vehicles, see p246) leave for the provincial capital (K20, five hours, several daily but fewer on Sunday) from near the market. The road is open all year, though during the wet season it is sometimes cut at

GULF & WESTERN PROVINCES

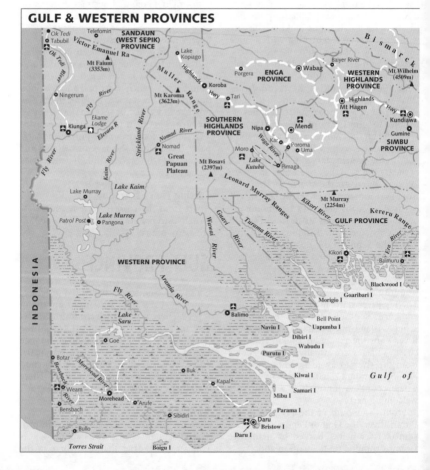

the Angabanga River, near Bereina. PMVs also connect to Malalaua regularly.

More interesting routes out of Kerema include trips by canoe and foot, see below.

AROUND GULF PROVINCE

The vast mangrove swamps and mountains are the main attraction of the Gulf Province. Travelling through this remote and unforgiving terrain won't be forgotten quickly. You could take any direction and go from village to village, eating sago and sleeping in local homes. The villagers are famous for their friendliness (post headhunting days) and it can be difficult to get away. If you plan on walking anywhere it's best to take a guide. The missionaries in

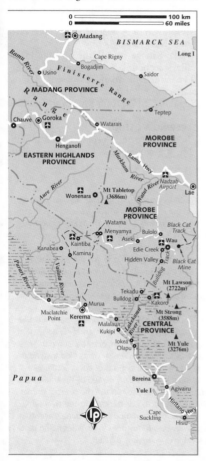

Kerema should be able to help with guides and reliable boat men.

Malalaua, a village at the end of the WWII-era Bulldog Track (p98) is easy to access by PMV or boat (K50). A more interesting trip would be to walk to **Kaintiba** via Kamina. The villages along this route have retained much of their indigenous culture and offer a view into the traditional way of life. Not far off the main track are villages where people still wear traditional clothes. If you wanted to attempt it, you'd take a canoe for much of the distance to Kamina. Kaintiba is in Anga country and is a tough, two- or three-day walk from Kamina where you climb through a range of vegetation including *kunaigras* and mountain forest. Several villages in this area also have missions. From Kaintiba you can fly back to Kerema or to Menyamya or Lae. You could even keep walking to **Menyamya** and take PMVs to Lae. A similar but longer canoe-and-walking trip (up to 10 days) takes you from Kerema and Menyamya.

For those gluttons for punishment, there is the most arduous boat trip of all, combining a series of canoes and other boats through endless swamp to Kikori, and then on to Daru. This could take several weeks and would require you to plan your first couple of days with the help of the missionaries in Kerema, and just hope for the best beyond that. Don't forget to take a good amount of food and buckets of mosquito repellent.

WESTERN PROVINCE

Western Province sees few tourists, but it's gaining a worldwide reputation as a birdwatching destination. However, be prepared for the expense of reaching the area.

DARU

Daru was the colonial headquarters for Western Division, the former name of the province, from 1893 and remains the capital today. It is on a small island of the same name, not far from the mouth of the Fly River. The main drawcard is the fishing, but some sailors moor here en route between Australia and PNG. The best contact is Max, the manager of the Kuki Hotel, who can arrange fishing trips in the mangroves for barramundi and black bass. Rates vary from about K475 to K2000 for a two-day trip (depending on how much fuel you use).

There's a **Bank South Pacific** (☎ 645 9062), but it's better to bring cash with you.

Sleeping & Eating

The best place in town is the **Kuki Hotel** (☎ 645 9476; marumari@daltron.com.pg; r K165, s/d all inclusive per person K237/265 ; 🍴 💻), where comfortable rooms have TV and phone. The hotel's **Crayfish Restaurant** (⏰ 6am-10pm) serves tasty food at fair prices, and caters for special requests.

Otherwise, the **Tawo'o Hotel** (☎ 645 9033; fax 645 9211; r with meals & laundry K121 or K220; 🍴) is not bad.

Getting There & Around

Unless you have a boat, you must fly to Daru. **Airlines PNG** (☎ 645 9039; at the airport) flies between Daru and Port Moresby most days and has a couple of flights a week to Kiunga, Tabubil, Kerema and other exotic locales.

There are no scheduled passenger boats from Daru.

AROUND WESTERN PROVINCE
Tabubil

Tabubil is the ordered, wealthy and expensive town that exists purely to support the vast Ok Tedi gold and copper mine. Like one of those isolated locations in apocalyptic films, it is accessible only by air or via a road to Kiunga and barge down the Fly River to the sea. The barge option isn't available to travellers. During extended 'dries' when the river level falls, the town can be cut off from supplies of food and diesel for months, and work at the mine reduces or ceases.

Tabubil is in a long, wide valley filled with rainforest and, in the early mornings, dense fog. It is safe and efficiently managed, and rows of Australian-style housing are occupied by employees. No outside visitors (expats or nationals) can stay in the houses without permission from the company.

Tabubil has a post office, well-equipped hospital, pharmacy and supermarkets in a complex near the centre of town. **Westpac** (☎ 548 9169) has a branch where you can withdraw money against your credit card. There is no ATM.

Like Kiunga (p159), the bird life in the valleys around Tabubil is quite amazing – there are more than 10 species of birds of paradise. Most birders engage Samuel Kepuknai (p159) from Kiunga as a guide.

SLEEPING & EATING

There is only one sleeping option in Tabubil, the comfortable but expensive **Hotel**

OK TEDI MINE

The open-cut Ok Tedi mine has been yielding gold and copper from Mt Fubilan, just beyond Tabubil, since 1984. For a time it was the largest gold mine outside South Africa, and if you can persuade Ok Tedi Mining Limited (OTML) to let you visit (having done the mandatory two-hour safety course), the immense size of the operation won't fail to impress. The logistics are extraordinary: to get the ore to ships off the PNG coast, a copper/gold slurry is sent 140km through a pipeline to Kiunga, where it's loaded on to barges for the 800km trip down the Fly River.

The mine has not been without controversy. In 1984 a tailings dam collapsed allowing 80,000 tons of pollution per day to flow into the Ok Tedi and Fly rivers. The resulting disaster endangered the livelihoods of people living along the river and damaged important breeding grounds for ocean fish near the river mouth.

A lawsuit was filed against BHP, the Australian company that developed and managed the mine. Thirty thousand villagers demanded compensation for the environmental damage. But BHP refused; it persuaded the PNG government to make it illegal for anyone to claim damages from BHP or its affiliates, such as Ok Tedi Mining Ltd, in such cases. The suit was filed instead in Melbourne and, soon after, BHP and the landowners agreed on a big out-of-court settlement.

In 2002 BHP opted out of Ok Tedi. Control was assumed by a company owned by the traditional landowners, who retained most of the mine's OTML management to run the show. Programmes to dredge the Ok Tedi and Fly rivers continue, aimed at reducing dieback along the riverbanks. OTML is also trying to establish other sources of income in preparation for the mine's eventual decommissioning, which is at least 10 years away. However, with fortunes in royalties being paid to local communities every month, encouraging local involvement is difficult.

Cloudlands (☎ 548 9277; cloudlands@online.net.pg; Newman Rd; r K132-380; ❄ ⌨). Rooms are clean if a little uninspiring, and there's a bar and a **restaurant** (meals K20-45; ⏱ 6am-10pm) that serves delicious pizzas, among other things. You can also eat at the nine-hole **Tabubil Golf Club** (☎ 548 8181; ⏱ lunch & dinner) and drink at the **Star Mountains Hash House Harriers Club** (☎ 6pm-midnight Mon, Wed, Fri, Sat).

GETTING THERE & AROUND

Getting to Tabubil is very costly: **Airlines PNG** (☎ 548 3244) flies daily to Port Moresby (K993; often via Daru). **Airlink** (☎ 548 8683) flies to Tari (K343), Mt Hagen (K524), Goroka (K661) and Madang (K794) five times a week. MAF (Mission Aviation Fellowship) also has irregular services in this area. There is an **MAF agent** (☎ 548 9025) at the Tabubil airstrip. If you're around for a few days it's worth waiting before you buy the return leg of your ticket; if you get drunk with the right people you might be able to 'hitch' a ride on a charter flight.

The road to Kiunga is serviced by PMVs (K20) that leave Tabubil at about 7am; the hotel can arrange for one to pick you up.

Kiunga

Kiunga mainly exists as the river port for the Ok Tedi mine and Tabubil. However, in recent years it has become a popular destination for bird-watchers, mainly due to the expertise of Samuel Kepuknai, an unassuming but passionate naturalist who's an expert on where to find the region's birds. Samuel is used by all tour operators running bird-watching trips to Western Province, but his company, **Kiunga Nature Tours** (☎ 548 1451; kepuknai@online.net.pg) can arrange private tours for a fraction of the price; he charges about K200 per day for guiding (per group).

Bank South Pacific (☎ 548 1073) has a branch in Kiunga, but carry money you'll need.

SLEEPING & EATING

The place to stay is the **Kiunga Guesthouse** (☎ 548 1084; bookings@gh.niungerum.com.pg; r all inclusive per person K140-275), where the cheapest rooms share a bathroom and aren't great, but the premier rooms are very nice. The guesthouse is also the best place to eat and is Kiunga's main store. There is talk of more accommodation options to come.

Samuel Kepuknai (see above) also runs the **Ekame Lodge** (r all inclusive per person K100) on the banks of the Elevara River, about 90 minutes by boat from Kiunga. This is a village-style place built specifically for bird-watching. Samuel virtually guarantees you'll see the twelve-wired bird of paradise, king bird of paradise, white-bellied *pitohui*, little paradise kingfisher and flame bowerbird, among others. The return boat trip costs K300.

GETTING THERE & AROUND

PMVs to Tabubil (K20) usually leave from Port Moresby around mid-morning. **Airlines PNG** (☎ 548 1125) flies between Port Moresby, Daru and Tabubil. **Airlink** (☎ 548 1390, ask for Moses) has flights to Mt Hagen, Goroka, Madang and Tari.

Bensbach

The Bensbach area is a vast floodplain, lightly populated because of lots of headhunting in earlier years. But the area is alive with birds and animals, including Rusa deer, wallabies, crocodiles and wild pigs. Bird-watchers and fishers are well catered for; the Bensbach River is renowned for its barramundi.

In the heart of all this is **Bensbach Wildlife Lodge** (www.pnghols.com; r all inclusive per person A$470), 96km north of the river mouth on the Bensbach River. The low-lying lodge is built of local materials and is quite comfortable. The drawback is the cash: to the daily rate, add a costly charter flight.

Island Provinces

A maze of wild jungles traversed only by a few tracks, frontier towns on the edge of the bush, and islands so remote they appear only as a speck of green in a vast blue ocean – these provinces won't disappoint you if it's an adventure you're seeking.

New Britain is an island steeped in history. The locals have seen German, Japanese and Australian empires come and go. The area is also known for the staggering Warwagira Festival of masked dance when sinister, anonymous figures from the villages swoop down like spirits upon the town to dance, sing and fire walk.

An angry chain of volcanoes traverses New Britain; you can see the cones smoking and hear the rock thunder. In 1994 Mt Tuvurvur and Mt Vulcan destroyed most of Rabaul in a furious rain of ash and rock.

West New Britain has a Wild West flavour; the migrant planters, loggers and the more bizarre species of expat struggle with the endless line of trees. Some of the world's best diving is here, near the mysterious Talasea peninsula.

New Ireland is even less developed than it's neighbour, little Kavieng – also a fantastic dive, surf and sailing destination – and is the largest town with hardly a vehicle in the sleepy streets. This is where you can inch down the coasts, staying in leaf-hut villages, snorkelling between limestone boulders on azure beaches and watching the spiritual art of the shark callers of Kontu. If you're game enough to venture into the deep south, you'll find a lost world in the utter wilderness of the Weitin rift valley, an area with flora and fauna unknown to science.

Tiny, far-flung Manus – a scuba-diver's dream supplied by the occasional cargo ship – seems like the world's end. Unless of course you want to take a canoe for a village stay on one of it's many islands.

Bougainville, the most troubled and beautiful isle of the North Solomons, is more akin to the Solomon Islands than New Guinea. It's rough, but as traditional as it gets.

HIGHLIGHTS

- Trekking through mysterious **Talasea** (p178) or spotting a killer whale while diving among the world's most diverse reefs
- Following the dancing procession of masked spirit men as they emerge from the sea at dawn during Rabaul's **Warwagira Festival** (p167)
- Taking a canoe across the gulf to **Manus** (p190) for a stay at one of the traditional villages on the outlying islands
- Diving with the sharks or taking a few days off to sail, surf and explore **Kavieng's** (p180) colourful history of sorcery
- Watching the ancient art of shark-calling on a trip through the wild and rugged beauty of the west coast of **Kontu** (p186)

| LAND AREA: 28,450 SQ KM | POPULATION: 523,000 |

ISLAND PROVINCES

NEW BRITAIN

New Britain Island, Papua New Guinea's largest, has a bit of everything you've come to PNG for. The colonial history, the mysterious cultures of the hinterland and the breathtaking wilderness are all here in one place.

East New Britain (ENB) Province ends in the densely populated Gazelle Peninsula where there has been lengthy contact with Europeans, education levels are high and the people are among the most economically advantaged in the country. By contrast, the other end of the island, West New Britain (WNB) Province, is sparsely populated, little developed and did not come into serious contact with Europeans until the 1960s. The migrant workers from the highlands, the 'colonial'-flavoured expats and the dense bush give WNB the flavour the east might have had just post-WWII. It's a frontier country with many a colourful, roguish Queenslander escaping from the more regulated life 'back home'.

One word comes to mind in New Britain in general: volcano. The whole region is a rumbling, billowing string of cones and craters covered in a riot of green. Fly over and you'll see smoke coming out of whichever one happens to be active – they really mean business.

In September 1994 Tuvurvur and Vulcan – the local volcanoes – erupted, spewing huge amounts of ash over Rabaul and the Simpson Harbour and Karavia Bay area. One of PNG's biggest and most beautiful cities vanished (see the boxed text, p174).

The impact on the densely populated Gazelle Peninsula has been enormous. Rabaul is now a Papuan version of Pompeii, destroyed by a few metres depth of the very ash that made this such an attractive plantation site for the early colonists.

History

The island of New Britain was settled around 30,000 years ago. The Lapita peoples, the world's first true ocean navigators, arrived about 4500 years ago bringing pottery and trade. Several hundred years ago, the Tolai people came from southern New Ireland and invaded the Gazelle Peninsula in northernmost New Britain, driving the Baining, Sulka and Taulil people south into the mountains.

In 1874–76 German traders established settlements in the Duke of York islands and Blanche Bay. At about the same time the Reverend George Brown started a Methodist mission at Port Hunter in the Duke of York islands and Emma Forsayth (Queen Emma; see p168) arrived from Samoa.

The area was renowned for cannibalism: in one case a captured European woman was married off to a chief who fed her late husband to her during the wedding *singsing* (celebratory dance/festival)! More missionaries were eaten than heathens converted in some districts. Michael Moran in *Beyond the Coral Sea* points out a curious parallel here with a biblical quote: 'He that eateth my flesh and drinketh my blood dwelleth in me and I in him'. It seems that the concept of acquiring your enemy's power or your loved one's spirit by eating them is not as foreign as it seems.

On 3 November 1884 a German protectorate was declared and the German New Guinea Company assumed authority, which it held until 1914 when Australian troops landed at Kabakaul.

At the end of WWI, the German planters had their plantations expropriated and were shipped back to Germany. Meanwhile Australians evacuated German residences, but not for long.

In 1937 the Vulcan and Tuvurvur volcanoes erupted, killing 507 people and causing enormous damage. Catholics fared better than Protestants, the former taking refuge in their grand and steep-roofed churches which didn't collect much ash. Before this eruption, Vulcan had been a low, flat island hundreds of metres offshore. It had appeared from nowhere during an 1878 blast (and had been immediately planted with coconuts). When the 1937 eruptions ceased, Vulcan was a massive mountain attached to the coast.

In 1941 Rabaul was completely crushed by the advancing Japanese. At the peak of the war 97,000 Japanese troops were stationed on the Gazelle Peninsula. They imported 800 Japanese and Korean prostitutes who were lined up in rows on the floor of the Cosmopolitan Hotel.

But the Allies never came. Over 20,000 tons of Allied bombs rained down upon the peninsula, keeping the remaining Japanese forces underground and impotent. When the war ended they were still there.

On 19 September 1994 Tuvurvur and Vulcan exploded again with relatively little warning, utterly destroying Rabaul (see the boxed text, p174). Only two people died (one of whom sat staunchly in his house and refused to leave) but 50,000 people lost their homes and one of PNG's most developed and picturesque cities was again flattened. The harbour was covered in a layer of pumice that only large ships could break through; chunks the size of sofas rained down in places, miraculously missing the locals. In the following weeks, buildings creaked under the weight of the falling ash and collapsed one after another. There was widespread looting and dogs ran wild.

Today, the region's seismic activity is measured more conscientiously than ever and the vulcanology observatory posts daily bulletins. Tuvurvur's spectacular emissions of smoke and noise are not presently considered dangerous.

Geography & Climate

New Britain is a long, narrow, mountainous island. The interior is harsh and rugged, split by gorges and fast-flowing rivers and blanketed in thick rainforest. The Pomio and Jacquinot Bay area receives more than 6500mm of rainfall each year, while annual rainfall in the Blanche Bay and Simpson Harbour area is about 2000mm. The dry season is between mid-April and November.

Culture

Most of the 184,000 people in ENB are Tolai who share many cultural similarities with southern New Irelanders.

Traditional enemies of the Tolai, the seminomadic Baining people of the mountains perform fire dances which are a spectacular event. Gigantic bark-cloth masks with emphasised eyes and features are worn by dancers who walk on, and *eat*, red-hot coals.

Secret male societies play an important role in village life, organising ceremonies and maintaining customary laws. Tolai ceremonies feature leaf-draped, anonymous figures topped by masks – *tumbuans* and *dukduks*, which are constructed deep in the bush under tremendous taboo. He who dances in the mask is no longer himself, but rather the collective kastom of the tribe's long history. The most feared spirits are

the *masalais*, which are spirits of the bush and water that live in certain rock pools and *dewel pleses* (thickets).

Shell money retains its cultural significance for the Tolai and is mostly used for bride price (p27). Little shells are strung on lengths of cane and bound together in great rolls called *loloi*.

EAST NEW BRITAIN PROVINCE

A basic network of coastal roads and two towns make this the most developed province in the New Guinea islands. If you need to book a flight, buy goods or receive medical treatment, this is the place. With the once-beautiful city of Rabaul levelled by the volcanic eruptions of 1994, Kokopo is now the main centre. Between the two, a strip of villages hug the shore of Blanche Bay, while behind them, beyond the copra plantations and the occasional town, the Baining Mountains give way to a green expanse of bush and volcanic peaks.

Kokopo

Kokopo is a friendly beach town which has retained its charm despite its recent expansion. Rabaul's government services and almost all of its businesses have relocated to Kokopo, causing some tensions.

ORIENTATION

A coastal road runs around Blanche Bay, from Tokua airport through Kokopo to Rabaul. Kokopo is strung along this coast road on the waterfront. At its western end are the picturesque lawns of the golf course.

INFORMATION

There are ANZ (towards Vunapope), Bank South Pacific (central) and Westpac (in Tacobar, 2km east of town) banks in Kokopo. To get to Westpac take PMV (Public Motor Vehicle) 8.

Ambulance (☎ 982 7333)

East New Britain Tourist Bureau (☎ 982 8657; fax 983 7070; 9am-1pm & 2-5pm Mon-Fri, 9am-1pm Sat) Near the ENB Historical and Cultural Centre.

Fire (☎ 982 8662/9516)

Nonga Base Hospital (☎ 982 7167) In Nonga, near the sub base, this is the biggest in the PNG islands. In a nonemergency, take PMV 1 to Rabaul market then PMV 6.

Police (☎ 982 8222)

Yudrowet Internet Cafe (per hr K25) Near Taklam Guesthouse.

ISLAND PROVINCES

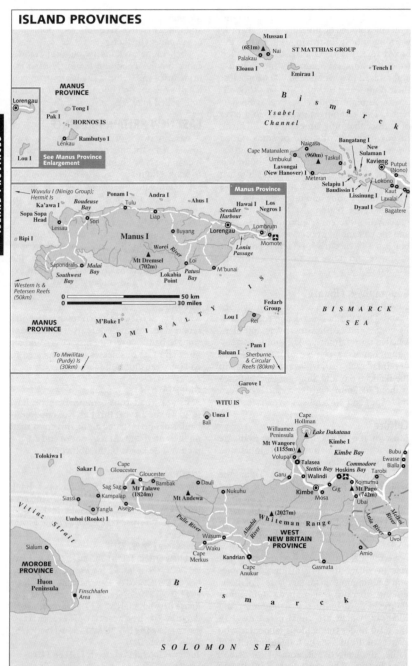

MANUS PROVINCE

Lorengau

Tong I
Pak I
HORNOS IS
Lénkau
Rambutyo I
Lou I

See Manus Province Enlargement

Mussau I
(651m) ▲ Nai
Palakau
ST MATTHIAS GROUP
Eloaua I
Emirau I
Tench I

B i s m a r c k

Ysabel Channel

Naigasa
Bangatang I
New Sulaman I
Cape Matanalem
(960m) ▲ Taskul
Umbukul
Kavieng
Putput (Nono)
Lavongai (New Hanover) I
Meteran
Lokono
Selapiu I
Baudissin I
Lissinung I
Kaut
Lavalai
Bagatere
Dyaul I

Manus Province

Wuvulu I (Ninigo Group); Hermit Is
Ponam I
Andra I
Ahus I
Hawai I
Los Negros I
Ka'awa I
Boudeuse Bay
Tulu
Liap
Seeadler Harbour
Lombrum
Sopa Sopa Head
Lessau
Sori
Buyang
Lorengau
Momote
Bipi I
Manus I
Loniu Passage
Sapondralis
Worei River
Loi
M'bunai
Malai Bay
Mt Dremsel (702m)
Patusi Bay
Southwest Bay
Lokabia Point

Western Is & Petersen Reefs (50km)

0 _____ 50 km
0 _____ 30 miles

MANUS PROVINCE

M'Buke I
Rei
Lou I
Fedarb Group

A D M I R A L T Y   I S

B I S M A R C K SEA

To Mwilitau (Purdy) Is (30km)

Baluan I
Pam I
Sherburne & Circular Reefs (80km)

Garove I

WITU IS

Unea I
Bali

Cape Hollman
Willaumez Peninsula
Lake Dakataua
Mt Wangore (1155m) ▲
Kimbe I
Kimbe Bay
Volupai
Talasea
Stettin Bay
Commodore
Hoskins Bay
Bubu
Ewasse
Bialla
Tolokiwa I
Garu
Walindi
Tarobi
Sakar I
Cape Gloucester
Gloucester
Bambak
Dauli
Nukuhu
Kimbe
Gig
Koimumu
Mt Pago (742m) ▲
Sag Sag
Mt Talawe (1824m) ▲
Mosa
Ubai
Siassi
Kampalap
Mt Andewa ▲
Mahoi River
Yangla
Aisega
▲ (2027m)
Whiteman Range
Umboi (Rooke) I
Pulie River
Alimbit River
Inia River
Uvol
Sialum
Wasum
WEST NEW BRITAIN PROVINCE
Vitiaz Strait
Waku
Cape Merkus
Kandrian
Amio
MOROBE PROVINCE
Cape Anukur
Gasmata
Huon Peninsula
Finschhafen Area

B i s m a r c k

SOLOMON SEA

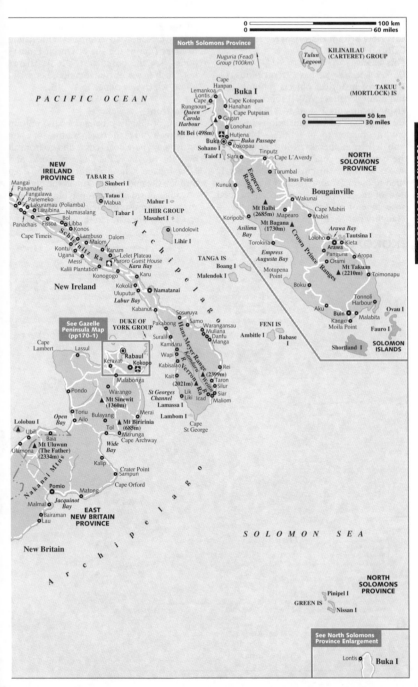

ISLAND PROVINCES

0 — 100 km
0 — 60 miles

North Solomons Province

Nuguria (Fead) Group (100km)

Tulun Lagoon

KILINAILAU (CARTERET) GROUP

TAKUU (MORTLOCK) IS

P A C I F I C   O C E A N

Cape Hanpan
Lemankoa
Lontis
Cape Rungnoun
Buka I
Cape Kotopan
Hanahan
Cape Putputan
Gagan
Lonohan
Queen Carola Harbour
Mt Bei (498m)
Hutjena
Buka — *Buka Passage*
Kokopau
Sohano I
Tinputz
Taiof I
Siara
Cape L'Averdy

0 — 50 km
0 — 30 miles

NORTH SOLOMONS PROVINCE

NEW IRELAND PROVINCE

TABAR IS
Simberi I

Mangai
Panamafei
Fangalawa
Panemeko
Lakuramau (Poliamba)
Laraibina
Namasalang
Bol
Panachais
Fissoa
Konos
Cape Timeis
Lambuso
Malom
Dalom
Kontu
Ugana
Messi
Kanam
Kalili Plantation
Konogogo

Sebelius Ra

Tatau I
Mabua

Mahur I
LIHIR GROUP
Masahet I

Londolovit
Lihir I

Tarumbal
Inus Point

Bougainville
Wakunai
Cape Mabiri
Mabiri

Mt Balbi (2685m)
Mapearo
Koripobi
Mt Bagana (1730m)
Asilima Bay
Torokina
Empress Augusta Bay
Motupena Point

Arawa Bay
Loloho
Tautsina I
Kieta
Arawa
Panguna
Orami
Aropa
Mt Takuan (2210m)
Toimonapu

Emperor Ranges

Kunua

Crown Prince Ranges

Boku

Tonnoli Harbour
Aku
Buin
Malabita
Kangu
Moila Point
Ovau I
Fauro I

SOLOMON ISLANDS

Shortland I

New Ireland

Lelet Plateau
Turoro Guest House
Karu Bay
Karu

Kokola
Uluputur
Labur Bay
Kabanut

Namatanai

Sosuruya
Samo
Warangansau
Muliana
Danfu
Manga

TANGA IS
Boang I

Malendok I

FENI IS
Ambite I
Babase

Pakabong
Surali
Kamdaru
Wapi
Kabisalao
Kait

DUKE OF YORK GROUP

See Gazelle Peninsula Map (pp170–1)

Cape Lambert
Lassul
Keravat
Rabaul
Kokopo
Malabonga

Pondo
Warango
Toriu
Ailo
Bulayang
Tol
Marunga
Cape Archway
Merai
Mt Sinewit (1360m)
Mt Bipinia (685m)

Open Bay
Lolobau I
Ubit
Baia
Mt Uluwun (The Father) (2334m)
Ulamona

Wide Bay
Kalip

Rei
Taron
Silur
St Georges Channel
Lik
Liki
Siar
Icad
Maliom
Lambom I
Cape St George

Hans Meyer Range

Crater Point
Sampun
Cape Orford

Pomio
Matong
Malmal
Jacquinot Bay
Bairaman
Lau

EAST NEW BRITAIN PROVINCE

Nakanai Mts

New Britain

S O L O M O N   S E A

A r c h i p e l a g o

NORTH SOLOMONS PROVINCE

Pinipel I
GREEN IS
Nissan I

See North Solomons Province Enlargement

Lontis
Buka I

(2399m)
(2021m)
Kamdaru Wei
Verron Ra

Lamassa I

St Georges

SIGHTS
East New Britain Historical & Cultural Centre
This **museum** (☎ 982 8453; fax 982 8439; admission K2; ☽ 9am-5pm Mon-Sat) has a tremendous collection of historical objects, photographs and many Japanese WWII relics. The Tok Pisin documents issued to allied airmen are accompanied by translations instructing the reader to obey the white men who fell from the sky. Most poignant is the courageous role played by the locals in a war whose origins were completely alien to them. Among the displays is a section of the 1940s-style soft-porn painted nose-cone of an American B17 bomber – 'Naughty but Nice'.

Queen Emma's Steps & House Site
Right where the road terminates at the Ralum Country Club is the site of Queen Emma's house (see the boxed text, p168). There's not much to see of Gunantambu, her grand home, which was ruined in WWII.

Waterfront
Dozens of dinghies (banana boats) pull up on the east end of the beach waiting for a fare or fishing. These boats come and go from all over the province, the Duke of Yorks and New Ireland. The operators usually sleep through the midday heat under the big trees or gather in small groups playing cards and string-band music on their salty ghetto blasters. The best beach is to the west of here.

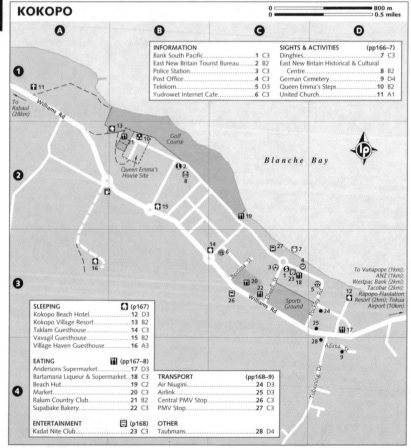

KOKOPO

0	800 m
0	0.5 miles

INFORMATION	
Bank South Pacific	1 C3
East New Britain Tourist Bureau	2 B2
Police Station	3 C3
Post Office	4 C3
Telekom	5 D3
Yudrowet Internet Cafe	6 C3

SIGHTS & ACTIVITIES	(pp166–7)
Dinghies	7 C3
East New Britain Historical & Cultural Centre	8 B2
German Cemetery	9 D4
Queen Emma's Steps	10 B2
United Church	11 A1

To Rabaul (28km)
Williams Rd
Golf Course
Queen Emma's House Site
Blanche Bay
Bertina St
Williams Rd
Elwell St
Brockley Rd
Sports Ground
Adima
Tobauing Dr

To Vunapope (1km); ANZ (1km); Westpac Bank (2km); Tacobar (2km); Rapopo Plantation Resort (2km); Tokua Airport (10km)

SLEEPING	(p167)
Kokopo Beach Hotel	12 D3
Kokopo Village Resort	13 B2
Taklam Guesthouse	14 C3
Vavagil Guesthouse	15 B2
Village Haven Guesthouse	16 A3

EATING	(pp167–8)
Andersons Supermarket	17 D3
Bartamana Liqueur & Supermarket	18 C3
Beach Hut	19 C2
Market	20 C3
Ralum Country Club	21 B2
Supabake Bakery	22 C3

ENTERTAINMENT	(p168)
Kadat Nite Club	23 C3

TRANSPORT	(pp168–9)
Air Niugini	24 D3
Airlink	25 D3
Central PMV Stop	26 C3
PMV Stop	27 C3

OTHER	
Taubmans	28 D4

ACTIVITIES
For information on diving in the area see p171.

Swimming
Kids swim at the beach near the hospital entrance at Vunapope and along the golf course beach which has a point reef that is good for snorkelling. But try anywhere along Kokopo's straight coast or beyond in either direction; ask a local first.

Fishing
Ask at Taklam Guesthouse (right) if you want to hire a boat or organise a trip.

Golf
Ralum Country Club (☎ 982 8240; admission free, single golf round K10) clubhouse has a bar, darts, snooker and a wonderfully antiquated bowling alley with a control panel of knobs and dials that looks like it came from a 1930s rocket-science project.

Rugby League
There are no millionaires on the sport field in Kokopo on a Saturday afternoon (February to September), but the game Australia exported to PNG is alive and kicking here – you can hear the bone-crunching tackles from across the road. It's a great atmosphere with kids climbing the mango trees, fans dodging splats from betel-nut splotches on the sidelines and even the linesman looking like he could bench-press a horse. It's well worth the K2; games start at 3pm. Cheer the team in red, white and blue – the local 'Royals'.

TOURS
Taklam Guesthouse has day tours (K192) of Rabaul that take in all the sights along the way including Vulcan, the submarine base and tunnels.

Heli Niugini (☎ 982 9422; 15 min K1000, maximum 5 people), just outside Vunapope, offers helicopter flights over Tuvurvur and Vulcan.

FESTIVALS & EVENTS
The **Warwagira Festival** (first two weeks of July) is a great occasion, in the last three days of which *dukduks* and *tumbuans* (masked forest spirits – *dukduks* are the taller ones) come out of the sea from canoes at dawn to dance. At night, Baining fire dancers per-form, fire walking in huge masks, with a live snake. Call the ENB Tourist Bureau (p163) or one of the hotels to confirm the date.

SLEEPING
Kokopo Beach Hotel (bungalows K250; 🟦) Affiliated with Taklam, this is the nicest place in Kokopo itself. The traditionally decorated beach bungalows are set in a garden and front onto the water. There's a thatched, outdoor bar and sitting area, and the setting is tranquil.

Rapopo Plantation Resort (☎ /fax 982 9944; s K264, d K170-302) The best bet if you want to be a bit out of town. It's right on the beach among fig and coconut trees and im-maculate lawns. The deluxe rooms are in a timber pavilion and are large with every commodity. The share-facility rooms aren't really worth it, but the self-contained apart-ments under construction (K330, sleeping five) look promising.

Kokopo Village Resort (☎ 982 8060; www.kokopo resort.com.pg; s K88-127, d K99-154, bungalow s/d K231/242; 🟦) Has plush, carved-wood bun-galows in the greenery. The bay views are terrific, as is the garden surround. Also has a restaurant. A good choice.

Village Haven Guesthouse (s/d K35/40) A set of huts on a hill with unrivalled views. It's rustic but clean and right in a village com-munity. There's a kitchen and shared bath-rooms, but no fans.

Vavagil Guesthouse (☎ 982 8833; vavagil@global .net.pg; s K83-108, d K94-121; 🟦) Economy rooms with shared facilities or simple, self-contained units. There's a kitchen for guests to use.

Taklam Guesthouse (☎ 982 8870; www.taklam .com.pg; s K79-250, d K95-280; 🟦) This has pokey but clean budget rooms with shared bath-room, and increasingly larger and better-equipped options up the scale. Chopsticks Restaurant (p168) is on site. The real plus is the excellent local information and tours.

EATING
There are some *kai* bars (cheap takeaway food bars) lining the streets, most of which are OK – Andersons has good chips. Generally restaur-ants open from 7.30am to 8.30pm.

Ralum Country Club (lunch/dinner K20/25) This is excellent value, as friendly as they come and flexible (staff will make you a vegetar-ian option). It has fish, fried chicken, chow mein and the like. The bar and grounds are a bonus.

ISLAND PROVINCES

ISLAND PROVINCES

QUEEN EMMA

Emma Forsayth was born in Samoa of an American father and a Samoan mother. She was expelled from a Sydney convent for performing a half-naked 'heathen' dance before the Virgin Mary's statue. Her first husband was lost in a typhoon before she started a trading business with her (common law) second husband, at Mioko in the Duke of York islands in 1878.

She was the image of promiscuity. From her Kokopo mansion, she threw wild parties for visiting German naval ships and traders, dancing with her Samoan protégés and serving delicacies and champagne ('enough to bathe in') in golden vessels. One German trader claimed 'she could accomplish miracles in love-making and drinking'. Men found her irresistible; early in life, one of her admirers had tried to sell a rival to a cannibal chief.

Emma extended her empire to include plantations, a number of ships and a string of trade stores. Whole provinces became hers in return for a few trinkets. She was faithful to one particular lover Agostino Stalio (a Dalmatian...), but after his death in a sea battle (a revenge mission) she married German sea captain Paul Kolbe. He died in Monte Carlo in 1913 and Emma died a few days later. Her empire soon fell apart.

But there's mystery about their deaths: the dates in the death notice don't correspond with those on their tombstones. It's thought that Coe Forsayth (Emma's son to James Forsayth) gave misleading information to Australian newspapers about his mother dying after Kolbe. It's significant that Kolbe predeceased Emma, because she was known to be anxious about claims on her estate by Kolbe and his German relatives. She wanted her son to inherit her fortune.

Emma's grave was only rediscovered in 1955 and her headstone was missing. Many years later, it was located in an old cemetery on South Head in Sydney, Australia, between the graves of JMC Forsayth (died 14 March 1941, 69 years) and Ida Forsayth (died 15 April 1947). Could JMC Forsayth be Coe? It seems likely.

Kokopo Village Resort (breakfast/lunch/dinner K22/30/40) Serves breakfast fry-ups and grilled fish or steaks for lunch. There's a broader menu in the evenings when generous mains include a crab salad.

Chopsticks Restaurant (breakfast/lunch/dinner K15/25/35) At the Taklam Guesthouse (p167), Chopsticks serves a wide choice of Chinese, seafood and steaks and a few veggie options. Portions are generous.

Kadat Nite Club (mains K25) Has steak and chips, fish and chips, and stew. It's open for dinner and dancing (right) too.

Beach Hut (mains K35) Some would say there's a bit too much atmosphere here. The music is loud, but it's on the water and the meaty menu, featuring many a T-bone, is popular with the locals.

You can fend for yourself at Supabake Bakery, Andersons supermarket and Bartamana Liqueur & Supermarket, and get great fruit and vegetables and some 'exotics' at the **Kokopo market** (closed Sun). Kokopo market is colourful and best on Saturdays. *Buai* (betel nut) and its condiments, *daka* (mustard stick) and *cumbung* (mineral lime, which looks rather like cocaine in its little plastic wraps) account for half of the stalls,

with produce – fruit, vegetables, smoked fish and crabs – most of the remainder.

At the rear, tobacco growers sell dried leaves; home-made cigars wrapped with sticky tape at the mouth-end sell for K0.20 each. You can buy meat (or plantain) and rice wrapped in a banana leaf for K1. You can pay your way with shell money here (K2 an arm's length). The main PMV stop is just across the main road from the market.

DRINKING

You're best off at the Ralum Country Club (p167) for atmosphere. It's lovely on the lawn, chatting to the minister's daughter, with the moon on the water...Otherwise kick-off at Chopsticks bar at Taklam Guesthouse (p167; they show the footy) before heading to friendly Kadat Nite Club where the Pacific reggae cranks and the ladies have a predatory reputation. Rare for a small town, this place really does get into full swing.

GETTING THERE & AWAY
Air

The Kokopo–Rabaul area is serviced by Tokua airport 10km east of Kokopo. Look out for the three murals of (from left to right) Tolai, Pomio and Baining dancers as you get off the plane.

Air Niugini (airport ☎ 983 9325, Kokopo ☎ 982 9033; fax 983 9052) flies return to Tokua airport and back once a day from Port Moresby (K661, two hours) and Hoskins (K309, 35 minutes). There are two weekly flights from Tokua to Kavieng (K312, 40 minutes) and three to Buka (K370, 45 minutes).

Airlink (☎ 982 8600) flies daily to Kavieng (K245, 1¾ hours) via Lihir. This sometimes includes a terrific low-level run up the east coast of New Ireland; you'd think the pilot was about to strafe the ground. On Monday, Wednesday and Friday, Airlink flies to Kandrian (K511, 45 minutes), Pomio in Jacquinot Bay (K302, 30 minutes) and Hoskins (K277), the latter flight passing just 100m over the smoking cone of Mt Uluwan on the way back to Kokopo.

Boat
Dinghies tie up on the beach near the post office. The two-hour trip to New Ireland via the Duke of York Islands costs K50 as a passenger, but you can charter a dinghy just about anywhere (K90 plus petrol).

GETTING AROUND
Car
Car hire (4WD/2WD per day K140/200 plus K0.90 per kilometre) is costly. **Budget** (☎ 983 9328), **Avis** (☎ /fax 983 9331) and **Travelcar** (☎ 982 9206) have offices at Tokua airport; **Hertz** (☎ 982 9153) is above Vunapope's ANZ bank. Most hotels will give you a 10% discount.

PMV
PMV No 1 – signed 'Tokua' on the widescreen – does the run to the airport (K1.50), but infrequently. This bus tends to meet the larger Air Niugini flights. Guesthouses and hotels can provide transfers (K25).

PMV No 1 also runs in the other direction out along the coast road past the Karavia barge tunnel (K1.50), to Rabaul (K2.50). Take No 2 to Bita Paka War Cemetery (K1) and Warangoi (K3). PMV No 3 goes to Vunadidir (K2) and Toma (K3), offering the chance to see the inland of the Gazelle Peninsula and perhaps a glimpse of the Baining mountains. PMV No 8 goes (sometimes) as far as the airport (K1.50) via Vunapope (K0.50) and Tacobar (K0.60). PMV No 5 goes to Keravat (K4) and Kabaira Bay (K5).

Around Kokopo
BITA PAKA WAR CEMETERY
Bita Paka War Cemetery contains the graves of over 1000 Allied war dead, many of them Indian slaves. The gardens are lovely. It's situated about 2km east of Vunapope – just before Kabakaul, turn off the coast road and walk inland for about 5km.

KOKOPO–RABAUL ROAD
The coast road goes past Raluana Point, around Karavia Bay before squeezing between Vulcan and the hills, and then around Simpson Harbour to Rabaul.

Queen Emma's matmat (grave) is signposted a few kilometres west of Kokopo in the pretty, well-maintained Forsayth family cemetery. The gravestones of her brother and her lover, Agostino Stalio, are in much better shape, the latter with a romantic inscription: 'Oh for the touch of a vanished hand and the sound of a voice which is still'.

Along this stretch of road are countless **Japanese barge tunnels**. The main tunnel contains five rusty barges, lined up nose to tail – bring a torch and K5 kastom price. They were hauled to the water along rails by slaves to load shipping cargo. Watch your step on the rotting boardwalk.

The huge form of **Vulcan** rises on the roadside. When Vulcan erupted in 1937 a boat was moored in the bay. The boat became landlocked 70m from shore. Thanks to the 1994 eruption, it is now buried for some future archaeologist to find and puzzle over.

MALMALUAN LOOKOUT
The Burma Rd leaves the Kokopo–Rabaul Rd and climbs to Malmaluan Lookout (at the Telekom tower). The views are OK, and there's an anti-aircraft gun and howitzer.

PETER TOROT'S CEMETERY & MEMORIAL CHURCH
As the Burma Rd begins to dip towards the coast, it passes through the Rakunai site of Peter ToRot's cemetery and memorial church (see the boxed text, p173).

It's moving when a multitude of families in pressed shirts, print dresses and bare feet walk many miles to Sunday church.

KERAVAT
The Lowland Agricultural Experimental Station is here. They're trying (among other

things) to introduce the durian fruit – beloved above all fruits in Southeast Asia – to PNG. Durians smell like *pekpek bilong cuscus* (cuscus droppings) if you're not used to them, or even if you are used to them.

Rabaul

Most of Rabaul is a weird wasteland, buried in deep black volcanic ash. Almost the entire old town is buried and barren and looks like a movie set for an apocalyptic film. There's now a bit of life a block or so inland along the whole road but east of here Rabaul is mostly abandoned. Thanks to the deep water (and Kokopo's shallow water), Rabaul's port facilities will keep the town alive.

At Matupit the thousand-strong village community still chooses to reside right underneath the belching monster. Tuvurvur's eruptions in 1994 miraculously left Matupit practically unscathed, thanks, they say, to the local *dukduks*. For more information on the history of this region see p162.

INFORMATION

There's a Bank South Pacific, and the Hamamas Hotel sometimes changes money. The post office is in Top Kai supermarket. Don't confuse it with Vunapope PO, also called 'Rabaul'.

Nonga Hospital (☎ 982 7167) On the way to the submarine base.

GAZELLE PENINSULA

SIGHTS
Simpson Harbour
The harbour – once crusted with pumice – is still magnificent, and the tethered ships lie quiet in the still water. The Beehives, the tiny craggy islands in its middle, look striking from any angle.

Namanula Road
This was the road that directly connected the northern coast to Rabaul, rising over the great caldera's rim. It runs east out of Rabaul off Mango Ave and used to meet the north coast road near Matalau. It's sometimes impassable now further up.

The **Japanese war memorial**, the main Japanese memorial in the Pacific, is dignified and testament to the forgiveness of the local people. There's a great view from here.

Tunnels & Relics
There are countless tunnels and caverns in the hillsides around Rabaul. **Admiral Yamamoto's bunker** (locked) is interesting if austere, with good information placards. There's a map on the ceiling for plotting world domination. Ask at the Hamamas Hotel for the key.

Just beyond Rabaul's old airport runway there's quite a mass of Japanese aircraft wreckage scattered among the palm trees and now semiburied in earth. Take the track to the right (kastom K5).

ACTIVITIES
Swimming
There is a pool at the Hamamas Hotel. The best beach for swimming is at pretty **Pila Pila** (p175) on the PMV No 5 route.

Diving
There are 10 (of 54) diveable wrecks situated in Simpson Harbour, but they're deep. George's Wreck near Rabuana is a shallow one. Right in Rabaul, at the end of old Turanian St, just beyond the swimming pool, there's a modern wreck. It's home for many colourful, small fish and you can snorkel right through the main holds.

You might rather some reef dives, or an overnight camping trip to the uninhabited paradise atolls of Cape Lambert. Contact the laid-back but capable Stephen Woolcott at **Kabaira Beach Hideaway** (☎ 983 9266; www .kabaira.com). You'll pay about K100 per dive – a *very* good price. The top end of the market (and better for harbour wrecks) is covered by **Rapopo Plantation Resort** (☎ /fax 982 9944; 2 dives K242, gear hire per day K45) in Kokopo.

Walking
There are excellent walking routes around Rabaul, and you can spend hours just walking around the town overawed by its complete annihilation.

You can hike down to Matupit and back (although someone will probably offer you a lift) and the views from the vulcanology observatory also make it a rewarding walk.

If you're fit you can climb Namanula Rd to meet the north coast road near Matalau. From here you can head north along the

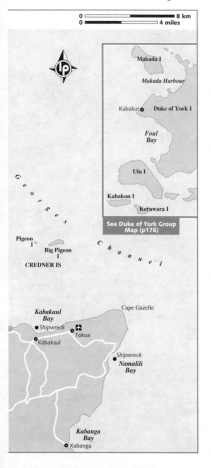

See Duke of York Group Map (p176)

ISLAND PROVINCES

ISLAND PROVINCES

coast road, which rises over a pass and meets the Nonga-Submarine Base Road. There are regular No 6 PMVs to Nonga hospital and some beyond. Or you could walk the whole loop over Tunnel Hill Rd and take in the **vulcanology observatory** (Map pp170–1) along the way. This would take about a day.

Climbing the Volcanoes

You can climb all the volcanoes (though we don't recommend Tuvurvur as it *might* blow up on you); they're all tracked, but the best idea is to take a guide from Hamamas Hotel (K20). You'll be up and down Kombiu in an hour if you're fit. It's also possible to camp (K50 including gear) on Kombiu (The Mother) – ask at Hamamas Hotel.

Be warned that the slopes of Vulcan are scored with deep cracks from mud-ash drying and contracting, which can be 4m to 5m deep. They can be hard to spot now they're vegetated. The best approach is on the northern face down near the water's edge.

TOURS

Hamamas Hotel offers great and affordable possibilities including local WWII heritage trips, hot-spring dips, village stays, canoe/walking trips to see the megapode colonies on Matupit Island (K20) and Indiana Jones–style multi-day jungle treks across the Baining mountains, through one of the most biodiverse forests on earth. The route follows the retreat of the Australians as they fled the

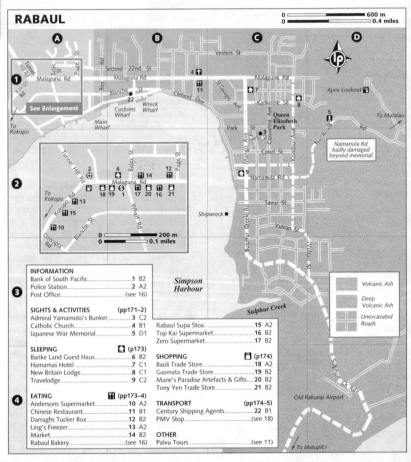

RABAUL

0 ———— 600 m
0 ———— 0.4 miles

INFORMATION	
Bank of South Pacific	1 B2
Police Station	2 A2
Post Office	(see 16)

SIGHTS & ACTIVITIES	(pp171–2)
Admiral Yamamoto's Bunker	3 C2
Catholic Church	4 B1
Japanese War Memorial	5 D1

SLEEPING	(p173)
Barike Land Guest Haus	6 B2
Hamamas Hotel	7 C1
New Britain Lodge	8 C1
Travelodge	9 C2

EATING	(pp173–4)
Andersons Supermarket	10 A2
Chinese Restaurant	11 B1
Darraghs Tucker Box	12 B2
Ling's Freezer	13 A2
Market	14 B2
Rabaul Bakery	(see 16)

Rabaul Supa Stoa	15 A2
Top Kai Supermarket	16 B2
Zero Supermarket	17 B2

SHOPPING	(p174)
Baoli Trade Store	18 A2
Gasmata Trade Store	19 B2
Marie's Paradise Artefacts & Gifts	20 B2
Tony Yen Trade Store	21 B2

TRANSPORT	(pp174–5)
Century Shipping Agents	22 B1
PMV Stop	(see 18)

OTHER	
Paivu Tours	(see 11)

Simpson Harbour

Sulphur Creek

Volcanic Ash
Deep Volcanic Ash
Unexcavated Roads

To Matupit I

Japanese. From the soldiers' accounts ('struggling over vines, tripping over logs, too tired to lift one's feet') it sounds like...fun.

Paivu Tours (☎ /fax 982 8556; Malaguna Rd) also offers a broad range of day activities and tours.

FESTIVALS & EVENTS

For details on the **Warwagira Festival** see p167. Rabaul's **Frangipani Queen Show** is held in mid-July and scheduled to go ahead.

SLEEPING

This is ground zero; staying here rather than Kokopo gives you the 'I was there' feeling. The locals will tell you that Kokopo is going to blow up in a few thousand years anyway.

Hamamas Hotel (☎ 982 1999; www.rabaulhotel.com .pg; Mango Ave; d K72-308; ❄ ⚖) This is the best choice; it's remarkably good value and has the best-informed local guides in the region. The budget rooms are better that you'd be used to, and from there on the beds get bigger and the rooms verge on cavernous at the top end. Pay K275 and up, and you can comfortably fit in four. All rooms have air-con, tea and coffee gear, TV, phone, fridge and private bathroom, and come with a terrific buffet-style breakfast. Hamamas has a pool, restaurant, public bar (try a few lava and brimstone stories), pokies room, pool table, coastal-defence cannon (fired with home-made gunpowder – recipe available), heavy machine gun (by the pool table), and a large bomb dangling from the lounge ceiling.

Kulau Lodge (Map pp170-1; ☎ 982 7223; fax 982 7226; cottages K160, apt K260) Excellent value on the beachfront of Talili Bay, past Pila Pila beach. There's a fine bush-materials restaurant (p174) and bar on the beach and the large cottages have private bathrooms. The deluxe two-bedroom apartments are *huge*, feature laundries and kitchens and sleep four or more. The No 5 PMV runs past to Rabaul, but you might wait an hour.

Kabaira Beach Hideaway (Map pp170-1; ☎ 983 9266; bed per person K30) Past Kulau Lodge, about 40 minutes from Rabaul on PMV 5. You can snorkel and dive from the beach, it's inexpensive, very friendly and rather lovely. Three meals a day are available for K30. The accommodation is on the beachfront in a simple house. You might even see a few exotic pets (Stephen has a possum, but he wanted a cassowary).

THE POPE & PETER TOROT

Much to the pride of the Catholic Church in PNG, one of its own has become the first saint in the Pacific.

Peter ToRot was born in 1912 in Rakunai village, New Britain, and was working as a village priest when the Japanese invaded. He was forbidden to perform any religious duties but refused to comply. He was arrested in April 1945 and in July that year was killed by lethal injection.

The papal tour of 1995 was planned around a visit to Rabaul for Peter ToRot's beatification but the volcanic eruptions forced a change of plan. Instead, the ailing John Paul II went to Port Moresby. ToRot's remains – his bones, rosaries and belt buckle – were exhumed and the beatification ceremony was held there. Tolai pall bearers danced around a small casket containing his remains. Other Tolai were outraged and many felt that exhuming ToRot's remains was insensitive to Tolai traditions.

Travelodge (☎ 982 1002; fax 982 1003; Namanuh Rd; r K120; ❄) This looks like a crumbling, idle mess from the outside, but the rooms are actually clean and pleasant.

Barike Land Guest Haus (☎ /fax 9821170; Malaguna Rd; s/d K60/80) This is a clean and simple family home with shared kitchen and bathrooms.

New Britain Lodge (☎ 982 9123; s/d K50/65) A passable cheapie 'in the broken heart of Rabaul'. You'll share bathrooms and get a fan. It's an extra K15 for dinner.

EATING

Apart from a few *kai* bars at the Malaguna end of town (Ling's Freezer and Zero Supermarket have good ones), Rabaul's eating options are pretty much confined to hotel restaurants. Kulau Lodge is a pleasant spot for a feed. There is a Chinese restaurant opening below Paivu Tours.

Hamamas Hotel (☎ 982 1999; www.rabaulhotel .com.pg; Mango Ave; breakfast/lunch/dinner K20/25/30) Has the best food and generous servings. The lunch and dinner menus here are semi-Asian. Chicken, beef, fish and seafood dishes are served, as well as pasta, good salads, tofu soups and a few eggplant variations for vegetarians.

Kulau Lodge (Map pp170-1; ☎ 982 7223; fax 982 7226; breakfast/lunch/dinner K12/12/20) You can have lunchtime sandwiches, salads and omelettes, grilled chicken, steak, lamb cutlets or reef fish. In the evenings, mains include lobster and mud crabs, seafood pastas, grilled pork chops and steaks, and chicken dishes.

Travelodge (☎ 982 1002; fax 982 1003; Namanuh Rd; lunch/dinner K17/27) Sandwiches, omelettes and hamburgers are on offer for lunch. In the evening there are steaks, lobster and garlic prawns.

Darraghs Tucker Box (Malaguna Rd; ☷ 9am-7pm) An above average *kai* bar with fish, chips and stews.

SHOPPING
The reception areas of the hotels and guesthouses sometimes sell *bilums* (string bags) and small carvings.

Browse through the few trade stores in Rabaul and in Kokopo for the ultimate T-shirts that the Tolai have perpetually had a taste for: 'My grandfather survived 1878, my father survived 1937 and I survived 1994'.

Marie's Paradise Artefacts & Gifts (Malaguna Rd) A good local crafts shop just east of Bank South Pacific bank.

GETTING THERE & AWAY
Air
Rabaul is serviced by Tokua airport (p168).

Boat
See p169 for information about dinghy travel around New Britain and through the nearby islands.

Shipping agents sometimes take passengers along the north and south coasts of New Britain towards Lae, or across to New Ireland and the North Solomons. They include the following:

Century Shipping Agents (☎ 982 1477; fax 982 1207; cnr Blanche St & Coastwatchers Rd) In Rabaul.

Consort Express Lines (☎ 982 1253; Kamarere St)

Pacific New Guinea Line (☎ 982 1955; George Brown St)

Rabaul Shipping wharf (☎ 982 1070) Vunapope (☎ 982 9480) Has departures to Pomio in Jacquinot Bay (K80) on Sunday, Kavieng (deck/bunk K105/180) on Tuesday and Buka (K105) on Wednesday. Also has two weekly passenger boats sailing from Rabaul to Lae (deck/cabin K175/290) via Kimbe (K80/130) twice a week. In Vunapope the office is above ANZ.

GETTING AROUND
To/From the Airport
Tokua airport is about 40km away. PMVs run out to Tokua and the better hotels and guesthouses can provide transfers for K30.

PMV
There aren't many on Sundays. No 1 goes from Rabaul to Kokopo (K2.50) to Tokua Airport (sometimes) and back. No 6 goes to the vulcanology observatory (inform the driver), submarine base and Nonga Hospi-

---

DEAD TOWN

Rabaul had a hustle and bustle, but it was a laid-back kind of place that was very friendly. It had the biggest market in the South Pacific, an orchid park, playgrounds and swimming pools.

There was a great music scene in Rabaul and PNG's thriving local music industry originated there. Rabaul's Pacific Gold Studios was the South Pacific's first recording studio. Now Rabaul is flattened – it collapsed under the weight of 1m to 2m of Tuvurvur's load.

For several days after the eruption there were severe earthquakes as Tuvurvur and Vulcan went at it, and Rabaul was evacuated. The dead of night would be broken by the sound of a building groaning as it eventually succumbed to the weight of ash on its roof.

However, the Hamamas Hotel is standing proof that most of the town could have been saved. Over several days, the staff made a joint effort to clear the flat roof of the piling ash. After all, Rabaul was never swamped by lava, only by ash – slowly piling ash that weighed as much as concrete. Rabaul might have been dusted off not too much the worse for wear with a round-the-clock shovelling effort and a bit of protection from the hundreds of looters who paraded around with new clothes and stereos immediately after the blast.

Raise your gaze a few degrees and you can see the rim of the old caldera with its five volcanoes, one still occasionally smoking, and remember where you are. Beneath the earth under your feet is the old town.

tal. No 5 goes to Kulau Lodge, No 5 goes to Rakunai (Peter ToRot's church) and No 4 goes to Malmaluan Lookout.

Around Rabaul
MATUPIT ISLAND
The September 1994 eruptions should have destroyed little Matupit but the prevailing winds brought Tuvurvur's load over Rabaul and left this island almost unscathed. It is beneath the volcano and from the beach you can watch Tuvurvur's conical form and see it belch huge plumes of smoke into the sky from just a kilometre away.

You can hire a canoeist to get you around to see Tuvurvur's southern slopes (which have giant lava flows) from the water. It's like a peek at a newborn planet. The megapode-egg hunters are here, burrowing almost 2m into the black sand to retrieve the eggs. The foolhardy still climb the slopes; ask at the Hamamas Hotel if you're one of them.

THE BEEHIVES (DAWAPIA ROCKS)
The two rocky pinnacles rising out of the centre of Simpson Harbour are said to be the hard core of the original old volcano. You can visit them by boat and there is some good diving and swimming. When Captain Blanche first visited Rabaul in 1882 these islands were much larger; the bigger one had a village of 200 people.

SUBMARINE BASE
Great for snorkelling and diving, the coral bed at Submarine Base is flat and almost horizontal until it drops down a 75m vertical reef wall. As you swim over this drop your heart races and it feels like you're leaping off a skyscraper. The Japanese used to provision submarines here during the war.

There are **tunnel and rail-track remnants** (admission K5) below and **guns and relics** (admission K5) in the hills above, but it was a 'base' in so far as the Japanese pulled their submarines up to the vertical wall and then surfaced allowing soldiers to walk off over the reef.

Catch PMV No 6 from the central PMV stop opposite Rabaul's new market on Malaguna Rd.

MATALAU & BAI
PMV No 7 services this area infrequently. There are lava flows near **Matalau**, natural staircases leading up Kombiu's slopes; they

are great to climb. These great slags were thrown from Tuvurvur and fell to earth over Kombiu's northern slopes (that's a long way). Mudslides are common and houses pitched on Kombiu's steep slopes are in real trouble – these people fear the wet season, and hold on and hope.

The road threatens to become impassable for several kilometres but finally terminates at **Bai**. It's swallowed by a great ravine of mud and trees and broken houses, its bitumen appearing like pie crust.

PILA PILA
Pila Pila (Map pp170–1) and nearby Ratung village are nice swimming beaches in Talili Bay. PMV No 5 runs past Pila Pila and Ratung.

WATOM ISLAND
Watom Island is an extinct volcano cone and the site of one of the earliest settlements in New Britain. Volcanic glass traded from Talasea (in WNB) has been found on Watom Island and dated at about 2500 years old.

The island is also a good place for walking or snorkelling; it can be reached from Kulau Lodge or Nonga beach, near Nonga Hospital. It's also possible to stay in villages on the island. There are no organised trips to the island, but it's worth asking at the Rapopo Plantation Resort.

THE PIGEONS
Between Rabaul and the Duke of York Group are the two 'Pigeons' or Credner islands. Small Pigeon is uninhabited.

Either island would make a pleasant excursion for a picnic or snorkel; two of the Marquis de Ray's (see p182) victims once used the place as a duelling ground. To get here you could hire a dinghy from the Kokopo waterfront for a few hours.

Jacquinot Bay
This region on the south coast of New Britain is beautiful, but little developed. There's **Manuginuna guesthouse** (contact Wesley Pagot ☎ 981 9321; r K50), near Pomio; bring your own food. You can get there by flying to Pomio from Rabaul (K302, 30 minutes), or ask at Rabaul wharf for MV *Explorer* (K60, 12 hours), which sails weekly to Pomio. Once there, walking is the only way to get around.

There are enormous caves and under-water lakes in the area, most notably around Bairaman village.

Duke of York Group

This is the *tambu* (forbidden or sacred) cockpit between New Ireland and the Gazelle Peninsula Tolais, a place of secret men's business, *dukduks* and *tumbuans*.

These islands are beautiful and accessible, but they are little developed. Mioko is the best one to visit. There are no vehicles on any of the islands except Duke of York Island. Some locals claim the islands are slowly sinking under the sea, but there's no scientific case to back this up as yet.

MIOKO ISLAND

The southwestern tip of the harbour was the site of **Queen Emma's first grand house**, but there's not too much to see now – just some steps really. You can see photographs of this house in the Kokopo museum (p166).

There are two open-pit **caves** on the island's eastern flank and a coastwatcher's lookout cut into the cliff top nearby on the easternmost point. For many years hundreds of people hid in these caves to avoid being press-ganged by the Japanese. You might see some splendid azure **butterflies** here the size of your hand. They're found nowhere else.

Nearby, a tiny **tunnel** runs between the two cliff faces of the island's eastern tip. You can crawl between (it's rough going) for two views of the open sea and sky, and

DUKE OF YORK GROUP

the cruel cliff below you. There's another passage leading into the darkness. If you want to snorkel, try the southern coast, but it's only good in flat conditions.

There's a **dukduk ples** (a place where the ritual costumes are built) on a beach; ask a villager for permission to see it, but be warned that women are sometimes refused.

DUKE OF YORK ISLAND

Port Hunter, at the northern tip of Duke of York Island, was the landing point for the Reverend Brown in 1875 and the site of his first mission. You can still see the crumbling chimney of his house.

KABAKON ISLAND

The closest of the island group to Rabaul, Kabakon Island has a curious history. A German health fanatic named Engelhardt established a nudist colony here in 1903, but it became a bit of a swingers' paradise.

He wasn't alone in fancying a break from the sexual straitjacket of the post-Victorian age. Many found the Pacific, where you could purchase a virgin or three (rather cheaply), preferable to protestant Europe, where you could purchase a device (rather expensively) to electrocute you if you became aroused in your sleep!

Engelhardt was soon dubbed Mr Kulau (Mr Coconut) by the locals because he ate nothing but coconuts and bananas. At one time he had 30 or more followers on the island, but coconuts and nudism must get boring – he died alone just before WWI after a singular combination of dietary deficiencies and sexual jealousy had destroyed the community. The attraction is the coral these days; there's a shallow reef between here and Ulu.

SLEEPING

There's a homestay programme on Mioko run via the Taklam Guesthouse (p167). You'll be accommodated in huts (K50) with running water and a pit toilet. Bring some food. On Ulu, there's also a small **guesthouse** (r K30) that has intermittent electricity; ask for Harvey Heurler.

GETTING THERE & AWAY

If you're lucky, you'll share the fare with locals, but otherwise, a (very splashy) 50-minute trip to the Duke of York Islands from Rabaul will cost K20, and the two-hour trip to New Ireland, K50. Only go on a calm day; there have been deaths in these waters when high seas have rolled dinghies.

You sometimes see whales, dolphins and dugongs in St Georges Channel and flying fish will launch themselves next to your boat and 'outrun' you for 70m or more. They really *do* fly for a while, flapping their fins.

WEST NEW BRITAIN PROVINCE

WNB has the country's greatest prolif-eration of volcanoes – five active and 16 dormant – and you can literally smell the sulphur in the air. It's also PNG's highest timber and palm-oil exporter with conse-quent tension between the province's vil-lagers and settlers.

GETTING THERE & AROUND

Hoskins airport is well serviced by the first- and second-level airlines, but beyond here you must either spend a lot of money flying to tiny airstrips or catch dinghies and trade boats along the coast and stay in villages. The unpredictable cargo ship *Elle Tanya* sails between Gloucester, Kandrian, Gasmata, Pomio and Rabaul. Ask at Kimbe wharf.

Beyond the Willaumez Peninsula you would have to prepare well for a freestyle trip into the unknown. Otherwise there are a few 4WD logging roads (in the dry season) leading towards the rugged and virtually unexplored mountains of the interior. The Walindi Plantation Resort (p178) might ar-range access – don't forget your wallet.

Hoskins

The picturesquely located 'major' airport of WNB is 40km east of Kimbe. There are a number of forested volcanoes surround-ing town, including the active Mt Pago. A short distance inland, at Koimumu, there's an active geyser field.

The friendly but grimy **Duko Tan Hotel** (☎ 985 0026; s/d K150/162; ❄) is five minutes' walk from the airport.

GETTING THERE & AWAY

Air Niugini (☎ 983 5287; fax 983 5669) flies to and from Hoskins once a day from Port Mores-by (K506) and Kokopo (K308). There are also two weekly fights to Kavieng (K353) and three to Lae (K419).

Airlink (☎ 983 5635) has flights once a week to the strips around WNB including Kan-

---

FISH BOMBS

PNG island villagers are always stumbling upon arms caches from WWII. The Bougain-villeans fought a war with their finds, but these locals bomb fish instead.

It's an extraordinary community event. Hundreds of villagers of all ages stand along the shoreline with coathanger-wire baskets and swimming goggles. A man sits, almost ceremoniously, in a canoe 100m offshore as the tension builds. The cordite-packed coke bottle slips into the water and the villagers hush for a few seconds before a dull thud sounds offshore.

Soon the water is boiling with a frenzy of dead fish and live people, who resurface with their wire loops of 50 fish strung up eye to eye, and baskets brimming.

Of course bombing fish is ecologically unsustainable. It's worst around Gloucester and Rabaul: the reef gets mashed, corals are destroyed and the local fish populations plummet. But you try telling the locals that.

---

drian (K166, 35 minutes), Gasmata (K150, 30 minutes) and also to Jacquinot Bay, ENB (K170, 40 minutes).

Kimbe

Kimbe is the provincial headquarters and a major centre for palm-oil production.

INFORMATION

There's the very reasonable Paradise local crafts shop and Bank South Pacific and Westpac banks all one block south (inland) of Kmart. East of here is the post office and daily market while the hospital is on the coastal road at the eastern edge of town.
Ambulance (☎ 983 5129)
Dr Tonar's Private Clinic (☎ 983 5562)
Fire (☎ 983 5411/5412)
Police (☎ 983 5422)

SLEEPING

You might rather stay just out of town (see p178) but there are good options in Kimbe itself.

Liamo Reef Resort (☎ 983 4366; fax 983 4371; s/d K205/249, beach bungalows K218-302; ❄ 🖵) On the beach at the east end of town. Tasteful, well furnished and serenely set in lovely gardens, right on a private beach. This is the only place that had Internet facilities for travellers at the time of research (per hour K40). Liamo also has a jungle lodge in far-off Baia (p178).

Kimbe Bay Hotel (☎ 983 5001; fax 983 5401; s/d with breakfast K181/204; ☒ ☐) On the main road opposite the wharf. Smart and comfortable but lacking in atmosphere.

Gorgor Guesthouse (☎ /fax 9834494; Sector 10; d K100) Near the primary school, this is basic but clean and very friendly. Two neat bathrooms are shared as is the kitchen.

Kimbe Tours & Guest House (☎ /fax 983 4886; r per person K100) This has similar facilities to Gorgor but is a bit more businesslike and a bit less warm. It's across from the opposite end of the lane that Gorgor is on.

EATING

Liamo Reef Resort (breakfast/lunch/dinner K20/20/30; ☹ 7am-9pm) The best place to eat; you'll get a *very* wide, international choice.

Kimbe Bay Hotel (dishes K25; ☹ 7am-7pm) Not as good or varied as Liamo.

J & D Trading (dishes K5-10; ☹ closes dusk) If you're counting the kinas, try this romantically-named place in the town centre on the main road. You'll get fish, chips and stews.

GETTING THERE & AWAY

For information on air travel see p177.

Boat

Lutheran Shipping (☎ 983 5630) and **Rabaul Shipping** (☎ 983 5365) sail overnight to Lae (deck/bunk K95/160, 9pm Thursday and Saturday) and Rabaul (deck/bunk K80/130, 3pm Tuesday and Saturday). Book at the wharf.

PMV

Many No 3 PMVs scuttle between Hoskins and Kimbe (K4, 40 minutes).

Talasea & the Willaumez Peninsula

Talasea is an active volcanic region. Lake Dakataua, at the tip, was formed in a colossal eruption in 1884. The locals have a fiery reputation too.

Ask at Walindi Plantation Resort for tours to the swimmable Garu hot river, rainforest trekking up the active Mt Garbuna, WWII plane wrecks and Pangula Island's geysers and fumaroles in the Wabua Valley (*wabua* means hot water).

Obsidian (volcanic glass) from here is believed to have been traded to New Ireland

about 20,000 years ago, possibly representing the earliest ever maritime trade in the world. Recently, Lapita pottery shards were also discovered here.

Apart from the superb natural surroundings and rare birds, the main attraction here is the unsurpassable diving. You might see anything from a tiny glass shrimp, to a pod of killer whales.

SLEEPING

Walindi Plantation Resort (☎ 983 5441; www .walindi.com; r per person US$155; ☒) This is the region's dive centre (daily US$120). It's *well* worth turning up and asking for stand-by rates. The resort is 15 minutes west of Kimbe on PMV No 1 (K2). Its attractive bungalows are set on a lovely beach among huge rain trees. It's also got a lodge on remote Muliagani island, just west of the peninsula. The Mahonia Na Dari conservation centre is next door to Walindi.

Queen's Head (☎ 983 4566; r per person K60) 'Binatang' Bob Prior's bizarre, mock-Tudor tavern ought to be in an English village, but has been enchanted onto a jungly beach a kilometre east of Walindi instead. It's simple but clean with a share kitchen, and…horse brasses…see it to believe it. Call direct or contact Walindi Plantation Resort or Air Niugini (p177).

Around West New Britain Province

Mt Langila, on Cape Gloucester at the southwestern end of the island, is still active and hiccups and rumbles every few months.

There's a **guesthouse** (s/d K35/55), which offers all meals (K30), at tiny **Kandrian**. Also try Akanglo Guesthouse, which is in a beautiful location five minutes by boat from Kandrian. You might see dugongs here. There's also the Awa Guesthouse, which is 45 minutes by boat from Kandrian. The **Department of West New Britain** (☎ 981 7305) has district offices in Kandrian that can arrange boats and will have more information.

Six kilometres east of far-flung **Gasmata**, there's a plush bungalow complex – **Lindenhafen Fishing Lodge** (☎ 983 4304; john@lindenhafen .com; all inclusive per person A$250; ☹ Oct-Apr; ☒). They'll charter a flight for you. There is daily game fishing, surfing or diving for A$200.

Liamo Reef Resort (p177) in Kimbe has a fishing lodge in remote **Baia**, available by arrangement.

NEW IRELAND PROVINCE

New Ireland has broad white-sand beaches and rivers of clear water tumbling down from the thickly forested central Schleinitz Range. Little Kavieng is the shy cousin of Rabaul.

In the rugged south is the spiritual home of Tumbuan culture. In the north are the intriguing traditions of Malangan, while Kabai culture dominates in the central areas. New Ireland is far less developed than New Britain; in fact the British/Irish connection holds up well. Once you cross St Georges Channel, which separates the islands, you'll notice the laid-back vibe, the more sedate pace of life and a greater emphasis on the old ways.

New Ireland is a beautiful and friendly place and, although little known and rarely visited, it has one of Papua New Guinea's longest records of contact with European civilisation. From the early 1600s, Europeans were sailing in and taking on fresh water at the island's southern tip at Cape St George. Later, the Germans developed lucrative copra plantations and the first real road in PNG – the mighty Boluminski Hwy. Many people fled here after Rabaul was destroyed.

New Ireland has the world's potentially largest undeveloped gold mine at Lihir Island. The province also includes a number of islands, the biggest being Lavongai (New Hanover) Island off the northwest end of the 'mainland'.

Kavieng and Namatanai are the only towns on New Ireland, although Namatanai barely qualifies. Outside Kavieng and Namatanai, there are coastal communities on each side of the island but no real settlements bigger than a trade store or two. Kavieng has the island's only port.

History

The remains of rock shelters found near Namatanai suggest that New Ireland was inhabited 30,000 years ago. Missionaries began arriving in 1875 along with 'blackbirders' who forcibly removed many New Irelanders to work on the plantations and canefields of Queensland (Australia) and Fiji.

A villainous crew, blackbirders often posed as missionaries to coax men aboard, killing them offhand if they revolted. One slaver even impersonated the bishop of Melanesia; the real incumbent – believed to be an imposter – was later killed in vengeance! Meanwhile, the shortage of males devastated village life in places.

Cannibalism and head-hunting were rife. Even a death from disease was often attributed, from certain 'signs', as the fault of another tribe which might be mercilessly attacked in revenge. In some communities, relatives smeared themselves with the blood of their deceased loved ones as part of the funeral rites.

During the German reign, large copra plantations made New Ireland one of the most profitable parts of the colony. The tyrannical Baron Boluminski became district officer of Kavieng in 1910 and built the highway that bears his name by forcing each village along the coast to construct and maintain a section. He made villagers push his carriage over any deteriorated sections.

New Ireland fell to the Japanese in 1942 and Kavieng was developed into a major Japanese base. Most of the Australians in Kavieng managed to escape but some chose to stay behind as coastwatchers (spies).

The Allies made no attempt to retake New Ireland but rather bombed it into oblivion. The Japanese surrendered in Namatanai on 19 September 1945.

Geography & Climate

New Ireland is mountainous and riddled with huge, flooded caves. Midway down the island, the Lelet Plateau rises to 1481m and further south near Taron the Hans Meyer Range reaches 2399m. A faultline provides passage for the Weitin and Kamdaru rivers.

The area between Namatanai and Kavieng receives about 3m of annual rainfall and has a dry season between May and November. December to March is the cyclone season and can bring high seas.

Culture

The people of New Ireland are Melanesian and speak 19 local languages. The north embodies the complex system of spiritual traditions of Malangan cultures. 'Malangan' also refers to the northern New Irelanders' carvings (see the boxed text, p180).

In the island's south are the Tumbuan traditions. The people from the south invaded the Gazelle Peninsula and settled the Duke of York Islands several hundred years ago. *Dukduks* and *tumbuans* are common to all three cultures. Around Namatanai and central New Ireland are the Kabai traditions, which are not as well understood.

As in most PNG islands, traditional clan power is wielded by chiefs and *bigmen* (important man or leader), but clan rites and land claims are passed on in a matrilineal system.

Getting Around
The cross-island roads, which are all dirt roads, are:

Fangalawa to Panamafei This, the most often used from Kavieng, is in good condition but so steep that some of it is sealed for safety.

Putput (Nono) to Kaut (Lokono) This is often used by trucks from Kavieng, but it's slippery in the wet.

Karu to Konogogo This crossing is also steep and the road isn't great. This is perhaps the most scenic of the lot; there's been very little logging here. You might well be able to stay at the Catholic church at Konogogo.

Lakurumau to Panachais This track might be impassable even in a 4WD but it would make an excellent and easy walk; it's not too steep. It's a day's hike for the reasonably fit. The track runs through a spectacular jungle-covered limestone gorge, though there are a few palm-oil plantations. You might find accommodation at Panachais school and Poliamba.

Lambuso to Ugana Very steep, definite 4WD territory, but rainforested with minimal logging.

Namatanai to Uluputur/Labur Bay Beginning at Namatanai, this is the least hilly of the crossings. From the west coast it should be possible to find a boat to the Duke of York islands.

KAVIENG
Kavieng is a sleepy little town. The harbour looks across a broad channel to Nusa Island. Errol Flynn lived here for a while, philandering with the locals and dynamiting fish.

Orientation
The town is spread out. Coronation Rd connects the airport road (Stanfield St) and the Boluminski Hwy with the waterfront. Just across from the beach are Nusa and Nusa Lik islands.

Information
Change all the money you'll need here at either bank. If you're heading south, add a margin. The hospital is about 1.5 km out of town.

Ambulance (☎ 984 2040)
Fire (☎ 984 2000/2029)
Malagan Beach Resort (per hr K45) The best bet for Internet access.
New Ireland Tourist Bureau (☎ 984 1449) Very informative indeed. If it receives some funds it might be able to book accommodation in village guesthouses for you by radio.
Police (☎ 984 2044/2054)
Post office (Coronation Rd; ⊗ 8am-5pm Mon-Fri)
Telekom (☎ 984 2626; Coronation Rd; ⊗ 8am-4pm Mon-Fri)
Zen 48 Hardware (Coronation Rd) Internet access. Next to the post office.

MALANGAN DEATH RITES

For centuries, it has been *kastom* for the Malagan to carve wooden masks and sacred figures for their mortuary rites. There are a few dedicated regular carvers on Tabar Island and Libba village near Konos, but otherwise carvings are only done by secret men's societies for mortuary ceremonies or rites of passage in the villages.

Different clans have different funerary traditions, including interment, cremation and burial at sea. The *tatanu* or *tanuatu* (soul) remains close to the body after death and it cannot go to the ancestors' world until the mortuary rites are performed. The spirit of a dead person enters the ancestors' world through the places that *masalais* (spirits of the bush and water) inhabit.

There's a terrific documentary film called *Malangan Labadama*, by Chris Owen, which shows a mortuary festival in all its extraordinary detail. Feasts are often performed for more than one person as they are terribly expensive. Those deceased long ago can be included in the rite, which includes chanting, masked dancing, clouds of lime and a huge feast.

Masks may depict the totem animal of a specific tribe in stages of metamorphosis. Such was the fearful power of the mask that, in the past, they were burned after the ceremony. Designs are strictly 'patented' according to clan rites, and a complex ritual payment must be made to pass a design on to another carver. Penalties for appropriation can be severe, but the real problem is, there are simply not enough young apprentices. One ancient master carver has even earned the nickname 'Last'.

Sights
NUSA PARADE
The northern end of Nusa Pde makes for a lovely waterfront walk; the huge fig trees just about meet overhead. If you keep heading north of the Malagan Beach Resort you will reach the intimate surrounds of **Patailu village**.

The southern section of Nusa Pde continues past the market and further along on the left are the **provincial government buildings**, built on the site of Baron Boluminski's residence.

Down at the shoreline, a small **workshop** houses the castings which were to hold the stone grinding wheel for a mill that was part of the Marquis de Ray's incredible scam (see the boxed text, p182).

Further south is the **Bagail Cemetery**, where Boluminski was buried. The tough guy's grave is right before you as you enter the cemetery.

HARBOUR & ISLANDS
Kavieng has a large and beautiful harbour. You can go down to the waterfront and catch a dinghy (banana boat) out to one of the many islands. Edmago and New Sulaman make for a good picnic and snorkel. You can negotiate a 'drop me off, pick me up later' trip. The cost is about K20 each way for the whole boat.

Activities
CYCLING
Tabo Meli's Rainbow Tours (adult/student K30/15, guide per day K50) arranges cycling tours and village accommodation. Contact the New Ireland Tourist Bureau.

If you want a better bike and village feasts along the way, try **Nusa Island Retreat** (tours per person all inclusive A$140-270). Price depends on the party size.

DIVING, SNORKELLING & FISHING
Lissenung Island Resort (www.lissenung.com; shore dives nonguests US$22, 2 boat dives US$80, gear per day US$50) is located on an offshore reef and there's free unlimited shore dives for guests (p182).

Scuba Ventures (☎ /fax 984 1244; scuba@globalnet .net.pg; per dive A$110, gear per day A$40) can take you down through some huge and virtually unexplored freshwater caves as well as local reefs and wrecks.

> ### OUTRIGGER CANOES
> Outrigger canoes are made by hand and vary in design and decoration. A tree is felled near the water's edge, from where it can be floated to the builder's home, but most of the work is done at the tree site. Once the log is to size and the top flattened with an axe, the builder floats the log home to hollow it out – an arduous process.
>
> When the canoe takes shape, the builder will float it and test its ride. The canoe is trimmed and charred over a fire to harden the timber and exude the resins to seal the pores. The charred material is scraped away and then the canoe is decorated, fitted with outrigging and given to some seven-year-old kid for transport to school.

SURFING
From November to March, long, barrelling reef breaks of up to eight feet roll into Kavieng; contact Nusa Islands Retreat (p182).

CANOEING, KAYAKING & YACHTING
You can try to hire a traditional outrigger from the Malagan Beach Resort or a modern Kayak from **Nusa Islands Retreat** (single/double kayak per day K66/88, guides per person K30). Ask about overnight trips and take advice about the strong local currents. Next door, **Tiki Turtle Eco Adventures** (contact Nusa Islands Retreat; www.tikiturtle .com; group of 5 per person per night A$200) can take you on anything from a half-day sail to a six-day trip up the rainforested rivers of Lavongai.

GOLF
Golf is pretty informal in Kavieng; pet dogs walk alongside the players and chase golf balls down the fairway. The golf course is a pleasant spot for a stroll.

Tours
Contact the **Malagan Beach Resort** (tours per half-day K60) for good-value tours of the surrounding area. It arranges harbour cruises, snorkelling and fishing trips and land tours that take you south along the coast.

Festivals & Events
The week-long **Malagan festival** is usually held in July or September and includes dances and feasting. In mid-July the local **Rugby Union grand final** causes a stir.

Sleeping

IN KAVIENG

Malagan Beach Resort (☎ 984 2344; www.malaganre sort.com; Nusa Pde; s/d K279/315; ❄) The rooms are comfortable and cosy if a tad small, but you get a bathtub! The grounds include a shady strip of beach overlooking Nusa Island; it's the most pleasant place in Kavieng itself.

Kavieng Hotel (☎ 984 2199; kavienghotel@daltron .com.pg; Coronation Rd; s K70-220, d K85-250; ❄) Well furnished with large rooms, but soulless and the budget rooms don't have bathrooms.

Kavieng Club (☎ 984 2224; fax 984 2457; Coronation Rd; s K77-154, d K88-198; ❄) Homely and good value – for PNG. All rooms have TV and fridge; the best rooms have cooking facilities. There's a bar, a garden area, snooker tables and TV lounge area.

Kavieng Guesthouse (☎ 984 2312; Emirau St; s K110-120, d K118-128; ❄) Spartan, well swept and well overpriced.

Peter ToRot Centre (☎ 984 2684; Tabar Terrace; dm K15, s/d K35/70) This is the cheapest with clean share bathrooms and some very uplifting hymns (but they don't rock on through the night).

AROUND KAVIENG

Nusa Islands Retreat (☎ 984 2247; www.nusaisland retreat.com.pg; s/d/tr A$110/120/140) Based on Nusa Lik Island, just 200m (K5) across from the international wharf. Its traditional-style, shared facility bungalows are well maintained. During the surfing season (November to April), there's share accommodation (A$60 per person). There's a good restaurant and the staff arrange a host of activities

including boating and diving. There are surf breaks close by. Recommended.

Lissenung Island Resort (☎ /fax 984 2526; Kavieng; www.lissenung.com; s/d US$35/70, r with bathroom US$85) Twenty minutes by boat (A$15) south of Kavieng on Paradise Island, which is not a misnomer. Very rare birds such as the green *electus* parrot have been spotted here. The bungalows are sparse but well-made traditional huts; you can snorkel or dive right off the beach. Meals are available for K35 per day. If rooms themselves are way too costly when lodging alone, the free shore-dives make it worth the price.

Eating

Malagan Beach Resort (☎ 984 2344; www.malagan resort.com; Nusa Pde; lunch/dinner K30/45; ❄ 6.30-7.30am, noon-2pm & 6.30-10pm) This has the most pleasant setting. There are good pasta dishes for lunch and some exotics like pork with pineapple chutney for dinner.

Kavieng Hotel (☎ 984 2199; kavienghotel@daltron .com.pg; Coronation Rd; breakfast/lunch/dinner K20/20/30; ❄ 6-9am, noon-2pm & 6.30-9pm) You'll find hot breakfasts, cheese or steak sandwiches for lunch, and substantial mains like crumbed lobster for dinner. The K45 Friday night seafood buffet is legendary.

Tsang Sang Bakery (Djaul St) This Chinese bakery has fresh bread and sweet cakes available from about 7am. There's not much left after 3pm. It's pretty basic and super cheap.

Health Store (Coronation Rd; ❄ 9am-4pm) Has groceries, staples and some vegetables, but you're better off at the market for anything fresh.

THE MARQUIS DE RAY & CAPE BRETON

The Marquis de Ray – 'Emperor of Oceania, King Charles the 1st of New France' – never set foot on New Ireland and yet he used the details of a ship's log to sell hundreds of hectares of land to gullible, would-be settlers. In 1879 he had raised A$60,000 on the basis of a flimsy prospectus with engravings of grand avenues flanked by birds of paradise. Many of his colonists paid with their lives as well as their savings.

The marquis had advertised Cape Breton, near Lambom Island off Cape St George, as a thriving settlement with fertile soil and friendly natives. In fact, it was a torrential, malarial and unfarmable thicket.

The marquis sent four shiploads of European land buyers to southern New Ireland, bequeathing aristocratic titles to them according to the amount of land they'd 'bought'. They only took a few weeks' supplies and such useful equipment as a mill for an area where grain would never grow, coops without chickens and tools without handles. The settlers soon started to die like flies.

The survivors were eventually rescued; a lot of their more stylish gear ended up in Queen Emma's mansion (see the boxed text, p168). The marquis ended his days in a French asylum.

ISLAND PROVINCES

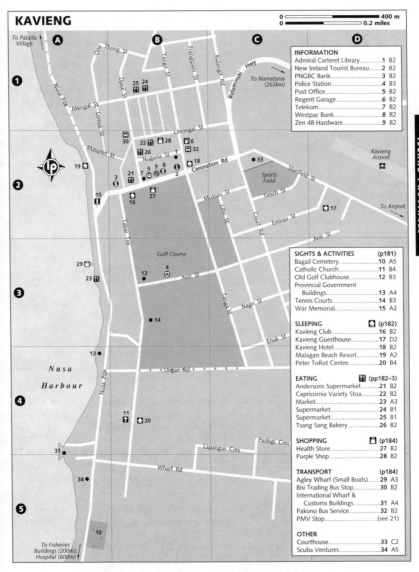

KAVIENG

0	400 m
0	0.2 miles

The market has a good range of fresh fruit and vegetables including the giant yellow hand grenade–like pandanus fruit; lobsters can cost as little as K10. Andersons supermarket has a decent *kai* bar selling fish, chips and sausages. There's another with good rice balls at **Capricornia Variety Stoa** (Lavongai St).

Drinking

The occasional band performs at the Kavieng Hotel, Kavieng Club or sometimes at the Malagan Beach Resort. Malagan's bar is the most genteel, but if you're wanting a game of pool with your *wantok* (fellow clanspeople), the hotel or the club is the better alternative.

Shopping

There are Malagan artefact collections at the Kavieng Hotel and Malagan Beach Resort. However, items are cheaper at the carver's in Libba village (opposite).

The **Purple Shop** (Lavongai St) has knick-knacks and T-shirts for very modest prices; it's fun to browse here.

Getting There & Away

AIR

Air Niugini (☎ 984 2135; fax 984 2337) and **Airlink** (☎ 984 2600) are represented at the airport terminal a couple of kilometres out of town.

Air Niugini flies return to Tokua (Kokopo/ Rabaul, 35 minutes) on Tuesday and Thursday (K312). On Wednesday it flies to Manus (K390, 50 minutes), returning on Sunday. Airlink flies to Tokua (K245, 30 minutes) daily via Lihir. The views are great.

BOAT

Dinghies and work boats run to the nearby islands. There are about two boats each week to Lavongai Island (passenger K30, charter K200).

Rabaul Shipping (☎ 984 2755) sails to Rabaul on Thursday afternoons (K105, nine hours) and carries on to Kimbe (extra K85, 10 hours) and Lae (extra K260, 19 hours).

CAR & PMV

There are two PMVs leaving Kavieng for Namatanai (K35, six to seven hours) from outside Anderson's supermarket at 9am and 10am (ish) every day except Sunday. There are also passenger trucks and PMVs leaving from Bisi Trading bus stop, which head some or all the way to Namatanai, or elsewhere, every day but Sunday.

Avis (☎ 984 1190; fax 984 2454) and **Hertz** (☎ 984 2374) have offices at the Malagan Beach Resort, with the **Regent Garage** (☎ 984 2090; fax 984 2106) behind the service station that also rents cars. The Kavieng Hotel will hire vehicles also. These last two are about K30 cheaper than Hertz and Avis which charge K200 daily plus K1 per kilometre. Take *all* fuel, tools, pump and a spare wheel with you.

Getting Around

PMVs (marked No 1 and 2 pretty much at random) around town cost K0.50 and some run to the airport.

EAST COAST

The east coast is more developed than the west, with the Boluminski Hwy running most of its length. The road is now sealed from Kavieng to Tandis village, 120km away. Don't count on getting to more than one, maybe two, places a day by public transport, and none on Sundays.

The coast consists of one breathtaking beach after another with limestone pinnacles jutting out of the ocean and lagoons of surpassing beauty. You might spot dolphins or sperm whales (September to January).

Boluminski Highway

The guesthouses (except the treehouse) are simple bush material huts that all cost K50 a night (fixed by tourism authority). Sometimes this will include food or you may be asked to pay extra. Otherwise there are small

---

SHARK-CALLING

Along the coast of New Ireland, especially the west coast between Konogogo and Kontu, the ancient art of shark-calling is practised. Because of the documentary film *The Shark Callers of Kontu*, by Dennis O'Rourke, Kontu attracts what little attention the west coast gets.

A loopshaped rattle made of coconut shells splashing in the water beguiles the shark into a handheld noose. The noose has a propellerlike wooden piece fitted to it to cause drag and 'lift' in the water as the shark fights and tries to dive. The buoyancy eventually exhausts the shark. The less artful bit comes next when the caller bludgeons the shark into some submission.

It's believed that the shark won't come if the caller is impure or does not respect the shark; shark and caller are connected. Shark callers 'own' certain sharks and only theirs will come to them. A new canoe must be initiated by an experienced caller who spills the blood of a shark over it before it can be used.

Unfortunately these days, the brutal and unsustainable practice of shark-finning by commercial vessels is decimating the population of sharks.

LIFE IN A (NEW) IRISH VILLAGE

You'll attract a lot of attention when you show up, but it'll trail off; there's a quiet respect for your privacy in most villages. Take something (preferably lasting and useful) for the kids if you can, but give it to the local school or *bigman* (leader) to redistribute. A football (there's no describing the joy), swimming goggles (you can carry quite a few and they're functional) and pens are all good gifts. Salt, sugar and tea will be appreciated by your hosts in the more remote places, but don't worry about this if you're on the tarmac road. Way off the beaten track, BYO rice or you'll eat them out of house and home.

A torch (flashlight), sleeping sheet, mosquito net, hammock, thongs (flip-flops; coral is sharp), book and toilet-paper roll are good to take along. Most villages have pit-toilets these days, but if not, ask about the customary spot in the river or sea. It's quite an experience if there's any phosphorescence (it's the village method and it's not too bad for low population densities. The ecofriendly option of digging your own pit 15cm deep and filling it with leaf litter and soil might get some funny looks).

If you can, stay for Sunday. Religious or not, you can't fail to be moved by the whole community dressing up and heading off to church, then returning to discuss the sermon. At night, if you're lucky, you'll hear very tuneful Tok Pisin hymns sung with absolutely no holding back to the tune of a strumming guitar; it's bizarrely reminiscent of Mark Twain.

---

trade stores around but they sell mostly *tinfis* (tinned fish) and rice. You'll also be welcomed in many places we haven't mentioned.

In **Matanasoi** (or Liga) village, about 5km along the highway from Kavieng airport, there's a limestone cave filled with crystal-clear water. The Japanese used this grotto for drinking water.

Twenty-three kilometres further is **Putput** and the fantastic **Treehouse Village Resort** (☎ 984 2666/1265; fax 984 2693; huts K140-170) – a series of huts perched in huge trees on the beach. There's even hot water, and a bar up a 200-year-old Kalapulim tree. The buffet (per day K80) is reputedly excellent, and the Kiwi proprietor Alun Beck has become a local chief, complete with red *laplap* (sarong). Another lodge is planned on the west coast.

Poliamba mill has a guesthouse for plantation workers but you might get a room. Sixty-six kilometres from town is Lossuk guesthouse, which has a shower. At the 84km mark is **Cathy Hiob's Homestay** (dinner K20) at **Laraibina** (ask for Munawai village). Cathy handfeeds some huge eels in the river, which slither right past your hands. Bring a tin of fish and K5.

There's a fantastic natural swimming pool upstream from the bridge at **Fissoa**, in the grounds of the Fissoa Vocational Centre. Just past Fatmilak, 115km further down, the large and attractive village of **Bol** has a spacious **guesthouse** (lunch/dinner K10/20) – one of the best and a good place to see community life. There's a nice wave here in surf season (November to March).

Just past Tandis, where the asphalt stops, is **Libba** village, 4km south of Bol (you can walk it). This is a great place to look at **Malangan art**. The village is home to master carver Ben Sisia. Ben charges K10 to see the Malagan house where a piece might sell for the K100 mark – be very respectful. Even the village church is carved in the local style, something the minister is, perhaps paradoxically, rather pleased with.

Konos is 140km from Kavieng, and has a village guesthouse by the Karawinai river. They can take you on a cross-island trek or arrange a boat to Tabar. There's a lovely beach at **Pinis Passage** just on the Namatanai side of Konos and a bit further at **Kartedan** is a refreshing swimming hole.

The turn-off to Lelet Plateau, just after **Malom** village, is 25km south of Konos. There's a fantastic village guesthouse further down at **Dalom**. It is well built, right on a gorgeous beach by a turquoise stream. This is a good surf spot. Try not to turn up on Saturday (the Adventists' Sabbath).

Beyond here are fewer plantations and more jungle. You can stay at simple **Karu Guesthouse** (meals K10), 220km from Kavieng. The paintings and carvings in the village church are creations of Kou, who has gone on to local fame as a singer.

A few hundred metres across Karu Bay from the village is the small Mumu Island

THE JOHNSON CULT

When the first elections for the House of Assembly were held in PNG in the 1960s, the islanders took to the spirit of democracy with gusto and decided they would vote for American president Lyndon Baines Johnson.

Lavongai went 'all the way with LBJ'. Islanders refused to pay taxes and instead, put their money in a fund to buy Lyndon Johnson. They raised a lot of money (10 shillings each) which they unceremoniously dumped at the door of the baffled Catholic mission. Unaccountably Johnson never turned up.

(also known as Mumugas Island), which the traditional owners have proclaimed as a conservation area. Turtles come ashore to lay their eggs around the end of July. You can get across in a canoe for about K3.

Namatanai

Namatanai is the second-largest town on New Ireland with a hotel, supermarket, Bank South Pacific bank and a few stores. It's just a transit point on a pretty bay. You'll only get electricity from 6pm to 10pm, despite the local hydro project. Namatanai was an important station in German days and the Namatanai Hotel is on the site of the old German station house.

SLEEPING & EATING

Namatanai Hotel (☎ /fax 984 3057; s/d K100/120) Right down by the waterfront. It's clean and friendly, but there isn't even hot water for this price. Meals are available for K19.

Kokobala Haus (s/d K60/80) Nearby, this place is a bit cramped but OK. Opposite Kokobala is a *kai* bar, which will probably be closed by the time you get here, and won't open until you leave.

GETTING THERE & AWAY

The bus stop is on the beach opposite the supermarket. PMVs for Kavieng leave here at 9am to 10am and arrive from Kavieng at about 5pm.

Dinghies travel between New Britain and New Ireland. From Namatanai, get a truck from the waterfront in the afternoon to any of a number of villages near Uluputur on the west coast (K5). Kabanut is a common destination and there's a plush guesthouse at nearby Kabahut. Sleep the night (often at the truck driver's place, K20) then catch a speedboat (K50) to Kokopo in New Britain in the morning.

WEST COAST

The beautiful, lonely, potholed west coast road is all unsealed with a stretch either side of Kontu that will challenge the toughest 4WD. In the wet season even a 4WD won't manage some river crossings. Between Kontu and Konogogo (Kono) **shark calling** is practised, but Kontu is the main centre for this.

There are just a few 'formal' places to stay on the west coast, but visitors are such a rarity you should have no trouble elsewhere. Most villages have a traditional *boihaus* (basically a guesthouse) and you may be invited to stay, although women might have trouble if there's a man staying already (which is unlikely). Always leave a gift of about K30, plus about K15 a meal or some food.

The Namatanai (east coast) crossing takes you to **Konogogo** (Kono). There's a basic store and a Catholic school where you can usually stay.

Further northwest is friendly **Messi** village, under a jungle-covered limestone escarpment (there are paths up if you want a view). The village is large for New Ireland, with a basic clinic.

Between Messi and Kontu there are many rivers; in the wet they (particularly the Ungana) can be impassable. The road gets very rough here even in the dry, and is 4WD-only from **Patlangat** onwards.

You might get lucky and find a lift with a 4WD utility. Or arrange a boat (passenger K20, charter K100). Otherwise, do as the locals do and walk the 10km.

Kontu is smaller than Messi. You can stay at **Lanarang Guesthouse** (r incl meals K36). The fascinating, ancient art of shark calling can be arranged for K45, but you'll pay K45 more if a shark is actually caught. Five or so kilometres north of Kontu at **Tembin**, there's the **Bibilang Guesthouse** (r K45), which also offers all meals for K40.

From Kontu, the road is barely navigable even by 4WD for 10km until you get to **Nalagalap**. Again, walk it, get a boat or find a 4WD. From Nalagalap you'll find transport to Kavieng via Kaut.

Keeping to the coast, the road wanders inland and rises through some spectacular rainforest. At **Cape Timeis** the road runs near clifftops from where there are stunning views. Further on, past Namasalang, you come to **Panamafei** village and the Fangalawa crossing to the east coast.

LELET PLATEAU

The 1200m plateau is cool enough to grow vegetables. There are no rivers – perhaps that's why rain magic is practised. There's an enormously deep cave, as yet unfathomed, as well as some bat caves near Mongop. You can stay at the **Puroro Guest House** (r K40), which offers meals for K40.

There's a road leading up from the Boluminski Hwy just after Malom village. Catch a truck heading across from Kavieng market on Wednesday or Saturday afternoon.

THE SOUTH

The southern 'bulge' of the island is an isolated wilderness. This is the birthplace of Tambuan culture. If you can seriously handle yourself in the bush, this presents a real adventure.

The tremendous Weitin rift valley is where the Pacific and Indian ocean plates meet, providing passage for two mighty rivers: the Weitin and the Kamdaru. There are high-altitude lakes, a huge number of rare orchids, frogs and, it's suspected, creatures unknown to science. There's a redundant hut for scientists at Icad near Siar. Once you get round to Kabanut on the western side, you'll find trucks heading to Namatanai.

Getting Around

Along the east coast you can continue in a conventional vehicle from Namatanai through Samo to Danfu. From there to Rei you usually need a 4WD. It's possible to walk, canoe and boat right around the southern tip of the island. A logging road goes south to Pakabong and extends to Wapi.

From the end of the road in Rei it takes about two days to walk to Srar village. From Srar to Maliom is a good, well-cut path. After Maliom the paths get difficult and some sections of the coast can only be negotiated by canoe. There is a path across the southern part of the peninsula or, if you are lucky enough to pick up a boat, you can go around to Lambom Island by the cape.

Cape St George is worth seeing. Canoes around Lambom to Lamassa are simple to find and there is a path to Pakabong. It is a better option to get a canoe from Kabisalao to Wapi.

CARGO CULTS

To many New Guineans, it seems the strange ways and mysterious powers of the Europeans could only have derived from supernatural sources. Cult leaders theorised that Europeans had intercepted cargo that was really intended for the New Guineans, sent to them by their ancestors in the spirit world. One cultist even suggested that the Whites had torn the first page out of their bibles – the page that revealed that God was actually a Papuan.

If the right rituals were followed, the cult leaders said, the goods would be redirected to their rightful owners. Accordingly, docks were prepared or crude 'airstrips' laid out for when the cargo arrived. Other leaders felt that if they mimicked European ways, they would soon have European goods – 'offices' were established in which people passed bits of paper back and forth. But when locals started to kill their own pigs and destroy their gardens, the colonial government took a firm stand. Some leaders were imprisoned while others were taken down to Australia to see with their own eyes that the goods did not arrive from the spirit world.

Seeing Black American troops during WWII with access to desirable goods had a particularly strong impact. In Manus Province in 1946, a movement started by Paliau Moloat called the New Way, or Paliau Church, was initially put down as just another cargo cult. But Paliau's quasi-religious following was one of PNG's first independence movements and a force for modernisation. He opposed bride prices for example and sought to dissuade the local populace's belief in the arrival of actual cargo from the sea.

Paliau was imprisoned in the early days, but in 1964 and 1968 he was elected to the PNG House of Assembly. Paliau Moloat was seen by his followers as the last prophet of the world. He died on 1 November 1991.

LAVONGAI & EAST ISLANDS

Volcanic Lavongai Island is mountainous and isolated. This is the abode of sorcerers. Michael Moran's *Beyond the Coral Sea* vividly describes five 'buried head to head in a star pattern' under Tsoi general store; the burial's opening ceremony featured (Moran tells) a broken glass–eating magician in a quasi-Christian shamanistic dance. You might see a ceremony like this if you're around at the right time or get invited to a private gathering.

Also on Tsoi Island, there's the **Mansava Adventure Lodge** (s/d K105/135) with bungalows in a paradise-like setting. Food costs K50. It arranges diving and snorkelling through the Lissenung Island Resort (p181) and can even organise river rafting. There's usually a boat (K30) to the island from Kavieng. Also consider sailing here with Tiki Turtle Eco Adventures (p181).

EASTERN ISLAND GROUPS

There are five island groups strung off the east coast of New Ireland – Tabar, Lihir, Tanga, Green and Feni. They are only 30km to 50km offshore.

Apart from Tabar, none of these have any formal lodging, and only Lihir has regular transport (Airlink fly there from Kavieng and Rabaul daily, and a boat from Namatanai will cost K30). They're all lovely, but rather impractical to visit.

Lihir Island has an enormous open-face gold mine that looks like a Mayan temple (the gold seems to fly straight to Port Moresby). Feni, Tanga and Green islands are covered in dense, steamy jungle and are almost untouched. There are also springs and geysers.

Tabar Islands

The Tabar islands are a stronghold of Malangan culture. Carvers Edward Sale, Leppan and Maris Memenga came from Tabar and their works (located on Tatau Island) are regarded as masterpieces. There's lodging and large meals available at **Andi's Guesthouse** (r K50).

You can get to Tatau from Konos or adjacent villages (K20 passenger, K200 charter). You might get stuck for a day or so on the way back. BYO petrol from Kavieng (seriously) if you can't afford another day in paradise.

MANUS PROVINCE

Remote Manus Province consists of Manus itself plus a scattering of tiny islands that barely break the water's surface. Take a short trip inland or a market boat to one of the islands and you'll find yourself in another century.

History

The tiny Western islands and Wuvulu Island are peopled by the descendants of Micronesian settlers from the north. Their fishing methods included fish traps and kite fishing.

German colonists arrived in 1911 and missionaries landed a while later, though they found it tough going and dangerous – the locals found them rather appetising.

The Japanese invaded in 1942 and were later evicted by the Allies who constructed a huge naval base and airstrip (at Momote) from which to invade the Philippines.

This display of Western technology had quite an impact on the local people (see the boxed text, p187). American anthropologist Margaret Mead described this impact in her book *New Lives for Old*, published in 1956.

Geography & Climate

Eastern Manus and Los Negros are uplifted coral formations while Southwest Bay is a flooded caldera. There are large limestone caves in the central area of the island. Other islands – Rambutyo, Lou, Baluan and M'Buke – are spent volcanoes.

Manus Province's daily temperatures are a moderate 24°C to 30°C. It's a rainy place with drier months from September through December. There are cyclones (and surf) from November to March.

Culture

The people of Manus Province are predominantly Melanesian; Micronesians dominate in the Western islands. The atoll-dwellers have no arable land and trade fish and lime for fruit and vegetables. Wuvulu islanders grow taro in ponds dug into the coral.

The Manus people (sometimes referred to as Titans) occupy the south and southwest islands and share a common language: Titan. They depend entirely on fishing. The Matangol live to the south, east and north,

LOMBRUM DETENTION CENTRE

In 2001 the Australian government implemented the 'Pacific Solution' to process asylum seekers who were arriving in Australia. Incarcerating them on Australian soil was proving problematic and embarrassing. A less visible and more secure containment area was sought.

The Howard government negotiated the construction of the facility at Lombrum on Manus, which at one point held 400 detainees, but trouble was brewing. It looked increasingly as if the immigration problem was being palmed off to a neighbour already indebted to Australia. The project had been agreed to by the then–prime minister, Sir Mekere Morauta, but Prime Minister Sir Michael Somare came to office in mid-2002 having campaigned against it.

Locals complained about the air-con and good food at the Lombrum site, while prisoners complained of being locked up like criminals on a remote island and isolated from the outside world. Many claimed they had been transported to Manus because they failed to ask for one specific form upon entering Australian territory, thus failing (technically) to apply for legal refugee status.

The number of inmates shrank, bizarrely, to just one: Aladdin Sisalem. Alone in a surreal village of portacabins, security guards and wire fencing, Aladdin began to wonder what on earth he was doing there. So did the PNG government and the Australian public.

Aladdin Sisalem was moved and the centre closed late in 2004 but Lombrum is currently on standby. It's a weird place, not really worth a visit. If you want to have a look at the portacabins, just drop by the local government department in Lorengau where a few of them are being used as offices.

depending on fish and some agriculture. The Usiai are inland people and exclusively gardeners and hunters. Ritual magic plays an important part in the *kawas* (trade) system, though this is fading. Margaret Mead first studied the Manus people in her book *Growing up in New Guinea* (1942).

Carving has virtually died out in the province, although the people of Bipi Island still do some – you can see examples in the Lorengau council office. Spears decorated with shark's teeth were produced in the Western islands.

MANUS & LOS NEGROS ISLANDS

One of the first things you'll notice about Manus and Los Negros islands is the distinctive call of the *chauca* bird. The birds are unique to the region, as is a variety of sea snail with a vivid green shell. There's a ridged white one too, less notable when alive perhaps, but unmissable when hollowed out, placed on the end of the penis and swung up and down. The ritual is an ancient one and is a part of ceremonial battle and dance. You might think this is bizarrely unique until you remember the cod-pieces of mediaeval knights.

Another local you'll hear is a *rokrok* (frog) with a bizarre croak that sounds like a faraway person nailing down a tin roof!

There are lots of crocodiles here too; they sometimes prey on villagers who harvester *saksak* (sago) in the rivers.

SIGHTS
Los Negros Island
The remains of the **US airbase** at Lombrum are interesting. There's a fine anti-aircraft gun as you enter, and rows of old hangers. General MacArthur's HQ is still in use by the PNG Navy.

The former Australian refugee detention centre is here too (see the boxed text, above). Near Loniu Passage is **Loniu Cave** (admission K5), where people hid during the war. Take a torch, dodge the bats and don't slip.

Momote airport has an Allied and a Japanese memorial plus some old transport hulks. If you look really closely, you'll even see bullet scars in a few trees.

Manus Island
Buyang, a village in the island's centre, is where you might see traditional dancing. Coastal **Worei**, in the south, is on the Worei River where you can take canoe trips.

ACTIVITIES
Diving
Ron Knight (☎ 470 9159/9285; Lorengau, Manus Island; dives K200) is a salt-encrusted salvage diver who

takes punters in groups of four or more. He supplies tanks, belts and great stories (avoid these before diving – they cover sharks, crocs, boatwrecks and high explosives).

The **Harbourside Hotel** (☎ 470 9408; www.dive pngmanus.com; Manus Island; per dive US$35, gear per day US$13) also arranges dives and has all gear. The marine environment here is world-class; look out for giant snails, seahorses and a lot of sharks. Whales are sometimes seen between January and March.

Swimming
You can swim with kids on both sides of the bridge or take a boat to **Salamei Beach** on **Rarah Island**, about two kilometres from Lorengau. Further on, try **Tulu** village, on the Manus coast west of Lorengau, or **Andra Island**. A waterfall and swimming hole is in the **Lorengau River** 5km upstream from town.

Surfing
There are some great breaks (November to March) all through the islands; the merciless reef off Ahus Island is terrific. It gets up to 12ft at times, so take care.

FESTIVALS & EVENTS
The **Manus Provincial Show** is celebrated over three days in late August.

SLEEPING
A hilltop guesthouse is at Sabon village, 10km inland from Lorengau, one near Lokabia Point near Worei and one near Lessau. They'll ask about K50 plus food. Each village on Manus or the islands has a *boihaus* for male guests; females can usually be housed too. Leave about K30 and bring some food.

GETTING THERE & AWAY
Air
Momote airport, on Los Negros Island, is linked to the capital Lorengau, on Manus Island, by 30km of sealed road. A bridge crosses the narrow Loniu Passage in between.

From **Momote airport** (☎ 470 9092), 35km east of Lorengau, Air Niugini connects to Kavieng (K390, out of Manus on Sunday, returning on Wednesday), Madang (K677, out of Manus on Monday, return on Friday) and Port Moresby (K677, out of Manus on Wednesday, return via Lae on Monday).

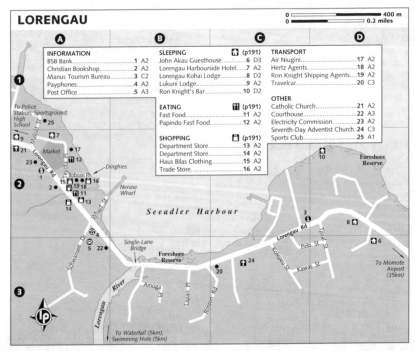

LORENGAU

INFORMATION			
BSB Bank	1 A2	
Christian Bookshop	2 A2	
Manus Tourism Bureau	3 C2	
Payphones	4 A2	
Post Office	5 A3	

SLEEPING 🏠 (p191)	
John Akau Guesthouse	6 D3
Lorengau Harbourside Hotel	7 A2
Lorengau Kohai Lodge	8 D2
Lukuni Lodge	9 A2
Ron Knight's Bar	10 D2

EATING 🍴 (p191)	
Fast Food	11 A2
Papindo Fast Food	12 A2

SHOPPING 🛍 (p191)	
Department Store	13 A2
Department Store	14 A2
Haus Bilas Clothing	15 A2
Trade Store	16 A2

TRANSPORT	
Air Niugini	17 A2
Hertz Agents	18 A2
Ron Knight Shipping Agents	19 A2
Travelcar	20 C3

OTHER	
Catholic Church	21 A2
Courthouse	22 A3
Electricity Commission	23 A2
Seventh-Day Adventist Church	24 C3
Sports Club	25 A1

Seeadler Harbour

Boat
Lutheran Shipping (contact Ron Knight ☎ 470 9159/ 9285; Lorengau; deck/bunk K160/100) usually operates the weekly ship MV *Maneba* via Lae.

GETTING AROUND
Boat
You can charter speedboats at the waterfront (per day excluding petrol K80). Hawai Island will take about 20L of fuel return. Give the fuel in advance, but try to pay the money later. The best way is to go as a passenger when the boats head back from the market at about 10am. Getting to Hawai will cost you just K3 this way. You'll have to spend at least one night there.

Car
Hertz (☎ 470 9351) at the airport and **Travelcar** (☎ 470 9491; Lorengau Rd) in town both cost K200 a day plus K1 per kilometre for a 4WD. John Akau Guesthouse and Lorengau Harbourside Hotel will shave about K30 off this.

PMV
You can catch PMVs between Lorengau and Lombrum, but that's all. The other roads have holes you could lose a car in. You'll have to hitch in from the airport (easy) or book ahead and get picked up. Airport transfers cost K20.

Lorengau
This provincial capital and only town is spread out along Seeadler Harbour. It's a very casual place, full of naked kids and *buai*-chewing teens with dreadlocks. It livens up on weekends when 'baptism of fire' sermons are preached to an enthusiastic crowd.

INFORMATION
There's a Bank South Pacific bank and hospital. There's no organised Internet here, but your guesthouse might let you use theirs.
Tourism bureau (☎ 470 9365; fax 470 9364)
Post office (Lorengau Rd; 8am-5pm Mon-Fri)

SLEEPING
Ron Knight's bar is floating on a couple of old ammunition barges he hauled up manually from deep under the harbour; it should have some pleasant rooms when completed (by mid-2005).
    Lorengau Harbourside Hotel (☎ 470 9262; fax 470 9392; Teyota Pl; s K193-237, d K215-282; ⊠) Odd

in that the tiled, cheaper rooms are nicer than the musty 'deluxe' options which open onto scruffy verandas. All come with fridge, phone and TV and you can pay by Visa here. Food is available and the bar closes at 10pm.
    Lorengau Kohai Lodge (☎ 470 9004; fax 470 9263; Lorengau Rd; s/d with fridge K100/120; ⊠) This is the most pleasant spot, with a cosy communal living room. Half the rooms have private bathrooms but – strangely – the price is uniform.
    John Akau Guesthouse (☎ 470 9289; johnakau@ daltron.com; s/d K50/80) This is cheap, clean, simple and homely. You can do your own cooking here, but you'll have to share the shower.
    Lukuni Lodge (☎ 470 9411; kuso@global.net.pg; Lorengau Rd; s/d 100/130; ⊠) A bit bare; there tends to be just a bed in each room. But it's a friendly place and central. You can use the kitchen.

EATING
Lorengau Harbourside Hotel (☎ 470 9262; fax 470 9392; Teyota Pl; breakfast/lunch/dinner K20/25/40; ⊠ 8am-8pm) Rather good, but pricey. It's got chilli mud crabs, pork with pineapple, and a generous 'burger with the lot'.
    Lorengau Kohai Lodge (☎ 470 9004; fax 470 9263; Lorengau Rd; breakfast/lunch/dinner K17/20/25) Non-guests can try the home cooking here.
    There are two stand-out *kai* bars in town.
Papindo Fast Food (⊠ 10am-dusk), where you can enjoy a lukewarm sheep's heart (dead), is no place for a vegetarian; the **fast food stall** (⊠ 10am-dusk) has popcorn. They both promise chips, but rarely deliver.

SHOPPING
All the consumer cargo that's shipped to Manus seems to end up in the department stores, Haus Bilas Clothing or the trade store. You can get hold of essentials like clothes, string, and anything plastic that's made in China.

OTHER ISLANDS
There are guesthouses on most islands. At **Andra** there's a reef-planting scheme to replace reef lost to *cumbung* traders. **Ahus** is the best snorkel spot with huge clams and a really good guesthouse; contact Ron Knight (p189). **Hawai** is close, and is a lovely island. There are hot springs on **Lou** and **Pam** has a real remote feel.

ISLAND PROVINCES

Wuvulu & Maron Islands

A favourite place of Jack Cousteau's, **Wuvulu Island** has to be the most remote part of the country. One traveller from Wewak returned a couple of days after he set off because the captain couldn't find Wuvulu! It's marked 'position approximate' on many maps. Wuvulu is famous for **killer whales**.

There are no rivers or creeks so visibility can be around 50m. The people are Micronesian and still make canoes large enough to hold 40 people. They need them too – transport is by monthly boat from Mussau Island (New Ireland). Ask at the tourism bureau in Lorengau (p191). Walindi Plantation Resort (p178) in WNB or **Blue Sea Charters** (www.blueseacharters.com) based in Madang (halfway along PNG's north coast) sometimes arrange liveaboard diving trips.

Maron is a bit closer – halfway there from Manus. There's a ruined German castle here – the result of a Baron Heinrich Wahlen's obsession to have a *really* remote hunting lodge. The deer he imported are still there. His harem of concubines, however, is long gone, as are the results of the Polynesian/Melanesian eugenic superrace he was trying to breed. The ride takes six hours by speedboat. Don't go if there's so much as a ripple.

SECESSION, WAR & PEACE

In the 1960s and early 1970s, the North Solomons began a push to break away from Australian colonial control, climaxing in land disputes over the proposed Panguna.

Before PNG independence, Bougainville pushed for an independent grouping of the Bismarck Archipelago. In 1974 secessionist movements sprang up.

In 1987 the Panguna Landowners Association was formed, led by Pepetua Sereo and Francis Ona. It demanded better environmental protection, huge back-payments of profits from the mine and US$10 *billion* in compensation. These demands were not met and in 1988 the Bougainville Revolutionary Army (BRA), an offshoot of the landowners' association, began to sabotage the mine. Relations between the locals and police sent to protect the mine deteriorated sharply. The BRA's numbers were bolstered by sympathisers from other parts of the country and even a religious cult.

Increasing attacks on mine workers resulted in the mine's closure in 1989 – an enormous blow to the PNG economy. A state of emergency was declared, the PNG army moved in and the conflict spread to the rest of the island. Whole villages were moved into 'care centres', areas outside BRA control. To ensure that the people moved, the army burned their villages and stories about rape and murder flooded out of Bougainville. The Panguna issue became a civil war – at the height of the conflict, there were 60,000 people displaced.

In 1990 the PNG government withdrew its forces and instituted a blockade, which led to great hardship for the Bougainvilleans. The BRA declared independence, forming the Republic of Meekamui on 17 May. Bougainville slipped back into primitivism. The BRA brought over supplies from the nearby Solomon Islands and the PNG army, in retaliation, caused international tension by raiding suspected BRA bases in the Solomon Islands, killing innocent people.

In February 1997 the Sandline Affair hit the headlines. In a highly secret operation then–prime minister Julius Chan contracted a mercenary company to put down the rebels. The plan was exposed and there was an international outcry. Days of heavy tension in Port Moresby saw rioting and looting in the streets with people calling for Chan to stand down. He did and the mercenaries – South Africans mostly – were deported. This act of lunacy cost US$36 million but perhaps it hastened efforts to find a peaceful outcome for Bougainville.

In March 2002 PNG Parliament passed legislation to give legal effect to the autonomy arrangements contained in a peace agreement, which includes a referendum for an independent Bougainville state in 2017. The PNGDF (PNG Defence Force) withdrew for the last time in April 2003. Weapons were surrendered to the UN, and certain amnesties and pardons were granted. People are still trying to go back to being normal. In mid-2004 the first divisions of local police graduated their training.

Francis Ona, meanwhile, still holds out in the mountains.

NORTH SOLOMONS PROVINCE

The islands that comprise the North Solomons (Buka, Bougainville and a scattering of smaller atolls) are closer to the neighbouring Solomon Islands than they are to PNG – just as the name suggests. The province is the farthest from the PNG mainland and the international border between the Solomons and PNG passes just a few kilometres south of Bougainville Island. This is the start of the string of islands down to Makira that makes up most of the Solomons. The Shortland and Choiseul islanders in the Solomons are very close to Bougainvilleans, culturally and racially – both have jet-black skin. Around PNG Bougainvilleans are known as 'blackskins' or 'bukas', and often the whole North Solomons region is referred to as Bougainville.

Bougainville Island is the main island: green, rugged and little-developed. Until the secessionist rebellion, the province had the most productive economy, best education and the most well-run government. Between 1972 and its 1989 closure, the Panguna mine made 45% of PNG's export earnings and paid the government about K55 million annually in taxes and dividends.

There is no longer any fighting and most of the province is safe to explore, but it's recovering from 10 years of conflict – there's little infrastructure and certainly no concessions to travellers. There's a bittersweet feel to Bougainville – it's probably PNG's most beautiful province but there's also been great suffering.

North Solomons has been granted a special autonomy status within PNG. Stability and prosperity have again returned to the region.

Though there are still a lot of aid workers, international police and Non-Governmental Organisations (NGOs) working in southern Bougainville, peace has been restored, the flights are full and people are happy to see visitors. There's huge potential for small-scale tourism.

History

There's evidence that humans settled on Bougainville at least 28,000 years ago.

Spanish mariner Luis Vaez de Torres passed through in 1606, but Bougainville acquired its name from French explorer Louis-Antoine de Bougainville who sailed up the east coast in 1768.

European settlements were established as the German New Guinea Company began trading in the late 1890s. Bougainville and Buka were considered part of the Solomons group, a British possession, until 1898 when they were traded to Germany. Australia seized the North Solomons, with the rest of New Guinea, at the start of WWI.

The Japanese arrived in 1942, swiftly defeating the Australians and holding most of the island until the end of the war. Buka became an important air base, and Buin, at the southern tip of Bougainville, was a base for ground troops. In 1943 American troops captured the port of Torokina and Australian forces were fighting their way south towards Buin. Of 80,000 Japanese troops only 23,000 were taken prisoner –20,000 are thought to have been killed in action and the remaining 37,000 died of disease and starvation in the jungles. There's a moving monument to the Japanese dead atop Sohano Island's cliff.

In 1964, a major copper discovery was made at Panguna and more than K400 million was invested in a mine and its ancillary operations. A new town, roads, a power station and a port were constructed, and thousands of workers descended.

Geography & Climate

Bougainville is volcanic, about 200km long and covered in jungle. The Crown Prince, Emperor and Deuro ranges make up the central spine and the volcanic Mt Bagana frequently erupts. Mt Balbi, the island's highest point at 2685m, is a dormant volcano; Benua Cave is perhaps the world's largest at 4,500,000 cu metres. The island has many natural harbours, and large swamps on its western edge.

Buka Island is formed almost entirely of raised coral. It's separated from Bougainville Island by Buka Passage, a tidal channel only 300m wide and a kilometre long. Buka Island is generally low-lying, apart from a southern hilly region. Another 166 islands spread over 450,000 sq km of sea. It's the most earthquake-prone area of the country.

The province is hot and wet, with some areas getting more than 5m of annual rainfall. The drier period in Buka is between May and October.

Culture

Intricately woven Buka baskets are made all over the country except seemingly here where they originated. The baskets are made from jungle vine, and the variation in colour is achieved by scraping the skin off the vine. They can be simple drink coasters or giant laundry baskets, and they're the most skilfully made baskets in the Pacific – solid and durable. They were originally made by the Siwai and Telei people of southwest Buka Island.

There are 23 languages in the North Solomons; Tok Pisin is the second main language but most people speak English well. The people of Takuu (or Mortlock) and Nukumani islands are Polynesian.

North Solomon Islanders have a matrilineal system of clan membership and inheritance rights. Most still live in bush-material housing in villages and grow cash crops.

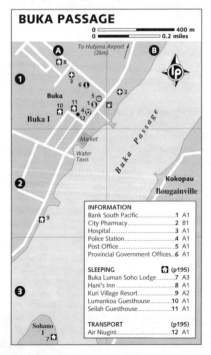

BUKA ISLAND

A road runs up the east coast of Buka Island, connecting the copra plantations. Queen Carola Harbour, on the west coast, used to be Buka's main port. Buka Passage has become the main port for the province.

Buka & Buka Passage

Buka used to be a tiny place but it now has many new buildings and residents. It has boomed in the last 15 years – during the war and afterwards – and now has several decent places to stay. Buka has the passage – perhaps the world's best water feature – and the people are very friendly, cheerful and interesting. Buka is the centre of activity in the province.

ORIENTATION

Most of the shops and services are on, or just off, the main waterfront strip of town. Dinghies congregate near the market and the passage is abuzz with these small crafts plying between the town, Kokopau village (opposite on Bougainville Island), Sohano Island at the southern mouth of the passage and the islands beyond.

INFORMATION

Many places in Buka don't accept credit cards – you might be expected to settle your accommodation bill in cash.

Bank South Pacific (☎ 973 9752) Down at the northern end of town. It has ATMs and extremely long queues.
Post office (☎ 973 9703) Next to the bank.

SIGHTS & ACTIVITIES

Riding in a dinghy in Buka Passage is a buzz. The water runs at about 8 knots when the tide is fast, making deep undulations on the water's surface. You can jump on a dinghy, pay the fare and go to lots of the islands near the southern mouth of the passage. Good swimming spots are on these islands and the fishing over the reefs is excellent.

There's great snorkelling in Buka Passage but be careful with the tide or you'll wind up lost at sea. Even when the tide is not running fast, you'll tire quickly just breaking even with the current. Those who aren't strong swimmers might choose to watch.

Sohano Island

Sohano Island is a few minutes by boat from Buka and was the provincial capital from WWII until 1960.

It's a beautiful place with lawns and gardens, a **Japanese monument** and war relics, steep craggy cliffs and panoramic views over town, the passage and Bougainville Island. There are some colonial-period buildings and a rather gentrified atmosphere on the island.

The weird **Tchibo Rock** stands just offshore from Sohano's northernmost point and figures in many local legends. It's said to have magical properties. The dinghy fare to Sohano Island is K1.

SLEEPING & EATING

There are several good places to stay in Buka and local accommodation is somewhat offbeat and quirky. There aren't a lot of travellers in Bougainville and the hotel clientele is mostly business workers and NGOs. Buka's power goes off pretty much every day but the guesthouses have generators, which kick in automatically.

Kuri Village Resort (☎ 973 9155; www.mena.org .au/kuri; s K182-196, d K208-226, f K270; 🔀) Kuri Village Resort is Buka's best place to stay with a fine outlook over the passage. The free-standing, self-contained bungalows are an odd mix of bush materials and pseudo-timber laminate interiors. They're comfortable nonetheless and the resort is the social centre of town. There's a sea-water aquarium where some giant turtles and large fish are kept, fed on meat and fruit – turtles like pawpaw. The set-menu meals are good and there's a bar. Tours are available and airport transfers are included.

Seilah Guesthouse (c/- Copra Marketing Board ☎ 973 9959; s/d K90/130) This is right in the middle of town near the Air Niugini office. Bathroom facilities are shared and meals are available.

Lumankoa Guesthouse (☎ 973 9779; fax 973 9806; s K88-94) Lumankoa is at the back of town. It's clean, straight and very friendly. Breakfast and dinner are included in the room prices. The bathrooms are shared but the better rooms have TV.

Hani's Inn (☎ 973 9930; fax 973 9930; s K99-132, d K154; 🔀) Hani's is near the hospital and it's a clean and comfortable place to stay. The cheapest rooms share bathroom facilities and set-menu meals are offered. Airport transfers are included.

Kuri Lodge (☎ 973 9938; www.mena.org.au/kuri; s K100; 🔀) Kuri Lodge is the sister lodge for Kuri Village Resort. The lodge is well set up

in a two-storey building at the rear of Buka. Facilities are shared, breakfast is included and other set-menu meals are available.

Buka Luman Soho Lodge (☎ 983 9937/9757; fax 983 9934; s K95-160, d K135-170; 🔀) Located on Sohano Island, this is a fantastic place to stay and very accessible by water taxi to Buka township. There are two wings – the older is fan-cooled and the newer wing is spectacularly sited on the clifftop overlooking the town and jungly shores of Bougainville (you could almost throw a stone across). There's a TV and fridge in the better rooms, which are large and very comfortable. Good meals are served in a dining room decorated with many WWII photos and other paraphernalia.

SHOPPING

There's not much to buy in Buka and ironically this is about the only place in the country where you can't buy *bukaware*. Maybe they got sick of weaving baskets. The market has the usual fare – nothing especially interesting.

GETTING THERE & AROUND

Air Niugini (☎ 973 9655), located just off the main road, flies in via Rabaul on Tuesday, Thursday and Saturday, while **Airlink** (☎ 973 9734) flies in on Monday, Wednesday and Friday. One-way full fares include Rabaul K309, Port Moresby K738 and Lae K710.

Water taxis are the way to get around the Buka Passage area. PMVs – Landcruiser Troop Carriers – ferry people down the coast road of Bougainville to Arawa, four hours away, for a steep K50. You have to go to Kokopau across the passage and book a seat by 9am even though the vehicles don't leave until 11am or noon.

BOUGAINVILLE

The road is in good condition running down the east coast of Bougainville to Arawa and Kieta. Not all of the rivers are bridged and the road fords several of them. From Wakunai there's a three-day trip to climb Mt Balbi (2685m). From its summit, you can see the active Mt Bagana (1730m).

DANGERS & ANNOYANCES

Francis Ona, former Bougainville Revolutionary Army (BRA) military commander, and a few of his diehards still control the area around the abandoned Panguna mine – the original source of discontent. This area is called the 'no-go zone', and it is not safe for any outsiders. Care needs to be taken elsewhere in Bougainville because, until very recently, there has been a lot of violence and retribution. Families turned on each other during 'the Crisis' – it's possible that old wounds could reopen.

GETTING THERE & AROUND
Travel on the Bougainville Island by PMV is possible, although quite expensive. You might be able to procure boats by negotiation, but this is a very remote area and there are no formal boat schedules or services. This area is devastated after 10 years of war – all the buildings are gutted and the roads are destroyed. They don't get travellers in southern Bougainville: it's basically a lawless and scary part of the country. See the boxed text on p244 for information on a route between Bougainville and the Solomon Islands.

Arawa & Kieta
Arawa and Kieta are virtually contiguous and were severely damaged during the conflict (see the boxed text, p192). Whole neighbourhoods have been abandoned. Coming north from the old airport you go through Kieta, then central Kieta and 10km east, over the Kieta Peninsula, to Arawa, the main town.

Four kilometres northwest of Arawa is **Loloho** on Arawa Bay, the port to which the copper concentrate was piped down from Panguna, the site of the power station and home to many of the mine workers. There's an attractive beach here.

SLEEPING
There are some guesthouses opening in Arawa and probably some informal accommodation available. It's likely that new places will open up over the next few years. The Arawa Women's Centre sometimes takes travellers also.

Arevai Guesthouse (☎ 641 1209; s K100) is a pretty basic place with shared facilities.

Panguna
Panguna is off limits – the 'no-go zone' as they say. High in the centre of the island the dormant mine is one of the world's largest artificial holes. Bougainville Copper Limited was the operator of the Panguna open-cut mine.

Copper was discovered at Panguna in 1964 (see the boxed text, p192). There's no chance that the mine will reopen again soon – Ona and his followers will see to that.

Buin
Buin suffered less damage than Kieta and Arawa during the conflict. It is very wet year-round, with more than 4m of annual rainfall. During WWII, Buin hosted a large Japanese army base and the area has many rusting relics.

There's a road south from Aropa to Buin that takes about three hours by vehicle. You could complete a circuit and come back through Panguna if you had your own transport, but the road fords several fast-flowing rivers, which would be pretty tough going after rain.

Around Buin
The Japanese had plans to resettle a huge number of civilian Japanese at an area called Little Tokyo. Tonnoli Harbour is beautiful.

The road from Aropa to Buin comes to an intersection; the road to the east heads back to Arawa through Siwai and Panguna, the west road goes to Malabita and the road straight ahead goes to Kangu. Beyond here there are various bunkers and pillboxes, and a gun pointing out to sea.

Admiral Yamamoto's aircraft wreck is the area's most historically interesting wreck. Admiral Isoroku Yamamoto, who planned the attack on Pearl Harbour, left Rabaul in a Betty Bomber on 18 April 1943 with a protective group of Zeros, not realising that US fighters were waiting for him near Buin.

The wreckage of the Betty still lies in the jungle a few kilometres off the Panguna–Buin road. It's signposted, near Aku, 24km before Buin. It's a one-hour walk from the road.

Solomon Islands

SOLOMON ISLANDS

The Solomon Islands is one of the friendliest places in the Pacific, but head-hunting, cannibalism and skull worship were common up to the 1930s. Outside the main centres, the archipelago is a wild chain of bushland, villages and lagoons. The vast blue ocean crossings will make you gulp before you climb aboard the pitching, monthly cargo ship with tattooed, scarred-up sailors swarming up and down the hatches.

If you're game enough, you can keep island hopping further and further, in little boats, until you're in an ancient Shortlands village that appears in no travel books at all. Some of the larger islands like Malaita have interiors that are barely charted, and still inhabited by full-*kastom* (custom) tribes.

Polynesian Rennell and Bellona are World Heritage–listed wildernesses of rare endemic species. Rennell is exceptional in that it thinly rings a huge freshwater lake. The Solomons is also home to the chicken-sized megapode (which lays its eggs in hot volcanic sand), crocodiles, flying foxes and rats larger than domestic cats!

Ghizo and Central Province are among world's top dive destinations, as is the world-renowned Marovo Lagoon. This and the other large lagoons are known for wood carvings. Take a boat passage through and you might see pilot whales, breaching dolphins chasing tuna, or a crowd of passengers paddling wooden dugouts to the ship as it throws a hawser round a coconut tree.

In Western Province the jungles are dotted with WWII fighter planes, each in a surge of tropical orchids. The lagoon floors are covered with wrecks, great for diving, and on the islands are skull shrines and the odd head-hunter king's coral fortress.

Press north and you'll reach Kolombangarra, a picture-book volcanic cone that you might be tempted to climb. Across the strait is Gizo, a kick-back Pacific town with a few bars on the beach, a few little island getaways and a few surf spots.

SOLOMON ISLANDS

HIGHLIGHTS

- Sailing to wild **Malaita Island** (p212) in a wooden ship, with breaching dolphins at the bow

- Kayaking and diving the islands of beautiful **Marovo Lagoon** (p209) and watching an active underwater volcano

- Relaxing and diving around **Lola Island** (p209) plus visiting a nearby skull shrine and ruins of a head-hunter king's coral fort.

- Exploring sunken war wrecks off the coast of **Gizo** (p205) and visiting the lonely missions of the nearby islands

- Paddling a traditional canoe and wildlife-watching through the huge, World Heritage–listed **Lake Te'Nggano** (p211)

Ghizo | Marovo Lagoon | Malaita
Lola Island
Lake Te'Nggano

| ▪ LAND AREA: 27,540 sq km (sea area: 1.35 million sq km) | ▪ POPULATION: 524,000 |

History

By 25,000 BC, hunter-gatherers arrived from New Guinea and Austronesian-speaking proto-Melanesians reached here in 4000 BC. Lapita people came between 2000 and 1600 BC. Polynesians from the east settled the outer islands between 1200 and 1600 AD.

Whalers and sandalwood traders started arriving in 1798. The Solomons was the most dangerous place in the Pacific. Black-birders (slavers) took over 29,000 Solomon Islanders to work in Australia and Fiji.

In 1893 Britain proclaimed the islands a protectorate and increasingly missionaries sought to eradicate local culture. The Kwaio Rebellion on Malaita in 1927 was crushed in the then-capital Tulagi. Basiana, the defiant rebel leader, declared before being hanged, 'Tulagi will be torn apart, and scattered to the winds'; 14 years later it was.

In April 1942 the Japanese occupied Guadalcanal. Allied troops heroically fought ashore in August, losing 1270 men. After six months the Japanese withdrew to New Georgia. During the Guadalcanal campaign, 67 warships were sunk – this area is now called Iron Bottom Sound. Around 7000 American and 30,000 Japanese lives were lost.

Honiara became the capital and independence was granted in 1978. By the late '90s the Guadalcanal locals were warring with Malaitan immigrants (see right), which ruined the economy. Law and order has returned.

Geography & Climate

The Solomons is the third-largest archipelago in the South Pacific. Volcanic activity and earthquakes occur alot. The dry season is from May to early December. Cyclones occur between January and April. Daytime coastal temperatures vary from 21° to 32°C.

Culture

Solomon Islanders' duties to their clan and village *bigman* (leader) are eternal and trans-geographic. The *wantok* system (p24) happens here, as in most Melanesian cultures. *Kastom* (or traditional ways) involve dances, songs and stories. *Kastom* fees are often charged for visiting an ancestral site. Many islanders believe in magic and devils. Most Solomon Islanders live in coastal villages. Each family has a coconut crop and vegetable plots. The bush provides food (pigs, nuts, ferns and fruits) and building materials.

ETHNIC TENSION

For years the Gwale people of Guadalcanal resented that their traditional land was being settled by migrants from Malaita.

Early in 1999 the Guadalcanal Revolutionary Army (GRA) began to terrorise Malaitan migrants, which led to thousands fleeing back home. The Malaitan Eagle Force (MEF) was formed and soon gained the upper hand. Hundreds died in the fighting.

Following mediation by Australia and New Zealand, the Townsville Peace Agreement was signed in October 2000. Conflict has ceased, thanks greatly to the Regional Assistance Mission to the Solomon Islands (RAMSI) presence throughout the whole country, implemented in July 2003.

The RAMSI force includes personnel from Australia, New Zealand and Fiji, and is mainly a policing project, thanks to which law and order has returned.

GUADALCANAL

Guadalcanal is the largest island in the Solomons group and boasts the national capital, Honiara. WWII battlefields are in every direction.

HONIARA

There's often a container ship in Honiara's busy port that is bigger than any of the city buildings. This centre is as hectic and urban as the Solomons get (not very). The capital is nothing less than a maritime crossroads between the far-flung island provinces.

The centre is along Mendana Ave from the SIVB to Chinatown. There is a map sales division of the Agriculture Lands Department where you should be able to get a map.

Information

Try NBSI, ANZ and Westpac banks. The latter two have Cirrus, Maestro and credit card–capable ATMs. The public library and, behind it, the **National Library** (☼ 27412) are both near Mataniko bridge. Neither opens on Wednesday.

Ambulance (☎ 911)

Central Hospital (☎ 23600) In Kukum.

En Vision Internet Café (per hr S$13.50; ☼ 9am-5pm Mon-Fri, 10am-noon Sun) Minimum fee S$6.

Fire (☎ 988 Honiara only)
Honiara Dental Centre (☎ 22746; Mendana Ave)
People First (per min S$0.35; ☺ 8am-5pm Mon-Fri, 9am-3pm Sat) Excellent Internet café.
Police (☎ 999)
Post office (Mendana Ave; ☺ 9am-5pm Mon-Fri, 9am-1pm Sat)
Solomon Islands Visitors Bureau (SIVB; ☎ 22442; info @sivb.com.sb; Mendana Ave; ☺ 8.30am-4.30pm Mon-Fri)
Solomon Telekom (per min S$0.74; ☺ 8am-4.30pm Mon-Fri) Has email, fax and telephones.

The Rennell and Bellona district office is located behind the magistrate's court, just south of the central market opposite Mendana Ave. It has information about the province, including rare passenger shipping going to and fro.

Sights

The sergeant at arms at the circular **National Parliament** (Hibiscus Ave; ☺ 8am-4pm) will give you a free tour.

The **National Museum & Cultural Centre** (☎ 22098; Mendana Ave; admission by donation; ☺ 8am-4.30pm Mon-Fri) displays dance, body ornamentation, currency and weaponry. There are some terrific 19th-century photographs, and petroglyphs from Poha.

The **Central Bank** (☎ 21791; Mendana Ave; admission free) shows woodcarvings and traditional money (Santa Cruz red-feather money!), Malaitan dolphin teeth and shell money.

The impressive and well-annotated **US War Memorial** is 20 minutes' walk up from Mendana Ave.

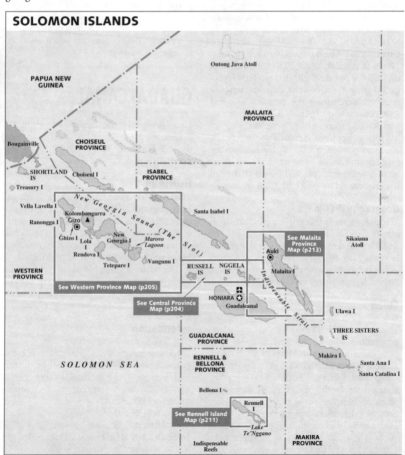

SOLOMON ISLANDS

Activities

Coastwatchers (☎ 95699; coastwatchers@fastmail .fm; Honiara Hotel; 2 dives S$400, gear hire per day S$300) dives the local wrecks, but Tulagi's better.

Tours

Battlefield tours (three hours) can be arranged through SIVB and **Guadalcanal Travel Services** (☎ 22587; gts@somomon.com.sb; Mendana Ave; per person S$200). **Lalae Charters** (☎ 25050; info@lalae.com.sb) offers fishing charters.

Sleeping

BUDGET

All places listed have communal kitchens, fan-cooled twin rooms and share facilities unless stated otherwise.

United Church Resthouse (☎ 20028; Lower Vayvaya Rd; dm S$61) A spotless, quiet, teetotal place run by good, honest church folk.

Chester Resthouse (☎ 26355; fax 23079; Lower Vayvaya Rd; tw S$140) Run by Anglican brothers, this place has a great veranda. It's very clean and you'll get used to calling staff 'brother'.

Bulaia Backpackers Lodge (☎ 28819; Chinatown; dm S$75, d S$150-200) Friendly. A good choice.

Solomon City Guesthouse (☎ 24862; Vayvaya Ridge Rd; s/d S$80/150; 🐾) Good for a cheap, basic single room.

St Agnes Transit Lodge (☎ 27785; s/d S$110/132) Spartan but functional.

Island lodge (☎ 20254; Cluck St; s/d S$140/180) Slightly shoddy, but OK.

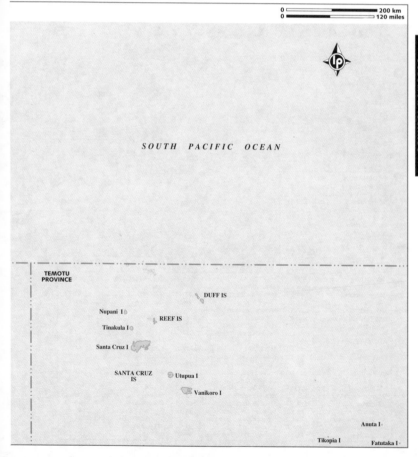

0 —— 200 km
0 —— 120 miles

SOUTH PACIFIC OCEAN

SOLOMON ISLANDS

TEMOTU PROVINCE

DUFF IS

Nupani I

REEF IS

Tinakula I

Santa Cruz I

SANTA CRUZ IS   Utupua I

Vanikoro I

Anuta I

Tikopia I   Fatutaka I

MID-RANGE

Quality Motel (☎ 25150; qml@solomon.com.sb; Lower Vayvaya Rd; tw S$180-320; ❄) Most rooms have TV; all have a fridge and telephone. It's the better of the two options.

Honiara Hotel (☎ 21737; honhotel@solomon.com.sb; Chinatown; dm/d S$140/from S$275; ❄) The rooms are a little dank, though well equipped with fridge, radio, TV and kettle. Going into the dorms is like venturing into a crypt.

TOP END

King Solomon Hotel (☎ 21205; kingsol@solomon.com.sb; Hibiscus Ave; d from S$532; ❄ ▣) The professional staff and comfortable rooms with all facilities make this the best place.

Solomon Kitano Mendana Hotel (☎ 20071; kitano@mendana.com.sb; Mendana Ave; s/tw from S$495/540; ❄ ▣) The staff are helpful and the rooms are well furnished but musty.

Pacific Casino Hotel (☎ 25009; paccashtl@solomon.com.sb; d S$400-800; ❄ ▣ ▣) Excellent facilities include a gym and squash courts. The rooms, however, are not worth the price.

Eating

Lime Lounge (mains S$40; ☽ 8am-9pm; ❄) The expats' hide-out with milk shakes, ice cream, coffee, cakes and aquatic mains in icy air-con. Off Mendana Ave, near the main wharf.

Solomon Kitano Mendana Hotel (breakfast/lunch/dinner S$40/70/100; ☽ 8am-9pm) Wide choice of Japanese and Western food. Excellent.

HONIARA

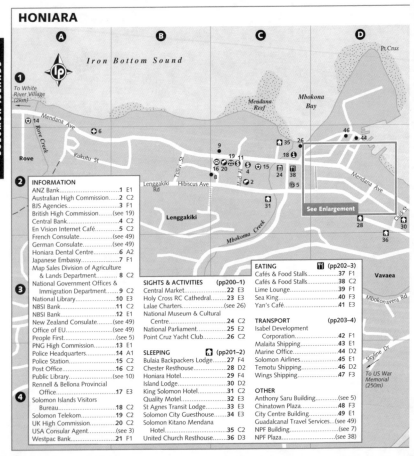

SOLOMON ISLANDS

INFORMATION	
ANZ Bank	1 E1
Australian High Commission	2 C2
BJS Agencies	3 F1
British High Commission	(see 19)
Central Bank	4 C2
En Vision Internet Café	5 C2
French Consulate	(see 49)
German Consulate	(see 49)
Honiara Dental Centre	6 A2
Japanese Embassy	7 F1
Map Sales Division of Agriculture & Lands Department	8 C2
National Government Offices & Immigration Department	9 C2
National Library	10 E3
NBSI Bank	11 C2
NBSI Bank	12 E1
New Zealand Consulate	(see 49)
Office of EU	(see 49)
People First	(see 5)
PNG High Commission	13 E1
Police Headquarters	14 A1
Police Station	15 C2
Post Office	16 C2
Public Library	(see 10)
Rennell & Bellona Provincial Office	17 E3
Solomon Islands Visitors Bureau	18 C2
Solomon Telekom	19 C2
UK High Commission	20 C2
USA Consular Agent	(see 3)
Westpac Bank	21 F1

SIGHTS & ACTIVITIES	(pp200-1)
Central Market	22 E3
Holy Cross RC Cathedral	23 E3
Lalae Charters	(see 26)
National Museum & Cultural Centre	24 C2
National Parliament	25 E2
Point Cruz Yacht Club	26 C2

SLEEPING	⌂ (pp201-2)
Bulaia Backpackers Lodge	27 F4
Chester Resthouse	28 D2
Honiara Hotel	29 F4
Island Lodge	30 D2
King Solomon Hotel	31 C2
Quality Motel	32 E3
St Agnes Transit Lodge	33 E3
Solomon City Guesthouse	34 E3
Solomon Kitano Mendana Hotel	35 C2
United Church Resthouse	36 D3

EATING	⚷ (pp202-3)
Cafés & Food Stalls	37 F1
Cafés & Food Stalls	38 C2
Lime Lounge	39 F1
Sea King	40 F3
Yan's Café	41 E3

TRANSPORT	(pp203-4)
Isabel Development Corporation	42 F1
Malaita Shipping	43 E1
Marine Office	44 D2
Solomon Airlines	45 E1
Temotu Shipping	46 D2
Wings Shipping	47 F3

OTHER	
Anthony Saru Building	(see 5)
Chinatown Plaza	48 F3
City Centre Building	49 E1
Guadalcanal Travel Services	(see 49)
NPF Building	(see 7)
NPF Plaza	(see 38)

King Solomon Hotel (breakfast/lunch/dinner S$30/60/80; 🕑 8am-9pm) Schnitzel, fettuccini, Malaitan crab and apple strudel feature here, along with all-day pizzas.

Pacific Casino Hotel (breakfast/lunch/dinner S$50/80/110; 🕑 8am-9pm) The restaurant has an extensive range of Japanese, Thai and Western food as well as a wine list.

Fortune Restaurant (lunch/dinner S$60/110; 🕑 8am-10pm) An excellent Chinese place, beside the Pacific Casino Hotel, with *yum cha* buffet from 11am to 2pm Monday to Friday.

Sea King (lunch/dinner S$60/90; 🕑 11am-9pm) Another great Chinese place specialising in seafood and some vegetarian options. Just seawards of Mataniko bridge.

Honiara Hotel (breakfast/lunch/dinner S$30/40/90; 🕑 11am-9pm) Along with French aspirations, it's got sashimi, but it's not *that* posh.

Point Cruz Yacht Club (☎ 22500; lunch/dinner S$40/60; 🕑 11am-9pm). Enter for good-value burgers, sausages and shepherd's pie for homesick colonists.

Yan's Café (Mendana Ave; dishes S$10; 🕑 10am-dusk) A better-than-average *kai* bar with fish, chips and noodles. Opposite the central market.

There are supermarkets near the city-centre building and arcades of ice cream, pastry and drinks stalls nearby.

Drinking

The **Point Cruz Yacht Club** (☎ 22500) is very pleasant. For a night out with the high rollers, head for a hotel bar or the casino at the Pacific Casino Hotel.

Shopping

There are craft shops on Mendana Ave, outside the Mendana and King Solomon Hotels, and in the National Museum & Cultural Centre.

Getting There & Away

See p236 for international destinations.

AIR

Solomon Airlines (☎ 20031) and GTS are agents for Air Niugini, Air Pacific and Qantas.

BOAT

Motor-canoes to neighbouring islands leave from Point Cruz Yacht Club. You can travel cheaply on cargo ships from Honiara to all over the Solomons. Ask at the wharf and check the daily reports at the **marine office** (☎ 21609) for schedules.

Temotu Shipping (☎ 27558; fax 27923; main wharf) and **Wings Shipping** (☎ 27942; Chinatown) both sail to Gizo (S$215, overnight) via Marovo Lagoon (S$125) weekly.

The *Sa Alia* sails between Honiara and Auki in Malaita (S$90, seven hours) every two days.

Getting Around

The taxi fare from the airport into town is S$50 . Generally major hotels provide transfers but the fee is the same.

There's a minibus driving up and down Mendana Ave every minute until 7pm (flat rate S$2).

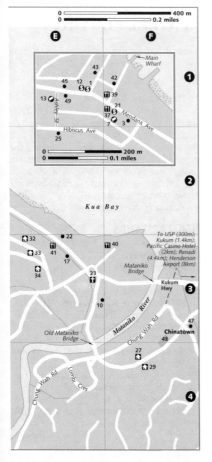

SOLOMON ISLANDS

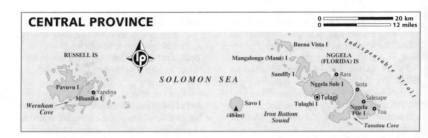

CENTRAL PROVINCE

Economy Car Rentals (☎ 27100; solmot@solomon .com.sb; Mendana Ave) has cars from S$228 per day, including insurance and kilometres.

Honiara taxis don't have meters; S$4 per kilometre is reasonable.

EAST OF HONIARA

Spectacular, double-sided **Mataniko Falls** thunders straight into a **cave** (kastom S$10) – formerly a hide-out for Japanese soldiers. It's a two-hour walk from Honiara. At Tuvaruhu, find a guide, cross the river and follow it south.

At **Mt Austen** you'll find a vandalised Japanese war memorial with views over Iron Bottom Sound (coined because many Japanese ships were sunk here during WWII).

About 6km from Honiara is the turn-off south to the **Betikama SDA Mission** (1.5km from the turn-off). There's a big carving shop and a museum including war memorabilia.

At the island's eastern tip is **Marau Sound**, a lagoon with some clusters of islands, reefs, shoals and coral gardens. Further into the lagoon is **Tavanipupu Island**, which has a top-class resort (due to open soon) in one of Guadalcanal's most stunning locations.

WEST OF HONIARA

About 5km west of the town centre, **Kakabona** marks the start of the nice beaches; they all charge S$10 *kastom*.

A few kilometres further at **Poha**, is **Vatuluma Posori Cave**, a renowned archaeological site. Some of the stone carvings from here are 2000 years old, though the best are on display at the National Museum & Cultural Centre (p200). A cross-island track begins here, but you'll need a guide and a couple of days.

Just a little way further, **Bonigi 1** and **Bonigi 2** beaches both have wrecks shallow enough for snorkelling. About 30km from Honiara is **Cape Espérance**, the site of the Japanese evacuation. The beaches from here on are lovely. Carry on and you'll eventually start to swing round to the south of the island and the spectacular **Weather Coast**, a panorama of fast rivers cascading from the craggy ridges onto volcanic beaches. Avoid the local wet season (July to September). It'll have to be a DIY trip; there are no facilities in this area.

CENTRAL PROVINCE

Central Province is made up of the Nggela (or Florida) Islands, Savo and the Russell Islands. Tulagi has superb diving.

Getting There & Around

Solomon Airlines flies to Yandina on Mbanika (Russell Islands) twice a week from Honiara (S$205). Cargo ships (the *Nolano* and *Bellama*; S$30) ply between Tulagi and the capital. Otherwise, buy passage on a market trader's motor-canoe (S$40). The cheapest way of moving between the islands is via Honiara on a passing vessel. If not, you'll be chartering costly private motor-canoes.

NGGELA ISLANDS

Widely known as the Florida Islands, the rugged silhouette of the Nggela group is clearly visible from Honiara. The main attraction here is the scuba diving, but it's also a great place to enjoy a remote beach without having to travel far from Honiara.

Tulagi was the colonial capital. **Vanita Accommodation** (☎ 32074; fax 32186; r per person S$85) is basic but it tries – you'll find a few flowers on the tables. **Dive Tulagi** (☎ 32131; www.tulagidive .com.sb; per dive S$200, gear hire per day S$250) caters for the serious wreck diver. There are also fantastic reefs, giant mantas and sharks here.

On **Mangalonga** (Mana) you'll find **Maravagi Resort** (☎ 29065; bungalows per person A$50), a classic, bungalows-on-a-paradise-beach place. It's looking a bit worn now, though. You can snorkel right from the shore.

SAVO

Savo is clearly visible to the northwest from Honiara. It has some striking hot springs, mud pools, geysers and megapode birds.

RUSSELL ISLANDS

Live-aboard dive boats such as the MV *Bilikiki* visit the Russell Islands from Honiara. The area has submarine caverns, prolific reef growth and many sunken war wrecks.

Mbanika and **Pavuvu** are the two largest islands. Yandina, on Mbanika's east coast, is the subprovincial headquarters.

WESTERN PROVINCE

Pristine lagoons, tropical islets, stunning diving and skull shrines make this part of the Solomons a must. The lush, forested islands, white sand bars, turquoise coral shallows and inky-blue seas are breathtaking.

Getting There & Away

Flights link Gizo and Seghe to Honiara daily.

By boat, weekly return journeys from Honiara to Gizo via Marovo Lagoon are run by **Wings Shipping** (☎ 27942; Honiara) and **Temotu Shipping** (☎ 27558; fax 27923; Honiara). The 48-hour return trip costs S$215.

GHIZO

The war wrecks and marine life found here make for superlative diving among some of the world's most biodiverse coral gardens.

Gizo

Gizo was a Japanese base during WWII.

INFORMATION

There's a hospital and immigration office.
ANZ (Middenway Rd) Accepts Visa and MasterCard.
Gizo Computers (Middenway Rd; S$2 per min) Internet access.
NBSI (Middenway Rd)
SI Systems (Middenway Rd; S$1.50 per min) Internet access.
Tourist Office (☎ 60560)
World Wildlife Fund (WWF; ☎ 60191; wwf@solomon .com.sb) Provides very informative books covering local marine, bird and terrestrial wildlife. It's most useful as a contact for visiting Tetapare, where it runs field trips.

SOLOMON ISLANDS

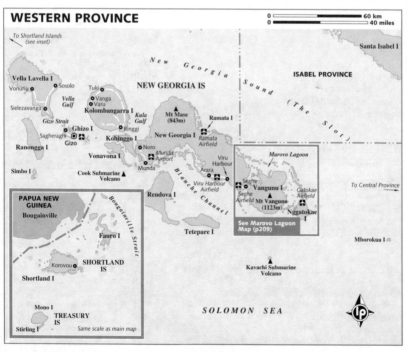

WESTERN PROVINCE

TOURS

Dive Gizo (☎ 60253; www.divegizo.com; Middenway Rd) has diving, treks, surf trips (excluding boards; November to March), sport-fishing charters, walks focusing on village life, and tours of nearby islands and skull shrines. Offices are at the Gizo Hotel and the main road, northwest of the city centre.

Solomon Watersport (☎ 60646; www.solomonconnect.com; Gizo Hotel) rents kayaks, sailboards and snorkelling gear. It also offers remote, multiday fishing charters.

SLEEPING

Unless otherwise stated, all places have share facilities, ceiling fans and communal kitchen. All air-con rooms also have a fridge.

Gizo Hotel (☎ 60199; gizohotel@solomon.com.sb; Middenway Rd; fan r per person/tr/delux tw S$350/570/ from S$650; 🗙 🗷) There's a pool and the rooms are 'hotel' standard, but you'd need a personal masseur thrown in to justify this price. Air-con rooms elsewhere cost half the price of fan rooms here.

Paradise Lodge (☎ 60024; plodge@solomon.com .sb; dm/tw S$66/176; 🗙) Large, airy, quiet and homely, with a nice kitchen and inspiring ocean views. Three meals are available for an additional S$100.

Motel New Georgia (☎ 60607; d/tr S$80/150; 🗙) One of the best. There's a restful common room and a pleasant little restaurant/bar downstairs but no kitchen.

Rekona Moa Moa Lodge (☎ 60368; fax 60021; s S$55-100, d S$66-110; 🗙) Clean throughout.

Gelvinas Motel (☎ 60276; fax 60323; Middenway Rd; tw S$250; 🗙) Helpful and central. The rooms are comfortable, but there are no cooking facilities. Each room has a balcony.

Harbourview Guesthouse (☎ 60594; r per person S$50) Neat, with a sweeping vista and quiet location.

Phoebe's Resthouse (☎ 60336; fax 60035; r per person S$60) Low-key and tidy. Offers sea views.

Trescol Motel (Middenway Rd; d S$100) A bit murky and crammed, but functional.

Eating

Gizo Hotel (dishes S$50-110; 🕑 6am-2pm & 6.30-10.30pm) Decent but overpriced. It serves English and continental breakfasts, and lobster and mud crab.

GIZO

0 — 200 m
0 — 0.1 miles

Ghizo Harbour

To Saeraghi

Football Field

Main Wharf

Malakepavi

To Paradise Lodge (1km)

Timpala Rd

SOLOMON ISLANDS

Tropix Restaurant (Middenway Rd; dishes S$35-70; 🕙 8.30am-5pm) Good food but small portions. The chips and burgers are good; there's also calamari.

JP Café (Middenway Rd; dishes S$12; 🕙 7am-4pm) A hole-in-the-wall place that's good value for rice, fish, chips and chicken.

Curry Hut (Middenway Rd; dishes S$15) Good for a quick fish or chicken curry for lunch and basics like boiled eggs later in the afternoon.

Motel New Georgia (dishes S$35) A pleasant little restaurant with Chinese-influenced mains such as sweet-and-sour fish.

PT 109 (Middenway Rd; dishes S$70) Right on the beach and pleasant with seafood mains.

You can buy bread at the **Daily Bread Bakery** (Middenway Rd), which opens just after dawn. At the market, buy *piné*, miniature coconuts which you can eat shell and all.

ENTERTAINMENT
There's a chest- and thigh-slapping Gilbertese Tamure dance at Gizo Hotel or PT 109 on weekends.

SHOPPING
Gizo Hotel and Dive Gizo sell stone and wooden carvings. A six-inch Nguzunguzu piece costs about S$200. The hawkers charge less if you bargain. Go easy, it isn't Wall St.

GETTING THERE & AWAY
Air
Gizo's airfield is on Nusatupe Island (canoe transfer S$20). From Gizo, Solomon Airlines flies daily to Honiara (S$495), stopping (except on Wednesday) at Munda (S$193) and Seghe (S$240, Tuesday, Friday, Sunday). Flights reach Choiseul (S$280, Tuesday, Thursday, Friday and Sunday), Ballalae (S$280, Friday and Sunday) and Ramata (S$195, Tuesday and Friday).

Boat
Solomons Connect (☎ 60646; Gizo Hotel) goes to Ringi (S$40) and Noro (S$35) on days excluding Tuesday and the weekend. The market means motor-canoe go between islands.

Around Gizo
At **Sepo Island**, a lovely retreat just 15 minutes from Gizo, in a beautiful traditional house, is **Oravae Cottage** (☎ /fax 60221; naomi@happyisles.com; r per person S$200). It's as pleasant a place as you'll find in Gizo. Return transfers cost S$200.

Six kilometres from Gizo, **Pailongge** has good surf breaks. **Saeraghi**, 11km from Gizo, has one of the Solomons' most beautiful beaches. **Titiana**, on the south coast, is another reef-break.

Nusatupe island is Gizo's airstrip and home to the **clam farm and research centre** (☎ 60022; admission S$40). Snorkelling over the sofa-sized giant clams is fantastic. Ask the staff how they get them to mate.

Seven kilometres southeast of Gizo, **Kennedy Island** is where John F Kennedy and crew swam ashore after their patrol boat was sunk. Kennedy towed his crewmate by clenching his life vest between his teeth. Dive Gizo (p206) arranges barbecues here.

ISLANDS AROUND GHIZO
Bring some rice and tinned goods for yourself and your hosts. You can arrange to stay with whoever takes you across by boat, so don't be put off by the remote islands. You could even keep hopping north to the **Shortland Islands**, a wilderness of dense mangroves, dolphins, and lonely Catholic missions on the PNG border.

Getting There & Around
Monday, Wednesday and Friday (market days) afternoons are a great time to catch stallholders' boats back to their islands. Rough one-way fares are: Kolombangara (S$15), Simbo (S$50), Ranongga (S$25) and Vella Lavella (S$20 to S$40). Dive Gizo arranges guided day trips to Simba (S$200 per person).

Kolombangara
Kolombangara's cone-shaped volcano rises to 1770m. It's a 14-hour return trip so take a tarpaulin (to camp) and a local guide (ask at KFPL, S$50). Start at Iriri village on the southwest of the island.

The **KFPL Forestry office** (☎ 60230; r S$100) at Ringgi *might* accept you as a guest. You could also negotiate a stay at Vanga Catholic Mission (by donation). You'll see Vanga products (herbal soaps etc) in the market; you may be able to get a ride to the mission from the market on its boat.

Simbo
This island has megapodes, two active volcanoes and a skull site at Pa Na Ghundu. Other skull sites are at Pa Na Ulu and Gurava.

SOLOMON ISLANDS

VELLA LAVELLA STRAGGLER

News travels slowly on Vella. In 1965 a particularly stoic Japanese soldier was spotted on the island. He hadn't been demobbed yet, so as far as he was concerned, he was still on duty.

The Solomons' Japanese ambassador turned up to act as the decommissioning officer, and after a leaflet drop informing the soldier that hostilities had actually ceased a fair while ago, he gave himself up and returned home to Japan with full honours.

Righuru has two petroglyph sites (rock carvings), and there's another at Vareviri Point.

Ranongga

This is where the soft carving stones you might see in Gizo are found. For visitors, butterflies and birds are the main attractions. There's a guesthouse at Buri in the north.

Vella Lavella

This huge, mountainous island is dominated by 790m Mt Tambisala. There are megapodes and a large thermal area in the Ulo River area. Parrots, butterflies, snakes and crocodiles abound.

NEW GEORGIA

The New Georgia area covers Vonavona, Kohinggo, Rendova and Tetepare islands. Launch off from Munda or Lola island.

Munda

Munda's 6km strip of contiguous villages was an important Japanese base during WWII, and many relics remain among the riot of orchids, hibiscus and frangipani.

The central village of Lambete has the guesthouse, wharf, airport, government offices, NBSI branch, police station, hospital and Telekom office. There's some very good archaeological information at the airport, including a tremendous 19th-century photograph of a head-hunting party.

There's a huge amount of **war material** (kastom S$10) in the bush behind Kia, a 25-minute walk east from Agnes Lodge.

Go West Tours (☎ 61080) has fishing tours, trips to Roviana Lagoon, Mt Bau and WWII sites. For diving, call Dive Gizo (p206) or Zipolo Habu Resort (p209) on Lola Island.

Agnes Lodge (☎ 61133; www.agneslodge.com; dm/d/cottages S$55/220/385; 🖳) is friendly but grimy and heftily overpriced. The **bar/restaurant** (mains S$20-50) is good, however.

GETTING THERE & AWAY

Solomon Airlines (☎ 61152; airstrip) connects Munda with Honiara (S$440, daily), Gizo (S$190, daily), Seghe (S$190, Wednesday and Sunday) and Ramata (S$190, Tuesday and Friday).

Wings Shipping visits Munda en route between Honiara and Gizo every Sunday, returning on Tuesday. Alternatively, take the Solomons Connect boat from Gizo to Noro, and catch a motor-canoe from Noro to Munda (20 minutes, petrol cost S$50).

Around Munda

Just north of the bridge over the Mburape River (9km from Lambete) is **Holupuru Falls**, a 10m waterfall and swimming hole.

Ancestral spirit stones stand atop mysterious **Mt Bau**. The site is about 9km inland from the coast at Ilangana on an overgrown bush trail towards Enoghae Point. Take a guide (S$50) and expect to pay *kastom*.

Noro has a NBSI branch, ANZ, police station and a waterfront *kai* bar. **Noro Lodge** (☎ 61238; tw per person S$110-165) is musty but spacious and peaceful. If you miss your connection between Gizo to Munda, this is where you'll end up staying the night.

Take the Wings Shipping or Temotu boat through **Roviana Lagoon** from Ghizo and you might well see dolphins and pilot whales. The notorious head-hunter Ingava ruled from a coral-walled fortress on **Nusa Roviana** until 1892. His people worshipped at a rock carved in the likeness of their dog-totem, Tiola. Remains of the **stone dog** and 500m of coral walls remain. Nusa Roviana is 4km east of Munda. There are skulls on nearby **Piraka** island. Go West Tours (left) or Zipolo Habu Resort (opposite) visit both for S$150.

Vonavona Lagoon

This beautiful lagoon extends northwest of Munda for 28km between Vonavona and Kohinggo islands.

Skull Island, an islet 1km from Lola, has an excellent **skull house** (kastom S$10) containing the skulls of many chiefs and warriors, and clam-shell valuables.

SOLOMON ISLANDS

The top spot for relaxing in the Solomons, **Lola Island** has a white-sand beach and great views of the volcano on Kolombangara.

Zipolo Habu Resort (☎ 61178; www.zipolohabu .com.sb; Lola Island; s/d/tr A$43/61/70; 💻) has scuba diving (two dives A$110), village tours, bush-walks, sport-fishing charters, water-skiing and surf charters (with board hire) from January to March. The rooms are big, leaf-house style with kitchen, fridge and running water. The hot showers work and the food is tasty. Three meals are available for A$50; return boat transfers from Munda are S$270.

Rendova

Rendova islanders are known as woodcarv-ers; many sell their wares at Munda. **Ren-dova Peak** (1063m) is a two-day climb – ask at Zipolo Habu Resort (left).

Tetepare

Uninhabited Tetapare is one of the Solo-mons' conservation jewels, with unlogged rainforest, leatherback turtles, dugongs and other rare wildlife. There is a research sta-tion, guides, bird-watching platforms and **huts** (kastom S$60 plus S$60 per person nightly). Book through **WWF** (☎ 60191; wwf@solomon.com.sb) in Gizo.

MAROVO LAGOON

Marovo Lagoon is the world's finest exam-ple of a double barrier-enclosed lagoon har-bouring hundreds of beautiful islets. World

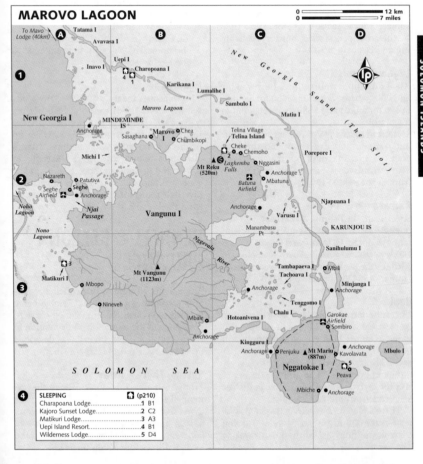

SOLOMON ISLANDS

MAROVO LAGOON

SLEEPING 🏠	(p210)
Charapoana Lodge	1 B1
Kajoro Sunset Lodge	2 C2
Matikuri Lodge	3 A3
Uepi Island Resort	4 B1
Wilderness Lodge	5 D4

Heritage listing for the lagoon was being debated at the time of research.

Radio-book these lodges through SIVB (p200) and Dive Gizo (p206). Unless stated otherwise, the lodges listed here are leaf-houses with twin rooms and share facilities.

Getting There & Around

From Honiara, Solomon Airlines flies daily to Seghe (S$370) and continues on to Munda (plus S$190) and Gizo (plus S$240).

See p205 for details on boat travel.

Seghe

Seghe, an old WWII airfield, has an **Internet post** (seghe@pipolfastaem.gov.sb), which can also book the lodge (put 'Seghe Lodge' as the subject). **Seghe Lodge** (r per person S$55), right by the airstrip, is simple, but *very* welcoming and clean.

Lagoon Islands

All lodges offer snorkelling, bushwalking and village trips. Count on S$50 for a guide, S$100 for a boat and S$80 to S$100 an hour for petrol.

Matikuri Lodge (s/d S$45/70; Matikuri) is simple but tranquil and can show you the local craft of paper making from banana leaves. Three meals cost S$65. Return transfers from Seghe cost S$130.

Ramata

Specialising in fishing, **Mavo Lodge** (r per week incl meals & transport A$1674) has an excellent reputation. Contact **Go Tours Travel** (☎ 0061-07-5591 2199; www.gotours.com.au) in Australia. Solomon Airlines flies to Ramata twice weekly from Honiara (S$420) and Gizo (S$190).

Uepi

The superlative **Uepi Island Resort** (www.uepi .com; full board from A$155; 🖳) is one of the Solomons' absolute best. Accommodation is in hotel-standard bungalows; there's a bar and a library of books and videos – everything but hot water. The dining area is airy and the terrific food includes pasta dishes. Seghe transfers are A$63 return.

There's phenomenal **diving** (per dive A$63, full gear per day A$40), fishing, a Monday carving fair and multiday, island-hopping **kayaking trips** (per day A$183).

Charapoana Lodge (d S$80, full board S$185) is neat and picturesque, and is the best of the budgets, with hearty meals and cheery rooms set in a mangrove tangle. All transfers and activities are arranged through Uepi next door, so this is a cheaper way to dive.

Vangunu

Local master carver John Wein owns **Kajoro Sunset Lodge** (d S$90, plus full board S$50). John's narratives on tribal history and excursions to *tambu* (sacred) sites are fascinating. A lot of his work is around the place and he's planning to build a war canoe to commemorate his great granddad, the illustrious chieftain Takijami ('talk once'). Takijami had a large axe, a healthy appetite and rarely had to repeat himself. John can also guide you to **Mt Reku**.

Take the weekly boat (from Ghizo or Seghe) to nearby Nggasini to avoid a S$300 canoe fee from Seghe.

Nggatokae

The **Wilderness Lodge** (☎ 0061 145 125 948, from Australia ☎ 0145 125 984; www.thewildernesslodge.org; full board A$70) is a large leaf-house. Activities include a hike to the top of Mt Mariu or up to the crater rim of Mt Vangunu. There's also sport fishing and nearby **Kavachi**, an active, and periodically spectacular, underwater volcano. Take the ship to Nggasini to save half the transfer fare. Seghe transfers from the lodge cost A$125.

RENNELL & BELLONA PROVINCE

The Polynesian outliers of Rennell and Bellona are uplifted coral atolls, Rennell being the largest on earth. Eastern Rennell – 'a stepping stone in the migration and evolution of species in the western Pacific' – as described by Unesco, is a World Heritage site.

Getting There & Away

From Honiara, Solomon Airlines flies to Rennell (S$346) via Bellona (S$326) twice a week (the Bellona–Rennell sector costs S$192) but *book at least two weeks ahead both ways*. You could become fluent in the local dialect before a ship turns up.

Getting Around

Chartering a (rare) utility costs S$600 for the 50km ride between the airport and the lake. Pre-arrange this with your accommodation.

RENNELL ISLAND

Surrounded by high cliffs, pristine **Lake Te'Nggano** is the South Pacific's largest expanse of fresh water. The lake itself is actually the old lagoon, and the tall cliffs that surround it are the old reef. Its western area has approximately 200 coral islets and swamps.

An **Internet café** (hutuna@pipolfastaem.gov.sb) is located at Hutuna. From there, you can contact the lodges. Insert the lodge name as the subject. Motor-canoe charters for lake excursions are available, while guided rainforest walks cost S$10 per person per hour.

Octopus Cave on the northern shore is lovely, as is **Tuangonga Bay** – a stunning beach from which it's possible to trudge to the cliff top for an unforgettable view of both lake and ocean.

Sleeping

The resthouses have share facilities and kitchens; book ahead. You can also stay at the community high school by the lake (contact deputy principal Rex Pugeika). Contact the **Internet post** (bellona@pipolfastaem .gov.sb) at Matamoana, which will pass your message to these people.

Moreno Guesthouse (r per person S$60) Friendly, clean and near Tinggoa airport.

Naitasi Lodge (r per person S$60) Rooms are in a lovely leaf hut on stilts over the lake.

Te'Nggano Lodge (r per person S$70) Near the clinic and close to the beach, this is simple and tidy.

Kiakoe Lakeside Lodge (r per person S$70) A little run-down. Canoe transfers are S$30 per person.

BELLONA

Little Bellona – aptly shaped like a canoe – is densely populated, with a fertile interior. The island is surrounded by forest-covered cliffs rising 30m to 70m.

Bellona's sacred rituals took place in the western part of the island, at the Nggabengga

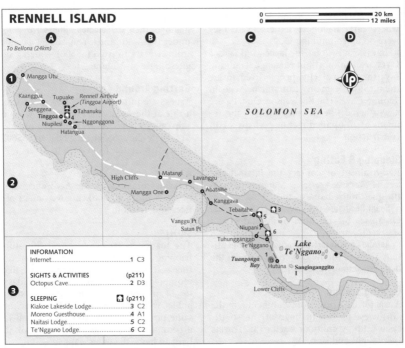

RENNELL ISLAND

To Bellona (24km)

Mangga Utu

Kaanggua   Tupuake   Rennell Airfield
                      (Tinggoa Airport)
Senggena   Tahanuku
Tinggoa
Niupilesi   Nggonggona
Hatangua

SOLOMON SEA

Matangi
High Cliffs   Lavanggu
Mangga One   Abataihe
              Kanggava
              Tebaitahe
Vanggu Pt
Satan Pt   Niupani
Tuhungganggo
Te'Nggano   Lake
Tuangonga   Te'Nggano
Bay   Hutuna   Sanginganggito
         Lower Cliffs

SOLOMON ISLANDS

A PLACE LIKE EDEN

The flora and fauna of Rennell and Bellona constitute a major transition point eastward into the Pacific from PNG. Species endemic only to these islands include the Rennell flying fox and pink-spotted fruit dove.

You'll see pied cormorants by the lake, and if you're really lucky, you might see one swimming underwater. Lake Te'Nggano has a unique sea krait and another sea snake which, strangely, comes on land when not feeding. There are – mystifyingly – no amphibians on Rennell.

A number of bird species are endemic to Rennell, including the Rennell fantail, white-collared kingfisher and the rare Rennell white spoonbill. Dawn and dusk see great flocks of frigate birds, cormorants and boobies circling over Lake Te'Nggano. This is an untouched paradise; with only the slightest knowledge of ecology or geology, you'll see things to make you gasp.

site in **Matahenua**. Around here are **caves** where early Bellonese settlers lived; they were occupied until the 1930s.

In eastern Bellona, the **Tapuna** and **Saamoa Caves** are 1km north of Matangi. Tradition says the original Hiti people lived inside them. Stone remains can still be seen in Tapuna Cave. The **Hiti Walls** at Ou'taha are a weathered line of coral rocks – the remains of an uplifted reef or perhaps a Hiti construction.

Sleeping & Eating

Radio ahead or contact the **Internet post** (bellona@pipolfastaem.gov.sb) at Matamoana with the guesthouse name as the subject.

Suani Resthouse (r per person S$75; Tangakitonga) Organises bicycle hire, bushwalking and snorkelling trips.

Aotaha Cave Resort (r per person S$120) Beautifully situated on the east coast; some of the beds are actually in a cave.

Getting Around

A tractor trail runs from Potuhenua in the northwest to Ana'otanggo at the southeastern tip. A utility or tractor (S$2) meets every flight and ship.

MALAITA PROVINCE

This large, varied province is basically a frontier for the traveller. The population of nearly 100,000 is all Melanesian except for about 2000 Polynesians who live on the lonely atolls of Ontong Java and Sikaiana.

MALAITA ISLAND

This island has a large and mysterious hinterland, a sort of reservoir for the old ways as well as a hide-out for the rare Malaitan Eagle Force (MEF) renegade (but there's very little crime to worry about these days). The highlands rise to 1303m Mt Kolovrat.

Many people worship ancestral spirits, and still more have scarified faces and tattoos. Strikingly, many also have blond hair.

You may be fed shredded *kwaa* (mangrove pods) here. It looks like porridge once it's been stewed with clams.

Getting There & Away

The *Sa Alia* plies the Honiara–Auki route (S$90, seven hours). Solomon Airlines flies daily from Honiara to Afutara (Auki airstrip is temporarily closed) for S$225. Auki has a branch of **Solomon Airlines** (☎ 40163) under the Auki Motel. You can get a canoe from Afutara to Auki (S$500) – there's no guesthouse at Afutara.

Getting Around

Trucks are infrequent. The best spot to get a ride at the Auki wharf or market when a ship calls in, but boats are more comfortable. You'll pay about S$500 for a boat and S$600 for a truck charter from Auki to Malu'u.

Auki

Auki has branches of the ANZ and NBSI banks, a hospital, market, government offices and Telekom.

SIGHTS

The market is large and busy with still-flapping fish, veggies and *kava* laid out on sheets. It often extends onto the wharf; like most Solomon Island markets, you're likely to get said 'inverse bargaining' here: the stallholder will offer you extra produce for the same price, convinced you'll waste half of it because you don't know how to cook it. Bargain hard (the other way).

Auki Island (kastom S$10), an artificial island 1km from town, was formerly the home of shark worshippers. There are skull shrines here that men can visit, but they are taboo for women.

Riba Cave (kastom S$40), a large cavern in Dukwasi village, is a 45-minute walk east (past the powerhouse) from Auki. You'll need a torch (flashlight).

Langa Langa Lagoon is famous for its artificial islands. One of these, **Laulasi** (kastom S$50), is 400 years old. This is headquarters for shell-money manufacture as well as ship building. The *Sa Alia*, which you probably arrived on, was built here. There are also skull shrines. The return boat charter costs S$250.

At the mouth of the Fiu River, 9km (15 minutes by canoe) north of Auki, **Onebulu Beach** is the best beach in the area.

Silas Diutee Malai (☎ 40423, message via the Sisters of the Church) has a vehicle and might act as your tour guide around the area.

SLEEPING & EATING

Auki Motel (☎ 40014; fax 40220; Loboi Ave; dm/d S$66/198; ❄) This is basic but spotless and welcoming. There's self-catering.

Auki Lodge (☎ 40131; Batabu Rd; s/d S$220/250; ❄) All rooms are self-contained but a bit grimy. The restaurant is up to par, but you can't self-cater.

Golden Dragon Motel (☎ 40113; Loboi Ave; dm/d S$55/165) There's a basic kitchen but rooms

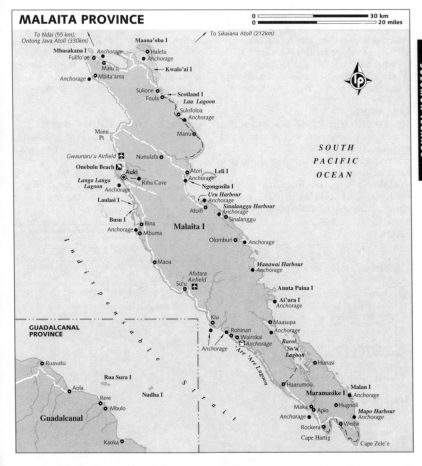

MALAITA PROVINCE

0 — 30 km
0 — 20 miles

To Ndai (55 km);
Ontong Java Atoll (330km)

To Sikaiana Atoll (212km)

Maana'oba I
Haleta
Anchorage

Mbasakana I
Fulifo'oe
Malu'u
Mbita'ama
Anchorage

Kwalo'ai I

Sulione
Foula
Scotland I
Lau Lagoon
Sulofoloa
Anchorage

Manu
Pt
Manu

Gwaunaru'u Airfield
Nunulafa

Onebulu Beach
Auki
Atori
Leli I
Anchorage
Langa Langa Lagoon
Anchorage
Riba Cave
Ngongosila I
Uru Harbour
Laulasi I
Anchorage
Sinalanggu Harbour
Anchorage
Atoifi
Sinalanggu

Busu I
Bina
Anchorage
Mbuma
Malaita I
Olomburi
Anchorage

Maoa
Manawai Harbour
Anchorage
Afutara
Airfield
Su'u

Anuta Paina I

Ai'ura I
Anchorage

Kiu

GUADALCANAL PROVINCE
Rohinari
Maasupa
Anchorage
Wairokai
Anchorage
Raroi
Su'u
Lagoon
Anchorage

Hunasi

Ruavatu

Rua Sura I

Aola
Rere
Nudha I
Mbulo
Haarumou
Malau I
Maramasike I
Anchorage
Maka
Apio
Hugnoli
Anchorage
Mapo Harbour
Anchorage
Rockera
Weihii
Guadalcanal
Cape Hartig
Cape Zele'e
Kaoka

SOUTH PACIFIC OCEAN

Indispensable Strait

Are'Are Lagoon

SOLOMON ISLANDS

are not quite as clean as at Auki Motel. You can also ask about this place at the **Auki Store** (☎ 40166), opposite.

Northern Malaita Island

It's a beautiful coastal trip, but it's hard to say whether the 'now proudly gun-free' signs on the roadside will make you feel less or more at ease! The To'obaita people of the hinterland are fire walkers, while on the coast, locals used to hunt dolphins by banging shells together underwater to drive them aground. The dolphins were eaten and also prized for their teeth. If you've mislaid your club and pliers, stock up on food before heading north.

Beautiful **Mbasakana Island** is surrounded by coral reefs and white-sand beaches.

Malu'u is the spot to get a canoe to Lau Lagoon. **Malu'u Lodge** (r per person S$50) has some reasonably pest-free, fan-cooled rooms, a kitchen and share facilities. A 4km hill-top trail behind Malu'u leads to **A'ama**, where there's a *biu* (tree house for initiated boys). Uala, 1km further on, has a **skull house**.

LAU LAGOON

This 35km-long lagoon has over 60 artificial islands. Some seaweed is harvested here and dugongs swim here. It's magical to sleep outside and see the coconut lamps of the fishing boats far across the water.

At times a cargo boat from Auki goes by; ask at the wharf. Auki Lodge (p213) can arrange a homestay on **Tauba Island** (r per person

---

ARTIFICIAL ISLANDS

One of Malaita's features is the large number of artificial islands, particularly in Langa Langa and Lau Lagoons. Some of these date from the 1550s and new ones are built each year.

Stones and dead corals from the lagoon are piled on a sand bar or reef, sand is spread around, houses are built and coconut palms are planted. The islands serve a dual purpose: protection from head-hunters and freedom from mosquitoes.

The largest islands exceed 1 sq km in size and can be very crowded; some are surrounded by a coral wall. Most, however, are tiny.

---

about S$70); return boat from Malu is S$250. Otherwise radio contact Mark Allardyce, who's on Berlin in the Tae Passage (Sulufou) area of the Lau Lagoon for a stay on **Lismore Island** (r per person incl food S$100). An option for Lismore is to call **Joseph Diau** (☎ 21838; joseph _diau@solomon.com.sb; Shell Oil Company, Point Cruz).

Central & Eastern Malaita Island

It's possible to visit some of the full-*kastom* Kwaio people of the rugged east-central part of Malaita. Their stronghold is between Uru Harbour and Olumburi. Bulaia Backpackers Lodge (p201) in Honiara is a good place to pre-arrange this. Ask for Ronnie Butala, who's a Kwaio himself.

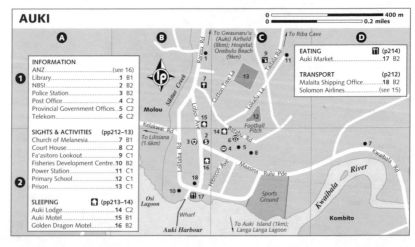

AUKI

0 ━━━━━━ 400 m
0 ━━━━━━ 0.2 miles

INFORMATION
ANZ.............................(see 16)
Library.................................**1** B1
NBSI......................................**2** B2
Police Station......................**3** B2
Post Office...........................**4** C2
Provincial Government Offices..**5** C2
Telekom................................**6** C2

SIGHTS & ACTIVITIES (pp212–13)
Church of Melanesia...............**7** B1
Court House...........................**8** C2
Fa'asitoro Lookout.................**9** C1
Fisheries Development Centre.**10** B2
Power Station.......................**11** C1
Primary School.....................**12** C1
Prison..................................**13** C1

SLEEPING (pp213–14)
Auki Lodge...........................**14** C2
Auki Motel...........................**15** B1
Golden Dragon Motel............**16** B2

EATING (p214)
Auki Market.........................**17** B2

TRANSPORT (p212)
Malaita Shipping Office..........**18** B2
Solomon Airlines..................(see 15)

To Gwaunaru'u (Auki) Airfield (8km); Hospital; Onebulu Beach (9km)

To Riba Cave

Faramani Rd

Sliakie Creek

Molou

Lobo Ave

Kelakwai Rd

To Lilisiana (1.6km)

Lailaba Rd

Cotton Tree La

Loiafu La

Ratabu Rd

Football Pitch

Hibiscus Ave

Maasina

Rulu Pde

Kwaibala Rd

Kwaibala River

Osi Lagoon

Wharf

Sports Ground

To Auki Island (1km); Langa Langa Lagoon

Auki Harbour

Kombito

Directory

CONTENTS

ACCOMMODATION

Papua New Guinea offers poor value in terms of accommodation. When compared with the cheap-as-chips places of nearby Indonesia and the rest of Southeast Asia, or even with the developed-world prices of Australia, it makes grim reading. The Solomons, thankfully, is not so bad.

Overall the quality is reasonable but in most towns your options are limited. Where there is enough accommodation to warrant it, we've divided into budget, mid-range and top-end categories (see the boxed text, p217). In both PNG and the Solomons there is a 10% VAT, and all prices in this book are inclusive of tax. Booking ahead is a good idea, especially for moderately priced hotels and guesthouses and especially at festival times, when everything is packed. Apart from festival weekends and national holidays (see p226), tourists make up such a small percentage of hotel guests that there is no clearly defined high or low season.

Don't expect to save money by bargaining; it's not common (see p230). Ask about weekend rates, which can offer huge savings. Hotels will often give free rides between the airport; especially useful where there's no public transport. When meals are included, 'all-inclusive' is shown in the accommodation listings.

Camping

Camping is not a traditional part of Melanesian culture. Travellers are welcomed into whatever dwelling is available, and refusing such hospitality in favour of pitching a tent can be quite offensive. All land has a traditional owner somewhere and you need to seek permission to camp – finding the landowner could take a while, and chances are that when you do they'll offer you room in a hut anyway. So unless you're planning on doing some seriously off-the-beaten-track trekking, don't bother bringing a tent.

Hotels & Resorts

The vast majority of hotels fall into the mid-range and top-end categories. In the mid-range category, prices and quality vary greatly, ranging from about K100 to K400 a night for a twin or double in PNG. Discounts for singles are usually small, if at all. You can expect a room with bathroom, cable TV, phone and air-con, and some will include one or more of tea- and coffee-making facilities, fridge, breakfast and free transport. In the Solomons there are fewer options, and outside Honiara it tends to be either a resort or village accommodation.

Top-end places are fewer and prices can get up as high as K700 for a double room. You'll usually have access to a swimming pool, the Internet or a business centre, and the usual range of pricey bars and restaurants. Service is usually pretty good, as you'd expect.

There are a few wonderfully indulgent resorts scattered around. Rather than being dedicated solely to sand and sun they usually boast some other attraction: diving, fishing, trekking and watching wildlife, or a combination. Some of the better resorts include the Tufi Dive Resort (p73), Tawali Resort (p78) in Milne Bay Province, Walindi Plantation Resort (p178) and Lindenhafen Fishing Lodge (p178) in West New Britain, Uepi Island Resort (p210) in the Solomon Islands, Madang Resort Hotel (p102) in Madang and Ambua Lodge (p129) in Tari, which is regularly patronised by David Attenborough. Rates are usually quoted in Australian dollars (though sometimes in US$) and are often more than A$200 per person, including meals. Wherever you head, don't forget to ask about specials and corporate and weekend rates.

Missions, Hostels & Guesthouses

When it comes to value for money (yes, it's a relative thing), the region's many mission guesthouses, community-run hostels and private guesthouses are hard to beat. Mission guesthouses are mainly for church types, but the lodgings are generally clean, homely and open to travellers. Quality varies and the cheaper ones have no air-con and share bathrooms. And you'll have to put up with a few rules – drinking and smoking are discouraged (or banned) and you can expect to hear grace before meals. But the managers

---

PRACTICALITIES

Newspapers

- PNG has two English-language newspapers: the *Post Courier,* owned by Rupert Murdoch's News Corp, and the Malaysian-owned *National.* Both are critical and quite aggressive where issues such as corruption and waste are concerned. They're available in most provincial capitals. The *Wantok* daily newspaper is written entirely in Tok Pisin; reading it will help familiarise you with the local language.

- In the Solomons, the *Solomons Star* is found in Honiara but rarely anywhere else.

Radio

- PNG has two government-funded national radio stations: Karai on the AM band and Kalang on FM. National commercial stations include NauFM ('now') broadcasting in English and YumiFM ('you-me') broadcasting 24 hours in Tok Pisin. BBC World Service can be heard in Port Moresby on 106.7FM.

- In the Solomons, national broadcaster SIBC can be heard on MW (1035kHz) and SW (5020kHz). The Australian Broadcasting Corporation (ABC) is at 630kHz MW.

- Short-wave frequencies for Radio Australia include 6080kHz or 7240kHz. For BBC see www .bbc.co.uk/worldservice/schedules/. Shortwave reception is often poor in PNG.

- For a full list of stations and frequencies in PNG and the Solomon Islands, see www.tvradio world.com/region2.

TV

- EmTV is the only local station in PNG. Most of its programming comes from Australia's Nine Network. There's no local TV in the Solomons. In both countries most places with 'cable' (actually satellite) can pick up CNN and BBC World plus a range of stations from rural Australia.

Electricity

- Electricity, when it exists and is flowing, is 240V, AC 50Hz and uses Australasian-style plugs.

Weights & Measures

- Both PNG and the Solomons use the metric system.

are usually pretty interesting people and great sources of information; best-described as Bible handlers rather than bashers.

Similar accommodation without the religion can be found in private guesthouses and a good number of places run by women's associations. Men are usually allowed to stay, but some YWCA establishments only take women.

These types of lodgings are found in many towns and cities, and in rural areas missions can be the only official accommodation around. Prices vary, but a bed (or sometimes a whole room) will usually be between about K60 and K110 per night with two meals in the communal dining room. Among the missions, Lutheran guesthouses are consistently good.

Rental Accommodation

With so many expats coming and going there is no shortage of rental accommodation in PNG and the Solomons. Much of it is attached to mid-range and, more often, top-end hotels. The formula is simple enough: provide large walls, plenty of security guards and the facilities of a hotel, and people will come. Weekly, monthly and yearly rates are very attractive when compared with hotel prices. Check www.pngbd.com/forum/f74s.html on the Papua New Guinea Business Directory.

Village Accommodation

Village accommodation comes in all manner of guises. It might be a basic leaf-house in the Solomons; a tiny thatched stilt house in the Trobriand Islands; one of the village guesthouses on the Huon Gulf coast, or around Tufi, Milne Bay, the Sepik or New Ireland. It might not be a village house at all, but a spare room in a school, space in a police station (preferably without bars), or just about any house you see. Just ask.

Village accommodation can be pretty rough but it's often the cheapest way to see the country, and in most villages you'll find a local who'll put you up. You must pay and K40 to K50 should be a fair amount to offer a family providing a roof and *kai* (food). But play it by ear, and ask locals before you head out of town what is suitable compensation; a live chicken might be the go. But they can be rather bothersome to cart around, so rice, bully beef, salt, tea or sugar should suffice.

A BED FOR THE NIGHT

Prices for a twin or double room fall into the following categories:

Papua New Guinea
Budget up to K100
Mid-range K100-400
Top end more than K400

Solomon Islands
Budget up to S$200
Mid-range S$200-400
Top end more than S$400

While men's houses *(hausboi)* are less common nowadays, it's possible couples will be asked to sleep in separate buildings to observe local custom. In some villages there is a *haus kiap* – a council house where local people might think you will want to stay. Try to resist this, as not only is staying with a family in a traditional house more enjoyable than sleeping by yourself, it's safer. As soon as you are involved with a community you become, to some extent, its responsibility.

High schools are often quite isolated and all have boarding quarters, so you could get lucky and find a spare bed. It's likely you'll have to sing for your supper or at the very least do a lot of talking! The school headmaster will be a good source of local information. Police stations around the country almost always allow you to camp on their grounds or use a spare room for no charge.

ACTIVITIES

If you're a lover of the outdoors it's hard to beat PNG. Offshore you can fish for the exotic or the aggressive, be the first to surf remote breaks and, in both PNG and the Solomons, enjoy arguably the most spectacular diving and snorkelling on earth. Onshore, PNG's trekking is both challenging and rewarding, the caving is extreme and bird-watching (see p221) attracts keen ornithologists from around the globe.

Boating

Few roads. Lots of rivers. More islands. It's a combination that makes boating in one form or another almost inevitable in PNG and the Solomons. And many of the

DIRECTORY

forms qualify as far more of an experience than simply getting from A to B. The one ingredient you need for almost every boat trip is time – don't leave home without it! Prices vary – wildly depending on the level of comfort you require (if comfort is even an option). For a guide, see p242.

RIVER JOURNEYS

PNG has some of the world's largest and most spectacular rivers. The Sepik is often compared to the Amazon and Congo Rivers, while the Sepik Basin (p131) is an artistic and cultural treasure house. Local people use rivers as highways, including the Sepik, the Ramu, the Fly and many rivers that flow into the Gulf of Papua. On these rivers there is often an assortment of craft, ranging from dugout canoes to tramp steamers.

For travellers there are a number of possibilities: you can buy your own canoe and spend weeks paddling down the Sepik; use PMV boats (unscheduled, intervillage, motorised, dugout canoes); charter a motorcanoe and guide/driver on the river; or take a tour boat, including luxury cruise ships (see p242).

SEA JOURNEYS

If you don't own a cruising yacht (and when you see PNG's islands and harbours you'll wish you did), there are four alternatives: use the regular coastal shipping, take a tour, charter a boat or crew a yacht. These options are covered on p242. With time, ingenuity and luck you can travel anywhere by boat.

With a dense scattering of beautiful islands, PNG is a great place for sea kayaking. Milne Bay Magic Tours (vickinev@spte .com.pg; p76) in Alotau has four kayaks that were originally paddled from Cairns. Apart from those, it's BYO everything, and be sure to take plenty of food and water.

Caving

Caves in the limestone regions of the Southern Highlands may well be the deepest in the world but actually getting into them requires something approaching a full-scale expedition. The Mamo Kananda in the Muller Range (near Lake Kopiago) is reputed to be one of the longest caves in the world at 54.8km. There are also caves around Bougainville (Benua Cave is thought to be the world's biggest cavern at

4.5 million cu metres), Pomio (East New Britain Province) and Manus Province.

Diving & Snorkelling

PNG and the Solomons offer some of the most-interesting, exciting and challenging underwater activities on earth. Many divers rate the region more highly than the Red Sea, the Caribbean or the Great Barrier Reef.

Those who like diving on wrecks will find literally dozens of sunken ships – either as a result of WWII or the maze of spectacular coral reefs. And the reefs are not only for divers, excellent visibility and an abundance of fish make them perfect for snorkellers, too, who can have much of the fun for a fraction of the cost.

PNG is the muck diving (diving in silty water where obscure marine life reside) capital of the world and Milne Bay is at its epicentre. Anyone who can swim can witness the extravagant coral, fantastic tropical fish and the detritus of history side by side underneath the Samarai piers (see p79); a truly unforgettable experience.

Other locations worth heading for include Alotau, Kavieng, Kimbe, Lorengau, Madang, Rabaul and Wuvulu Island. In most of these places dive operators offer courses, equipment and tours.

The best time to dive varies depending on the location. As a rough guide, Milne Bay is best from October to March, when the winds are lightest. Head to Kimbe and Kavieng from April to September, though it's possible to dive these two most of the year.

There are several good live-aboard dive boats available for charter in PNG and these allow you to enjoy a range of locations during a single trip. Prices vary, but at several hundred US dollars a day none of them is cheap (see the websites for the latest rates). The years of diving experience on board, however, is usually worth it.

Some boats and their base ports:

Barbarian II (www.niuginidiving.com) Lae, Morobe.
Chertan (www.chertan.com) Alotau, Milne Bay.
FeBrina (www.febrina.com) Walindi, New Britain.
Golden Dawn (www.mvgoldendawn.com) Port Moresby.
Marlin 1 (www.marlin1charters.com.au) Alotau, Milne Bay.
Moonlighting (www.blueseacharters.com) Madang.
Paradise Sport (www.mikeball.com) Cairns.
Star Dancer (www.usdivetravel.com/V-PNG-StarDancer .html) Kimbe, New Britain.
Telita (www.telitadive.com) Alotau, Milne Bay.

Some dive resorts and good dive shops:
Alotau Dive & Tours (alotau@png-japan.com.jp; in Japanese only) At Alotau, Milne Bay (p76).
Aquaventures PNG (www.aquaventures-png.com.pg) Jais Aben Resort near Madang (p102).
Dive Centre (www.divecentre.com.pg) Port Moresby (p51).
Dive PNG Manus (www.divepngmanus.com) Lorengau, Manus (p190).
Kabaira Beach Hideaway (www.kabaira.com) Near Rabaul, New Britain (p171).
Lissenung Island Resort (www.lissenung.com) Near Kavieng, New Ireland (p181).
Loloata Island Resort (www.loloata.com) Near Port Moresby (p63).
Niugini Diving Adventures (www.pngdiving.com) Madang (p102).
Scuba Ventures (www.scubakavieng.com) Kavieng, New Ireland (p181).
Tawali Resort (www.tawali.com) On the north coast, Milne Bay Province (p78).
Tufi Dive Resort (www.tufidive.com) East of Popondetta, Oro (p73).
Walindi Plantation Resort (www.walindi.com) Near Kimbe, New Britain (p178).

For more on diving see Lonely Planet's *Diving & Snorkeling Papua New Guinea*.

Fishing

Fishing, and particularly sport fishing in PNG's many river estuaries, is fast becoming a major tourist drawcard. There are dozens of virtually untouched rivers chock-full of fish, with species such as barramundi, mangrove jack and the current flavour of the month, the Papuan black bass, the most popular targets. There's no shortage off the coast, either. Yellowfin tuna, mackerel, sailfish and blue, black and striped marlin are just some of what's available.

You can't just get in a boat and go. Everything and every piece of PNG is owned by someone, including streams and reefs, and unless they have permission from traditional owners, anglers can easily get into trouble. It's obviously a lot easier to arrange your fishing via a tour company or lodge, but this can also be very expensive. Some lodges worth looking at:
Bendoroda Fishing Lodge (www.pngblackbass.com) In Oro (p71).
Lindenhafen Fishing Lodge (http://www.angling adventures.com.au/lindenhafen.html; john@lindenhafen .com) In West New Britain (p178).

> ### SAFETY GUIDELINES FOR DIVING
>
> Before embarking on a scuba diving, skin diving or snorkelling trip, carefully consider the following points to ensure a safe and enjoyable experience:
>
> - Possess a current diving certification card from a recognised scuba diving instructional agency (if scuba diving).
> - Obtain reliable information about physical and environmental conditions at the dive site (eg from a reputable local dive operation).
> - Be aware of local laws, regulations and etiquette about marine life and the environment.
> - Dive only at sites within your realm of experience; if available, engage the services of a competent, professionally trained dive instructor or dive master.
> - Be aware that underwater conditions vary significantly from one region, or even site, to another. Seasonal changes can significantly alter any site and dive conditions. These differences influence the way divers dress for a dive and what diving techniques they use.

Several fishing clubs operate in PNG and the Lae Game Fishing Club's website (www .laegamefishing.org.pg/) is excellent, with rules, records, upcoming competitions and contacts for the other clubs – click through 'GFAPNG corner'.

The **PNG Tourism Promotion Authority** (www .pngtourism.org.pg) has a good page of fishing contacts on its website. Most of the dive boats also do offshore fishing trips; for a list of dive boats, see p218.

Surfing

There's something pretty cool about finding a remote break and being among the first people to surf it. One surfer we heard from was so impressed he described his PNG surfing holiday as: 'Awesome, dude. I'm beyond stoked'. Quite!

It's possible to surf all year round in one part of PNG or another, but the best waves are during the November to April monsoon season along the north coast and islands. Beach, point and plenty of reef breaks are out there, and reaching them is becoming easier. The **Surf Association of Papua New Guinea** (www.surfingpapuanewguinea.org.pg) has a decent website with links to surfing tours.

The best places to head are Kavieng (p181) and the eastern coast of New Ireland, Wewak (p137) and, probably the pick of the lot, Vanimo (p141), where you will soon become acquainted with the laid-back Lido Surf Club, whose members will be happy to show their new *wantoks* (clanspeople) the best breaks. The reef break off Ahus Island, north of Manus (p190), is reputed to host a 12ft-high swell and be a life-and-death event. There is accommodation of varying standards available at or near all these places, and if you find a wave you just can't bear to leave you can always stay in a nearby village.

It's best to avoid June, July and August when the prevailing winds are southeasterly. One of the problems of surfing in PNG is that most accessible beaches are in the lee of reefs or islands and don't open onto the ocean. If you have access to a boat and can get out to the reefs, there are plenty of waves. These reef breaks aren't for the inexperienced.

Websites worth looking at include that of the ecologically sound Nusa Island Retreat (p182) at Kavieng and **World Surfaris** (www .worldsurfaris.com).

The waves tend to be fast-breaking over reefs but rarely more than about 2m. You'll only need one good all-round board and a vest to keep the sun off.

Trekking

PNG is a trekking (also known as bushwalking) paradise. The country is criss-crossed with tracks, many of which have been used for centuries by the local population, and it is rarely more than a day's walk between villages. Some of the walks are tough but, especially on the coast, it's possible to avoid the steep ascents and descents characteristic of PNG.

In the bush your expenses plummet. Your major costs will be paying for guides, where they are necessary, or buying petrol for outboards on rivers. Expect to pay a guide K25 to K50 per day. You'll also have to provide or pay for their food and possibly some equipment. The best way to find a reliable guide is to ask around the local expat population – they will usually be able to put you in touch with someone who knows someone…

A number of companies offer organised treks. The treks are not cheap but are worth considering if you have limited time. It's hard to guarantee itineraries at the best of times in PNG but professional companies will probably have a better chance of sticking to them than you will on your own.

The Kokoda Track (p64) is far and away the most popular trek in PNG. Mt Wilhelm (p119) is climbed reasonably frequently, and some people then walk from there to Madang (p120). The Highlands are full of interesting treks of varying durations. Among the more notable is Lake Kopiago to Oksapmin (p130). Apart from the Kokoda Track, the Black Cat

---

SAFETY GUIDELINES FOR TREKKING

Before embarking on a trek, consider the following points to ensure a safe and enjoyable experience:

- Pay any fees and possess any permits required by local authorities.
- Be sure you are healthy and feel comfortable walking for a sustained period.
- Obtain reliable information about physical and environmental conditions along your intended route (eg from park authorities).
- Be aware of local laws, regulations and etiquette about wildlife and the environment.
- Trek only in regions, and on tracks, within your realm of experience.
- Be aware that weather conditions and terrain vary significantly from one region, or even from one track, to another. Seasonal changes can significantly alter any track. These differences influence the way trekkers dress and the equipment they carry.
- Ask before you set out about the environmental characteristics that can affect your trek and how local, experienced trekkers deal with these considerations.

Track (p98) and the Bulldog Track (p98) will appeal to those with a military or historical bent…and a wide masochistic streak.

The Solomons are obviously less of a trekking mecca, but on Guadalcanal and from Gizo there are some decent walks.

MAPS

If you want topographic maps you're strongly advised to contact the **National Mapping Bureau** (NMB; ☎ 327 6223; natmap@datec.com .pg; Melanesian Way, Waigani) well before you leave home to make sure they have the maps you want; see also p228.

Even with a map, it's best to employ a guide. Maps can't speak local languages, and they don't know shortcuts. Guides (hopefully) do.

Windsurfing

The very characteristics that make surfing difficult in many areas make windsurfing viable: sheltered harbours, strong winds between June and August and, if you're interested, waves outside lagoons. One of the best and most accessible places to head is Hula Beach (p63), about 100km southeast of Port Moresby, though don't head there alone. If you don't have your own board, ask around the yacht clubs and resorts.

Wildlife Watching

PNG is home to thousands of species of flora and fauna (p34) and seeing some of it, especially the rich birdlife, is becoming easier as local guides learn what birders want.

Birders report that in a three-week trip you'll see about 300 species. A small number of local guides are well-worth seeking out. You can plan and execute your trip with these guys for a fraction of the cost of a tour. Samuel Kapuknai (p159) is *the* man in remote Western Province, while former hunter Daniel Wakra of Paradise Adventure Tours (p51) knows the sites around Port Moresby very well. Paul Arut is the expert at Kumul Adventure Resort Hotel (p126) in Enga Province, and Steven Wari from Warili Lodge (p129) in Tari is another reputable guide.

In the Highlands (p109) and the Sepik (p131) several lodges, such as Ambua Lodge (p129) at Tari, have programmes specifically for bird-watchers. You'll find similar tours on the Sepik River, around Madang and at Bensbach (p159) in Western Province.

JUNGLE TREKKING TIPS

Trekking through the jungle tracks of PNG can be a highlight of any visit. But to the uninitiated each step can become a new experience in discomfort. The following tips will help limit the pain.

- Practise climbing before you leave home, as it's the climbs and ascents that hurt most.

- On overnight trips bring two sets of clothing: one for hiking and one for wearing at night. Keep your night clothes in a plastic bag, as everything in your bag will be wet from rain or sweat.

- In dense vegetation wear long pants with your sturdy boots. Otherwise, shorts and a T-shirt will do.

- Carry talcum power and/or Lanoline to nip chaffing in the bud; or better, wear no underwear at all.

- Carry and drink plenty of water. Oral rehydration salts are a must, especially if you sweat a lot.

- Have your glasses treated with an anti-fog solution before you leave.

- Be aware of local laws, regulations and etiquette about wildlife and the environment – or take a guide to do that for you.

Most of the main tour operators (see p240 and p247) have bird- and wildlife-watching trips.

Also look at these specialist companies:
Eagle Eye Tours (www.eagle-eye.com) US-based group with one or two tours per year.
Sicklebill Safaris (www.cassowary-house.com.au) Regional birding expert Phil Gregory's company.

Some books and websites on birds and other wildlife (you can find the books on www.abebooks.com):
Birds of New Guinea By Bruce M Beehler et al.
http://www.camacdonald.com/birding/papapua newguineahtm.htm Excellent links to trip reports, lodges, and other PNG-specific birding sites.
Mammals of New Guinea By Tim F Flannery.
www.birdingpal.com Find a local birder for the latest information.
www.papuabirdclub.com Birding in West Papua.
www.surfbirds.com Thorough trip report about Kiunga.

PNG is not just about birds. Among the exotic animal species is the tree-kangaroo, which is probably the best-known of PNG's mammal species but can be very difficult to spot in the wild. There are also countless insect and butterfly species. The famous Queen Alexandra's Birdwing butterfly, for example, is only around at certain times of the year. And your chances of seeing exotic stick insects are very slim without a good guide. Your best bet is to visit one of the following:

Crater Mountain Wildlife Management Area (p117)
Insect Farming & Trading Agency (p99)
Ohu Butterfly Habitat (p105)
Rainforest Habitat (p91)
Wau Ecology Institute (p99)

If you fancy a tour, check out **Eco-Tourism Melanesia** (www.em.com.pg).

BUSINESS HOURS

Opening and closing times can be erratic, but you can rely on most businesses closing at midday on Saturday and all day Sunday. In this book hours will accord with the following lists unless stated otherwise.

Papua New Guinea

Banks (☽ 8.45am-3pm Mon-Thu, 8.45am-4pm Fri)
Government Offices (☽ 7.45am-12.30pm & 1.45-4.06pm Mon-Fri)
Post Offices (☽ 8am-4pm Mon-Fri & 8-11.30am Sat)
Private Businesses (☽ 8am-4.30 or 5pm Mon-Fri, 8am-noon Sat)
Restaurants (☽ lunch 11.30am-2.30pm, dinner 6 or 7-10pm or whenever the last diner leaves)
Shops (☽ 9am-5 or 6pm Mon-Fri & 9am-noon Sat)

Solomon Islands

Banks (☽ 8.30 or 9am-3pm Mon-Fri)
Government Offices (☽ 8am-4.30pm Mon-Fri)
Post Offices (☽ 9am-5pm Mon-Fri & 9am-noon Sat)
Private Businesses (☽ 9am-4.30 or 5pm Mon-Fri, 8am-noon Sat)
Restaurants (☽ lunch 11.30am-2.30pm, dinner 6 or 7-10pm or whenever the last diner leaves)
Shops (☽ 9am-5 or 6pm Mon-Fri & 9am-noon Sat)

CHILDREN

People who bring their *pikininis* (children) to PNG or the Solomons are often overwhelmed by the response of local people, who will spoil them mercilessly given half a chance. And travelling with children offers a whole different perspective; a chicken's-eye view of the world (being lower to the ground).

Practicalities

There are few really child-friendly sights, but the practicalities of travelling with children aren't too bad. Top-end and mid-range hotels should have cots, and most restaurants have high chairs. You'll be lucky, however, to find dedicated nappy-changing facilities anywhere, and forget about safety seats in taxis – working safety belts are a novelty.

As you'd expect in a country where bare breasts are everywhere, breast-feeding in public is no problem. A limited range of nappies and baby formula is available in larger towns. There are no day-care centres catering to travellers, though larger hotels can usually recommend a babysitter.

For more on family travel, read Lonely Planet's *Travel with Children.*

CLIMATE CHARTS

The wet and dry seasons in PNG are not as black and white as elsewhere in Asia. In practice, for most places the wet just means it is more likely to rain, the dry that it's less likely.

Rainfall is generally heavy but varies greatly. In dry, often dusty Port Moresby, the annual rainfall is about 1000mm and, like areas of northern Australia, the wet is short and sharp and followed by long dry months. Elsewhere, rainfall can vary from a little over 2000mm, in Rabaul or Goroka for example, to over 4500mm in Lae. In extreme rainfall areas, such as West New Britain Province or the northern areas of the Gulf and Western Provinces, the annual rainfall can average more than 8m a year.

The island provinces and the Solomons have a more steady climate, with the 'dry' season from December to late May having milder temperatures (about 21°C to 28°C during the day) and infrequent, light rainfall. The heat and humidity rise during the 'wet' monsoon season, from late May to December. However, other parts of the Solomons are affected by their own microclimates, such as Honiara (with the heaviest rainfall occurring between December and April and fairly stable temperatures year-round) Cyclones can blow between January and April. For more information, see p9.

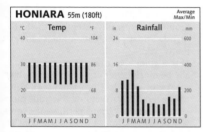

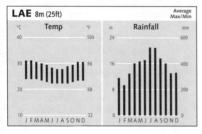

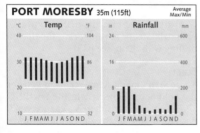

CUSTOMS

Visitors to either country are allowed to import 200 cigarettes (or 50 cigars or 250g of tobacco), a litre of spirit and a 'reasonable' amount of perfume duty free.

Of more interest is what you can and can't take out. Problems can arise when you get home, particularly to Australia, with a bagful of wooden artefacts, or anything containing animal parts, such as feathers. As a rule, polished wood won't cause much alarm, but anything with bark on it will need to be treated, or confiscated. Ditto for feathers or any other bits of dead animal.

Anything created before 1960, traditional stone tools, certain shell valuables from Milne Bay and any item incorporating human remains or bird of paradise plumes cannot be exported. If you are uncertain of what your purchases are made of, get them checked at the National Museum in Port Moresby (p51).

If any of these things are judged to be quarantine risks you will have to pay to have them irradiated, a costly process that could take up to a week. This can be done by customs in, say, Australia, or PNG Arts (p54) in Port Moresby can arrange it. Don't forget that if you're flying home via Australia your goods will be subject to Australia's strict regulations, a particular problem if something needs to be irradiated and you're due to fly out the next day!

DANGERS & ANNOYANCES

There are undoubtedly 'law and order' issues in PNG, but it is not some sort of wild west where gun-law rules and stepping outside is putting your life in danger. No, that's just the perception perpetuated by a lazy Australian media, which provides this region's information to international media. If you use your common sense, especially in larger towns, the chance of encountering the notorious *raskol* (bandits) is small.

Having said that, when things do go wrong in PNG and, to a much lesser extent, the Solomons, it can be pretty frightening. Violent crime is not unusual, but the victims are rarely tourists.

So what does this mean for the traveller? Most importantly, don't be paranoid. We have heard from travellers who have been robbed and attacked, but the vast majority of feedback (including from lone women; see p233) is overwhelmingly positive. Of course, what's dangerous to one person is everyday to another, and each traveller will decide for themself what they figure is safe and what is not. Those who have travelled to developing countries in the past probably won't be overly concerned. But for inexperienced travellers the lack of structure and the number of unemployed standing idly around the cities can be intimidating.

Bear in mind that everything is more relaxed outside Port Moresby, Lae and Mt Hagen. In villages people quickly get to know you and you rapidly lose the anonymity that makes a stranger a target. The average person's natural friendliness and hospitality is more evident and villagers will take some level of responsibility for you, which makes a world of difference.

It's important to speak with locals for an up-to-date assessment. Remember, however, that an expat's range of horror stories is refined from many friends and won't take into account that, actually, nothing will probably happen. It's worth asking expats: so how many times have you been robbed?

The mantra is common sense. Fortunately, common sense is not rocket science, but specific tips include:

- Don't flaunt your wealth – wear unremarkable clothes and keep your camera hidden. Carry a *bilum* (string bag) rather than a daypack – they attract less attention and make you look less like a tourist (notice how many expats use a *bilum*). If you're going to, say, a city market, don't take anything you're not prepared to lose.
- *Raskol* money – always keep at least K50 in your pocket as '*raskol* money' to appease any would-be thief. Hide the rest in a money belt or, better, leave it in the hotel safe. Have some emergency cash (in kina) stashed in your boot.
- Speak to the people – make an effort to communicate with everyone you meet. Not only will this add to your enjoyment, but also to your security – you will be identified as 'belonging' and have access to first-hand advice.
- Pay Friday – don't walk the streets at night, especially if you're a woman, and

be wary of drunks and young men in groups. Be especially careful on the fortnightly Friday pay nights – things can get pretty wild.

- Hire a guide – outside towns you'll usually be much better off with a guide who speaks the Tok Ples (local language). You will be less likely to get lost, the guide can take care of the various permissions you will need (to camp, to cross someone's land etc) and you'll have automatic introductions to local people.
- If you get held up – as in this situation anywhere, stay calm. Most robberies are fairly unsophisticated affairs in which *raskol* demand money with menaces and you promptly hand it over. One man we met even managed to persuade his assailants to leave his camera and then posed with them (all smiling, and why not?) while his run-in with *raskol* was recorded for posterity.

Apart from crime, the main annoyance is the zillions of mosquitoes – for tips on dealing with them, see p251.

Scams

There aren't many actual scams in PNG or the Solomons. However, in the few PNG cities that have taxis there's a chance you'll encounter one of the developing world's favourite cons: 'Sorry, no change'. If you're waving anything more than K10 or K20 around, then it might not be a scam at all. But if you only need K5 or K7 in change, for example, they will almost certainly have it.

Few of the cabbies you meet could be described as the Artful Dodger, and countering this most basic of scams is equally unscientific. With a knowing smile, say something like: 'Oh, come on. Surely you must have K5. Maybe there's some money in the ash tray'. At this point, open the ash tray and there's a good chance your K5 will be there. Always maintain your sense of humour and if there's no cash in the ash, then get the driver to take you to a shop where you can get change yourself.

DISABLED TRAVELLERS

PNG and the Solomons have little infrastructure to cater for the needs of disabled travellers. Access ramps are virtually non-

---

DANGER, WILL ROBINSON...

For the latest travel warnings and advice you can log onto the following (overly cautious) websites:

Australian Department of Foreign Affairs and Trade (www.dfat.gov.au/travel)

Canadian Department of Foreign Affairs & International Trade (www.voyage.gc.ca/dest/index.asp)

German Federal Foreign Office (www.auswaertiges-amt.de/www/de/laender infos/reise_warnung_html)

Japanese Ministry of Foreign Affairs (www.mofa.go.jp/anzen/)

Netherlands Ministry of Foreign Affairs (www.minbuza.nl/default.asp?CMS_ITEM=MBZ458731)

New Zealand Ministry of Foreign Affairs & Trade (www.mft.govt.nz/travel/)

UK Foreign and Commonwealth Office (www.fco.gov.uk/travel)

USA Department of State/Bureau of Consular Affairs (www.travel.state.gov)

existent and only the most upmarket hotels are likely to have lifts (elevators).

For general information check out the following websites:

Access-Able Travel Source (www.access-able.com)
Radar (www.radar.org.uk)
Society for Accessible Travel & Hospitality (www .sath.org)

DISCOUNT CARDS
Air Niugini offers a 25% discount to students under 26 who have a valid ISIC card and university ID. The very occasional sight in PNG offers student discounts.

EMBASSIES & CONSULATES
Papua New Guinea
A round of belt-tightening a few years back saw many of PNG's foreign missions closed. Diplomatic representation abroad includes:

PAPUA NEW GUINEAN EMBASSIES & CONSULATES
Australia Canberra (☎ 02-6273 3322; www.pngcanberra .org; 39-41 Forster Cres, Yarralumla); Brisbane (☎ 07-3221 7915; pngcg@kundubne.org; Level 11, Suite 8, 320 Adelaide St, Brisbane, Qld 4001)
Belgium (☎ 02-779 0609; kundu.brussels@skynet.be; Av de Tervuren 430, 1150 Brussels)
Fiji (☎ 330 4244; kundufj@connect.com.fj; PO Box 2447, Government Bldgs, Suva)
Indonesia Jakarta (☎ 021-725 1218; kundujkt@cbn .net.id; 6th fl, Panin Bank Centre, Jalan Jendral Sudirman 1, Jakarta); Jayapura (☎ 967-531250; kundudjj@jayapura .wasantara.net.id; Jalan Serui No 8; Jayapura)
Japan (☎ 03-3454 7801; fax 03-3454 7275; Mita Kokusai Bldg, 3rd fl, 313, 4-28 Mita 1-Chome, Minato-Ku, Tokyo)
Malaysia (☎ 03-4257 5405; fax 03-4257 6203; 11 Lingkunga Thant Ampang, Kuala Lumpur)
New Zealand (☎ 04-385 2474; pngnz@globenet.nz; 279 Willis St, Wellington)
Philippines (☎ 02-811 3465; kundumnl@pdw.net; Corinthian Plaza, Paseo de Rozas Cnr, Makati)
Solomon Islands (☎ 20561; fax 20562; PO Box 1109, Honiara)
UK (☎ 0207-930 0922; 14 Waterloo Pl, London SW1R 4AR)
USA (☎ 202-745 3680; www.pngembassy.org; Suite 805, 1779 Massachusetts Ave, NW, Washington DC 20036)

EMBASSIES & CONSULATES IN PAPUA NEW GUINEA
All embassies are in Port Moresby.
Australia High Commission (Map p50; ☎ 325 9333; www.embassy.gov.au/pg.html; Godwit St, Waigani); Hon-orary Consul (Map pp92-3; ☎ 472 2466; Trukai Industries, Mataram St, Lae)
France (Map p46; ☎ 321 5550; 12th fl, Pacific Pl, Champion Pde, Town)
Indonesia Embassy (Map p50; ☎ 325 3544; fax 325 0535; Kiroki St, Waigani); Consulate (☎ 857 1371; fax 857 1373; Vanimo)
Japan (Map p46; ☎ 321 1800; 1st fl, Cuthbertson House, Cuthbertson St, Town)
New Zealand (Map p50; ☎ 325 9444; nzhcpom@ dg.com.pg; Magani Cres, Waigani)
Solomon Islands (Map p50; ☎ 323 4333; Unit 3, GB House, Kunai St, Hohola)
UK (Map p50; ☎ 325 1677, emergency ☎ 683 1627; www.britishhighcommission.gov.uk/papuanewguinea; Kiroki St, Waigani)
USA (Map p46; ☎ 321 1455; ConsularPortMoresby@ state.gov; Douglas St, Town)

Solomon Islands
SOLOMON ISLANDS EMBASSIES & CONSULATES
Solomon Islands diplomatic representation includes:
Australia High Commission, Canberra (☎ 02-6282 7030; solomon.emb.gov.au; JAA Bldg, 19 Napier Close, Deakin, NSW, 2600); Sydney (☎ 02-9361 5866; fax 02-9361 5066; Level 5, 376 Victoria Rd, Darlinghurst, NSW, 2010); Melbourne (☎ 03-8531 1000; fax 03-8531 1955; 1 Southbank Blvd, Melbourne, Victoria 3006)
EU (☎ 02-732 7085; 106255.2155@compuserve.com; Ave Edourd 17, 1040 Brussels, Belgium)
Japan (☎ 03-5275 0515; fax 222-5959 5960; 16-15 Kirakawa-cho, Z-Chome, Shyoda-ku, Tokyo)
USA (☎ 212-599 6192; 800 Second Ave, Suite 8008, New York)

EMBASSIES & CONSULATES IN THE SOLOMON ISLANDS
All foreign embassies and consulates are in Honiara
Australia (☎ 21561; fax 23691; Mud Alley St)
European Union (☎ 22765; ecsol@solomon.com.sb; City Centre Bldg, Mendana Ave)
France & Germany (☎ 22588; fax 23887; Tradco office, City Centre Bldg, Mendana Ave)
Japan (☎ 22953; fax 21006; NPF Bldg)
New Zealand (☎ 21502; fax 20562; City Centre Bldg, Mendana Ave)
Papua New Guinea (☎ 21737; fax 20562; Anthony Saru Bldg, Ashley St)
UK (☎ 21705; bhc@solomon.com.sb; Telekom House, Mendana Ave)
USA Consular Agent (☎ 23426, mobile ☎ 94731; fax 27429; BJS Agencies Limited in Honiara)

FESTIVALS & EVENTS

Shows and festivals are held on weekends, so the dates change from year to year, but usually only by a few days. Generally, however, *singsings* (celebratory festival dance) are local affairs with no fixed yearly schedule, so you'll have to depend on word-of-mouth to find them. Check www.pngtourism.com and www.visitsolomons.com.sb for more precise dates. See also Holidays (p226) for other dates worth watching out for.

January–May
Whit Monday (eighth Monday after Easter) Celebrated all over the Solomons with marching, dancing and singing.

June
Port Moresby Show (mid-June) Traditional and modern events.

July–September
Milamala Festival (July-August) The Trobriand Islands' famous Yam Harvest festival of Trobriand cricket, yams and free-ish love.
Goroka Show (early August) This is *the* big Highlands *singsing* and well worth adjusting your travel plans around. A huge gathering of clans in traditional dress and *bila* (finery).
Mt Hagen Show (late August) Another major gathering of Highlands clans.
Hiri Moale Festival (mid-September) This festival in Port Moresby celebrates the huge Papuan trading canoes.

October–December
Kundiawa Simbu Show (11-12 October) Traditional *singsing* and agricultural show.
Milne Bay Kenu Festival (first weekend in November) A new but spectacular festival with sailing canoes from the province and beyond racing to Alotau.

FOOD

For information on the regions' eating and eateries, see (p40).

GAY & LESBIAN TRAVELLERS

Homosexuality is illegal in both PNG and the Solomons, but the law is rarely, if ever, enforced. Homosexual men and women are around, but there is nothing remotely like a 'gay scene'. Tapping into the local gay community is very difficult – even the Web throws up very few leads.

Homosexuality is far from a topical issue in Melanesian society. This is hardly surprising; churches have been reinforcing the idea that homosexuality is morally reprehensible for years. You'll see many local people hold hands as they walk down the street – women with women and men with men – but this is simply an expression of friendliness and affection.

There is no danger of physical violence based on sexual preference, but it's still wise not to be openly affectionate in public (straight couples aren't either).

HOLIDAYS

In addition to the national holidays listed here, each province has its own provincial government day (usually a Friday or Monday) and there is usually a *singsing* to mark the occasion. Like anywhere, accommodation is harder to find during holiday times, particularly Christmas and Easter. The following national holidays apply to both PNG and the Solomons unless otherwise stated.
New Year's Day 1 January
Easter March/April, variable dates. Includes Good Friday and Easter Monday.
National Remembrance Day April 25 (PNG only)
Queen's Birthday second Friday of June
Solomon Islands Independence Day 7 July (SI only)
PNG Independence Day 16 September (PNG only)
Christmas Day 25 December
Boxing Day 26 December

INSURANCE

Especially in PNG and the Solomons, where help is often an expensive helicopter ride away, a travel insurance policy to cover theft, loss and medical problems is essential. There is a wide variety of policies available and travel agents often know which is most suitable. Read the small print to check it covers potentially 'dangerous activities', such as diving and trekking.

You might prefer a policy that pays doctors or hospitals directly rather than you having to pay on the spot and claim later. If you have to claim later make sure you keep all documentation. Some policies ask you to call back (reverse charges) to a centre in your home country where an immediate assessment of your problem is made.

Check that the policy covers ambulances or an emergency flight (medivac) home.

INTERNET ACCESS

These are two of the least Internet-aware countries around, though the Solomons is at the forefront of an innovative shortwave

Internet. Outside the major cities and a few expensive hotels, expect to be locked out of cyberspace for extended periods unless you're carrying your own equipment. Be sure to set up your email account's auto-response.

For websites on PNG and the Solomons, see p11.

Papua New Guinea

For those without a computer of their own, one or two Internet cafés exist in each of PNG's main centres charging K25 to K40 an hour. All top-end hotels and a growing number of mid-range places have a computer you can use to get online.

If you're carrying a laptop, a few top-end places have dedicated Internet connections in their rooms. Connection is by RJ-45 socket (it's best to carry your own) and is usually made using **Daltron's** (www.daltron .com.pg) Webtaim prepaid Internet package, which you must buy from the hotel for about K70 and install. If you're planning on tripping around a bit it's a better idea to buy the Daltron package yourself (K66). In theory, Webtaim allows you to connect to the Net from any phone line in the country by dialling a single, low-cost number. In practice, we found it seldom worked outside Port Moresby and, worse, each new attempt to contact the server cost us a K1 phone fee from the hotel. One way to avoid this is to find a Telikad phone with an RJ-45 connection (many hotels have one), connect your computer and use your Webtaim account together with a Telikad (see p231). To do this on Windows, open the Connect Webtaim Internet dial-up connection box, which will have been created when you loaded the software, and in the Dial box change the phone number to '123, 1, XXXXXXXXXXXX (your 12-digit Telikad number), 1880200#'. The commas create a pause while the Telikad voice prompt talks you through the connection process.

Solomon Islands

There are a couple of good Internet cafés in Honiara charging about S$14 per hour. Outside the capital you'd expect it to be something of a black hole where cyberspace is concerned. Instead, the Solomons is at the forefront of a new Internet technology – digitally interpreting shortwave radio. The **People First aid project** (www.peoplefirst.net.sb) pro-

vides a text-only Internet link to some of the remotest outposts in the islands. Which means you can send a text-only email from all the way out on Rennel for about S$10.

LEGAL MATTERS

Visitors to PNG have little reason to fear trouble with police. The occasional after-dark road block shouldn't be a concern and aside from that there's no reason why you'll be stopped. If by chance you are, you're unlikely to be asked for a bribe and shouldn't offer one, at least not until you've refused several times and there seems to be no other option. Always be deferential.

Unfortunately, however, while most police are courteous enough (even friendly!) don't expect them to do much about any crime perpetrated against you. For years police have been outnumbered, outgunned and outmotivated by gangs of *raskol,* and the number of crimes solved is piteously low. Police frustration is common, and don't be surprised to hear of swift justice being applied when a *raskol* is caught (see The Millenium Job, p48). If you need the police to go anywhere you might need to pay for their fuel. The whole country is hoping things will change with the arrival of more than 200 Australian officers as part of the Enhanced Cooperation Programme.

Travellers could attract unwanted attention by buying marijuana, which grows wild in the Highlands. The government takes its antidrug stance very seriously, and has even managed to convince much of the public that *raskol* do their thing because they have been whipped into a violent frenzy by smoking too much weed! We're not quite sure what kind of reefer that is, but whatever…penalties are stiff.

COMING OF AGE

For the record:

- The legal voting age in PNG and the Solomons is 18.

- You can drive legally at age 18 (to rent a car you must be 25).

- Heterosexual sex is legal at age 16 in PNG and 15 in the Solomons.

- To legally buy alcohol you must be 18.

DIRECTORY

MAPS

There are two maps of PNG that should be available to purchase online, if not necessarily at your local bookstore. Hema Maps' *Papua New Guinea* (1:2,600,000) 2nd Edition (1992) is the most common, and is readily available in PNG as well. More recent is ITMB's *Papua New Guinea* (1:2,000,000). This is probably the pick of the two.

If you're planning on trekking, or just want more detailed maps, you're advised to contact the **National Mapping Bureau** (NMB; ☎ 327 6223; natmap@datec.com.pg; Melanesian Way, Waigani), order the maps you want and then collect them from the office in Port Moresby when you arrive. The topographic maps range in scale from 1:2000 (K10 per sheet) through 1:50,000, 1:100,000 and 1:250,000 (all K15 per sheet). They have the whole country covered though they're often out of stock, out of paper or out of date. Some of the provincial Lands and Survey departments also sell these maps but the helpful office in Port Moresby is your best bet. It should be borne in mind when reading old maps that villages in PNG tend to move around over the years. If you are planning to walk the Kokoda Track, the NMB's *Longitudinal Cross Section of the Kokoda Trail* (1995) is worth the K10.

Hema Maps publishes *Solomon Islands* (1:1,200,000), and ordinance survey maps of the Solomons are available at Ministry of Lands & Housing offices; the **Honiara branch** (Map pp202-3; ☎ 21511) has most of them.

Finally, the **Ex Kiap website** (www.exkiap.net/other/png_maps/index_png_maps.htm) has maps covering the whole country.

MONEY

Perhaps appropriately for such a diverse country, travelling in PNG requires a diverse approach to money. Cash, credit cards and travellers cheques will all be useful, and it pays not to put all your eggs in one basket. Credit cards are increasingly accepted, but you don't need to go too far off the track before you're fully reliant on cash.

Both the PNG kina and the Solomon Islands dollar have seen a steady decline in value against major currencies. That might make your trip a bit cheaper than it seems in this guide, but expect inflation to take prices of imported goods up at the same rate as the local currency falls.

Traditional currencies, such as shell money and leaf money, are still occasionally used. You'll see women on the Trobriand Islands carrying *doba*, or leaf money, which is dried banana leaves with patterns incised on them.

See the Quick Reference (on the inside front cover) for exchange rates.

ATMs & Credit Cards
PAPUA NEW GUINEA

Credit cards are accepted in most top-end and many mid-range hotels, and in a few restaurants and stores in Port Moresby and other larger cities. Visa and MasterCard are the favourites, with Amex, JCB and Diners Club not so widely accepted. Credit-card payments often incur an additional charge.

ATMs are fairly common in cities, but only those at **ANZ** (www.anz.com/png/importantinfo/atmlocations.asp) and **Westpac** (www.westpac.com .au) branches allow you to withdraw cash against your Visa or MasterCard. ANZ has many more ATMs than Westpac, and in our experience they are far more likely to issue cash. Both ANZ and Westpac machines are linked to the Cirrus, Maestro and Plus networks, though it is dangerous to be relying solely on getting money this way. If the machines are broken, head inside and you should be able to get a cash advance against your credit card over the counter.

Bank South Pacific has plenty of ATMs, but for now they're not linked to international networks.

SOLOMON ISLANDS

Major credit cards are accepted in larger hotels and most restaurants and stores that see tourists. There are ATMs at the ANZ and Westpac banks in Honiara. That's it.

Cash
PAPUA NEW GUINEA

PNG's currency is the kina (*kee*-nah), which is divided into 100 toea (*toy*-ah). Both are the names of traditional shell money and this connection to traditional forms of wealth is emphasised on the notes, too. The K20 note features an illustration of that most valuable of village animals, the pig. Most banknotes are plastic and look very similar to Australian banknotes – the colours are even the same.

In remote areas having enough small bills is important. People are cash-poor and won't have change for K50. You'll need cash for small purchases and PMV rides and it doesn't hurt to give a child a kina for showing you that WWII relic.

SOLOMON ISLANDS
The local currency is the Solomon Islands' dollar (S$). As in PNG, be sure to have plenty of small notes for when you leave town.

International Transfers
The easiest way to transfer money to PNG is by Western Union. For a list of BSP branches that are Western Union agents, see www.bsp.com.pg/personal_banking/per_western_union.htm.

Neither Western Union nor an alternative money-transfer system operates in the Solomons.

Taxes
There is a 10% value added tax (VAT, but sometimes called GST) on top of most transactions in both PNG and the Solomons. It's worth asking your hotel whether this is included in the quoted rate, as quite often it is not.

Tipping
Tipping is not customary anywhere in PNG or the Solomons.The listed price is what you'll be expected to pay.

Travellers Cheques
You can change travellers cheques in every major town in PNG, although chances are it will take ages. It will cost a bit too, with all the banks (in typical Australian-bank fashion) applying hefty charges for changing your cheques. For the Solomons, use Visa, Amex and Thomas Cook.

PHOTOGRAPHY
Papua New Guinea and the Solomon Islands are pretty close to a photographer's nirvana. The stunning natural colours and locations are just the start, and shooting a cultural show (see p226) could end up a career highlight. You could easily burn dozens of rolls of film, or gigabytes worth of memory. Negative film (about K13 or K15 for a roll of 36) is widely available but you'll need to bring your own slide film. If you're shooting digital it's worth bringing some sort of portable storage device, as

you'll have a hard time finding an Internet café (or like) where you can download images and burn to a CD. Also bring batteries, cables and, most importantly, a cleaning kit and a large, sturdy plastic bag big enough to hold all your gear when it starts pissing down with rain. Silica gel sachets are handy for soaking up excess moisture.

Divers should consider giving themselves a series of uppercuts if they arrive without an underwater camera, preferably with a light. Enough said.

Bring some faster film (ISO 400 or greater) if you'll be anywhere in the jungle, where it can be pretty dim. Photographing dark-skinned people also requires some different rules: a flash is almost an imperative, otherwise the contrast with a light-coloured background can cause underexposure.

You'll find people are generally happy to be photographed, even going out of their way to pose for you, particularly at *singsing*. And it's a lot of fun showing people their just-taken images if you're shooting digital.

Some people, usually men dressed in traditional style, do request payment if they are photographed – K10 is a popular price. People are aware that Western photographers can make money out of their exotic photos and see no reason why they shouldn't get some of the action. If you've gone ahead and taken a photo without getting permission and establishing a price, you may well find yourself facing an angry, heavily armed Highlander demanding K20 in payment. It would take some nerve to argue.

Never take a photograph of, or even point a camera in or at, a *haus tambaran* (or any other spirit house) without asking permission from a male elder. For more tips see Lonely Planet's *Travel Photography*.

POST
Papua New Guinea
PNG has a fairly efficient postal service and you can usually rely on your mail or parcels getting home, even if it takes quite a while. There is poste restante in most post offices, though the larger ones will be more reliable. Letters or cards up to 50g cost K2.70 to Australia and the Pacific, K4.60 everywhere else; a 5kg package costs surface mail/airmail K135/158 to Australia, ranging up to K200/351; and you might not have lost your head buying that 20kg

skull rack, but it will cost you an arm and a leg, at least, to post it home – K290/313 to Australia, K540/585 to the UK and USA, and K540/841 to most of the rest of the world. Allow at least three months for surface mail to the USA or Europe.

Note that there is no postal delivery in PNG, so everyone and every business has a PO Box. Hence when you look in the phone book all addresses are listed as PO Box something, rather than a street address. The same applies in the Solomons.

Solomon Islands

Post is cheaper than PNG and fairly reliable – you can rely on it getting there, and rely on it taking at least two weeks, and that's just to Australia.

SHOPPING

You're not coming to PNG or the Solomons to buy a new camera or kit yourself out in a new wardrobe (except, perhaps, a *koteka*; see the boxed text, below), but there is no shortage of interesting arts and crafts to take home. The best advice to shoppers is to buy one good piece you really like – it might even cost several hundred kina – rather than armfuls of small inferior carvings and artefacts. *Bilums* and Highland hats are easy to get home in your luggage, but lugging more than one or two unwieldy artefacts around the country is going to be a hassle.

The style of carving and artefacts varies so widely that general rules are hard to establish but look for the carver's deft touches and see how well the recesses are finished. Look at the details and feel the weight in the timber – sometimes inferior timbers are blackened and passed off as high-quality ebony.

There are good stores in Port Moresby (p54), Lae (p94) and Wewak (p138), but buying direct from the artist is usually cheaper and not only gives you a fuzzy feeling, but also a good story.

Bargaining

There's no tradition of bargaining in Melanesian culture so don't expect to be able to cut your costs much by haggling. Bargaining is, however, starting to creep into some aspects of society, souvenir shopping being one. It's a rather grey area and impossible to give definitive advice, but if you tread sensitively you should be OK. For example, artists who are used to dealing with Westerners (eg at the Ela Beach Craft Market, see p54) will have experienced bargaining to some degree so will probably not be too offended if you make a lower bid for their work. But forget about the old 'offer one third and work up to a half' maxim, it's more like they ask K300, you offer K200 and you get the piece for K250. Maybe. Some artists are used to being asked for a 'second price', and might even come at a 'third price' if asked. What you should never do is demean the quality of the work in an effort to reduce the price – this is highly offensive.

Elsewhere in society, taxi drivers in PNG are used to haggling to a limited extent (though not in Honiara in the Solomons, where they're very honest indeed), and you could try your luck in hotels, but not in village accommodation.

BIZARRE SOUVENIRS

You can see it now…'Gee Bill, that's a mighty fine skull rack you've got there. Which village did that come from?' The skull rack, once common in homes around the Gulf country as a convenient, practical way to present the skulls of ancestors and vanquished enemies alike, would definitely be a conversation starter back home.

But they're heavy, and hard to find, so we reckon you shouldn't leave PNG without a *koteka*. *Koteka* are traditional penis gourds still worn by many Highland men. They're light, readily available in most traditional art stores and come in all manner of sizes, so if you're buying it for personal use you should be able to find one to fit.

And *koteka* can be more than just ornamental. We heard of a Christmas party for one of Port Moresby's larger firms at which, after a few drinks, five *koteka* were presented to the most senior partners. They were a big hit! However, it's worth noting that presenting the smallest *koteka* to anyone known to have (or suspected of having) a small-dick complex might not be a good career move.

SOLO TRAVELLERS

It makes sense that anyone travelling alone in the Solomons and, more particularly, PNG is at a greater risk of running into trouble. Expats will tell you that in cities such as Port Moresby, Lae and Mt Hagen the golden rule is 'safety in numbers'.

These destinations, however, remain exotic enough that they attract quite a few soloists trying to get as far off the beaten track as possible. For men, this sort of travel can be especially rewarding and rambling from village to village is a great way to get around. Assuming you've got your head screwed on and take the usual common sense precautions, outside the aforementioned cities you should be fine.

Women don't have it quite so good. For more information, see p233.

TELEPHONE & FAX
Papua New Guinea

Telecommunications in PNG can be very unreliable and in the more remote parts of the country a working telephone line is pretty rare. The complex networks of relay stations that link many towns and villages are also precarious. In larger centres there's no guarantee of getting a line. Phones at Lae's Nadzab Airport had been down for months at the time of research.

FAX

Kwik piksa leta (fax) is still pretty big in PNG, where email is still in its infancy. You can send faxes from post offices for a few kina and they can be a useful way of making accommodation bookings. Fax numbers are listed in telephone directories.

MOBILE PHONES

Mobile phones have finally arrived in PNG, but the **B-Mobile** (www.pacificmobile.com.pg) digital GSM network was so limited when we visited that it was not really worth connecting to it. At the moment the network covers Port Moresby, Lae, Goroka, Mt Hagen and Madang, but you can expect it to expand – see the website for coverage details. All mobile numbers begin with ☎ 68.

B-Mobile (spot the 'Feel The Buzz' signs) does cater for tourists with its Visitor Pack. For K50 you get a SIM card valid for three months (longer with extensions), and K28 worth of credit. Calls are charged at K0.40 per 30 seconds for domestic calls between 7am and 8pm, and K0.15 per 30 seconds at other times. International calls are costly.

The visitor pack operates on a pre-paid card system, and cards are widely available in major centres. It comes with SMS messages, voicemail and caller ID as standard. You need to show your passport and onward ticket at purchase.

PHONE CODES

There are so few phones in PNG and the Solomons that there are no local telephone codes for long-distance domestic calls. PNG's international code is ☎ 675. Some other codes:

international directory assistance	☎ 0178
PNG directory assistance	☎ 013
reverse charge calls from other phones	☎ 016
reverse charge calls from payphones	☎ 0176
ships at sea	☎ 300 4646
to call a HF radio phone	☎ 019

For a full list of phone codes, see the front of the phone book.

PHONECARDS & TELIKAD

Most PNG cities have phone-card public phones, but people rarely buy a phone card that needs to be inserted into a phone. Almost everyone has a Telikad. The Telikad has a 12-digit code on the back and comes in denominations of K5, K10, K20 and K50, but the K5 card is hard to find.

Telikads are widely available and easy to use. Just dial ☎ 123 from *any* fixed-line phone, including any type of public phone, then 1 for English, your 12-digit code and then your number. Telikads are great for using in hotels, but only for long-distance calls as most hotels will still charge you K1 for the call, even though you're paying for it.

There are a few coin-operated pay phones around. They take K0.20 coins and above. Unused coins are refunded.

SATELLITE PHONES

In PNG and the Solomons there are two functioning networks: **Iridium** (www.iridium.com), which is worldwide and uses a Motorola phone; and **Aces** (Asia Cellular Satellite; www.acesinternational.com) which only covers parts of Asia. The compatible phone is made by Ericsson. Aces is a fair bit cheaper, but less reliable.

DIRECTORY

Solomon Islands

Public phones are reasonably common in larger centres and phonecards widely available; Solomon Telekom is the most reliable supplier. Cards come in denominations of S$10 and are the same as the PNG 'punch-in-the-number' variety; the cheapest way of making an international call is from a public phone using a phonecard. Faxes can be sent internationally via Telekom offices. Your hotel might do it cheaper. Telekom will also receive faxes, but they must be collected by the customer.

The Solomons IDD code is ☎ 677. There are no area codes and no mobile phone network. For information on satellite phones, see p231.

TIME

The time throughout PNG is 10 hours ahead of UTC (GMT). When it's noon in PNG it will be noon in Sydney, 9pm in Jakarta, 2pm in London, 9pm the previous day in New York and 6pm the previous day in Los Angeles. There is no daylight saving (summer time) in PNG. See World Time Zones, p255. Time in the Solomon Islands is 11 hours ahead of UTC.

You will inevitably encounter 'Melanesian time' at some point, the habit throughout Melanesia (and all the South Pacific) of putting a low premium on punctuality.

TOILETS

Most toilets are 'thrones', though often what you're sitting on is far from gold-plated. In remote villages you might find a long-drop consisting of a pit with a hollow palm trunk on top, and a toilet seat on top of that. And that's relatively extravagant. If you're in a village and can't spy the loo, be sure to ask someone. Even if there's no throne, there will be a place where people usually defecate; if you accidentally take a crap in the village garden the locals might get shitty.

TOURIST INFORMATION

In both PNG and the Solomons there is not much in the way of organised, Western-style tourist offices that hand out maps and brochures. Instead, the best information is almost always gathered by chatting with the locals; be it in the street, a PMV, a hotel or guesthouse, a bar – anywhere. Most are genuinely happy to point you in the right direction; sometimes they'll drop everything and take you there!

There are, of course, a few tourism offices around. Among the more useful:

Madang Visitors & Cultural Bureau (☎ 852 3302)
Milne Bay Tourism (☎ 641 1503; www.milnebay tourism.gov.pg)
Morobe Tourism Bureau (☎ 472 7823; www .tourismmorobe.org.pg)
PNG Tourism Promotion Authority (☎ 320 0211; www.pngtourism.org.pg) Focuses on marketing campaigns, but the website has useful info and links. A few international offices can be accessed from the website.
Solomon Islands Visitors Bureau (☎ 22442; www .visitsolomons.com.sb)

VISAS

Visitors must have a valid passport or internationally recognised travel document valid for at least six months beyond the date of entry into PNG or the Solomon Islands.

In PNG there are heavy penalties for overstaying any visa.

Papua New Guinea
TOURIST VISAS

Far and away the easiest and cheapest way to get a 60-day tourist visa is to apply on arrival at the airport. The process is simple enough: once inside the terminal change money to get your K100, fill out a form, take your cash and one passport photo to the immigration desk and Bob's your aunty's live-in lover. Note that on weekends or at random other times the exchange bureau inside immigration can be closed, and you'll be sent into the arrivals hall (without your passport or luggage) to change at the Bank South Pacific.

If you happen to be near one of the few PNG diplomatic missions (p225) you could apply in person and the visa costs only K75. But for most people, the costs of postage and the hassle are not worth the K25 saving. Wherever you apply, be sure to ask for the full 60 days, as extending is a nightmare. You might need to show onward ticketing and adequate funds to support yourself.

People coming in by yacht pay K200 for a visa (which must be obtained in advance) and a K300 customs clearance fee when they leave.

WORKING VISAS

Applying for a business visa requires all manner of letters from home (including letters of invitations from businesses) and PNG, as well as details of your business. Approval can take months, so start early. A multiple-entry visa allows up to 60 days stay each time and costs K500. If you are seeking an employment visa, you must provide certain medical results, details for a police clearance, a copy of your employment contract and a copy of a Work Permit issued by the PNG Dept of Labour & Employment.

A short-term visa costs K550. Church and aid volunteers can enter on a special K50 visa but the issuing authorities are required to wait for special immigration department approval. Researchers, filmmakers and journalists must submit their visa applications with a special application form from the **National Research Institute** (☎ 326 0300; fax 325 0531; PO Box 5854, Boroko). They cost K50 (visas for journalists cost K500).

VISA EXTENSIONS

Tourist visas can be extended for one month for a fee of K200. To do it yourself, go to the Department of Foreign Affairs' **immigration section** (☎ 323 2010; ground fl, Moale Haus, Wards Strip, Waigani; 🕑 9am-noon Mon-Fri), where you'll battle hordes of agents who are on first-name terms with the staff. Extending a visa takes one to two weeks, though occasional travellers do it faster.

Stories abound of travellers trying to extend visas by mail from other parts of the country and having, after weeks of waiting, to trek back to Port Moresby to retrieve their passports. Don't bother.

If money is not too tight using an agent will save you a lot of grief. **Kaia Reva** (☎ 308 7000; kreva@deloitte.com.pg) of Deloitte Touche Tohmatsu in Port Moresby has a reputation for getting the job done no matter what sort of visa you're after. Other, perhaps cheaper, agents can be found in the *Yellow Pages* under 'Visa Services'.

VISAS FOR INDONESIA

Visas for Indonesia can be bought in Port Moresby or Vanimo (see p225). For the lowdown on crossing the Vanimo–Jayapura border see p239.

Solomon Islands

In theory, entry visas are not required as a three-month visitors permit is granted upon arrival to most nationalities, and especially to Commonwealth, US and most EU passport-holders. However, the guidelines are ambiguous for nationals from former or continuing communist countries, the Indian subcontinent, Nauru and Kiribati. Nationals from these countries should seek advice from a Solomon Islands embassy (p225) before travelling. If you do need a visa and there's no Solomon Islands embassy around (pretty good chance of that), head for a British embassy.

Visitors permits can be extended for a further three months at the **Immigration Office** (☎ 22585; Mendana Avenue; Map pp202-3) in Honiara.

WOMEN TRAVELLERS

Plenty of women travel to PNG and the Solomons and while doing so with a man, or a friend, is usually safer than doing so alone, quite a few solo women have written to us with glowing reports of their trip. Lone women can find PNG trying, but if you've travelled to developing countries by yourself in the past (Africa, the Middle East, Indonesia…) you probably won't find PNG or the Solomons particularly difficult. Of course, lone women need to be more aware of where they go, what they wear and how they act. Pay close attention to the common-sense precautions outlined in Dangers & Annoyances (p223).

We haven't heard of any women travellers being sexually assaulted, but women are raped with disturbing regularity in PNG so you should avoid any situation where you're alone with a man you don't know well. At night, don't go *anywhere* alone, and avoid secluded spots at any time.

Men sometimes assume you're fair game if travelling alone and it's not uncommon to experience some low-level harassment, such as whistling, hissing etc. Ignore it.

It can sometimes be difficult for women to have a normal conversation with a man without being misinterpreted as a flirt. Similarly, a Western man who attempts to initiate a conversation with a local woman can cause embarrassment and confusion.

You need to think about what you wear, but not too hard. Three-quarter length pants and T-shirts are common and you can get away with shorts if they're not too far above the knee – showing thighs is considered sexually provocative.

VOLUNTEERING IN PNG

By Jon Cook & Fiona Young

The decision to come to PNG and the clutter and chaos of leaving home (should we bring a wok? can we bring seeds into the country?) seem a long time ago and a long way away. We were offered positions in PNG but didn't know much about the place – few of our friends and family had been there. Our thoughts are of living with a different community and learning some different ideas about life. From farewell meals in restaurants, we find ourselves in a place of chickens, pigs and children running free; of betel nut, coconut, banana and pawpaw trees; of dust and mud and heavy rain.

Faced with the prospect of everyday life in this new place, we have no idea of where to start. Each attempt to master a basic skill such as to 'scrape' dry coconuts, or cut grass with a 'grass knife' provokes bemusement, concern and occasionally sheer hilarity. We are met with expectations: we are fed meat, when everybody else is eating bananas, and given chairs when everybody else sits on the floor.

We begin to make attempts to become a part of communities here, and people respond immediately with warmth. Any effort to learn the language brings delighted encouragement – as well as relentless correction. Joining the work of preparing a feast earns big kudos and suddenly the floodgates open; we are brought food, adopted into families, and welcomed into homes.

This access to people's lives informs our work. We are seen as experts, but know little of what people here need to know to live – nothing of the uses of animals and plants here, how to make shelter or feed a family without needing money. So we stumble along, and try to offer what we can.

Diseases are different, resources are different, and people's priorities are different. A community meeting to discuss health may need to resolve how to manage pit toilets in a village that regularly floods. Or may result in a decision to build a fence to keep out sorcerers.

This is how things are for us now. We don't know how the next week will go, let alone the next year. We feel sure, though, that the community will keep us interested. And we know we are alive.

Jon Cook and Fiona Young were placed together by Australian Volunteers International to work with a Catholic diocese in rural Central Province. Jon is the only doctor at a rural health centre. Fiona is a community development worker, supporting women's groups and community participation and action on health issues.

Skimpy tops, however, should be avoided. You won't see local women in Western-style swimwear, and unless you're at a resort it's best to use a *laplap* (sarong) as a wrap. Take your cue from local women.

Public displays of affection are almost unknown, and a Western couple making physical contact in public – even holding hands – is regarded as an oddity and, especially in traditional rural societies, may be regarded with contempt. This can put the woman in danger. In villages you'll notice a distinct difference between the way local people see themselves and how they expect Westerners to see them. Women will cover their breasts as soon as you arrive, a hangup which is a hangover from the time of the conservative *mastas* (colonial white adult males) and their haughty attitudes towards locals.

Many towns have women's groups (which sometimes have guesthouses) and these are good places to meet local women and learn about their lives. Usually it's OK for men to go as well, but check first as this is unusual.

WORK

There are about 20,000 expats living in PNG and they work in just about every facet of the economy. Mining, logging, financial services, aviation and tourism are full of expats, often earning quite good money. At the other end of the spectrum, aid agencies and projects in PNG and the Solomons attract quite a few volunteer workers (see p235).

Potential employees will need to get a work permit/visa, which can be a convoluted process (see p232).

Volunteer Work

There are several organisations operating volunteer projects in PNG, and a couple in the Solomons. These are often in remote communities, so this sort of work is not for those who will faint at the sight of a spider.

Their activities range from teaching and medical assistance to advisory roles with local area councils. Most are either associated with the churches or with international volunteer organisations. Most of the organisations listed here have projects in both PNG and the Solomons.

Australian Business Volunteers (www.abv.org.au)
Australian Volunteers International (AVA; www.australianvolunteers.com)

Canadian University Service Overseas (CUSO; www.cuso.org)
German Development Service (DED; ☎ 325 5380; www.ded.de)
Japan International Co-operation Agency (JICA; ☎ 325 1699; www.jica.go.jp/png/)
Volunteer Service Abroad (NZ VSA; ☎ 325 4136; www.vsa.org.nz)
Voluntary Service Overseas (British VSO; ☎ 852 1924; www.vso.org.uk/about/cprofiles/papua_new_guinea.asp)

Some other useful websites that have details for those interested in volunteering:
Global Volunteers (www.globalvolunteers.org)
Volunteer Abroad (www.volunteerabroad.com)

Transport

CONTENTS

GETTING THERE & AWAY

ENTERING THE REGION

Most people can enter both Papua New Guinea and the Solomons with nothing more than a passport with six months' validity, an onward ticket and enough money to support themselves. Make sure you have at least some cash on you to pay for your visa. For details, see p232.

AIR

The vast majority of visitors to PNG and the Solomon Islands will arrive by air.

THINGS CHANGE...

The information in this chapter is particularly vulnerable to change. Check directly with the airline or a travel agent to make sure you understand how a fare (and ticket you may buy) works and be aware of the security requirements for international travel. Shop carefully. The details given in this chapter should be regarded as pointers and are no substitute for your own careful, up-to-date research.

Airports & Airlines

The good part of flying into either PNG or the Solomons is that you don't have to shop around looking for a ticket. And that is also the bad news. A complete lack of competition means airfares are sky high.

PAPUA NEW GUINEA

The national airline is **Air Niugini** (airline code PX; www.airniugini.com.pg) and it's the only carrier that operates scheduled services to PNG. **Qantas** (QF; www.qantas.com) has a code-share agreement with Air Niugini that awards Qantas Frequent Flyer points on international flights, but Qantas planes no longer go to PNG. Air Niugini flies to Cairns, Brisbane and Sydney in Australia, plus Narita, Manila, Singapore and Honiara. At the time of research, these were the only cities from which you could fly to PNG.

Jackson's Airport (POM) located in Port Moresby is, for the time being, the only international airport in PNG. There's talk of Mt Hagen and Alotau reopening; if they do, flights will probably be to Cairns only.

SOLOMON ISLANDS

Solomon Airlines (IE; ☎ 20031; www.solomonairlines .com.au), the national carrier, is vying for the title of least reliable airline on earth, though to be fair its international services are better than the domestic flights. From its base at Henderson Airport (HIR), 11km east of Honiara, Solomon Airlines flies five days a week to Brisbane and has one or two flights weekly to Nadi in Fiji, Port Vila in Vanuatu and Auckland in New Zealand, some being code shares (one plane carrying passengers from other airlines) with Air Pacific.

Tickets

If you buy your flight to PNG with Air Niugini you qualify for discounts on the airline's domestic services.

Almost all flights to Honiara go via Australia or Fiji. So if you're coming from Europe, Asia or anywhere in between – head for Oz. From North America, also look at **Air Pacific** (FJ; www.airpacific.com) or anyone else flying to Fiji.

AIR FARES

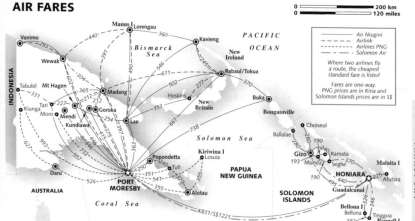

VISIT SOUTH PACIFIC PASS

The Visit South Pacific Pass could save you a lot of money. This pass uses several regional airlines, including Air Niugini, Solomon Airlines and Qantas, and allows travel between Australia, New Zealand, PNG, the Solomons, Vanuatu, New Caledonia, Fiji, Tonga, Niue, Samoa and French Polynesia. The pass costs a very reasonable US$220 to US$370 per sector, depending on length. You must buy a minimum of two sectors when you purchase the pass, and it must be bought before you begin your trip to the region (preferably when you buy your flight to the region). Additional sectors can be bought from offices of the airlines involved once you arrive. Sadly, it is not available to residents of any of the countries mentioned above. And yes, that includes Australia and New Zealand. For full details see www.solomonairlines.com.au/fares.htm.

Asia

There are no flights between PNG and neighbouring Indonesia. Garuda Indonesia and a couple of Indonesia's new budget airlines do fly to Jayapura, just across the border from PNG; travel agencies in Jakarta and Denpasar can help, otherwise you have to fly via Singapore or Cairns.

Air Niugini has a weekly flight between Manila and Port Moresby leaving on Wednesday. There are also flights from Singapore on Monday and Thursday, and Narita on Saturday.

From anywhere else in Asia you'll need to first get to one of the cities listed here or somewhere in Australia.

An agency worth considering is **STA Travel** (Bangkok ☎ 02-236 0262; www.statravel.co.th; Singapore ☎ 6737 7188; www.statravel.com.sg; Tokyo ☎ 03 5391 2922; www.statravel.co.jp). Another resource in Japan is **No 1 Travel** (☎ 03 3205 6073; www.no1-travel.com). **Schenker Travel** (☎ 2545 1033; eliza.lau@schenker.com.au), in Hong Kong, is efficient and reliable.

Australia & New Zealand

Air Niugini operates code-share services with Qantas between Australia and PNG. There are a range of fares and some complex discount structures (see www.airniugini.com.pg for details) and it pays to book ahead. The following prices are for the full-fare/cheapest discounted return seats: Sydney (A$2111/938, twice a week); Brisbane (A$1721/845, six days a week); and Cairns (A$1030/577, daily). You can book at either Qantas or Air Niugini offices or through a travel agency. To the Solomons, Solomon Airlines flies to Honiara from Brisbane (A$795 one way) five times per week, and from Auckland (NZ$986 one way) via Port Vila every Saturday. Agencies worth looking at include **Flight Centre** (☎ 133 133; www.flightcentre.com.au) and **STA Travel** (☎ 1300-733 035; www.statravel.com.au). For online bookings, try www.travel.com.au.

From New Zealand to PNG, connect with an Air Niugini flight in Australia.

Flights to Australia can be very cheap if you plan ahead. **STA Travel** (☎ 0508-782 872; www.statravel.co.nz) has branches throughout the country and www.travel.co.nz is a good online source.

Continental Europe

The easiest and probably the cheapest way from Europe to PNG is to put together a ticket to Singapore or Australia and then on to Port Moresby on an Air Niugini flight. There are millions of deals to Australia or Singapore, some of the cheapest with airlines such as **Gulf Air** (www.gulfairco.com), **Emirates** (www.emirates.com) or **Aeroflot** (www.aeroflot.com) cost about UK£250/400 one way/return. Most round-the-world tickets take in Singapore and Australia; you could tack on a flight to PNG or the Solomons. The Singapore option is obviously shorter, but coming via Australia gives you far more dates (more than a dozen flights per week versus two from Singapore to Port Moresby).

Some reliable agencies:

FRANCE

Anyway (☎ 0892-893 892; www.anyway.fr in French)
Nouvelles Frontières (☎ 0825-000 747; www.nouvelles-frontieres.fr in French)
OTU Voyages (www.otu.fr in French) This agency specialises in student and youth travellers.

GERMANY

Just Travel (☎ 089-747 3330; www.justtravel.de)
Lastminute (☎ 01805-284 366; www.lastminute.de in German)

OTHER COUNTRIES

Airfair (☎ 020-620 5121; www.airfair.nl in Dutch) In the Netherlands.
Barcelo Viajes (☎ 902-116 226; www.barceloviajes.com in Spanish) In Spain.
CTS Viaggi (☎ 06-462 0431; www.cts.it in Italian) Italian agency, specialising in student and youth travel.

The Pacific

If you're flying around the Pacific islands look closely at the Visit South Pacific Pass (p237), which is also one of the cheapest ways of getting between the Pacific and Australia or New Zealand. Island hopping all the way to Port Moresby becomes eminently affordable with this pass.

Otherwise, Air Pacific operates from Nadi to Honiara (S$854 one way), from where Air Niugini flies to Port Moresby. The only other way of getting to PNG from the Pacific is via Australia (p237).

The UK & Ireland

Flying via Australia is the obvious way to PNG from the UK and Ireland, and is especially attractive given the plethora of cheap deals on offer. Return tickets from London to Australia can cost as little as UK£400; or you could consider a round-the-world ticket taking in Australia and starting at about UK£550. You'd then have to tack on the PNG flights, but if you make your way to Cairns these are relatively cheap.

The other option is flying to Singapore, then Port Moresby. Again, there is always some sort of deal to Singapore – Emirates and other Middle Eastern airlines have some great offers.

To get to the Solomons, make your way to Australia (see p237) and take a flight from Brisbane.

In the UK, advertisements for many travel agencies appear in the travel pages of the weekend broadsheet newspapers, in *Time Out*, the *Evening Standard* and in the free magazine *TNT*. Or check out the following:
Bridge the World (☎ 0870-444 7474; www.b-t-w.co.uk)
STA Travel (☎ 0870-160 0599; www.statravel.co.uk) For travellers under the age of 26.
Trailfinders (☎ 020-7938 3939; www.trailfinders.co.uk)
Travel Bag (☎ 0870-890 1456; www.travelbag.co.uk)

The USA & Canada

There are a couple of options from North America: fly to Australia, then on to Port Moresby; or fly to Narita (Tokyo), Manila or Singapore, then on to Port Moresby. Deals between a number of US and Canadian cities and Australia's east coast are common and a good return to Australia is about US$1000. From North America you could fly to the Solomons via Brisbane (see p237) or, if you coordinate with Solomon Airlines' infrequent flights, travel via Nadi in Fiji or Port Vila in Vanuatu.

The via-Asia options might prove cheaper, but with only one or two flights to PNG a week they can be inconvenient. Deals to Narita can be particularly good (US$550 from the west coast, US$650 from New York), and if you're flying from the east coast might cut

out a couple of stops. Some agencies recommended for online bookings:
www.cheapflights.com
www.expedia.com (www.expedia.ca in Canada)
www.orbitz.com
www.travelocity.com (www.travelocity.ca in Canada)

In Canada there's also **Travel Cuts** (☎ 800-667-2887; www.travelcuts.com), the country's national student travel agency.

LAND
Border Crossings
The only land border crossing in either PNG or the Solomon Islands is between Vanimo, in Sanduan Province and Jayapura in Papua Province (West Papua), Indonesia. At the time of research this **border** (🕑 8am-noon & 1-4.06pm) was open and operating pretty smoothly, but it has a history of closing at short notice so check Lonely Planet's **Thorn Tree** (http://thorntree.lonelyplanet .com) bulletin board before making plans.

Entering PNG you must first get a visa in Jayapura (or any other PNG mission; see p225). This is fairly straightforward, but will take at least a couple of days. The occasional bus (1½ hours) leaves for the border. You might need to change buses a few times and if you're in a hurry consider hiring an *ojek* (motorbike), or perhaps two to help with luggage, to take you straight there. You must get stamped out of Indonesia at the immigration office opposite the Dafonsoro Hotel in Jayapura, *not* at the border itself. You'll need to pay a 50,000Rp 'fee' and the stamp must be within 24 hours of your departure. The office is open (or can be opened) most of the time.

The border itself is uneventful, and once through there's usually some vehicle hanging around that will give you a lift to Vanimo. A taxi can be arranged in advance through **Visser Car Rentals** (☎ 857 1366) in Vanimo. There is only one PMV (K10, 50 minutes) a day and times are random.

Leaving PNG is a little more difficult. If you haven't already got an Indonesian visa in Port Moresby (p225) you'll need to spend a day in Vanimo doing that. The **Indonesian Consulate** (☎ 857 1371; fax 857 1373; 🕑 9am-noon & 2-4pm Mon-Fri) takes 24 hours to issue a 30-day visa; you'll need K35 and two photos. This can usually be extended by two weeks in Indonesia. It's best to say you're heading for Bali or Manado as they are less contentious destinations than anywhere in West Papua. If you have trouble, the manager of the Vanimo Beach Hotel (p142) can help out – if you're staying there. You will need to buy some Indonesian rupiah before you get to the border; go to **Jacane Trading** (☎ 857 1133), beside the BSP Bank, head upstairs and knock on the door.

The lone red PMV to the border leaves from outside Vanimo Trading when it's full. If you can't wait, ask around and you might find a ride. Formalities on the PNG side are easy. At Indonesian immigration put your 20,000Rp bribe inside your passport on the Indonesian visa page. Once it's been discreetly pocketed, you're on your way. You might be stopped at several military checkpoints on the way to Jayapura.

So you've paid your bribe and you're into Indo, all sorted, right? Not quite. Once you get to Jayapura you must go directly to the abovementioned immigration office, fill out a form and present your passport and 50,000Rp to the official who will stamp you in. This can't be done at the border and if you don't get the stamp you will have dramas leaving Indonesia.

If you plan on travelling elsewhere in Papua Province (West Papua) you will need a Surat Keterangan Jalan (SKJ), or travel permit. This is issued by the provincial police office in Jayapura for a small fee and two photos.

SEA
There are plenty of boats plying the waters around PNG and the Solomons, but very few are actually scheduled services to other countries. For information on travelling between Bougainville and the Solomon Islands, see the boxed text on p244.

Papua New Guinea
Unless you're on a private boat or cruise ship, it's very difficult coming to PNG by sea. The only regular service is the *MV Libby II,* which makes a weekly run between Vanimo and Jayapura (K70 one way). It departs at 4am Friday, arriving in Jayapura at 7.30am, and caters mainly to Vanimo residents weekend shopping in Jayapura. The road trip (p239) is so much easier. The return boat trip is on Sunday morning. Book through the Vanimo Beach Hotel (p142).

TRANSPORT

Unless you are a Torres Strait Islander, it is illegal to island hop between Thursday Island (known as TI to locals) and PNG. You can exit Australia from TI but you must go directly to PNG, usually Daru, where you can pass through immigration if you already have a visa.

PRIVATE BOATS

PNG and the Solomons are popular stopping points for cruising yachties, either heading through Asia or the Pacific. In PNG you can clear immigration at Alotau, Daru, Kavieng, Kimbe, Lae, Lorengau, Madang, Misima Island, Port Moresby, Rabaul, Samarai and Vanimo. You must get a visa before you arrive.

See www.noonsite.com for a full rundown, and p243 for details on crewing yachts.

CRUISE SHIPS

There is no shortage of 'Pacific island paradises' in PNG and the Solomons, but finding a cruise ship to take you there is nigh on impossible. Samarai Island in Milne Bay Province used to see one or two ships a year, but not anymore. Pretty much the only cruising available is aboard two domestic ships, the *MTS Discoverer* and the *Sepik Spirit* (see p242).

Solomon Islands

The Solomons is similarly popular with private yachties but, like PNG, doesn't see much in the way of big boats. Places where you can complete immigration formalities include Honiara, Gizo, Graciosa Bay (Ndende Island, Santa Cruz), Noro and Yandina. Boats can stay in the Solomons for three months and this can be extended to a total of six months. For a swathe of detail see the excellent www.noonsite.com.

TOURS

The three main PNG-based inbound tour operators are Melanesian Tourist Services, Trans Niugini Tours and Niugini Holidays. They offer a wide variety of tours but prices are usually disconcertingly high. As with tours anywhere, taking this option should give you a pretty smooth trip, but you can do much the same thing for about half the price (or less) if you're prepared to send a few emails and organise it yourself. For

smaller operators, see p247. For Kokoda Track tours, see p67.

Dick Lang's Desert Air (☎ 08-8264 7200, 1800 004 200, both in Australia) Operates all-inclusive air safaris. A unique option, visiting some off-the-beaten-track places. Itineraries in 2005 are timed around the Goroka and Mt Hagen shows.

Eco-Tourism Melanesia (☎ 323 4518; www.em.com .pg) Focuses on village-based tours and cultural, wildlife, bird-watching tours.

Field Guides (www.fieldguides.com/png.htm) Well-organised but expensive bird-watching tours, focusing on birds of paradise. US-based.

Melanesian Tourist Services (☎ 675-311 2050; www.mtspng.com) Operates the *MTS Discoverer* (see p242) and several high-end resorts, which you'll stay at on its tours. Runs diving and Sepik tours.

Niugini Holidays (☎ 1300 850 020, 02-9290 2055, both in Australia; www.nghols.com) Probably the biggest range of tours, from specialised family tours through surfing, fishing, diving, trekking, war veterans tours and more. Not necessarily the best.

South Pacific Tours (☎ 323 5245; spt@onthenet .au) A range of general travel services, including diving, adventure and trekking tours. Not always as well organised as it could be.

Trans Niugini Tours (☎ 675-542 1438; www .pngtours.com) Based in Mt Hagen, these guys operate the *Sepik Spirit* (see p242) and several luxury lodges. There are general tours, wildlife tours, treks, cruises and tours of the cultural shows. It can be expensive (some say unreasonably so). If you're on a budget, look elsewhere.

GETTING AROUND

AIR

PNG is probably more reliant on air transport than any other country on earth. The population is scattered, often isolated in mountain valleys and on tiny islands, but even the most remote villages now have some familiarity with the ubiquitous *balus* (aeroplane). About 2000 airstrips have been cut out of the bush or into hill tops and coral islands during the last 80 years or so and the aeroplane has become almost symbolic of the way technology has intruded so successfully into what was a loose collection of hunter-gatherer societies. Less than a quarter of these airstrips are regularly used today, but many involve the sort of hair-raising landings you won't easily forget. The pilots are extremely skilful – keep telling yourself this as you approach flat-topped ridges masquerading as airports.

Aircraft are often small (Mission Aviation Fellowship is into Cessnas) and strips can be almost unrecognisable if you don't know to look for them. One we landed on looked and felt more like a rally track; another has a 15-degree bend halfway along; and the strip at Wau is on a nine-degree slope. All of them are great fun!

Aviation in PNG and the Solomons will probably prove more informal than you're used to (alert: understatement of the year!). Outside Port Moresby you can pretty much forget about X-rays and metal detectors; you might get a cursory pat down, but probably not. For lighter aircraft, not only is your baggage weighed (16kg is the limit but 20kg is usually accepted), so are you. Fortunately, excess baggage charges are reasonable. At remote strips you might have to buy your ticket direct from the pilot – cash only.

Outside the main centres don't rely on being able to pay for anything on credit. Even in big towns there's no guarantee. Air Niugini refused our plastic at Jackson's Airport in Port Moresby because 'the phone lines are down' – a common problem.

Unpredictable weather combined with mechanical problems and complex schedules can frequently lead to delays, or cancellations. It's not unheard of for passengers to stand around scanning the horizon all day. In the Solomons your domestic flight has about a 50% chance of arriving on the right day. So have a book (or two) handy, and make friends with the locals.

Flying in this part of the world is far more than just getting from A to B and provides some of the most memorable moments of your trip (or your life). It would be even more of a joy if it wasn't so damned expensive.

Airlines in the Region

While Air Niugini operates larger planes to the larger centres, the smaller second- and third-level airlines service everywhere else. Airlines PNG (formerly called Milne Bay Air) and Airlink are the main secondary airlines in PNG, with North Coast Aviation, covering destinations out of Lae, and MAF (Mission Aviation Fellowship) dealing with the smallest communities, and doing it pretty well. In theory, tickets on Air Niugini, Airlink and Airlines PNG can be booked at any travel agency linked into

the international computer reservations network. If not, try a Qantas office.

Following is a list of airlines operating scheduled flights in PNG and the Solomons. Local offices are listed on the airline websites or under the relevant destinations in the regional chapters; the websites also have up-to-date fare tables. Other airlines do charter services; see the Yellow Pages.

Air Niugini (☎ 327 3444; www.airniugini.com.pg)
Airlines PNG (☎ 325 0555; www.apng.com)
Airlink (☎ 325 9555; www.airlink.com.pg) Airlink doesn't fly Sundays.
MAF (Mission Aviation Fellowship; ☎ 325 2668; www.maf.org.au)
North Coast Aviation (☎ 472 1755; norco-lae@global.net.pg)
Solomon Airlines (☎ 20031; www.solomonairlines.com.au)

Discounts

Neither Airlink nor Airlines PNG offers any discounts – a return fair is twice the price of a one-way fare, all year round.

Air Niugini, on the other hand, has a bag full. The See PNG fare offers a 20% discount on all advance purchases of domestic tickets to non-PNG residents who can produce their international ticket (so don't forget it). This is the only discount available if you're buying the ticket outside PNG; it's valid year-round. Following is a summary of other deals, all of which can only be bought *inside* PNG and some of which are not applicable at peak times such as Christmas and Easter. For more details see www.airniugini.com.

Nambawan Fares These are probably the most useful fares for travellers, as they offer round-trip tickets at a 30% discount. You have to stay a minimum of seven days and maximum of 30. This fare is upgradeable to full economy class.

Wantok Fares 50% off the normal economy class round-trip fare. This fare is instant purchase with a minimum stay of seven days and maximum stay of 30 days.

Weekend Fares These round-trip tickets cost 60% of the standard fare. You have to fly out on Friday or Saturday and back on Sunday or Monday. These seats are often booked out in advance. The Weekend and Nambawan Fares must be paid for within three days of making a reservation.

These fares may not be available at all times, and must be issued on Air Niugini ticket stocks – which means you have to buy them from an Air Niugini office. Be certain of your travelling dates as changing them (or cashing them in) incurs a K110 penalty.

TRANSPORT

THOSE MAGNIFICENT MEN & THEIR FLYING MACHINES

The development of the Wau and Bulolo gold fields in the 1920s launched aviation in New Guinea. Cecil John Levien realised the gold fields would never be successful as long as getting men and supplies up from the coast involved a long, hard slog across difficult terrain populated by unfriendly tribes. So his Guinea Gold company set up Guinea Airways.

Its pilot, 'Pard' Mustar, had to do far more than just fly the first DH-37 biplane. First he arranged for an airstrip to be constructed at Lae (the local jail provided prisoners to build it), then walked from Salamaua to Wau to supervise the airstrip construction there. Next, he had to travel back to Rabaul where the DH-37 had arrived in pieces as sea cargo, assemble it and fly to Lae – a 650km journey, much of it over sea or unexplored jungle, in a single-engine aircraft of dubious reliability.

In April 1927 Mustar took off on his first flight to Wau – and couldn't find it! He returned to Lae, took more directions and advice and tried again with an equal lack of success. Finally, on his third attempt, and with an experienced guide on board, he made the first of many 50-minute flights.

Mustar quickly realised the need for more capacity and reliability, and before the end of 1927 he went to Germany to buy a Junkers W-34 at the astronomical cost of UK£8000. It may have been expensive, but at the time it was the latest thing in cargo aircraft and could lift over a ton. A second W-34 soon followed, and with these aircraft Guinea Airways operated a service that proved the real possibilities of air transport just as convincingly as the much better publicised flights of Lindbergh or Kingsford-Smith. Wau became the busiest airfield in the world and more air freight was lifted annually in New Guinea than in the rest of the world put together!

Mustar left New Guinea but in 1929 was called back to attempt a scheme that, to many people at the time, must have seemed like something in the realms of science fiction. He had to find a way of flying gold dredges weighing 3000 tons into the gold fields. Mustar's answer was to dismantle the dredges and buy another Junkers, the G-31, a three-engine, all-metal monster that cost UK£30,000 and could lift three tons. In the early 1930s a fleet of these aircraft carried not just gold equipment but also workers and even the first horses ever to be transported by air.

Air Passes

You can use the Visit South Pacific Pass to get between Port Moresby and Honiara; see p237 for details.

BICYCLE

In the odd town or island, such as New Ireland, it's possible to rent a bike (about K10 per day), but don't expect anything flash.

BOAT

Island hopping through PNG and the Solomons is a pretty cool way of travelling, especially if you have no concern for time. Unless you take a cruise, the only certainties of travelling this way are that you'll have a truly memorable, exotic experience, and you'll spend a lot of time sitting under palm trees waiting for your freighter, banana boat, luxury yacht or outrigger canoe to finally set sail. But hey, life could be worse.

The main ways of getting around by sea are by large boats, small boats, charters and yacht crewing.

Boat Charter

Many dive operators charter their boats, some for extended cruises. A cheaper alternative, if you're not looking for comfort and the chance to dive, is to try to charter a work boat. Chartering is definitely possible in Milne Bay, Lae and the islands – for a group of five or six, it isn't ruinously expensive. For a list of dive boats, see p218.

Cruise Boats

There are two luxury cruise boats working the north coast, islands and Sepik River in PNG. The **MTS Discoverer** (www.mtsdiscoverer.com) is a catamaran that sleeps 40. It operates out of Madang Resort (p102) and has cruises to places including the Trobriand Islands, the Sepik River and, occasionally, the Louisiade Archipelago.

The smaller *Sepik Spirit* is run by **Trans Niugini Tours** (www.pngtours.com) and has nine rooms. It does mainly Sepik River cruises, mainly packaged with the company's luxury lodges in the Highlands and on the river.

Neither are cheap, with costs running to more than US$300 per person per night, twin share.

Large Boats

Sailing from one exotic locale to the next, via who-knows-where, on a slowly rolling freighter has a certain Joseph Conrad–style romance to it. And while cargo boats generally don't take travellers, it's worth trying your luck. Lae is the best place to look; ask around the port to see what's going. You'll almost always have more luck getting on a freighter by talking directly to the ship's captain (and perhaps investing in a few SP Lagers) rather than the office people. Accommodation is usually in a spare cabin and you should ask about food and water (you'll probably have to BYO). Bring plenty to keep yourself entertained as freighter 'schedules' are unreliable due to delays in loading/unloading cargoes. If freighters load (or expect to load) dangerous cargo such as petrol, they will not accept passengers.

If you don't have time to sit around waiting, there are regular passenger services linking the island provinces with Lae and, to a lesser extent, Madang.

Three boats have recently started scheduled services to the islands of Milne Bay (p77), making those more accessible than they have been for years. There are no passenger vessels linking the north and south coasts or running along the south coast.

The main operators along the north coast and to the islands are Lutheran Shipping and Rabaul Shipping (Star Ships). Based in Lae, Lutheran Shipping has a virtual monopoly on passenger shipping along the north coast. Boats run at least once a week from Lae to Oro Bay, Finschhafen, Madang, Kimbe and Rabaul (see p95). From Rabaul there are regular boats to Kavieng and Manus. Schedules are released at the end of the month for the following month, and you can only make a booking once the schedule is out. Even then, the departure is far from guaranteed.

Some boats, such as the twin-hull *Gejemsao*, are passenger-only and quite comfortable. Others carry cargo and passengers and have tourist class (air-conditioned seats and berths) and deck class (air-vented seats and berths). Deck class can get crowded; both classes have video 'entertainment' and it's worth avoiding bunks near the video.

There are simple snack bars. Students are entitled to discounts of at least 25%.

In the Solomons cargo ships leave Honiara in all directions and it's best to ask at the wharf or check at the **Marine Office** (☎ 21609) to see what's going. Ships sail at least once a week to Gizo via Marovo Lagoon and to Auki.

See the appropriate regional chapters for further details.

Small Boats

In addition to the freighters and passenger boats, local boats and canoes go literally everywhere. For these you have to be in the right place at the right time but, with patience, you could travel the whole coastline by village hopping in small boats.

Trade boats – small, wooden boats with thumping diesel engines – ply the coast, supplying trade stores and acting as ferries. They are irregular but if you're prepared to wait, they can get you to some off-the-track places. Don't expect comfort, bring your own food and make sure the operator is trustworthy before you commit yourself to a day or two aboard. If you're in a major centre, such as Alotau, ask around the port and at the big stores, which might have a set schedule for delivering supplies to the area's trade stores. Negotiate the fee before you leave.

For shorter distances, there are dinghies with outboard motors, often known as speedies or banana boats. These are usually long fibreglass boats that leap through the waves and are bone-jarringly uncomfortable. The cost of running outboard motors makes them expensive if you have to charter one, but there will often be a PMV boat (a public transport boat; see p246) with reasonable fares – about K20 per hour's travel. Note, banana boats are no fun at all when the wind picks up and the open seas should be avoided. People die reasonably frequently in open-sea banana-boat crossings; try to stay within sight of shore.

For shorter distances, such as from Tufi to the surrounding villages, you might take an outrigger canoe and will be expected to assist with the paddling.

Yacht Crewing

There are thriving yacht clubs located in Port Moresby, Lae, Madang, Wewak and Rabaul, and it is possible you might be able

THE GUN RUN

The route between the Solomon Islands and Bougainville, for years the main thoroughfare of smuggled guns to the Bougainville Revolutionary Army (BRA), is once again open to civilian traffic. Actually, 'open' is a slight overstatement; it's basically illegal and there is no PNG immigration post in Bougainville so you can't get an exit stamp. The PNG government does not advertise this route, but the lack of a stamp won't matter to the Solomon Islanders and the trip is one to tell the grandkids...

To do it, get to Buka and take transport south to Buin. From there, on Thursday or Saturday, squeeze into a 10m-long motor-canoe for the three-hour trip to the Shortland Islands. If you can find someone at Korovou you might get an entry stamp there, but you probably won't. Spend the night in the village of the guy whose boat you came in, then, on Friday or Sunday, fly to Ghizo from Ballalae airstrip, which you can reach from anywhere in the Shortlands by canoe. To arrange the flight, radio the Solomon Airlines agent in Maleai from the village you're staying in. When in Ghizo, go to the immigration officer and get stamped in.

Disadvantages

It was technically illegal at the time of research – seek advice locally (or perhaps from other travellers on the Thorn Tree at www.lonelyplanet.com) before attempting it. While locals regularly travel this way for trade purposes, a visitor may not enjoy the same privileges. Buin is a cowboy town full of brawling *raskols* (bandits) and knives. The crossing can be dangerous due to waves, overcrowding and drunken steering.

Advantages

From the islands, it's much cheaper than flying 1000km out of your way to Port Moresby, and 1000km back. You get to see Bougainville (p195). The Shortlands (p207) are an incredible and truly remote place to visit.

to find a berth, if you have some experience. Yachties often look for people to share costs and for the company. Be sure to at least have a couple of drinks with your host before agreeing to go anywhere.

CAR & MOTORCYCLE

Driving yourself around PNG and/or the Solomon Islands is not really a viable way of travelling. PNG really only has one road – the Highlands Hwy – that connects two or more places you might want to visit, and in the Solomons you need no more explanation than the 'Islands' part of the country's name.

In PNG it's pointless bringing your own vehicle as even a dirt bike would need to be shipped between many locations due to the lack of roads (see p245). The same applies to buying a vehicle; it's not worth the hassle.

You could, however, hire a car or 4WD in Lae or Madang for the trip up the Highlands Hwy, or perhaps to drive around New Ireland. All the major cities have an array of car-hire companies.

Driving Licence

Any valid overseas licence is OK for the first three months you're in PNG. International driving permits are accepted in the Solomons, as are most driving licences. People drive on the left-hand side.

Fuel & Spare Parts

Fuel can be hard to find and is expensive. In PNG a litre of petrol costs K2.70 per litre, while diesel is K2.27 per litre in cities, but expect prices to rise dramatically once you leave town. As for spare parts, start praying.

Hire

Four-wheel drives can be hired in most PNG cities, including on the islands, and in Lae and Port Moresby you can hire a plain old car. You must be 25 to hire a car and have either a credit card or K2500 cash as a deposit. Hiring anything will cost you an arm and probably both legs, and the rates are even higher when you add the per-kilometre charges, insurance and tax.

For example, a compact car (the cheapest option) costs about K140 per day, plus K0.72 per kilometre, plus 10% VAT, plus any fee for personal insurance. A 4WD is about K200 per day plus K1.10 per kilometre. Probably the cheapest way of hiring is with an accommodation and car-rental package; **Coral Sea Hotels** (www.coralseahotels.com. pg) and Budget do some good deals.

One-way rentals are available at locations along the Highlands Hwy. The following companies have offices around PNG; see destination chapters for details.

Avis (☎ 324 9400; www.avis.com.pg)
Hertz (☎ 302 6822; sales@leasemaster.com.pg)
Travel-Car (☎ 323 9878; queenemmalodge@daltron .com.pg)

The Solomon Islands has less than 1500km of roads. Cars can be hired in Honiara, but nowhere else.

Insurance

Most hire companies supply full insurance as standard in their rental agreements, but be sure to ask before you drive off. This is particularly important as some travel insurance policies don't cover driving off-road.

Road Conditions

Perhaps the most pertinent point about the roads in PNG is that there aren't very many. Port Moresby, for example, is not linked by road to any other provincial capital except Kerema, and that road is subject to seasonal difficulties. The most important road is the Highlands Hwy, which runs from Lae to Lake Kopiago, via Goroka, Mt Hagen and Tari. Madang is also connected to the highway via the Ramu Hwy.

The road conditions are variable, to say the least. Many are full of potholes and only passable by 4WD, and only then in the dry. Others are recently sealed all-weather affairs. If you're planning on getting out of the towns a 4WD is a necessity.

Road Hazards

Roads in PNG come with a range of hazards. There is the deterioration factor: many are becoming almost impassable due to lack of maintenance. There's the wet-season factor: it rains, you get bogged. And then there's that one you can't do much about: the *raskol* (bandit) factor. Your chances of

being held up are admittedly quite slim, but it's worth reading the Dangers & Annoyances section (p223) for tips on what to do if it happens to you.

Bear in mind the tourist office's recommendations if you are involved in an accident: don't stop, keep driving and report the accident at the nearest police station. This applies regardless of who was at fault or how serious the accident (whether you've run over a pig or hit a person). Tribal concepts of pay back apply to car accidents. You may have insurance and you may be willing to pay, but the local citizenry may well prefer to take more immediate and satisfying action.

Road Rules

Cars drive on the left side of the road. The speed limit is 60km/h in towns and 80km/h in the country. Seat belts must be worn by the driver and front-seat passengers. Most cars won't have seat belts in the back.

HITCHING

Hitching is an important part of travelling in the region. The lack of scheduled transport means jumping onto a bus, truck, tractor, outrigger, freighter, plane – or whatever else is going your way – is a time-honoured way of getting around. You'll often be expected to pay the equivalent of a PMV fare. If your bag is light, it's also sometimes possible to hitch flights at small airports.

Keep in mind that hitching is never entirely safe in any country and we don't recommend it. Travellers who decide to hitch are taking a small but potentially serious risk, and solo women should absolutely *not* hitch in PNG or the Solomon Islands. People who choose to hitch will be safer if they travel in pairs and let someone know where they are planning to go.

LOCAL TRANSPORT IN URBAN AREAS

Local transport is not particularly sophisticated in PNG and the Solomons. The vast majority of trips are made by minibuses known as PMVs (public motor vehicles), though in a few places you'll find more exotic means of transport, such as outrigger canoes for getting around Tufi or dugout canoes for paddling between villages on the Sepik River. They operate on the same principal as a PMV; they're cheap and leave when full.

TRANSPORT

TRANSPORT

A few (very few) towns and islands rent battered bikes to travellers for a few kina a day.

Minibus (PMV)

In most urban areas a fleet of minibuses, universally known as PMVs, provides public transport along a network of established routes. Stops are predetermined and are often indicated by a yellow pole or a crowd of waiting people. You can't just ask to be let off anywhere. The destination will be indicated by a sign inside the windscreen or called out by the driver's assistant, aka 'conductor', in a machine-gun-style staccato.

PMVs have a crew of two: the driver, who usually maintains an aloof distance from the passengers; and the conductor, who takes fares and generally copes with the rabble. On most occasions, the conductor sits in the seat nearest the door, so when the PMV stops, he's the man to ask about the destination. If it's heading in the right direction and there's a centimetre or two of spare space, you're on. Don't be surprised if you have to wait for your change; it will come when the conductor gets his change sorted.

If you tell the conductor where you want to go he'll let the driver know when to stop. In town, PMVs usually cost 50t per trip, irrespective of length.

Taxi

Considering PNG's reputation for nocturnal danger, it's surprising there are not more taxis. Port Moresby and Alotau have plenty and there are two in Vanimo. That's it. Lae, Wewak, Madang, Popondetta, Goroka and Mt Hagen have no taxis, making it difficult to get around after dark when you don't want to be walking. To fill the gap, hotels often have minibuses that will run you around.

If you do manage to get a taxi you'll find most of them are complete shitboxes – windscreens that look like road maps, broken seats, smelly drivers, no radios. Prices aren't excessive (starting at about K5 and averaging about K1.5 per kilometre) but you'll have to negotiate the fare before you get in, and don't expect to be offered change when you get out (see p224). The one shining exception is **Scarlet Taxis** (☎ 323 4266) in Port Moresby, where the cars and drivers

are clean and well kept, there is a radio dispatch network and the meters work.

In the Solomons, Honiara has plenty of taxis and Gizo and Auki have a few.

PMV

PMV is the generic term for any type of public transport and wherever there are roads, there will be PMVs. Whether it's a dilapidated minibus, a truck with two facing wooden benches, a tractor in the Solomons, a pick-up with no seats whatsoever but space in the tray, or any other means of transport (boats are also referred to as PMVs, see p245), the PMV is one of the keys to travelling cheaply in PNG. It's also one of the best ways to meet local people.

There's no real science to using PMVs, just turn up at the designated departure point and wait for it to fill up. Many rural routes have only one service a day so ask around a day ahead for the intelligence on when it leaves and from where (usually the market). It might also save you waiting for hours…most PMVs start in one town very early in the morning, drive to another (usually larger) town, then wait a couple of hours while the morning's passengers go to market before returning.

Out of town you can assume that anything with lots of people in it is a rural PMV. The conductor will tell you where it's headed and take your money, usually at or just before the end of the trip. If you want to get off before the end, just yell 'stop driver!' Market days (usually Friday and Saturday) are the best days for finding a ride. On secondary roads, traffic can be thin, especially early in the week.

Most of the time, travelling in a PMV is perfectly safe; your fellow passengers will be most impressed you're with them and not in some expensive 4WD. There is, of course, a risk of robbery, especially on the Highlands Hwy. Lone women travellers are also at greater risk and should think twice about travelling by PMV. If you do, find a vehicle with women passengers and get a seat nearby.

COSTS

PMVs are refreshingly cheap. For example, from Lae to Madang costs K30; from Madang to Goroka is K30 and Mt Hagen to Madang is K50. Remember that oil price fluctuations affect the whole world…not just the price of fuel in your home town.

TOURS

From rough-and-ready village tours to luxury lodge and cruise-boat affairs, there is a PNG tour to suit almost everyone. Of particular interest are the specialist tours catering to those with a penchant for watching wildlife, bird-watching, trekking and village-based tours. Smaller operators are usually cheaper and offer a more personal experience, though not necessarily a better-organised trip – try to contact them before coming to PNG and allow a couple of weeks organisation time.

The following companies have good reputations. For tours of the Kokoda Track, see p67, and for bigger companies, see p240.

Frontier Travel PNG (☎ 325 7371; www.frontier travelpng.com.pg) Frontier can organise good four- and five-day tours of the Sepik.

Paradise Adventure Tours (☎ 542 1696; www .paradisetours.com.pg) This Mt Hagen–based operation has had good feedback on its Highlands, Sepik and bird-watching tours. Good value.

PNG Frontier Adventures (☎ 856 1584/1400; www .pngfrontieradventures.com) A British/PNG partnership, these guys are Sepik experts. They can provide everything from a single guide to a full-blown tour. Recommended.

PNG Highland Tours (☎ 732 1602; png.gold@global .net.pg) A range of Highlands tours organised by the friendly Norman Carver, including climbs of Mt Wilhelm.

Sepik Adventure Tours (☎ 856 2525; www.ambunti lodge-sepiktour.com.pg) Alois Mateos has vast experience and knowledge of the Sepik and can arrange all manner of tours. A genuinely nice guy.

WALKING

The best and cheapest way to come to grips with PNG is to walk (see p220). With a judicious mix of walks, canoes, PMVs, coastal ships and the odd plane, PNG can change from a very expensive country to a reasonable one. Accommodation and food is normally available in the villages – meaning floor space and sago or sweet potato. See p217 for information on staying in villages.

TRANSPORT

Health Dr Michael Sorokin

CONTENTS

With sensible precautions and behaviour, the health risks to travellers in Papua New Guinea and Solomon Islands are low. Mosquito-transmitted disease is the main problem. The countries share two serious health hazards: malaria and saltwater crocodiles. The region is rabies-free.

Both countries lie in the tropics and are under-resourced in terms of medical infrastructure. Although steadily improving, overall standards of health and healthcare are not good.

BEFORE YOU GO

Prevention is the key to staying healthy while abroad. See your dentist before departing, carry a spare pair of contact lenses and glasses, and take your optical prescription with you. Bring medications in their original, clearly labelled, containers. A signed and dated letter from your physician describing your medical conditions and medications, including generic names, is also a good idea. If carrying syringes or needles, be sure to have a physician's letter documenting their medical necessity or obtain a prepared pack from a travel health clinic.

INSURANCE

If your health insurance doesn't cover you for medical expenses abroad, consider sup-plemental insurance. (Check the Subwwway section of the Lonely Planet website at www .lonelyplanet.com/subwwway for informa-tion.) Find out in advance if your insurance plan will make payments directly to provid-ers or reimburse you later for overseas health expenditures. (In PNG and Solomon Islands, most doctors expect payment in cash.)

Check whether your insurance covers evacuation to the nearest major centre (eg Brisbane) – the extra premium is not usu-ally inordinately expensive.

RECOMMENDED VACCINATIONS

The World Health Organization (WHO) recommends that all travellers be covered for diphtheria, tetanus, measles, mumps, rubella and polio, regardless of their destin-ation. Since most vaccines don't produce immunity until at least two weeks after they're given, visit a physician at least six weeks before departure.

MEDICAL CHECKLIST

It is a very good idea to carry a medical and first-aid kit with you. Following is a list of items you should consider packing.

- Antibiotics (prescription only), eg cipro-floxacin (Ciproxin) or norfloxacin (Utinor, Noroxin)
- Antibiotic plus steroid eardrops (prescrip-tion only), eg Sofradex, Kenacort otic
- Antidiarrhoeal drugs (eg loperamide)
- Acetaminophen (paracetamol) or aspirin*
- Anti-inflammatory drugs (eg ibuprofen)
- Antihistamines (for hay fever and aller-gic reactions)
- Antibacterial ointment (prescription only; eg Bactroban) for cuts and abrasions
- Antimalaria pills
- Antigiardia tablets (prescription only; eg tinidazole)
- Steroid cream or hydrocortisone cream (for allergic rashes)
- Bandages (including a long compression bandage), gauze, gauze rolls, waterproof dressings
- Adhesive or paper tape
- Scissors, safety pins, tweezers**
- Thermometer

REQUIRED & RECOMMENDED VACCINATIONS

When travelling to PNG and Solomon Islands, vaccination for yellow fever (and the certificate to prove it) is required if you are entering from a yellow fever–endemic country. Vaccinations are also recommended for hepatitis A, hepatitis B and typhoid fever.

For PNG, it is recommended that some visitors are vaccinated against Japanese B encephalitis (see p251).

Side Effects of Vaccinations

All vaccinations can produce slight soreness and redness at the inoculation site, and a mild fever with muscle aches over the first 24 hours. These are less likely with hepatitis A inoculations and a little more common with hepatitis B and typhoid inoculations. Japanese B encephalitis vaccine has been associated with allergic reactions that require an antihistamine. Yellow fever vaccine is dangerous for anyone with an allergy to eggs and in about 5% of cases causes a flu-like illness within a week of vaccination.

- Pocketknife**
- DEET-containing insect repellent for the skin
- Permethrin-containing insect spray for clothing, tents and bed nets
- Sun block
- Oral rehydration salts (eg Gastrolyte, Diarolyte, Replyte)
- Iodine tablets (for water purification)
- Syringes and sterile needles, and intravenous fluids if travelling in very remote areas

*Aspirin should not be used for fever; it can cause bleeding in cases of dengue fever.
**Not in carry-on luggage.

If you are travelling more than 24 hours away from a town area consider taking a self-diagnostic kit that can identify, from a finger prick, malaria in the blood.

INTERNET RESOURCES

There is a wealth of travel health advice on the Internet. For further information, the Lonely Planet website (www.lonelyplanet .com) is a good place to start. The WHO publishes a superb book called *International Travel and Health,* which is revised annually and is available online at www.who.int/ith at no cost. Other websites of general interest are MD Travel Health (www.mdtravel health.com), which provides complete travel health recommendations for every country, updated daily, also at no cost; the Centers for Disease Control and Prevention (www.cdc.gov); Fit for Travel (www.fitfor travel.scot.nhs.uk), which has up-to-date

information about outbreaks and is very user-friendly; and www.traveldoctor.com .au, which is a similar Australian site.

It's also a good idea to consult your government's travel health website before departure, if one is available:

Australia (www.dfat.gov.au/travel/)
Canada (www.hc-sc.gc.ca/pphb-dgspsp/tmp-pmv/pub_e.html)
UK (www.doh.gov.uk/traveladvice/index.htm)
USA (www.cdc.gov/travel/)

FURTHER READING

Good options for further reading include *Travel with Children* by Cathy Lanigan, and *Healthy Travel Australia, New Zealand and the Pacific* by Dr Isabelle Young.

IN PNG & SOLOMON ISLANDS

AVAILABILITY & COST OF HEALTH CARE

The quality of health care varies over the region and within each country. In the main centres – Port Moresby and Lae (PNG) and Honiara (Solomon Islands) – you can expect primary care of a high standard that is limited by the lack of access to sophisticated laboratory and radiological procedures. Specialists in internal medicine, surgery and obstetrics/gynaecology are also available in these centres, while in Port Moresby there are paediatric, orthopaedic and psychiatric specialists as well.

In secondary centres, eg Madang (PNG) and Gizo (Solomon Islands), the quality of service can be lower – not often because of lower-quality diagnostic and treatment facilities. Small hospitals, health centres and clinics are well-placed throughout these centres but staffing and facilities will vary. Intergovernmental or church mission aid and doctors may be in some of these facilities.

Private medical practitioners will usually expect payment in cash. Consultation fees for a general practitioner are often slightly less than those charged in a Western country. Where hospital facilities (government or private) exist, a cash deposit will be required. In the Solomons payment by credit card to a government institution may not be accepted. Public hospital outpatient services are free or of negligible cost, but apart from serious emergencies waiting time can be very long.

Commonly used drugs, including oral contraceptives and antibiotics, are available in the main centres, where there are private pharmacies, but do not expect large supplies. If necessary, special drugs can be flown in. For diabetics it may not be possible to obtain exactly the type of insulin preparation or drug that you are using and, although alternatives will be available, it is much safer to have enough of your own supply. The more up-to-date antiepileptics and antihypertensives may also be hard to find.

Tampons and pads can be obtained easily in major centres. In smaller centres they may have been sitting on the shelf for some time.

Private dentists practice in Port Moresby. Elsewhere, limited government dental services may be available.

Medical help will be available within a day's journey. Self-medication for minor skin infections or cuts and for simple diarrhoea is reasonable. In the case of fever in a malarious area it is always best to try and rule malaria out. If you don't have a diagnostic kit (which is not foolproof anyway), almost all clinics will have the ability to do a blood-smear check. Your medical adviser may have decided to prescribe self-treatment medication for malaria rather than preventive antimalarials, in which case you should still try to get an accurate diagnosis and certainly get to a major medical centre for treatment.

The region is generally not an ideal holiday destination for a pregnant woman. Malaria can cause miscarriage or premature labour and prevention cannot be guaranteed even when taking antimalarials. As far as vaccinations are concerned, the three recommended ones (for hepatitis A, hepatitis B and typhoid fever) do not contain live organisms so are not a problem, but the mumps/measles/rubella vaccine does contain live virus material and should not be given during pregnancy. Also because of possible allergic reactions, Japanese B encephalitis vaccination is not recommended during pregnancy.

Travel with children can present special problems. In tropical climates, dehydration develops very quickly when a fever and/or diarrhoea and vomiting occur. Malaria is much more dangerous to children than to adults, as is dengue fever. Insect repellents are essential.

INFECTIOUS DISEASES
Dengue Fever

Dengue fever is spread through mosquito bites. It causes a feverish illness with headache and severe muscle pains similar to those experienced with a bad, prolonged attack of influenza. There might also be a fine rash. Mosquito bites should be avoided whenever possible – always use insect repellents. Self-treatment includes paracetamol, fluids and rest. Danger signs are prolonged vomiting, blood in the vomit, and/or a blotchy dark red rash. Dengue Fever is not a danger in the Highlands.

Filariasis

Also known as elephantiasis, filariasis (found only in the Solomon Islands) is another mosquito-transmitted disease. It can cause a fever with lymph gland enlargement, and prolonged exposure (over a period of months) can lead to chronic limb swelling. Though rare, it hasn't been eliminated and is another reason for anti-mosquito precautions. It's treated with the drugs albendazole or ivermectin. These drugs are used by governments in periodic mass-treatment campaigns, and long-stay expatriates who are offered this would be wise to accept.

Hepatitis A

Hepatitis A is a virus causing liver inflammation. Fever, debility and jaundice (yellow colouration of the skin and eyes, together with dark urine) occur and recovery is slow. Most people recover completely over time but it can be dangerous to people with other forms of liver disease, the elderly and sometimes to pregnant women in their third trimester. It is spread by contaminated food or water. Self-treatment consists of rest, a low-fat diet and avoidance of alcohol. The vaccine is almost 100% protective.

Hepatitis B

Like hepatitis A, hepatitis B is a virus causing liver inflammation, but this virus is more serious and often progresses to chronic liver disease and even cancer. It is spread, like HIV, by mixing body fluids through sexual intercourse, contaminated needles and accidental blood contamination. Treatment is complex and specialised but vaccination is highly effective.

HIV/AIDS

HIV infection is on the rise in the whole region of West Melanesia. Government reports usually underestimate the extent of the problem, so when the international conferences discuss the incidence reaching epidemic proportions you can take it that the danger of unprotected sex is huge. Condom use is essential. If you require an injection for anything check that a new needle is being used or have your own supply.

Japanese B Encephalitis

This disease is found in the southern region of PNG including Port Moresby, but excluding the Highlands, is a serious virus transmitted by mosquitoes. Early symptoms are flu-like and this is usually as far as the infection goes, but sometimes the illness proceeds to cause brain fever (encephalitis), which has a high death rate. There is no specific treatment. Effective vaccination is available (involving three costly inoculations over a month). Allergic and sensitivity reactions to the vaccine, though rare, can occur. Vaccination is usually recommended for anyone staying more than a few weeks and/or going to work in villages.

Malaria

Malaria, found in all areas of PNG below 1000m, and in Solomon Islands (except the outlying atolls and Honiara), is a parasite infection transmitted by infected anopheles mosquitoes. While these mosquitoes are regarded as night feeders they can emerge when light intensity is low (eg in overcast conditions under the jungle canopy or the interior of dark huts). Both malignant *(falciparum)* and less-threatening but relapsing forms are present here. Since no vaccine is available we have to rely on mosquito-bite prevention (including exposing as little skin as possible, applying topical insect repellents, knockdown insecticides and, where necessary, bed nets impregnated with permethrin) and taking antimalarial drugs before, during and after risk exposure. No antimalarial is 100% effective.

Malaria causes various symptoms but the essence of the disease is fever. In a malarious zone it is best to assume that fever is due to malaria unless blood tests rule it out. This applies up to a few months after leaving the area as well. Malaria is curable if diagnosed early.

Typhoid Fever

Sporadic in the region, typhoid fever is a bacterial infection acquired from contaminated food or water or both. The germ can be transmitted by food handlers and flies, and can be present in inadequately cooked shellfish. It causes fever, debility and late-onset diarrhoea. Untreated it can produce delirium and is occasionally fatal, but the infection is curable with antibiotics. Vaccination is moderately effective but care with eating and drinking is equally important.

Yaws

This is a bacterial infection found in Solomon Islands that causes multiple skin ulcers. It was thought to have been eliminated, but there has been a recent resurgence. The infection spreads via direct contact with an infected person. Treatment with penicillin produces a dramatic cure.

TRAVELLER'S DIARRHOEA

Diarrhoea is caused by viruses, bacteria or parasites present in contaminated food or water. In temperate climates the cause is usually viral, but in the tropics bacteria or parasites are more usual. If you develop diarrhoea, be sure to drink plenty of fluids, preferably an oral rehydration solution (eg Diarolyte, Gastrolyte, Replyte). A few loose stools don't require treatment, but if you

HEALTH

DRINKING WATER

To prevent diarrhoea a sensible precaution is to avoid tap water unless it has been boiled, filtered or chemically disinfected (with iodine tablets) and to steer clear of ice. The municipal water supply in capital cities in both countries, and in the majority of towns in PNG, can be trusted. If you're trekking, drink only from streams at a higher altitude than nearby villages – local guides know which water is safe.

---

start having more than four or five stools a day, you should take an antibiotic (usually a quinolone drug) and an antidiarrhoeal agent (such as Loperamide). If diarrhoea is bloody, persists for more than 72 hours or is accompanied by fever, shaking, chills or severe abdominal pain, seek medical attention.

Giardiasis

A parasite present in contaminated water, giardia produces bloating as well as a foulsmelling, persistent, although not 'explosive', diarrhoea. One dose (four tablets) of Tinidazole usually cures the infection.

ENVIRONMENTAL HAZARDS
Acute Mountain Sickness

Areas of PNG's Highlands higher than 2500m, including Mt Wilhelm (4509m), are high enough for acute mountain sickness (AMS), or altitude sickness, to be a risk. Lack of oxygen at high altitudes affects most people to some extent. Less oxygen reaches the muscles and the brain, requiring the heart and lungs to compensate by working harder. The major risk factor in AMS is the speed with which you make your ascent. AMS is a notoriously fickle affliction and can affect even trekkers accustomed to high altitudes. AMS has been fatal at 3000m, although 3500m to 4500m is the usual range.

Acclimatisation is vital and usually takes from one to three days. Once you are acclimatised to a given height you are unlikely to get AMS at that height, but you can still succumb when you travel higher. If the ascent is too high and too fast, your body's compensatory reactions may not kick into gear fast enough.

Mild symptoms of AMS usually develop during the first 24 hours. They tend to be worse at night and include headache, dizziness, lethargy, loss of appetite, nausea, breathlessness, difficulty sleeping and irritability. More serious symptoms include breathlessness at rest, a dry irritative cough (which may progress to the production of pink, frothy sputum), severe headache, lack of coordination (typically leading to a 'drunken walk'), confusion, irrational behaviour, vomiting and eventually unconsciousness.

TREATMENT

Treat mild symptoms by resting at the same altitude until recovery, usually a day or two. Take paracetamol or aspirin for headaches. If symptoms persist or become worse, however, *immediate descent* is necessary – even 500m can help. The most effective treatment for severe AMS is to get down to a lower altitude as quickly as possible – any delay could be fatal.

The drugs acetazolamide (Diamox) and dexamethasone are recommended by some doctors for the prevention of AMS. However, their use is controversial. While they can reduce the symptoms, they may also mask warning signs; severe and fatal AMS has occurred in people taking these drugs. Drug treatments should never be used to avoid descent or to enable further ascent.

Bites & Stings
LAND CREATURES

Snakes (eg the death adder or highly venomous taipan) seldom attack humans without reason, so when walking in areas in PNG where visibility is not clear (such as long grass, leaf-covered ground or at night), be alert and careful. Compression by pad and bandage over the bite and immobilisation of the limb with any form of splint is the first-aid treatment. Victims should stay still unless there's no other option. Antivenoms are usually available from major medical centres.

The redback (jockey spider) is a distinctive small spider (known for the orange-red stripe on its back) that can cause a very painful bite with occasional generalised poisoning heralded by marked sweating of the affected limb, severe pain, weakness and vomiting. An ice pack is useful as a first-aid measure. An antivenin is available. Check with local village clinics.

Leeches are present in swampy jungle areas and easily fix themselves onto skin.

They aren't dangerous except to the rare person who may be allergic. Liberal application of insect repellent to skin, clothing and boots will prevent leech infestation. Pulling a leech off the skin may result in extensive bleeding – it is better to induce the leech to remove itself by applying an insecticide (or burning it with a cigarette tip!).

MARINE CREATURES

Saltwater crocodile attacks, though rare, are well recorded. Crocodiles can swim into tidal rivers; heed local warnings.

The notorious box jellyfish (seawasp) has been recorded in the waters of the Torres Straits, but much more common are the whip-like stings from the blue-coloured Indo-Pacific man o' war. If you see these floating in the water or stranded on the beach it is wise not to go into the water. The sting is very painful and is best treated with vinegar or ice packs. Do not use alcohol.

Poisonous cone shells abound along shallow coral reefs. Stings can be avoided by handling the shell at its blunt end and by using gloves. Stings mainly cause local reactions, but nausea, faintness, palpitations or difficulty in breathing are signs that flag the need for medical attention.

Sea snakes may be seen around coral reefs. Seasnakes are extremely unlikely to attack and their fangs will not penetrate a wetsuit.

Coral Ear

This is a common name for inflammation of the ear canal. It is caused by water entering the canal activating any fungal spores that may be lying around predisposing to bacterial infection and inflammation. It usually starts after swimming but can be reactivated by water dripping into the ear canal after a shower, especially if long, wet hair lies over the ear opening.

It can be very, very painful and can spoil a holiday. Apart from diarrhoea it is the most common reason for travellers to consult a doctor. Self-treatment with an antibiotic plus steroid eardrop preparation is very effective. Stay out of the water until the pain and itch have gone.

Coral Cuts

Cuts and abrasions from dead coral cause similar injuries from any other sort of rock, but live coral can cause prolonged infec-

tion. Never touch coral. If you do happen to cut yourself on live coral, treat the wound immediately. Get out of the water, clean the wound thoroughly, getting out all the little bits of coral, apply an antiseptic and cover with a waterproof dressing.

Diving Hazards

Because the region has wonderful opportunities for scuba diving it is easy to get over-excited and neglect strict depth and time precautions. Few dives are very deep but the temptation to spend longer than safe amounts of time at relatively shallow depths is great and is probably the main cause of decompression illness (the 'bends'). Early pains may not be severe and may be attributed to other causes, but any muscle or joint pain after scuba diving must be suspect. Keeping well hydrated helps prevent the bends.

At the time of writing, privately run compression chambers could be found at Port Moresby and Tawali Resort in Milne Bay Province, but transport to a chamber can be difficult. Supply of oxygen to the chambers is sometimes a problem. Novice divers must be especially careful. Even experienced divers should check with organisations like Divers' Alert Network (DAN) about the current site and status of compression chambers, and insurance to cover costs.

Food

Only eat fresh fruits or vegetables if cooked or peeled; be wary of dairy products that might contain unpasteurised milk. Eat food that is hot through and avoid buffet-style meals. Food in restaurants that are frequented by locals is not necessarily safe but most resort hotels have good standards of hygiene, but individual food handlers can carry infection. Food that is piping hot is usually safe. Be wary of salads.

Heat

This region lies within the tropics so it is hot and for the most part humid.

Heat exhaustion is a state of dehydration associated with salt loss. Natural heat loss is through sweating so it is easy to become dehydrated without realising it. Thirst is a late sign. Heat exhaustion is prevented by drinking at least 2L to 3L of water per day and more if you're very active. Salt-replacement solutions are useful, as muscle weakness and cramps are due to salt as well as water loss and can be made worse by drinking water alone. The powders used for treating dehydration due to diarrhoea are just as effective when it is due to heat exhaustion. Apart from commercial solutions, a reasonable drink consists of a good pinch of salt to a half-litre (pint) of water. Salt tablets can result in too much salt being taken, and can cause headaches and confusion.

HEAT STROKE

When the cooling effect of sweating fails, heat stroke ensues. This is a dangerous and emergency condition characterised by muscle weakness, exhaustion and mental confusion. Skin will be hot and dry. 'Put the fire out' by cooling the body with water on the outside and with cold drinks for the inside. Then seek medical help.

Sunburn

Exposure to the ultraviolet rays of the sun causes burning of the skin with accompanying pain and misery and the danger of skin cancer. Cloud cover does not block out UV rays. Sunburn is more likely a problem for those taking Doxycycline as an antimalarial. The Australian 'slip, slop, slap' slogan (slip on a shirt, slop on sunscreen and slap on a hat) is a useful mantra. Treat sunburn with cool, wet dressings. Severe swelling may respond to a cortisone cream.

TRADITIONAL MEDICINE

Treatments involving local herbs, roots and leaves have evolved over centuries, with each village having their own traditional healers. Some of these folk remedies have effective ingredients, and governments and research institutions are researching many of them. Claims such as AIDS cures and aphrodisiacs can be ignored. Tree-bark concoctions for fever are like aspirin. Chinese herbs are available in all of the main towns.

Buai, or betel-nut chewing (p40) is widespread in PNG and Solomon Islands. It has an astringent effect in the mouth but claims about other healing properties remain unproven. Prolonged use predisposes to mouth cancers.

HEALTH

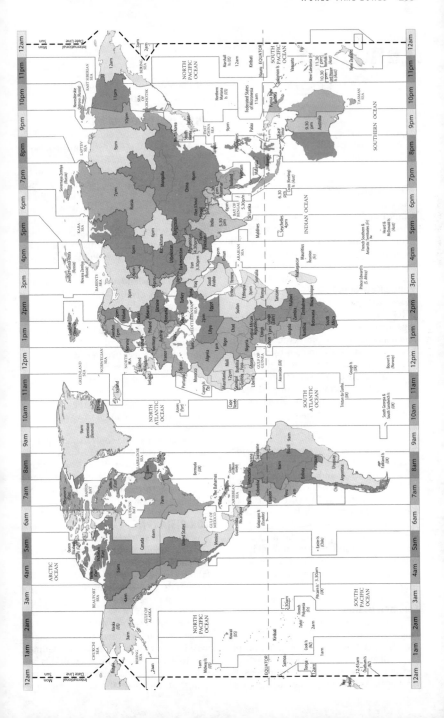

Language

CONTENTS

WHO SPEAKS WHAT WHERE?

After the national pidgins of Papua New Guinea and the Solomons, English is the most universally understood language, but while it's quite common in the cities and large towns, in rural areas you'll need some basic pidgin in order to communicate.

Papua New Guinea

More than 800 languages are spoken in PNG – a whopping 12% of the world's indigenous languages. Linguists divide these languages into 14 major groups. Austronesian languages are spoken by a sixth of PNG's people and dominate in the islands and around the coast. Kuanua, the *tok ples* (native tongue, literally 'talk of your place') of East New Britain's Tolai people, has the most speakers. Austronesian languages usually have a number system based on five.

Various dialects in the Highlands and Sepik regions are are closely related, non-Austronesian languages that can be broadly understood across old clan boundaries.

In the early days of British New Guinea and then Australian Papua, the local language of the Port Moresby coastal area, Motu, evolved into Police Motu, and was spread through Papua by the native constabulary. It's still widely spoken in the southern Papuan part of PNG and you can easily pick up a Motu phrasebook in Port Moresby.

Solomon Islands

Officially, there are 67 listed indigenous languages and about 30 dialects in the Solomon Islands. It is quite common for people from villages separated by only a few kilometres to speak mutually incomprehensible languages. As a result, the national language of the Solomons is Solomon Islands Pijin, or Pijin for short.

PIJIN (SOLOMON ISLANDS)

Early 19th-century sailors stimulated the evolution of Pijin. The recruitment of labour (including Solomon Islanders) from the 1860s to 1900s to work in mines, and in Oceanic canefields and plantations, spread the language all over the Pacific. By the 1930s, Pijin was being spoken by missionaries in many areas, helping to spread it further. While English is now the official language of the administration, many government staff use Pijin in everyday conversation.

Solomon Islands Pijin – like similar languages in PNG, Vanuatu, West Africa and along the old China coast – has been condemned by all and sundry, including the UN. It has been called 'baby talk', a 'bastard language' and a 'mongrel lingo'. Pijin speakers use two versions. One is a simplified form used by islanders to their English-speaking employers. The second is the true Pijin, which they use among their fellow countryfolk. Since the 1970s, linguists have been treating this version with respect.

This language guide only includes phrases in the pidgin of PNG, Tok Pisin, as it is very similar to Pijin. Listen closely to what people say, use your English inventively, and you'll find it easy to communicate in both PNG and the Solomons.

TOK PISIN (PNG)

Tok Pisin (or as it has also been called, New Guinea Pidgin English, Tok Boi, Neo-Melanesian) has its origins in the Pacific labour trade. Between 1880 and 1914, thousands of New Guineans worked for periods of three years or more on the German plantations of Samoa, where Pidgin English had developed as the working language of a multicultural and multilingual workforce. On returning to New Guinea, they took with them knowledge of this language. Pidgin English also became the language of the plantations the Germans established in coastal New Guinea and the islands of the Bismarck Archipelago, where young men from the more remote interior and the highlands were employed. Until very recently, the majority of Tok Pisin speakers had acquired their knowledge of the language as part of their work experience away from their home village.

Tok Pisin has grown into a language with many functions, and is now learned as a second language in most villages. For a growing number of children in the big towns, it has become creolised (adopted as their first language). The simple plantation language of the 1920s and 1930s has changed into the national language of independent Papua New Guinea, and as such is used regularly by more than two million speakers, not only in former German New Guinea, but also in former Papua.

The spread of Tok Pisin is due not so much to deliberate policies (in fact both the German and Australian governments opposed its use for quite some time), but its perceived usefulness as a common language in a country where more than 800 languages are spoken. Tok Pisin is the major lingua franca of PNG, and even in very remote villages it's rare not to find someone who speaks it.

Much maligned as a broken English, bastard language or comic opera talk in colonial days, Tok Pisin is a vibrant and expressive language used in all areas of daily life, including the PNG parliament, education, churches, and the media. It has been a written language since the 1920s, and although an official writing system exists (used in the *Nupela Testamen* and *Wantok* newspaper), non-standard spellings still abound. The most widely written and spoken variety of Tok Pisin is that of the Madang region.

Most Tok Pisin words are of English origin, but many words referring to local phenomena originate in local languages such as Tolai (spoken around Rabaul). Tok Pisin speakers are tolerant of variation and visitors will find the language invaluable when they move away from the towns and want talk to Papua New Guineans socially.

For a more detailed guide to the pidgin languages of Oceania, including Solomon Islands Pijin and Tok Pisin, get a copy of Lonely Planet's *Pidgin Phrasebook*.

The best places to look for books in Tok Pisin are the Christian bookshops in PNG; there is usually one in every town and they have all sorts of literature, including, needless to say, a Pidgin bible.

It is worthwhile buying the *Wantok* weekly newspaper, written entirely in Tok Pisin. As well as being a decent newspaper, reading it is a good way to learn the language. There are also comic strips, which are easy to follow even for beginners. EmTV broadcasts many programs in Pidgin, which will also help you pick it up.

Pronunciation

Only a small number of Papua New Guineans speak Tok Pisin as their first language (about 100,000) and they are mainly in towns or nontraditional settlements. Second language Tok Pisin speakers are often influenced in their pronunciation and grammar by the conventions of their mother tongue.

Note that **p** and **f** are virtually interchangeable in both spelling and pronunciation, as are **d** and **t**, **j** and **z**. The combination **kw** represents the English 'qu'. Vowels and diphthongs are pronounced clearly, even when unstressed and at the end of a word.

a	as in 'art'
e	as in 'set'
i	as in 'sit'
o	as in 'lot'
u	as in 'put'
ai	as in 'ais;e'
au	as the 'ou' in 'house'
oi	as in 'boil'

Avoiding Confusion

Be wary of words that may sound similar to English but have a different meaning in Pidgin. For instance, *kilim* just means to hit (hard); to kill somebody or something you have to *kilim i dai*.

Be careful of the sexual phrases – *pusim* means to copulate with, not to push. And while you can *ple tenis* (play tennis), *ple* is also a euphemism for intercourse. A man's trunk or suitcase may be a *bokis,* but a woman's *bokis* is her vagina, and a *blak bokis* is not a black suitcase but a flying fox or bat!

You'll love the standard reply to 'how far is it?' – *longwe liklik*. It doesn't actually mean a long way or not a long way - it translates more like 'not too near, not too far'.

Accommodation

Do you have a single/double room?
Yu gat rum slip long wanpela/tupela man?
How much is it per night?
Em i kostim hamas long wanpela de?
Can I see the room?
Inap mi lukim rum pastaim?
I like this room.
Mi laikim (tru) dispela rum.
Is there a mosquito net?
I gat moskita net i stap?
Where's the toilet?
Haus pekpek i stap we?
I want to stay ... day(s).
Mi laik stap ... de.
I'd like to check out today/tomorrow.
Mi laik bai mi lusim hotel tede/tumora.

Is there a ...?	*I gat rum ...?*
bath/shower	*waswas (i stap)*
laundry	*bilong wasim (ol) klos*

Conversation & Essentials

Hello.	*Gude.*
Goodbye.	*Lukim yu.*
Yes.	*Yes.*
No.	*Nogat.*
Please.	*Plis.*
Excuse me/Sorry.	*Sori.*
Thank you (very much).	*Tenkyu (tru).*
How are you?	*Yu stap gut?*
I'm well.	*Mi stap gut.*
What's your name?	*Husat nem bilong yu?*
My name is ...	*Nem bilong mi ...*
Where are you from?	*Ples bilong yu we?*
I'm from ...	*Ples bilong mi ...*
What's your job?	*Wanim kain wok bilong yu?*
I'm (a/an) ...	*Mi ...*
I (don't) understand.	*Mi (no) save.*
More slowly please.	*Yu tok isi isi plis.*
Can you draw a map?	*Inap yu wokim/droim map?*
I need help.	*Mi laikim sampela halp.*

man/woman	*man/meri*
child	*pikinini*
relative	*wantok*
sister	*susa*
brother	*brata*
a little	*liklik*
big	*bikpela*
forbidden	*tambu*

Directions

Where is ...?	*... i stap we?*
Straight ahead.	*Stret.*
Turn left/right.	*Tanim lep/rait.*
How far is it?	*Em i longwe o nogat?*
Is transport available?	*I gat bas, teksi samting?*

behind	*bihain long*
in front of	*ai bilong*
near	*klostu*
far	*longwe*

Numbers

1	*wan*
2	*tu*
3	*tri*
4	*foa*
5	*faiv*
6	*sikis*
7	*seven*
8	*et*
9	*nain*
10	*ten*
11	*wanpela ten wan*
12	*wanpela ten tu*
13	*wanpela ten tri*
14	*wanpela ten foa*
15	*wanpela ten faiv*
16	*wanpela ten sikis*
17	*wanpela ten seven*
18	*wanpela ten et*
19	*wanpela ten nain*
20	*tupela ten*
21	*tupela ten wan*
22	*tupela ten tu*
30	*tripela ten*
40	*fopela ten*
50	*faivpela ten*
60	*sikispela ten*
70	*sevenpela ten*
80	*etpela ten*
90	*nainpela ten*
100	*wan handet*

Shopping & Services

I'd like to buy ...
Mi laik baim ...
How much is it?
Hamas long dispela?
What's that?
Wanem dispela?
I'm just looking.
Mi lukluk tasol.

That's very cheap.
Pe/Prais i daun (tru).
Is that your lowest price?
I gat seken prais?
I'll take it.
Bai mi kisim.

I'm looking for ... *Mi painim ...*
  a bank *haus mani/benk*
  the church *haus lotu*
  the hospital *haus sik*
  the market *maket/bung*
  the police *polis stesin*

Time & Dates

When/At what time? *Wanem taim?*
What time is it? *Wanem taim nau?*
It's (eight) o'clock. *Em i (et) klok.*

morning *moningtaim*
afternoon *apinun*
evening (7 – 11) *nait*
night (11 – 4) *biknait*
today *tede*
tomorrow *tumora*
yesterday *asde*

Sunday	*Sande*
Monday	*Mande*
Tuesday	*Tunde*
Wednesday	*Trinde*
Thursday	*Fonde*
Friday	*Fraide*
Saturday	*Sarere*

Transport

How much is it to ... ?
Em i haumas long ... ?
How long is the journey?
Hamas taim long go long ... ?

I'd like a ... ticket *Mi laik baim tiket long ...*
to ...
  one-way *i go long tasol*
  return *go na i kambek*

What time does *Wanem taim ... i kamap?*
the ... arrive?
What time does the *Long wanem taim neks ... i go?*
next ... leave?
  boat *bot*
  bus *bas*
  plane *balus*

Also available from Lonely Planet:
Pidgin Phrasebook

Glossary

arse tanket – a bunch of tanket leaves stuck into a belt to cover a man's backside, also called *arse gras* (Highlands)

bagarap – broken; literally 'buggered-up'
bagi – red shell necklace used for trade in the *kula* ring islands
balus – aeroplane
banana boat – trade boat or dinghy
baret – artificial channel or canal constructed across loops in a river (Sepik)
bigman – important man, a leader
bikpela – big, great
bilas – jewellery, decorations, finery
bilum – string bag
boi – boy
BRA – Bougainville Revolutionary Army (Solomon Islands)
buai – betel nut
buk tambu – the bible
bukumatula – bachelor house (Trobriand Islands)

dewel – devil
diwai – wood
doba – leaf money from Milne Bay Province
dukduk – spirit and ritual costume

garamut – drum made from a hollowed log
GRA – Guadalcanal Revolutionary Army (Solomon Islands)

haus lain – long house (Highlands)
haus sik – hospital
haus tambaran – spirit house
haus win – open-air structure like a gazebo; literally 'house of wind'

inap – enough

kai bar – cheap takeaway food bar
kaikai – food
karim leg – courting ceremony involving crossing legs with a partner; literally 'carry leg' (Highlands)
kastom – custom
kaukau – sweet potato
kiap – patrol officer (of colonial origin)
kina – unit of PNG currency, large shell traded from the coast as an early form of currency
kokomo – hornbill bird
kula ring – ring of trading islands in Milne Bay Province
kumul – bird of paradise
kunai – grass, grassland

kundu – hourglass-shaped drum covered with lizard or snake skin
kwik piksa leta – fax; literally 'quick picture letter'
laplap – sarong
liklik – small
liklik haus – toilet; literally 'small house'
loloi – rolls of shell money strung on lengths of cane (East New Britain)
lotu – religious service, worship
lusim – to leave

malangan – ritual of making totemic figures (also called *malangans*) to honour the dead; also known as *malagan*
masalai – spirit of the bush or water, a devil (East New Britain and New Ireland)
masta – white adult male (colonial)
mausgras – beard, moustache, whiskers
MEF – Malaitan Eagle Force (Solomon Islands)
meri – wife, woman
misis – European woman
missinari – missionary
moga – ceremony surrounding the giving away of goods to display one's wealth (Highlands)
Motu – the indigenous people of the Port Moresby area, the language spoken by these people
mumu – traditional underground oven
mwala – decorated armlets made from cone shells used for trade in the *kula* ring islands

nambawan – number one, the best
natnat – mosquito

OPM – Organisasi Papua Merdeka, or Free West Papua Movement

payback – compensation paid for a wrongdoing, but in reprisal more than revenge
pekpek bilong cuscus – cuscus droppings
pikus tri – fig tree
pinis – finish
pis – fish
pisin – bird
pitpit – wild sugar cane
PMV – public motor vehicle
pukpuk – crocodile

raskol – bandit, criminal or thief
ria – volcanic fjord, as found near Tufi
rokrok – frog

saksak – sago
salvinia – weed *(Salvinia molesta)* found in many waterways
save – understand, think
singsing – celebratory festival/dance
solwara – ocean, sea
spia – spear
story board – narrative carving done on a wooden board
susu – milk, breast

tambaran – ancestral spirit, also called tambuan, tabaran or tabuan
tambu – forbidden or sacred, shell money (Tolai)
tapa – beaten bark cloth
taro – tuberous root vegetable similar to a sweet potato
tasol – that's all, only
tee – ceremony where men give away goods to display their wealth (Enga)

toea – unit of PNG currency (100 toea = 1 *kina*), a shell necklace also used as currency
Tok Pisin – the Pidgin language
Tok Ples – local language, first language, pronounced 'talk place'
Tolai – the main inhabitants of East New Britain's Gazelle Peninsula, pronounced 'tol-eye'
tumbuan – large, feather-draped body mask
tupela – two, both
turnim het – a courting ceremony involving rubbing faces together, literally 'turn head' (Highlands)

voluntia – volunteer

wantok – fellow clanspeople, kith and kin; literally 'one talk' or 'one who speaks the same language'

yam – tuberous root vegetable similar to a sweet potato

Behind the Scenes

THIS BOOK

Lonely Planet cofounder Tony Wheeler researched and wrote the first two editions of Papua New Guinea. Mark Lightbody researched the 3rd edition. Richard Everist updated the 4th edition and Jon Murray updated the 5th. The 6th edition was written by Adrian Lipscomb, Rowan McKinnon and Jon Murray. For this edition Andrew Burke was the coordinating author assisted by authors Rowan McKinnon and Arnold Barkhordarian. Bestselling author and environmental scientist Tim Flannery wrote the Environment chapter. Veteran Pacific journalist Sean Dorney wrote the Snapshot chapter and Dr Michael Sorokin wrote the Health chapter. Australian Volunteers International (AVI) volunteers Jon Cook and Fiona Young wrote the 'Volunteering in PNG' boxed text for the Directory chapter.

THANKS from the Authors

Andrew Burke Almost everyone I met in PNG was overwhelmingly helpful, but special thanks go to Gail Thomas, Eric Uwea, Erik Anderson and the POMP crew in Port Moresby; the irrepressible Gretta Kwasnicka-Todurawai, Serah Clarke and Wayne and Lee Thompson in Alotau; Alex Scholten and Jonika Paulsen for their fast feedback and enthusiasm in Lae; and Chris Marshall for inviting me into the copilot's seat for a hair-raising (but very safe) day around the airstrips of Morobe. On the Trobriand Islands Lydia was a wonderful host. My Kokoda endurance test was aided by Russell, Kingsley and Grace Eroro, and the expert help of Clive Baker. Samuel Kepuknai was a great help in Kiunga. Thanks also to Donna Harvey-Hall, Nathan Kumin,

Adrian van Roren, Lara Andrews, Ross Wittig, Phil Franklin, Bob Finall, Maine S Winny, Heni Dembis, Vicky Neville, Peter Taramuri, Trevor Michie, Phil Taudevin, and Paddy and Rochelle Freeney. Thanks to my fellow authors Rowan McKinnon and Arnold Barkhordarian for going many bumpy extra miles in the name of research, while at Lonely Planet HQ the dedication of Marg Toohey, Melissa Faulkner and Helen Rowley was greatly appreciated. As usual, thanks to my family for their unselfish support, and especially my 65-year-old Dad who struggled and sweated up the Kokoda Track with me. And last but definitely not least, an enormous thanks to my *nambawan meri*, Anne Hyland, for her unfailing love, faith and support over many years. I'm looking forward to the day she'll be my *meri bilong mi.*

Rowan McKinnon Thanks to Jane and my kids for letting me go to PNG and for remembering me when I returned. Thanks too to my commissioning editor, Marg Toohey, who was fantastic to work with, as were Corie Waddell and my co-authors Andrew Burke and Arnold Barkhordarian. Thanks to Peter Vincent and Nathan Kumin at the PNG Tourism Promotion Authority; Diane Cassell, John Gele, Simon Lusam, Bugau Damon and Lesley Schoon in and around Madang; Louisa Noble and the staff of the Madang Visitors & Cultural Bureau. *Tenkyu tru* to Brian and Maggie Wilson, and Barbara at Haus Poroman Lodge; Peter Noah, Richard and the village boys who adopted me; Susan and Richard Baker; Simon Saka and the Kambot boys for the generous hospitality and a splendid hang-

---

THE LONELY PLANET STORY

The story begins with a classic travel adventure: Tony and Maureen Wheeler's 1972 journey across Europe and Asia to Australia. There was no useful information about the overland trail then, so Tony and Maureen published the first Lonely Planet guidebook to meet a growing need.

From a kitchen table, Lonely Planet has grown to become the largest independent travel publisher in the world, with offices in Melbourne (Australia), Oakland (USA) and London (UK). Today Lonely Planet guidebooks cover the globe. There is an ever-growing list of books and information in a variety of media. Some things haven't changed. The main aim is still to make it possible for adventurous travellers to get out there – to explore and better understand the world.

At Lonely Planet we believe travellers can make a positive contribution to the countries they visit – if they respect their host communities and spend their money wisely. Every year 5% of company profit is donated to charities around the world.

over after several cases of warm SP Lager. Special thanks to my Mosbi *wantoks* Digby Ho Leong and John Wong.

Arnold Barkhordarian Thanks to Peter Ratusia at Seghe Lodge for help booking flights and frying aubergines after I'd seen one too many cooking bananas; Helen Newton of Honiara; SIVB Honiara; Martin and Lily Laurie of Shortland Island's Nuhu village for offering friendship to a stranger; the sober members of the crew in the boat from Buin to Nuhu for spotting the reef, the drunk ones for convincing me to go in the first place; 'Binatang' Bob Prior of Kimbe, my *wantok tru*, for his advice, life story and help; Stephen Woolcott at Kabaira Beach Hideaway; Dive Gizo and the guys at Walindi for the orca, sea snake and shark experiences; everyone at Bol village for making a 48-hour wait for the truck pleasurable with their great stories, and the truck driver for stopping. Thanks to Brian the pilot from Airlink for missing Mt Uluwan (not by much, but it made all the difference); the anonymous helicopter pilot; John Wein from Kajoro Sunset Lodge for his radio help, boat rides and head-hunting stories; Miki, Emily and family for sharing transport and companionship in Malaita; Eiran for his continued research into the PNG walderbeast; and Sara 'pointy' Hutchison for her deep knowledge of anthropology and all her butterfly effects.

CREDITS

Coordinating the production of *Papua New Guinea & Solomon Islands* were Emma Koch and Melissa Faulkner (editorial), Helen Rowley (cartography) and Sonya Brooke (layout). Jacqueline McLeod chose the colour images. Overseeing production were Andrew Weatherill, Glenn van der Knijff and Celia Wood (project management), Martin Heng (managing editor) and Corie Waddell (managing cartographer). Piotr Czajkowski provided GIS data, and Lachlas Ross, Paul Piaia and Chris LeeAck gave technical assistance for the mapping. Quentin Frayne compiled the language chapter. This title was commissioned and developed in Lonely Planet's Melbourne office by Marg Toohey. The cover was designed by Jane Hart and Sonya Brooke prepared the finished artwork.

The following people assisted with editing, proofing and indexing: Andrew Bain, Imogen Bannister, Kyla Gillzan, Brooke Lyons, Lucie Monie, Fionnuala Twomey and Gina Tsarouhas. Adriana Mammarella oversaw layout. Vicki Beale, Katherine Marsh and Laura Jane assisted in layout. Thanks to Meg Worby who gave useful feedback on the author brief, Adrian Campbell for his advice on the Kokoda Track, and Carol Chandler and Graham Imeson from Print Production.

THANKS from Lonely Planet

Many thanks to the following travellers who used the last edition and wrote to us with helpful hints, useful advice and interesting anecdotes.

A Alexander Abraham, Mark Alexander, Manlio Altomare, John Andrew, Sam Argov, Sarah Argov, Harold & Susan Armitage, Tonas Artzi **B** Norman Ba'abi, Judith Babka, Andrew Barber, Michael Barber, Nigel Barlow, Matthew Barnes, Mike Barnett, Peter Barter, Christoph Beiglboeck, Keith Bickley, Andrew Binnie, Rick Blue, Anthony Blythen, Michael Bohm, KR Bond, Jim Bowar, Maggie Bowes, Bill Boyd, Anne Burgess, Lisa Burman, Damon & Jill Burn, Ken Burrage, Philippe Busslinger **C** K Camer, Ruth Cameron, Beryl Canwell, Dan Cassell, Eduardo Castro, Pete Chorney, Pren Claflin, David Colquhoun, Katy Cooke, Murray Cox, Danny Cracknell, Stephen Cross, Jenny & Mark Crowley, Suzanne Cullen, Margaret Cunningham **D** Daisy Daurobona, Fatima & Luigui de Carvlaho, Simon de Trey-White, Nicole Demosky, Freya Desbiolles, Robert Dew, Vah Camp Dieter, Marleen Dirkzwager, Suzanne Dooley, John Dopi, Saba N Dozio, Charles Drace-Francis, Annette Dusel **E** Andrew Eckel, Erez Engel **F** Paul Falworth, Tania Fiegert, Hanne Finholt, Carolyn Flaagan, Denzel Fohombari, Kevin Ford, Stan Ford, Alan Foster, Don Foster, Paul Franckowiak, Steven Frost, Liat & Eran Fuchs **G** Suat Gapas, Robert S Garing, Rick Gartner, Irene E Gashu, Yossi Ghinsberg, Tad Glawthier, Jean & John Glenister, Christian

SEND US YOUR FEEDBACK

We love to hear from travellers – your comments keep us on our toes and help make our books better. Our well-travelled team reads every word on what you loved or loathed about this book. Although we cannot reply individually to postal submissions, we always guarantee that your feedback goes straight to the appropriate authors, in time for the next edition. Each person who sends us information is thanked in the next edition – and the most useful submissions are rewarded with a free book.

To send us your updates – and find out about Lonely Planet events, newsletters and travel news. Visit our award-winning website: **www.lonelyplanet.com/feedback**

Note: We may edit, reproduce and incorporate your comments in Lonely Planet products such as guidebooks, websites and digital products, so let us know if you don't want your comments reproduced or your name acknowledged. For a copy of our privacy policy visit www.lonelyplanet.com/privacy

Glossner, William Goldberg, Rogier Gruys **H** Felix Hammann, Debbie Harrison, Edith & Tyler Hartzen, Adam Hays, Johan Hedstrom, Vincent Hefter, Arthur Hendi, Steven Herr, Randy Hess, Andrew Hii, Art Hilado, Susan Hills, John Hird, Melanie Hirsch, Kevin Hodges, Darja Hoenigman, R Hogenschurz, Linda Honey, Steve How Lum, Laura Hughes **I** At Ipenburg, Yuval Itan **J** Alan Jacobs, Tony Jacoby, Elizabeth Jansen, Jenny & Craig Jarrett, Marie Javins, B Jeans, Grant L Joblin, Berit Johns, Adrian Jowett, M Juedes **K** Chris Kauffman, Colum Keelaghan, Kai & Irma Keller, Marilyn Kelly, Kakal Keltim, Mette Kirk, Les Knebl, Joseph Kone, Don Kossuth, Pratish Kotecha, Alex Kryska, Gabriel Kuhn, Axel Kummel, Gretta Kwasnicka Todurawai, Brandt Kwiram **L** Brian Leach, Burkhard Leicht, Kimberlee Lenander, Jacinta Lesek, Daniel Levitis, Jennifer Lilley, Libor Lindmajer, Eva Lindström, Stefan Johannes Link, Karin Lowing, Kirsten Lund Larsen **M** Helen McGregor, Garry McKellar-James, Michael McKeown, Peggy Mcnamara, Alan McNeil, Sandy MacTaggart, Dale Malpezzi, Melvyn Maltz, Melanie Manley, Cyril F Manning, Doug Marmion, Mary-Claire Marriot, Andrew May, Mark Mehrlander, Wayne Melrose, Mark Meredith, Jurgen Merzaros, Nina & Benedikt Metternich, John Michalski, Yolande & Etienne Michiels, Alexander Millar, Ben Miller, Rex Mirams, Mark Moller, James Moloney, Marcus Morris, Katherine Moseby, Katrin Muller, Juliette Muscat **N** Michael Nagual, Ken & Margery Nash, Gary Nethery, Helen Newton, Edward Nielsen, David Nugi **O** Kaspar Oberli, Melissa Olson, Samuel Opa, Elizabeth Orians, Kellie Orr, Iain Overton **P** Lin Padgham, Rickard Palsson, Hae Seoung Park, Gail Parker, Seth Parks, Russell Parker, Brent & Alicia Pav, Santos Penha, Ilan Peri, Adam Phillipson, Adrian Pitts, Jeanne & Peter Pockel, Rita Pohnisch, Dina Priess **R** Dave Radford, Mary Raymond, Wendy Rayner, Bjarke Refslund, Sara Richards, Tom Ridenour, Lorraine Riddle, Sue Robb, Nancy Roper, Christophe Rosat, Roger Roth **S** Merrav Sadot, Mansur Safai, Martin Salmingkeit, Richard Samuelson, Jane & Dave Santos, HE Sawyer, Brigit & Andy Schaerenburkard, Guido Schaffner, Erik Schäffer, Rosalie Schultz, Michael Schmittmann, Douglas Scott, Warren Christopher Seeto, Gil Shalem, Karen Shenoff, Rob Sherry, Jonathan Sibtain, Karyn Simkins, Eregari Singri, Susan Sjoberg, Kate Skovron, Barbara Slone, John Small, J Smelling, Bill Smith, Meg Smith, I Smits, Laura Sobel, Carol Solomoniks, Dana Spatenkova, Zoltan Stabo, Sidney J Stafford, Richard Stanaway, Eran Stark, Norma Stehle, Peter Steiner, Lynn Stephenson, Wolfgang Sterrer, Bob Stevens, Michael Sullivan, Stuart Symons **T** Vicki Tay, Wayne Thompson, John Thorp, Anja Tibutt, Tim Timoney, Alex Tsang, Tara Tuatai, Inbal Tubi, Gemma Tucker, Darrell Tully, David Twine, Russ Ty **U** Mathias Ulmer **V** Dieter van Camp, Klaas van Wijk, Thierry Vanheerswynghels, Ilse Vanroy **W** Laszlo Wagner, Peter Wagner, Christopher Paul Webster, Alain Werner, Bjarne & Gitte Werther, Emma White, Michael White, Douglas Whitman, Tim Wild, James Williams, AF Wilson, Simon Wilson, Manfred Wolfensberger, Kilian Wolters, J Woods **Y** Guy Yoger, Daniel Yokota, Gayne C Young **Z** Craig Zwicky

ACKNOWLEDGMENTS

Many thanks to the following for the use of their content:

Globe on back cover © Mountain High Maps 1993 Digital Wisdom, Inc.

Kokoda Track map has been adapted from *Diary & Guide: The Kokoda Trail Papua New Guinea* by Bob McDonald.

Index

MAP LEGEND

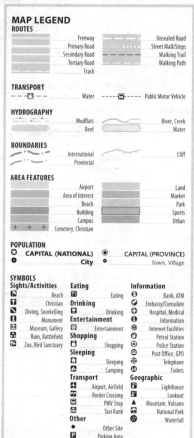

ROUTES

Freeway	Unsealed Road
Primary Road	Street Mall/Steps
Secondary Road	Walking Trail
Tertiary Road	Walking Path
Track	

TRANSPORT

Water — Public Motor Vehicle

HYDROGRAPHY

Mudflats	River, Creek
Reef	Water

BOUNDARIES

International	Cliff
Provincial	

AREA FEATURES

Airport	Land
Area of Interest	Market
Beach	Park
Building	Sports
Campus	Urban
Cemetery, Christian	

POPULATION

CAPITAL (NATIONAL)	CAPITAL (PROVINCE)
City	Town, Village

SYMBOLS

Sights/Activities
- Beach
- Christian
- Diving, Snorkelling
- Monument
- Museum, Gallery
- Ruin, Battlefield
- Zoo, Bird Sanctuary

Eating
- Eating

Drinking
- Drinking

Entertainment
- Entertainment

Shopping
- Shopping

Sleeping
- Sleeping
- Camping

Transport
- Airport, Airfield
- Border Crossing
- PMV Stop
- Taxi Rank

Other
- Other Site
- Parking Area

Information
- Bank, ATM
- Embassy/Consulate
- Hospital, Medical
- Information
- Internet Facilities
- Petrol Station
- Post Office, GPO
- Telephone
- Toilets

Geographic
- Lighthouse
- Lookout
- Mountain, Volcano
- National Park
- Waterfall

LONELY PLANET OFFICES

Australia
Head Office
Locked Bag 1, Footscray, Victoria 3011
☎ 03 8379 8000, fax 03 8379 8111
talk2us@lonelyplanet.com.au

USA
150 Linden St, Oakland, CA 94607
☎ 510 893 8555, toll free 800 275 8555
fax 510 893 8572, info@lonelyplanet.com

UK
72–82 Rosebery Ave,
Clerkenwell, London EC1R 4RW
☎ 020 7841 9000, fax 020 7841 9001
go@lonelyplanet.co.uk

Published by Lonely Planet Publications Pty Ltd
ABN 36 005 607 983

© Lonely Planet 2005

© photographers as indicated 2005

Cover photographs by Lonely Planet Images: A man in traditional dress from the Southern Highlands, Papua New Guinea, Jerry Galea (front); The crystal waters of Kanggava Bay on Rennell Island, Peter Hendrie (back). Many of the images in this guide are available for licensing from Lonely Planet Images: www.lonelyplanetimages.com